INTERLOCKING BASINS OF A GLOBE:

ESSAYS ON DEREK WALCOTT

INTERLOCKING BASINS OF A GLOBE:

ESSAYS ON DEREK WALCOTT

EDITED BY

JEAN ANTOINE-DUNNE

PEEPAL TREE

First published in Great Britain in 2013
Peepal Tree Press Ltd
17 King's Avenue
Leeds LS6 1QS
England

ISBN13: 9781845232207

CONTENTS

To Patricia Ismond
A teacher, friend and mentor
December 21, 1944 — June 27, 2006.

ACKNOWLEDGEMENTS

All works are to some extent collaborative. A collection such as this begins and ends because many individuals have given it shape. First of all thank you to Derek Walcott whose generosity resounds in this volume. He has given permission to publish drawings and excerpts from manuscripts held at The University of the West Indies, St Augustine and The Thomas Fisher Rare Book Library, University of Toronto. He has allowed the use of one of his paintings for the cover of this book: he has read at least one of the essays and noted his approval; he attended the Academic Conference celebrating his life and work at the University of the West Indies, St Augustine in 2010, the gathering from which these essays emanate. Not only did Walcott bring from St Lucia some of his own paintings at our request, he was also present and applauded the production of several of his works by the Department of Creative and Performing Arts, listened to papers and joined in the proceedings. He even called together a gathering of filmmakers and met with this group on several occasions as the beginnings of a new Caribbean Film Collective. Thank you Derek. I want to say a special thank you to Sigrid, whose patience and grace every time she takes yet another call is phenomenal. Thank you Lizzie and Anna for your hospitality and support.

Thanks are due to Professor Edward Baugh for his encouragement and help in making this volume a reality. Thanks, too, to Andra Ramdeen and Nadia Whiteman, my research assistants.

The librarians at St Augustine and the Fisher Library have been at all times courteous and outstanding in the help they have given. Mrs. Hellenese -Paul, librarian at the West Indianna Library, was instrumental in putting together an exhibition of Walcott manuscripts and drawings at that Celebration in 2010. We acknowledge with gratitude the generosity of the Thomas Fisher Rare Book Library of the University of Toronto in allowing the reproduction of Derek Walcott's drawings for this publication. Thank you to John Shoesmith of the Fisher Library Digital Collections for his assistance in this regard.

In Toronto I met Jennifer Toews whose caretakership of the Walcott papers led to a wonderful exhibition in 2011 where Derek was again honoured. I must record my personal debt to Jennifer without whom my own essay could not have been written. Thank you also to Albert Masters, librarian at the Thomas Fisher Rare Book Library.

Dr Bhoendradatt Tewarie, former principal of the St Augustine Campus, [illegible] and Professor Clement Sankat continued the project. The Dean of the Faculty of Humanities and Education supported the Walcott conference and it was [illegible]

PAULA MORGAN AND BARBARA LALLA

DEREK WALCOTT: PROLOGUE

In January 2010 the University of the West Indies, St Augustine hosted a conference on the theme "Interlocking Basins of a Globe" in honour of Derek Walcott. This was the final in a series dedicated to Caribbean Nobel laureates and conceived as a gift from the institution to the nation of Trinidad and Tobago. The three conferences in this series rolled out within the broad time frame of other significant markers – the 50th Anniversary of the University of the West Indies (2010), the 50th Anniversary of the UWI St Augustine campus (2011) and 50th Anniversary of the Independence of Jamaica and Trinidad and Tobago and of the collapse of the West Indian Federation (2012). The deliberations were simultaneously laudatory, appraising and critical. Segments that were open to the public attracted a substantial cross section of the nation's population. The Walcott conference 2010 and the conference held in honour of V. S. Naipaul (2007), demonstrated that contrary to the lament of the poet/persona of the 1969 poem "Homecoming: Anse La Raye"[1] as a people we have become capable of creating rites for those who have returned and that it has come to mean something when writers assert "I am your poet, yours" (The *Gulf*, p. 51). The enthusiastic representation of a substantial cross section of the population in these celebrations, and the publications which have emerged as a result are testimonies to the willingness of Caribbean people to take a backward glance as a basis for future engagement.

The response recalls the problematic Walcott outlined over half a century earlier in his 1957 article "The Society and the Artist" in which the youthful writer celebrates the manner in which the diverse peoples of the emerging nation were developing a national imaginary which allowed them to "possess the land in thought and share it".[2] He then defined artists as master craftsmen in the project of synthesizing difference and crafting Caribbean ontologies and modes of belonging. Walcott, while applauding the conceptual and visionary act of self-fashioning, "we are now learning to think. To see ourselves, not as others see us, but with all the possibilities of the new country we are making" (p. 15), decried the lack of social recognition of the pivotal role being played by the artist: "I do not think there is any minority in the entire archipelago [illegible] men and their younger inheritors who think they write for themselves, who long for the metropolitan centres of civilization, temporarily conquer them, and then [illegible]

The lifelong and passionate pursuit of this Herculean work of the imagination has borne much fruit. The artist as teacher and scholar, prophet and avenger has culled the terrible lessons of New World civilization to create a mirror in which new island societies can trace their becoming. More significantly he has figured the pathways of this vulnerable yet robust archipelago as lessons to the globe on grappling with, and for the most part overcoming, grim adversities and crafting creative ways to be human. Several issues remain: Where is Walcott's Adamic man half a century later? What remains of the sense of infinite creative potential? What have his bedrock energies and multitudinous creative fusions produced? Has the numinous power survived and been put to good use? What have been the challenges to the masculinist nature of this early formulation? And what brave new worlds remain to be invented and named? It is the foundational work of Mr Walcott and his dedicated fellow architects of a uniquely Caribbean imaginary which has empowered a new generation to address these kinds of issues.

For this we give thanks.

Paula Morgan

Introducing Derek Walcott

In traversing spatial, ideological and linguistic boundaries as he re-charts Caribbean history, Derek Walcott evades descriptors that fix and contain, such as post- or antimodernist, or postcolonial. It is difficult to categorize him as anything but *Caribbean*.

Currently Professor of Poetry at the University of Essex, Derek Walcott was born in St Lucia (1930), of black and white forebears, and absorbed the poetry of the British canon in which his mother immersed her sons even as the theatre of their social setting unfolded around them – a setting he has ever celebrated. "Thank God," he says, "I was born in it…"[1] and he composed verses at fourteen, published by eighteen, and set out to producing "the mighty line of Marlowe and Milton". But the disparate past and riven present made their demands.

Graduating from the University College of the West Indies in Jamaica (1953) in English, French, and Latin, Walcott accepted a Rockefeller fellowship to study American Theatre and within three years founded what would become the Trinidad Theatre Workshop. Two decades later, teaching at Boston University, he established Boston Playwrights' Theatre. By then he had won the Obie Award for *Dream on Monkey Mountain*, had written *O Babylon!*, and *Remembrance & Pantomime*. In these, as in other much loved plays, like *Ti-Jean*, Walcott meshed native content and form in celebrating and contesting European literary tradition. His adaptation of Homer's *Odyssey*, staged by the Royal Shakespeare Company, sold out in London. Reflections on both his own exilic experience and his personal involvement in the Trinidad Theatre workshop merge in another play, *A Branch of the Blue Nile*.

Yet it was for his poetry that the Nobel Prize (1992) crowned an array of other honours (like the American Poetry Award and the Queen's Medal) – verse fraught with departure and with loss and conflicted homecoming. *The Castaway* reveals the artist as Crusoe separated from ancestral cultures and as Adam articulating meaning in a new world. Later, *The Gulf* separates the US from St Lucia, adult poet from childhood beginnings; but in *Another Life* the poetic consciousness bridges gulfs within the Caribbean psyche. The tension between cultural traditions and their complex synthesis would later produce *The Star-Apple Kingdom*'s polyphonic tracking of the archipelago in its epic dimensions of space and time.

Walcott's preoccupation with abandonment and wandering had taken form early, as in "Sea Grapes",[5] in the Odyssean figure, haunted by the guilt of betrayal and torn between yearnings for home and adventure ensuing from the ruin of Troy – that monumental myth that has infused European culture and percolated into our own time and space. These themes *Omeros* took up, relocating such quests to the Caribbean, replacing heroic warriors with fishermen, weaving their journeys among other texts and subtexts of Caribbean history in the aesthetics of a new Aegean crisscrossed with multiple identities.

All this he achieved through unrelenting labour, awaking with sunrise (as he portrays the artist in "The Flock")[6] and working, as those who know him best testify, "all the time", filling notebooks with drawings that detail his plays, covering the lawn with sets, turning the house into a theatre – yet, in between, devouring glossy magazines, drumming, indulging his incorrigible sweet-tooth, and – most fervently – painting.

For, in verse and prose, Walcott's brilliantly vivid style draws on the visual artist's sensibility, whether representing in verse the journey of an impressionist painter or conveying such questing in his own paintings. Walcott's style is also unashamedly inspired by English literary genius – Shakespeare, Eliot, Lowell – but expressed in Caribbean rhythm and idiom whether speaking through Shabine, the sailor, or as artist (mulatto of style). This divided Caribbean speaker torn between two voices rejects cheap solutions to cultural interface – solutions such as a consumable Caribbean [illegible] is a down-to-earth genius. Though scholarly and meticulous he revels in dining out with friends, in the company of his children, in the exchange of [illegible] generous, supportive of young actors and aspiring poets.

As critic and essayist he is as penetrating, lucid and fearless, as he is in verse. But humane. Thus his critique of imperial culture rejects bitterness for exuberance, denounces without vengeance, balances scepticism of the canon against a dream (realised) of joining this canon and, in so doing, crucially defining our own. Derek Walcott's technical intricacy, density of thought, erudite allusion and multi-dimensional argument, sensitivity to the sonorous and the vivid produces verse and prose that define a liminal space. Assessing the West Indian mind as "historically hungover",[7] Walcott reaches above the inertia of mere fact for imaginative truth in clearing a path to history between revenge and remorse. In this sense he detoxifies the "blood of both" and recombines them to a restorative. Looking back into himself, into history as into a mirror, he thanks his forefathers "that exiled from your own Edens you have placed me in the wonder of another, and that was my inheritance and your gift."[8]

Barbara Lalla: Introducing Walcott at the Celebration in 2010.

End Notes

1. Derek Walcott, *The Gulf* (London: Cape, 1969), p. 50; and *Collected Poems* (New York: Farrar, Straus and Giroux, 1987) p. 127.
2. Derek Walcott, "Society and the Artist" [1957] *Critical perspectives on Derek Walcott*, Ed. Robert D. Hamner (Washington, DC: Three Continents Press, 1993), p. 15-17
3. Leif Sjöberg, "An Interview with Derek Walcott" in *Conversations with Derek Walcott*. Ed. William Baer (Jackson: University Press of Mississippi, 1996), p. 82.
4. "What the Twilight Says", *What the Twilight Says: Essays* (New York: Farrar, Straus and Giroux, 1998), p. 28.
5. *Sea Grapes* (London: Cape, 1976), p. 9; and *Collected Poems*, p. 297.
6. *The Castaway & Other Poems* (London: Cape, 1965), pp. 14-15; and *Collected Poems*, pp. [illegible].
7. "What the Twilight Says", p. 10
8. "The Muse of History," ibid. p. 64.

JEAN ANTOINE-DUNNE

INTRODUCTION

Derek Walcott's literary affiliations and his grounding in the Caribbean are key ideas in this volume of essays that celebrates the extraordinary and prolific life and work of the Caribbean poet laureate. No matter from what viewpoint you look at this man – poet, essayist, playwright, film aficionado, journalist– he soars, yet remains grounded in the care and love of his original place. His often noted affiliation to James Joyce suggests a mutual desire to encircle the earth and shape it within the context of modernism's nostalgia and to use form to suture the gaps and fissures of modern existence. But Walcott is not so easily pigeonholed. In fact, if there is a sentence that resonates within Walcott's *oeuvre* it is that he is Janus faced – seeing with "twin heads"[1] – and therefore is an artist whose work reflects the multifaceted nature of Caribbean and New World experience, and the tensions and compromises that exist as a result of the interlocking of these various elements.

Walcott's proprietorial attitude to the Antilles is traced in Rohlehr's essay which, addressing Walcott's conflicted relationship to the islands in at times ironic ways, offers a close reading of Walcott's sixty-year-long career. This goes beyond an analysis of the idea of Walcott as "mulatto of culture" to which Rohlehr has often returned[2] and accesses a range of material from newspapers to poetic texts in a commentary that follows Walcott's journeys from St Lucia to Jamaica to Trinidad and from America and Europe back to the Caribbean.

The extensive range of Rohlehr's essay enables him to trace Walcott's varying moods and his reactions to cultural and political events, many of which relate to Walcott's own position as a member of the Caribbean bourgeoisie. In particular, the sixties and seventies see Walcott engaged in a war of words with those who, according to Rohlehr, claimed to speak for the citizens of the failed Federation – a function and role that Walcott had, Rohlehr argues, reserved for himself. Walcott's themes include revolution and compromise and his essays, plays and poems reference Trinidad, Cuba and the Americas as he seeks to investigate and reflect on the turn from colonization to post colonization and from a white-centred ethos to a sense of self more fully cognizant of the inter-racial and changing dynamics of the

Caribbean. His interventions led to his founding of the Little Carib Basement Theatre with Beryl McBurnie in 1959 and the Trinidad Theatre Workshop, which in themselves gave rise to tormented essays such as "What the Twilight Says: An Overture". What Rohlehr does [illegible] [illegible] *Prodigal* where Europe's own genocides take centre stage; and to place this work within the context of Walcott's desire to be the voice of the people and the crafter of a new aesthetic [illegible] tions, the at times paternalistic and increasingly conflicted and isolated voice and figure of the poet who, while articulating his life-long love and commitment to the islands, nevertheless consistently identifies his need to leave.

Cricket becomes the metaphor for man and poet, for Rohlehr and for Walcott, as they negotiate the changing attitudes to Caribbean politics, cultural and economic life and the failing fortunes of the West Indian cricket team. The image of Walcott astride two worlds is brought on at the close of Rohlehr's essay in the double-edged role of poet laureate who will poeticise the failing fortunes of the West Indies team and eulogise the dying victories of England. That he does this admirably and with candour and wit is indeed the sign of Walcott's power over language.

Walcott's love affair with language – his witty playfulness that leads with all the delight of a calypsonian to puns, innuendos and *double entendres* that are often hidden, as in *The Prodigal*, in the very belly of the texts – is always to the forefront in the various discussions. Walcott has written much about the language of poetry and the viability of the calypso as a form of poetic language. He has excelled in twinning the pithiness and the rancour of the calypsonian against the wit and satire of say Pope or the British dramatic tradition in plays and film scripts such as *Pantomime*[4] and in the much cited "The Spoilers Return".[5]

His love for the classics and his equally contradictory refusal to be bracketed off as a mimic man of Homer, Europe or Africa echo throughout his texts and not just in *Omeros*. Several chapters in this collection revisit Walcott's stance on Afrocentrism, his long and careful apprenticeship to European classical traditions, his battle with language as a reservoir of culture and history. Perhaps the most deliberately focused on such issues are the essays by Rachel Friedman and Rhonda Cobham-Sander. Friedman's essay argues not so much for influence but parallelism in Walcott's long relationship with the Homeric texts, or what she calls his "conversations" with the works he has read. *The Odyssey: A Stage Version*,[6] and *Omeros*[7] provide two examples of the delineation and elaboration of what Walcott has described in "The Muse of History" as "*simultaneous* concepts, not *chronological* concepts".[8] Friedman uses the classics and the figure of [illegible] to explore the ways in which oral literature of all ages relies on tribal memory and draws on equivalent archetypes.

The idea that a writer may use and reference the work of another, whether culture or individual, without slavishness is key to understanding Walcott's work and is also fundamental in seeing him as a Caribbean writer who has long been in dialogue with many other Caribbean writers, and whose quarrels with Naipaul and Brathwaite, for example, have led to significant thematic and formal elements and experiments. Rhonda Cobham-Sander's essay aptly entitled, "'Any Enemy So Was a Compliment': Walcott, Brathwaite and the Formal Possibilities of Creole" complicates Pat Ismond's by now classic essay "Walcott versus Brathwaite".[9] The polarities codified in this 1971 essay have shaped much of the discourse on the relationship between Walcott and Brathwaite and on Walcott's so called indebtedness to European forms and ideas. Cobham-Sander argues that while there has been incredible tension between these two major Caribbean poets, Walcott has absorbed many of the lessons taught by the African oriented Brathwaite, his apparent rival. Her analyses uncover several of the creole formations, ideas and narrative styles that Brathwaite has bequeathed to Walcott. Her essay traces Walcott's appropriation of the narrative of return and journeying in *Masks*[10] and sees this as the template for Achille's journey back to Africa, led by a swift to his ancestral home. But this is just the most obvious in a series of parallels and conversations between these two extraordinary innovators in Caribbean literature. Her reading places Achille and Hector and their irascibility and petty squabbles at the centre of an epic poem that is really about what it is to be a Caribbean person and a Caribbean poet. Their squabbling over a rusted can becomes metaphorically a re-visitation of those decades of rivalry between Brathwaite and Walcott. Both share with Naipaul a sense of Caribbean void, but for them this must yet give way to creative potential. This newness is to be found in the use of the creole and in the patterns that emerge when two languages dance and argue with each other: what emerges is a "crispness" of language when Walcott "stitches together rhymes across the two languages; for example, between "bitch" and "campêche" and when [p]atterns in one language also find their echo in the rhythms of the other." This Cobham-Sander argues is a lesson learnt from Brathwaite whose poems in *The Arrivants* demonstrate a capacity to make creole or nation language engender narrative tension as in "The Dust"[11] where sound and shape give expression to the existential dilemmas of black Barbadian women. Walcott's long-standing debate about the malleability of creole in poetic and narrative expression is here aligned to Brathwaite's daring experimentation in form and language. But the use of the creole and the play of two lines, European and Caribbean in tandem, also reinforce the battle between European and African and between old worlds and new. This leads to the shaping of new metaphors such as that of the coral to signify the creation of new civilisations out of the mutations and interchanging processes of creolisation as

Brathwaite has famously articulated in his much debated *Contradictory Omens*.[13] That Brathwaite actually made the coral his own metaphor long before Walcott appropriated it gives the reader much to think about.

But the gift of [illegible] Walcott [illegible] to emerge most fully in two late works, *The Prodigal* and *Tiepolo's Hound*. *Tiepolo's Hound* in particular engages with the idea of a poem that "paints in [illegible] him to Paris and in effect colonises Europe. The impact of his sense of light and colour on European Impressionism and Post Impressionism speaks to Walcott's own sense of the burgeoning impact of Caribbean art and expression on world literature. The idea of painting in dialect fully fleshes out the concrete visuality of the calypsonian's use of language, in particular the use of simile.

The Prodigal may be read as a culmination of these several themes and quests in Walcott's work. Not least among these is the poet's desire to journey, his constant movement and the sense of betrayal that this has given rise to in works such as *Arkansas Testament*. In *The Prodigal* there is no choice made as Edward Baugh points out. There is only an acknowledgment that home is where the heart is, or to quote both Baugh and Walcott, journeys follow maps "made in the heart". Ultimately the poet is a wanderer, but with a sense of home. Edward Baugh's analysis of Walcott's relationship to his islands situates Walcott's work in the debates about nationalism, citizenship and origins that fuelled the writings of the sixties and seventies. He notes that in the early seventies at the ACLALS conference in Jamaica, important since it marked the beginnings of sustained scholarship on Caribbean literature, scholars and writers "closed the door" on the debate about what constitutes Caribbean (or in this case, Anglophone Caribbean literature or West Indian literature). They were led by Edward Kamau Brathwaite who declared West Indian writing and culture to be distinctly African, and who articulated the need to write a counter discourse to Western literature, using Caliban rather than Prospero as the model. However, according to Baugh, by the nineties that "door" was resolutely reopened, and writers and academics perceived themselves as part of a global world, an idea fostered perhaps by the buzzword of globalization, and the seductive potential of a "global village". This Baugh links to a new "cordiality" formed by a new confidence.

Baugh's essay traces the development of Walcott's theme of "here" and "elsewhere" and even notes the overlap of disparate spaces in Walcott's spiritual positioning of these oppositions in the recent collection *White Egrets*. The critic argues persuasively that Walcott's [illegible] in the work of the late sixties and seventies was directly the result of a particular moment in history. He also cites *Omeros* as a specific turn towards Africa as a space of reconciliation. One must note, however, while agreeing with this assessment, that Achille's return to Africa in *Omeros* is not without ambiguity.

Equally poised between Walcott as articulator of a Caribbean aesthetic and Walcott as Janus faced is Harold McDermott's essay, which seeks to trace the ambiguities and the dependencies of Walcott's thought. Arnold and Eliot are identified as key influences here, but what is interesting is the gradual development of Walcott's position as a New World writer at one with writers such as Chamoiseau, whom he idolizes, and Borges and Lowell for example. His various arguments, as these emerge in the essays, suggest his tracking of ideological positions held by Caribbean intellectuals over the past six decades, and show his love of correspondences and the openness to influence that he shares with many other great poets.

If there is a lesson to be learnt from such analyses of Walcott's passionate attachment to place, his evolving ideas and reactions to West Indian Federation, négritude, creolisation and its discourses and what he saw as the cant of European critical theory, then one could say that his work yearns for a form within which these several differences and disparate parts might cohere. This is the rationale for Antoine-Dunne's analysis of the importance of film form and film sense in Walcott's work. Film as montage provides a formal principle for examining and delineating the conflictual relationships between races, cultures and histories as these exist within the Antilles. But film as myth-making and transformative process also gives to Walcott the capacity to "fly", to create new myths and to soar beyond the confines of the corporeal, the temporal and the ideological. His concept of simultaneity finds its most articulate expression through film. First there is the formal strategy in his use of superimposition which allows him to see all sides equally and with balance, not as a mere repetition of events but as happenings that elucidate the elemental nature of the human. In *Omeros* as film script, as novel poem, as dramatization of history, and as epic, Walcott deliberately deploys the lessons learnt from montage, in particular, classic montage. Here, Helen *is* Helen of Troy whose beauty caused the destruction of a civilisation and whose face launched a thousand ships. Helen is also St Lucia, over whose beauty Dutch, British and French fought and whose battles are part of the history of the Caribbean. She is fought for by the present day Achille and Hector. Their lust and their carnality are the stuff of legend – of the Homeric. Their leap out of time is enabled by the use of the swift as a movie projector, and the illusions thus engendered transcend the actual and enable the viewer/reader to experience the past and present as one occurrence. Helen's rage and resistance enable this sense of simultaneous time as they link her to W.B. Yeats's passionate intensity and the transformations thus engendered. Her beauty and the repercussions of that beauty lead to a series of "magical" leaps that are part of the transformative process articulated by the poem *Omeros*.

The most concrete expression of film's enabling of "*simultaneous* concepts" as opposed to "*chronological* concepts"[13] is in the market scene in *Omeros* where the pain of history is heard in the "iron roar of the market" [illegible] gutted fish are "slaves head-down on a hook" and "the gutted carcasses/ of crucified rebels, from orange-tiled villas".[14] There we find the fullest expression of what Walcott describes in "The Muse of History" [illegible] instant archaism" where "violence is felt with the simultaneity of history. So the death of a gaucho does not merely repeat, but is, the death of Caesar. Fact evaporates into myth." ("Muse", *What the Twilight Says*, p. 38).

Walcott opens his Nobel speech, *The Antilles: Fragments of Epic Memory*,[15] with a nod to film, and the filmic becomes his vehicle for understanding how a response to the past becomes more than nostalgia; this is because it speaks to the simultaneity of memory and the co-existence of past and present. Kenneth Ramchand examines Walcott's description of the Hindu dramatic production, Ramlila, as an act of faith that transcends nostalgia, as the expression of a tradition that constantly renews itself, possessing a vitality because it is not imprisoned by a sense of history, but because it is open to both the religious traditions of its ancestry and to the newness and creativity of that belief transplanted to a new world. *The Antilles* in this sense continues the preoccupations of the 1974 essay "The Muse of History" in its refusal to be contained by chronology and its advocacy of poetry that both forgets and courts the haunting spectres of the past. What Ramchand foregrounds is the function of memory in the transmission of the Trinidad Ramlila and the relationship between memory, religious ritual and performance. The "play" generates intense emotion through the spiritual devotion of its participants. This remembrance and this devotion are read as acts of possession and defiance.

Ramchand's essay returns us to "the Figure of Crusoe"[16] with its memorable image of poetry as a burning of the past. For him the archetypes of Ramlila speak to the poet Walcott of acts of purification by fire as preludes to the new. Ramlila brings together in the poet's mind the function of art and of religion as vehicles through which the human person arrives at a state of intense feeling, an emotion that transcends time and space and crosses race, creed and culture.

The many sides to Walcott leave us with a very open-ended poetry – a poetry that is always surprising in its stitching together of disparate parts and its self-referentiality. His poetry can be accused of being anti-woman, or reactionary in its alignment to a European [illegible] particular class, or even self-indulgent. Yet Walcott's friendships, and in particular his long standing relationship and shared [illegible] with Seamus Heaney,[17] situate him as a postcolonial writer in the very strictest sense of such labels.

But the many avenues and ways of entering the highly complex writings with their multiple references to prior work and to the work of others often leave the Caribbean person and the St Lucian, according to St Lucian critic Antonia MacDonald, with a sense that Walcott's poems in particular are not really for the ordinary Caribbean citizen. Her essay seeks to redress the problem evident in a body of work that states that it is there to "give those feet a voice"[18] and yet is often unread by the people the poet eulogises. MacDonald carefully unravels and contextualizes two early and well known poems in "Students, I present the young poet, Derek Walcott" in an attempt to make Walcott's early years as a poet relevant to the experiences of the young Caribbean person.

For Walcott, the encroaching years seem to have brought, as he has put it, "regrets" and a sense of death that exceeds the many white cities in his head, and that calls forth fading images of his early life and those friendships in St Lucia. Increasingly his poetry negotiates the space between death and life and death and the after death as Monsignor Patrick Anthony aptly puts it. But whether one compares his religious sense to the faith and Catholicism of Dunstan St Omer, he who is named Gregorias in *Another Life*, or whether one sees in this relationship a kind of envy of that sustaining belief, there is no gainsaying the fascination that the spiritual domain holds for Walcott. Both George Handley and Monsignor Anthony in their respective ways discuss Walcott's "flights", his desire to soar above the body as in "The Season of Phantasmal Peace",[19] or the angels that ascend, descend and reappear in Santa Cruz Valley in the work *The Prodigal*. Dolphins and angels are images of Walcott's final phase; his desire to make right and to leave and bequeath a legacy to these islands that will not diminish with death and with the passing of time, but that will remain a part of our collective memory.

Endnotes

1. Derek Walcott, *Another Life* (London: Jonathan Cape, 1973), p. 139.
2. Gordon Rohlehr, *Transgression, Transition, Transformation. Essays in Caribbean Culture* (Port of Spain: Lexicon, 2007).
3. Walcott, *The Prodigal* (New York: Farrar, Straus and Giroux, 2004).
4. Walcott, *Pantomime* in *Remembrance & Pantomime* (New York: Farrar, Straus and Giroux, 1980).
5. Walcott, "The Spoiler's Return", *The Fortunate Traveller* (London: Faber & Faber, 1982), pp. 53-60; and *Collected Poems* 1948-1984 (New York: Farrar, Straus and Giroux, 1986), pp. 432-438.
6. Walcott, *The Odyssey: A Stage Version* (London: Faber and Faber, 1993).

7. Walcott, *Omeros* (London: Faber and Faber 1990).
8. "The Muse of History" [1974], *What the Twilight Says: Essays* (London, Faber and Faber, 1998), pp. 36-64.
9. Patricia Ismond, "Walcott versus Brathwaite", *Caribbean Quarterly* 17, nos. 3-4 (September-December 1971): 54-71.
10. Edward Kamau Brathwaite, *Masks* (Oxford: Oxford University Press, 1968); and in *The Arrivants: A New World Trilogy* (Oxford: Oxford University Press, 1973).
11. Edward Kamau Brathwaite, *Rights of Passage* (Oxford: Oxford University Press, 1967) and *The Arrivants. A New World Trilogy.*
12. Kamau Brathwaite, *Contradictory Omens: Cultural Diversity and Integration in the Caribbean* (Kingston: Savacou Publications, 1974).
13. Walcott, "The Muse of History", *What the Twilight Says: Essays*, pp. 36-64.
14. Walcott, *Omeros*, pp. 37-38.
15. Walcott, *The Antilles, Fragments of Epic Memory. The Nobel Lecture* (London: Faber and Faber 1993).
16. "The Figure of Crusoe" [1965], *Critical Perspectives on Derek Walcott*, Ed. Robert Hamner (Washington, DC: Three Continents Press, 1993), pp. 33-40.
17. See Heaney's production of *The Cure at Troy* in Derry 1990 and the collaboration between Walcott and Heaney in London in their version of "The Burial at Thebes", an opera, at the Globe, London, 2008.
18. Walcott, *Omeros*, p. 76.
19. "The Season of Phantasmal Peace", *The Fortunate Traveller* (New York: Farrar, Straus and Giroux, 1981), pp. 98-99; and *Collected Poems*, pp. 464-465.

GORDON ROHLEHR

"THE MAN WHO LOVED ISLANDS: DEREK WALCOTT'S LITERARY CARETAKERSHIP OF THE ARCHIPELAGO"

I

In 1948 Derek Walcott published a poem entitled "Travelogue"[1] in which he sought to warn visitors against being fooled by glamorous portraits of Caribbean islands, "these worlds/ We dreamed of in travelogues and gorgeous poster" (*25 Poems*, p. 17). Noting a certain fierceness and sorrow in these slowly healing archipelagic societies, he unmasks mediocrity beneath their glamorous façades, and an intense struggle towards self-betterment in the face of smallness, frustration and narrowness of opportunity.

> Its people are small and build their architecture
> Of futures, in small rooms late at night, in courses
> On accountancy, the violin and shorthand.
>
> Observe how later here your same boredoms will grow
> Concealed like cancer, in magistrate, tennis champ-
> Ion, in doctor, doctor's wife and pensioner (*25 Poems*, p. 17)

An informed tourist-guide, Walcott discloses that the islands have been moving towards "a kind of democracy and politics" (p. 17), but remain internally divided along lines of racial and ethnic tribalism. Walcott at eighteen then declares a mission to transform his class-, caste- and race-stricken society, and exhorts all others who share his dream to join him and work towards its realization.

> Let all on islands of the heart construct a day
> Of the federated archipelago, black
> And white live apart, if so, but dream the same dream (*25 Poems*, p. 18)

Walcott's as yet indistinct community of dreamers, each isolated on his island of the heart, would have to contend with the harsh struggle for upward mobility taking place in the islands, whose civilization is little more than:

A civilization of tennis and country club
Hovels, and men who pulled themselves up by the braces
The blackest is seen at bars with knight, complexions rub

In an inescapable democracy of races.

The word "inescapable" suggests that the traditional denizens of the country clubs throughout the archipelago, the white proprietorial élite, had, since the [illegible] would [illegible] presence of an upwardly mobile black meritocracy in their clubs, bars and sports teams, but could not escape the inevitable process and consequences of democratic change.

The cricket field was one forum where this "inescapable democracy of races" seemed to be taking place. Yet in reality, nowhere was race and class prejudice more evident than in that forum where plantation autocracy was still very much in control of the venues of performance, the selection process and the game itself as a shaping cultural agency. Cricket had emerged with the victory over England in 1950 of the West Indies cricket team as a symbol of West Indian unity and the potential that resided in the hoped-for Federation, in which Walcott seems fervently to have believed. But cricket, itself as much a plantation product as sugar or cocoa, could not alter the deep structure of racialism, class and colour prejudice upon which Caribbean societies had been erected.

So Walcott in 1951 in *Poems* sees in cricket the ambiguity of an apparent social togetherness and the thinly concealed reality of a society divided by its ancient prejudices. He was at that point in time a student of the University College of the West Indies, Jamaica.

And cricketers, advancing before the language of applause
Are cheered by yellow, pink, black hands,
Suspiciously united in one cause,
As though the gunman, Duty, behind them stands. [...]
[...]
Bully my gift to a nervous crowd of roars
Conceals my anger under lip-thin laughter,
And when the pavilion of pigments applauds after
Some skin-surpassing stroke, I itch to scratch the sores

Under the green epidermis of the lawn.[3]

Here Walcott, recognizing the lot he shares with the emerging cricketers as an icon of the new Caribbean nationalism, declares his violent mistrust of the evolving bourgeoisie of [illegible] who applaud his talent. This mistrust has remained an essential element of his relationship with audience, public, literati and glitterati, over the more than six decades of his creative life.

This essay seeks to determine the difficulties Walcott faced in carrying out his mission of caretakership of the emerging sensibility of the archipelago; the challenges that have confronted him between "Travelogue" (1948) and his anthologies of travelogues, *The Fortunate Traveller* (1981), *Midsummer* (1984) and *The Prodigal* (2004), in which he often assumes the persona of traveller, wanderer and pilgrim, a man and mind in perennial transition between worlds, women, loves and destinations. "Islands," Walcott has written, "can only exist / If we have loved in them."[4] His quarrel with the Federation that was eventually inaugurated in 1958 was that it prohibited freedom of movement between the islands, with the more developed (or less underdeveloped) islands setting up nationalist barriers – this even before they had been properly proclaimed nations – against immigrants from the smaller islands. Walcott regarded such barriers as making "a mockery of the heart". They were walls that literally and metaphorically restricted love, interface, exchange, sharing, intercourse between people of the archipelago, and the fact that such walls had been approved and established by "our first parliaments"[5] augured ill for the Federation itself.

The collection of poems *In a Green Night* (1962) contains several poems, e.g. "Pays Natal", "En Mi-Careme" and "A Sea Chantey" that illustrate Walcott's love for the islands. Yet the important "Tales of the Islands", a sequence of ten sonnets, reflects little of that love, providing portraits of human and ecological dereliction that culminate in the narrator's departure from the island and "all that I love" (*In a Green Night,* p. 30). "Tales of the Islands" renders St Lucia with, if not the "scrupulous meanness" James Joyce employed in his portrayal of genteel decadence in *Dubliners*, a severity of seeing that is its equal. The repeated images of Walcott's "Tales" are those of paralysis; of stymied filth-clogged lives reaping the wages of sin, which we learn is life rather than death. The threads of the intermeshing web of themes in "Tales" are religious hypocrisy, decadence, disease, prostitution, necromancy, madness, drug abuse, drunken stupor and a state of undeadness. Its sounds are howl of bolom and loupgarou and of jalousies slammed tight against such noises; snicker of cynical laughter at the distress of the poor-white Miss Rossignol ("Tales" III, p. 27), and the failed black writer.

The final poem, a poem of parting and perhaps escape/flight, is an aerial portrait of the island, restored to a sort of imaginary pristine purity via the distance that each symbolic and widening gyre of the aeroplane establishes between the hitherto impassive narrator and the idealized island residing in his mind and heart. He prays, ironically, that nothing will change, after having consistently depicted scenarios of unchanging stasis and spiritual death. One would think that he could owe no fidelity to such a place. When he speaks of each mile covered as dividing "us", he may be talking not of the island, but of his first love Andreuille/Anna who is herself poised to leave St Lucia.

In Walcott's portrayal of Anna in "Pays Natal", "En Mi-Carême", in his essay "Leaving School" and *Another Life*, one sees the roots of a tendency to render highly idealized women as landscape, and landscape as idealized female essence. Anna is not just one of innumerable daughters of the canny owner of "a spacious [illegible]" [illegible] family home, but a creature of light, shade, colour and form imaginatively constructed from all of the heroines in the literature that Walcott has read both before and after 1949 [illegible] Tolstoy's Anna Karenina, [illegible] Florence Nightingale, the nurse in Hemingway's *A Farewell to Arms* and Lara of the novel *Dr. Zhivago*. Besides being a composite of all of these fictional women, Anna is a collection of what might be termed "visual illusions" derived from the portraits of women and landscapes done by various European painters.

Loving the island and loving in the island; loving the island and loving its iconic women, or the idea, fantasy and illusion with which Walcott invests these women, are the same thing. Walcott at eighteen, forty-three, fifty-four or seventy-four displays a remarkable consistency in his conflation of woman, landscape and painting into fantastic idealized objects of the poet's desire. Thus, Anna of *Another Life*, a creature of purity, holiness and almost sacred love is forerunner of the Swiss Alpine Ice Maiden in *The Prodigal* who is in reality a waitress at the lodge where he is staying, but who "becomes", through Walcott's depiction of her, a Muse of the place and, simultaneously, an object of his sexual fantasizing.

Similarly, Paola, Sandra, Roberta – young women enrolled in a class Walcott the Wanderer is teaching in Milan – become in his imagination figures in an art gallery

> immortal models
> of those framed miracles of portraiture
> and their invisible strokes, this one
> with the Botticellian cheekbones, that one
> with the gaze of the ferret-stroking girl
> by Leonardo

They are, simultaneously, objects of Walcott's Yeatsian

> […] implacable lust that came with old age –
> [illegible]
> in the name of their common art, common craft,
> an old white eagle beating priapic wings. (*The Prodigal*, p. 32)

Later, Roberta and Esperanza are described as "women who contained their cities" (*The Prodigal*, p. 48), thus completing the link between woman, landscape and painting as the conflated object of Walcott's passion. That link had already been forged in *Another Life* when Anna and the island were perceived as one,[8] and when to leave the island's dreadfully constricting space was, because of Anna, to leave all he loved.

Anna, Walcott writes in that magical, autobiographical essay "Leaving School":

> gave off a nimbus whose quality was golden, the colour of the light itself, and it made her the generator of those canoes that returned at dusk and of the stillness of the water. [...] I surrendered my heart to her as wholly as I had surrendered my imagination to her landscape. (pp. 129-130).

Yet, despite the completeness of this surrender of heart, Walcott's desire was unfulfilled by Anna, the Madonna and Muse of the poems of that formative period. There were the dark ladies of his profane carnal desire, the "two shilling whores" ("Leaving School", p. 134) who in "Tales of the Islands" are framed in a "queer" – the word meant only "strange" in those days – green light. There was, Walcott reminds his alter ego, "the Indian woman you finger-poked in the doorway"[9] and "the Negro whore on the drawing-room floor/ under the silent portraits of your parents,"[10] who was, most likely, a domestic servant in another life.

These literally and metaphorically "dark" women lack names, faces, or representation in painting; though they do have literary predecessors in the equally faceless prostitutes sought out by Joyce's Stephen Dedalus during his blind tormented plunge into a world of flesh. Walcott confesses that the "current hero" of his early force-ripe manhood was "the blasphemous, arrogant Stephen Dedalus" ("Leaving School", p. 133).

> Like Stephen, I had my nights of two shilling whores, of 'tackling in the Alley', and silently howling remorse. Like him, I was a knot of paradoxes: hating the Church and loving her rituals, learning to hate England as I worshipped her language, sanctifying A. the more I betrayed her, a Methodist-lecher, a near-Catholic-ascetic, loving the island and wishing I could get the hell out of it. ("Leaving School", p. 134)

This "knot of paradoxes" will be constantly in evidence in Walcott's six decades of literary caretakership of the archipelago.

II

The scope of Walcott's coverage of the Caribbean has been astoundingly wide. Beginning with his native island from which he has constantly departed, of which he always dreams while lost in alien landscapes, and to which he always returns in reality and imagination, Walcott has written a trilogy of plays about Haiti, sequences of poems on Guyana and the Virgin Islands, a play and long poem on Jamaica and perhaps a dozen plays and scores of poems inspired by his residence in and encounter with the complex universe of Trinidad and Tobago. This shortlist excludes a play such as *Marie Laveau*, set in nineteenth century New Orleans, which is in some ways a kind of Caribbean island planted on North American soil. Through this distinguished caretakership he has raised issues of home, exile, identity, the necessity for healing from history, and reconciliation. He has in the process defined and redefined notions of the artist's mission, and probed the paradox of alienation from and commitment to the still unfederated islands of location and dislocation, of rootedness and transitionality.

Walcott's sojourn in Jamaica (1950-1954) and then (1957-1958) in[illegible] "Pays Natal", [illegible] Passion", and "Brise Marine". Walcott's biographer Bruce King mentions several poems written by Walcott about his relationship with Faye Moyston, his first wife, including a sequence of thirteen sonnets dedicated to her, but apparently never published.[12] Faye was no replacement for Andreuille as Muse of place and the fifties were not a decade of fresh encounter with the compelling and new Jamaican landscape and people, but rather a consolidation of modes of contemplation and envisioning already evident in the foundational St Lucian years (1944-1950). "Pays Natal" and "En Mi-Careme" are superb examples of Walcott's Andreuille-inspired St Lucian poems where woman, painting, landscape, colour and light combine to create the characteristic Walcott Muse.

Sojourn in Jamaica with its echoes of Garveyism, nascent Rastafari movement and stirrings of pan-Africanism in the politics, forced Walcott to contemplate the possible consequences of Africans of the Diaspora coming into consciousness of their history of servitude. "Ruins of a Great House" and "A Far Cry from Africa" reveal Walcott's agonized wrestling with the social and political dimensions of blackness and Africanity, and the implications of the exploding liberation struggle in colonial Africa for multi-ethnic Caribbean societies. Caretakership began to assume the form of prophetic warning against any revolution inspired by an ideology of racial revenge. Walcott's plays, *Henri Christophe* (1950) and *Drums and Colours* (1958), strategically located at the beginning and towards the end of the 1950s decade, both enter into the nightmare of Caribbean history whose heroes, Columbus, Raleigh, Toussaint, seem to end up mad or incarcerated or mad and incarcerated, and whose redemption could lie only in a reconciliation of its warring elements.

The fifties deepened Walcott's reputation, distinct since the very early years, of being a gifted child, genius, visionary and architect of New World Caribbean sensibility [illegible] and Painter [illegible]. The role had its difficulties and Walcott was aware of them. He would by the early seventies portray himself as Janus-faced, looking backwards into the past, forwards into the future and perhaps sideways into the ambiguous present.

> [illegible],
> I saw with twin heads
> and everything I say is contradicted (*Another Life*, p. 139)

True to his Eurocentricity, Walcott identifies himself as Janus; but Janus, Anansi, Legba and Eshu are different names for the Crossroads sensibility that writers of Walcott's pioneering and pathfinding generation would affirm, arriving at such affirmation from radically different directions and journeyings. Wilson Harris, Kamau Brathwaite, Denis Williams, Derek Walcott: all are avatars of Eshu-Elegbara, Afro-Greek, Afro-Saxon, mulatto, mestizo bouncing up on common mourning-ground.

The fifties culminated for Walcott in the honour that the "founding fathers" of the West Indian Federation bestowed on him, of writing the historical pageant *Drums and Colours*[13] to mark the inauguration of the Federation. It was regional affirmation of his profile of gifted, redemptive son, an heroic role that has been bestowed variously on artists, athletes, cricketers and politicians. The sixties were a new beginning. Walcott's exposure to Trinidad's volatile, hybridized, infinitely transgressive and optimistic society led to a new marriage, Muse, family and landscape of possibility.

He immediately stamped his authority on the place, premiering *Ti Jean and His Brothers* (1958)[14] his play based on St Lucian folklore. Ironically, perhaps, when *Ti Jean and His Brothers* was revised and resuscitated in the middle of 1970, just after the lifting of the curfew that had accompanied the State of Emergency, it was celebrated as a play about three phases of Black revolt, culminating in the burning of the Devil's plantation and the defeat of oppression to cries of "Ay Ti" – yes Ti Jean and Haiti.[15] Yet Walcott might have meant otherwise as his other meditations on Black Power – *In a Fine Castle*, *Dream on Monkey Mountain*, "What the Twilight Says: An Overture" and Chapter XIX of *Another Life* – clearly illustrate.

Walcott founded the Little Carib Basement Theatre in 1959, working at first in tandem with Beryl McBurnie and some of the leading actors from various theatre groups in Trinidad, but gradually shaping a company that was to become a creature of his own will, intelligence, direction and even misdirection. His preferred style of leadership was distinctly patriarchal and authoritarian and the Theatre Workshop would in time come under threat when various members began to question whether the company was fulfilling its original mandate of performing a repertoire of distinguished Caribbean and contemporary modern plays, or simply becoming an extension of its director's will and showcase of his work alone.

Walcott in 1960 sealed his commitment to his adopted country, Trinidad and Tobago, by marrying one of its daughters, Margaret Maillard. *In a Green Night*, published in 1962, the year of Independence for both Trinidad and Tobago and Jamaica, provides no clue to Walcott's early experience of this new island in which he had chosen to put down roots. That text was really the fruit of his St Lucian, and to a lesser extent, his Jamaican years. It is in the ominously named *The Castaway* (1965) that one gets a clear picture of the nature of Walcott's encounter with this new domain of what he still considered – despite the dissolution of the Federation – to be his caretakership of the archipelago.

If Walcott's efforts with the Theatre Workshop provided the challenge of constant experimentation with oral and performance styles and the necessity to cope with the strengths and limitations of his company of actors and to accommodate his appeal to that limited sector of the [illegible] Trinidadian public [illegible] *[illegible] and Other Poems* (1965) was increasingly about alienation, void, the old theme of "nothing" already pervasive in *In a Green Night*; drought, infernal heat, light intensified to glare, and the reduction of voice, song and commitment to nothing – "Nothing, the rage with which the sandfly's head is filled."[16]

Stasis, inertia, paralysis, the keynotes of his earlier St Lucian phase, become pervasive here and counterpoint all that urgent activity in drama: the amazing energy he displayed as a feature columnist and culture and art critic; his flirtation with calypso-judging and carnival-drama, the latter of which would end in frustration and bitter polemic about folk culture and its accessibility or otherwise as a basis for Art; the poetic potential or limitations of Calypso and the performed word; the orchestral inadequacies of the steelband and the near impossibility of creating theatre out of the theatrical. Janus-faced, Walcott sought simultaneously to appropriate and build from the folk arts and to reject them as inadequate to the Afro-Greek/Creole-Classical aesthetic ideology to which he still clung, the scaffolding he still sought to erect towards the construction of an hybridized, crossroads sensibility.

Walcott's audience had never been the general population. In Jamaica and Trinidad it had consisted of the educated middle-class, Walcott's class, who had recognized his talents and acclaimed his excellence, basking in the sheen of his charisma. Walcott instinctively mistrusted anointment from this audience and community as was evident since an early poem like "[illegible]" ([illegible]) where even the St Lucian bourgeoisie had fallen under his withering scrutiny. Mistrust did not wane during the first decade of the Trinidad years. It intensified. In "What the Twilight Says: An Overture", he declared his contempt for

> [illegible] who had accepted the limitations of their society, but whose solicitude concealed insult.
>
> You had to endure their respect, their vapid, reassuring smiles at parties and those dinners you were summoned to to electrify with abuse. You went, knowing how dead they would be behind eyes that, [illegible] in the sunny features, showed the [illegible]. They were ones that denied their [illegible]. The idea of a theatre and the possibilities of their cities bored them, because they had accepted failure as logic.[17]

If this is how Walcott really felt about his patrons, his public, why did he not simply decline their invitations? The answer is that he needed them as much as he despised them; and conversely, they might have deplored his ungraciousness as much as they savoured the prospect of basking in the glare of his charisma. The severity of Walcott's attack increased when he unmasked those black and brown new men with white wives as his rivals and competitors for the caretakership of the people's interest. They are now defined as enemies or rather as a single collective undifferentiated "enemy".

> [...] the enemy was those who had elected themselves as protectors of the people, frauds who cried out against indignities done to the people, who urged them to acquire pride which meant abandoning their individual dignity, who cried out that black was beautiful like transmitters from a different revolution without explaining what they meant by beauty, all of these had emerged from nowhere suddenly, a different, startling "canaille." ("What the Twilight Says", p. 35)

Walcott's naming of "canaille" – mongrels, pot hounds – has progressed from what he calls a new brown meritocracy, to black and brown men, presumably members of the same meritocracy, with white wives, to enemies advocating black pride, excavating historic injustices done by white people to black people, and preaching a new gospel, one that was alien to the Afro-Graeco-European aesthetic, that "black is beautiful". The enemies, coming from "nowhere" suddenly, are clearly recognized by Walcott as being different from the patrons who would invite him to dinner. Yet he lumps all groups, *tout moun*, together and excoriates them collectively with the same tongue-lashing.

There were no black or brown men with white wives among the leadership of the 1970 Black Power movement in Trinidad. Most of the younger men were unmarried, while the spouses of the older leaders, black and East Indian (for example George Weekes and Winston Lennard) trade union leaders, were also Afro- and Indo-Trinidadian. What the "enemies" represented was the beginning of a counter-discourse to the understandably contradictory Janus-faced text of Walcott's hitherto unchallenged stewardship over the people of the archipelago whom he simultaneously loved and despised. "What the Twilight Says: An Overture" and Chapter XIX of *Another Life*, where he condemns the same undifferentiated assemblies of "enemies" in the name of hyper-idealized "My Anna, my Beatrix", are one part of Walcott's response to the threat to his authority to represent and the authenticity of the terms of his caretakership.

The other side of Walcott's response was the hermetic self-alienation implicit in his donning of the Crusoe mask; the consolation of exile in the midst of the mediocre, the unworthy, the insincere, the fraudulent and the merely indifferent. Walcott's Crusoe, elaborately decoded by Walcott himself,[18] is a mask and persona behind and through which Walcott creates on his happy desert island of useless, shallow Trinidadians; that is, until the advent of Black Power jolts him from his occupation of abandoning dead metaphors" and creating new ones out of the landscape into which he has been exiled. The Swamp [illegible] [illegible] metaphors that Walcott imagines into existence from his Crusoe-like withdrawal. Withdrawal from society becomes a pre-condition for the [illegible] exclusively as a dedication to craft and hard dry sculpture, and a recognition that "if the poem begins to shrivel" he should no longer distend his heart.[20]

In the title poem of *The Gulf and Other Poems* (1969) the Crusoe stance of exile at home is replaced by the location of the narrator in the air; which foreshadows the poems of the last three decades where the protagonist views the world of history and political affairs from the air or through the changing window-frames of moving vehicles. "The Gulf" depicts a journey over the American South and the Gulf of Mexico; one that will possibly end somewhere in the Caribbean. As in Chapter X of "Tales of the Islands", this location affords the narrator a panoramic view of the world beneath him: the still strife-torn stage of Civil Rights and Black revolution that will break out in the Caribbean during the decade of the seventies. Read alongside such poems as "Ché", "Negatives", "Elegy" and "Blues" (all in *The Gulf*), "The Gulf" is a resolute rejection of revolution as a possible solution of the archipelago's problems.

"Elegy," dated precisely June 6th 1968, the date of US Senator Robert F. Kennedy's assassination, begins:

> Our hammock swung between Americas
> we miss you, Liberty. Che's
> bullet-riddled body falls,
> and those who cried the Republic must first die
> to be reborn are dead,
> the freeborn citizen's ballot in the head. (*The Gulf*, p. 31)

The Kennedy brothers, John and Robert are [illegible] Malcolm X or Martin Luther King, but one senses that Walcott's "Elegy" is written with a sad awareness of all of these assassinations and a surmise about whether they might not all have originated from the same source.

Walcott's initial concern seems to be with the symbolic significance of Che Guevara's death. Che was, above all others, [illegible], a gifted, redemptive son: doctor, bourgeois hero, abandoning his country and class comforts for Marti's greater cause, the bringing into being of "Nuestra America", a larger concept than the North American Revolution, embracing as it did both North and South America and the islands in between. Born in Argentina, Che fights for the liberation of Cuba from the American-endorsed Batista régime; becomes chief ideologue of the Castroite revolution whose ideals he seeks to transport to Bolivia, another but a far less congenial outpost of his notional "Nuestra America". He fails and is killed, a martyr for the Revolution.

No one could possibly doubt the authenticity of Che's commitment. He bears no resemblance to the come-from-nowhere bourgeoisie that two years later Walcott berates for their false stewardship and predictable betrayal of the masses. Che, who spoke of the true revolutionary as being driven by a deep feeling of love, transcends race in his commitment. But Che is dead, as are the dreamers of a new world-order emerging out of the apocalyptic destruction of the old Republic. What his death signifies for Walcott is not immediately clear: perhaps it is the death of all revolutionary possibility, or the futility of choosing the path of revolution; what Victor Questel termed in his assessment of the failure of the so-called February Revolution of 1970, "the ash of effort".[21]

The bulk of "Elegy," however, focuses not on Che and Latin American Revolution, the quest for "Our America", but on the equally dreadful implications of the failure of the North American Revolution, then just under two centuries old. Part of this failure has been the inscription of genocide as the founding American experience, and the mythologisation of genocide via Western movies. Walcott measures the potential consequence of historical atrocity now that ancient wounds are being reopened and genocide's victims break into voice.

> Some splintered arrowhead lodged in her brain
> sets the black singer howling in his bear trap
> shines young eyes with the brightness of the mad,
> tires the old with her residual sadness (*The Gulf*, p. 31)

The 'her' here is America whose unhealing wound has begun to fester. The fact that this wound is caused by an "arrowhead" tells us that Walcott's concern is as much with freeborn – i.e. white – America's paranoia that the pacified Native American can still erupt at any time, as with the growing "madness" that can possess a radicalized youth to seek, perhaps, Che's martyrdom in the cause of Revolution. The aggressively defensive reaction of the freeborn citizen, himself a product of the American Revolution, to this ingrained fear of a latter-day reprisal is to fire a bullet into the head of any contemporary revolutionary. The products of Revolution become in time its most conservative enemies.

Walcott shares the fear that a revolution of reprisal might be in the offing, and that the alternative possibility of humane reconciliation and peace that he has always advocated may, with all the assassinations that have stained the decade of the sixties, be indeed remote. He concludes "The Gulf" with the declaration:

> I have no home
> [...]

[illegible]

boils for that day when in the Lord God's name
the coals of fire are heaped upon the head
of all whose gospel is the whip and flame

age after age, the ministering dead. (*The Gulf*, pp. 29-30)

This grim conclusion does not mean that he has abandoned his [illegible] [illegible] swinging between the equally failed revolutionary models of North and South America, but that he is prepared to redefine the terms of his stewardship: to abandon the concept of "home" if societies and sects continue to propagate ideologies that are driven by lust for revenge, retribution and murder. Towards the end of the 1960s, Walcott began to see clear signs that Trinidad and Tobago was developing into the sort of society he could no longer call "home", and the question then arose of why then did he remain.

"They'll keep on asking, why did you remain?" (*The Gulf*, p. 70) he writes in "Hic Jacet", the last poem in *The Gulf and Other Poems*. The tense of the verb "did" suggests that the "they" of the subject are friends and fellow-artists who migrated long ago and are curious as to why Walcott has not done so as well. He answers the question first negatively and then positively. He stayed not to win the acclaim and adulation of "hoarse and hungry thousands" (*The Gulf*, p. 70). His dialogue with the people, whom he says he loved before they became popular, has been neither the pragmatic one of the politician seeking votes and acclamation; nor the hypocritical one of the academic recently returned and seeking roots he had never previously affirmed; nor the parasitic one of a new "frock-coated, iridescent" race of "dung beetles" who have begun to crawl over the people.

This third cohort, termed dung beetles perhaps because they reside in filth, relish filth and privately believe that the people are filth, are also described as "iridescent", because they change colour with every change of light. Their lavish clothes betray their [illegible] and inauthenticity. As noted above, Walcott the next year, in "What the Twilight Says: an Overture", vehemently dismisses this new set of would-be leaders and lovers of the people as [illegible] and [illegible]. He [illegible] identifies them as the chief [illegible] of [illegible] dangerous Black nationalist ideology.

Walcott next declares that he did not remain "to spite some winter-bitten novelist / praised for his accuracy of phlegm". The reference here is clearly to V.S. Naipaul, who had in *The Middle Passage*, *A Flag on the Island* and *The Mimic Men* [illegible] and [illegible] Caribbean islands. Walcott in "Hic Jacet" distinguishes between his own commitment until death and burial to the people, and Naipaul's contemptuous spitting on and rejection of them. This is deeply ironic when one considers that the islands have been inspiring rage and nausea in Walcott as well, who is much nearer to choosing exile than he can foresee.

Walcott now provides positive reasons for his choice of Caribbean parochialism over metropolitan exile when he says he stayed:

> [...] for something rooted, unwritten
> that gave us its benediction
> its particular pain

He stayed, that is, because of his commitment to writing his previously unwritten island into identity and visibility. He had, since *The Castaway*, recognized the blessing – "benediction" – he calls it – of having been given "a green world, one without metaphors" to name, paint, inscribe and endow with its first meanings. He stayed because:

> I loved them all, the names
> of shingled, rusting towns

He liked smallness, provincialism and its power to make one feel that one's work could make a difference to people's lives.

> I pretended subtly to lose myself in crowds
> knowing my passage would alter their reflection (*The Gulf*, p. 70)

Such almost egoless self-mergence with people and landscape is restorative. The poet alters the people's self-contemplation: the landscape and manscape restore his soul. It is a claim that Kamau Brathwaite also makes in *Mother Poem*.[22]

One year earlier Walcott had declared, in an interview with fellow-poet and playwright Dennis Scott: "Now my personal life is calm and my poetry is not that involved or tormented." He presented himself then as having moved beyond the alienation of the mid-sixties.

> I have written my last kind of Crusoe poem and now I am very keen on looking at how a table looks good in the morning – you know – across the table with your wife looking down on your children. This is what fascinates me now.[23]

This settled domestic phase, as we have seen, does not last too long, what with the grappe of assassinations mentioned above, particularly that of Martin Luther King who Nina Simone in her elegiac song describes as "the King of love",[24] whose murder has opened the American nation to the possibility of blindly retributive violence.

Startled, Walcott is anything but calm or self-assured as he lurches into the 1970s. It is his Janus-faced capacity for self-contradiction that he reveals when in one breath he seeks to clarify the terms of his exemplary rootedness and commitment to his family and the people, while in another revealing dire divisions between himself and a mediocre, hypocritical and potentially malicious public. His Muse becomes "Irascibility" [illegible] helps him to recognize, call out and verbally excoriate his enemies.

> Irascibility, muse of middle age,
> how often you have felt you have wasted your life
> among a people with no moral centre,
> to want to move from the contagion of too many friends,
> the heart congealing into stone,
> how many would prefer to [illegible]
> [illegible]
> and [illegible] catch in the corner of [illegible]
> the uncertified odour of your death? (*Another Life*, pp. 122-123)

By the start of the seventies Walcott had begun to portray himself as the [illegible] lover of islands, [illegible] and continuously reborn creative soul now at risk of contamination from his diseased friends; and a protector of the moral centre that his people lacked. Loving such folk had begun to prove impossible and as a strategy of self-protection it had become necessary to harden his heart, to be stoical, self-contained, impermeable; to become more inaccessible than Crusoe in his cave or stockade. To continue overseeing a society where even one's friends wished to see one reduced to failure, dereliction and even death, was to take upon oneself the ordeal of Sisyphus. These island-rocks were truly hard places, impossible surfaces for the planting of a new civilization. They certainly had not proven to be the "islands of the heart"[25] he had longed for in "Travelogue" (1948).

In *In a Fine Castle* (1970) – later rewritten and published as *The Last Carnival* (1986), Walcott explores the dilemma of a French Creole family caught in the trauma of the 1970 Black Power uprising in Trinidad and faced with the choice of either remaining and standing their ground or fleeing their ancestral mansion and the island itself. It is Walcott's dilemma, barring the fact that he had been bequeathed no fine castle but rather "genteel Methodist poverty"; and like his main character, the black journalist Brown, Walcott deeply empathized with the situation of the French Creoles.

One of the play's central images is a painting by W[illegible] depicting a community of people fleeing an island but looking back longingly on the place they are escaping, even as their feet approach the ship's gangplank. The prospect of leaving the island, then, was clear in Walcott's mind in 1970 when Black Power catalysed the subliminal terrors he shared with the [illegible] paranoia.

For the play's epigraph he quoted the first stanza of Baudelaire's "Voyage à Cythère", a translation of which he provided on the programme:

> What is this sad, dark island? Cythera.
> A place, they told us, famous in old songs,
> [illegible] Eldorado where the old hope never [illegible].
> [illegible] a new place full of the old [illegible][26]

The last line is almost totally an invention of Walcott's. Baudelaire's verse reads "Regardez, après tout: c'est une pauvre terre" and is meant to mark the narrator's flat disillusion at the difference between the Cythère of legend and reality. Walcott's rendition draws attention to the element of stasis and unchange in the so-called New World of the Caribbean, where a new generation of monarchs have failed to rectify any of the wrongs bequeathed them by their forefathers.

By the latter years of the 1970s, the threat of Black Power or any other type of uprising had been securely contained by multiple detentions, strategic executions and liberally disseminated narcotics. Walcott, who had by turns castigated and championed the threatened bourgeoisie, wrote out of and against the void that had reopened in his mind. Black Power simmered down into a sad memory of unresolved issues in the tragic-comic *Remembrance* (1980); while in *Pantomime* (1980) Walcott reduced all the burning and burnt-out issues of the seventies to absurdity. Re-interpreting the Crusoe/Friday myth in the light of the post-colonial Caribbean situation, Walcott portrays independence as a temporary reversal of roles in the pantomime of history, as master and former slave take turns in seeing who can push the other over the ledge. In this neo-colonial Theatre of the Absurd, meaning and the meaningless collide and collapse into each other. Laughter is a kind of pain; the serious is confused or conflated with the trivial. Words lose their value; action is reduced to gesture and laughter, a reflex reaction to the ensuing paralysis, becomes a form of the violence it pretends to mask, while the impulse to violence is held in paralysed check by a foreknowledge of the emptiness and futility which lie at the nether end of Friday's rage.

What can one do with or in such a society, whose capacity for reducing effort to futility seems much more complex and intricately engineered than in the simple, almost innocent world of postwar indigence where Walcott began his tour of duty? David Rudder, the calypsonian, commenting on Trinbagonian society in the mid-1990s, described it as a place "where you run from the pain but the jokes pull you back again."[27] Walcott in 1978, when *Pantomime* premiered in Port of Spain, was as ready to run from the pain as he was to revel in the jokes, which he knew quite well had become only another aspect of that pain. The Trinidad Theatre Workshop, his grand design since the sixties, seemed to be in a state of collapse. His second marriage was in shambles. A new fresh Muse had moved towards centre-stage of both the Theatre Workshop and the private life of its director. It was like a re-run of the end of the Jamaican phase. It was time to go. The John D. and Catherine MacArthur Prize Fellow Award (1981) would make possible an honourable exit from Port of Spain, in much the same way as the Colonial Development and Welfare Scholarship (1950) had thirty-one years earlier enabled his flight from Castries.

One of Walcott's major poems published in 1981, "The Spoiler's Return", is both a denunciation of what Trinidad had become after nearly two decades of Independence and a rationalization of the act of withdrawal from a tainted and fallen world, and descent into Satan's much better organized and managed calypso-tent Hell. What is most curious about Spoiler, the protagonist is his final accusation hurled at society with mock politeness:

> All you excuse me, Spoiler was in town;
> you pass him in the road and never knew him!

This is not at all true if we consider how the poem begins with Spoiler "high", probably drunk as well as elevated somewhere on a bridge overlooking the city. Limers passing by do in fact greet Spoiler with the question: "When you come back?" That he is so high, spaced-out; so self-obsessed, that he does not answer that question, but rather the question in his own head: "Where have you been these last twenty years?"

So himself answers himself, "Hell"; he mesmerizes his curious and – he thinks – rude questioners with his dead cold snake's eyes and begins his monologue of denunciation and perceived decay, indifferent to the presence or absence of his stunned audience. Society has not ignored Spoiler; Spoiler has withdrawn from society into his own preferred and private hell of classical literature, rough scathing satire and vintage kaiso – Satan's tent – where he receives greater and more consistent recognition than ever he was given in "four-cup Port of Spain" (*The Star-Apple Kingdom,* p. 6). Walcott, with Spoiler, with Shabine of the matronly wife and young concubine, needed to rationalize his own escape.

Shabine, however, is different from Spoiler in that the trajectory of his journey is not from morally elevated space downward into invisibility, but rather outward and upward – he is travelling from the South to the North of the archipelago, saying his adieux along the way. Shabine seeks absolution through movement, madness, self forgiveness and eventually by benevolent, prayerful rededication to islands, even as he seeks the solitude of the single lamp above the schooner's prow. Spoiler, self righteous and morally whole from start to finish, seeks judgment and condemnation after the style of Juvenal, Swift, and local Grand Inquisitor V.S. Nightfall, to whose crow-like voice, he joins his own.

Here, however, there is no hope in even the promised escape and in "A Sea Change" (*The Fortunate Traveller*, p. 19) Walcott assumes the persona of a hapless tourist, lured to these pitiable shores by the deception of the tourist brochure, and shocked at the reality he encounters. He has circled back to "Travelogue" (1948) and *Poems* (1951) where as sardonic narrating voice he circled visions in those unconventional verses round the archipelago's tourist islands the sores hidden beneath "the green epidermis of the lawn" (*Poems*, 1951, p. 26).

Walcott's voice against the notion of tourism as development had, since the late 1960s, become harsher and more acridly dismissive. By 1968, tourism had begun to occupy centre-stage along with Carnival and the Folk Arts as the joint objects of State-sponsored development. Walcott bitterly complained that:

> the wider life opens to the tourist, the harder it grows for the artist to concentrate on his own truth, when every island nation now advertises itself as a cut-rate resort, when what is offered is not only an escape from, but a suspension of reality, pitched in a tone shared by politician and travel agent. The archipelago has surrendered its future to tourism, to a nightmare of Caterpillar shovels regurgitating every beach into a paradise.[29]

Twelve years later in "A Sea Change" the truth he discloses is exposed in the island's development programmes.

> Islands hissing in rain,
> light rain and governments falling.
> Follow, through cloud, again,
> the bittern's lonely calling.
>
> Can this be the right place?
> These islands of the blest,
> Cheap package tours replaced
> by politics, rain, unrest? (*The Fortunate Traveller*, p. 19)

Here the persona might be Columbus discovering too late his mistake, or Shakespeare's bewildered, guilt-ridden Neapolitans shipwrecked on Caliban's and Prospero's island. Or the persona might be Walcott or Garth St Omer, returning to St Lucia after some years' absence, being mistaken for tourists and learning life's ultimate truth: that there are "homecomings without home". (The *Prodigal*, p. 31) Or the persona may be Walcott, a retired, self-exiled but deeply concerned caretaker, seeking still traces of pristine innocence, but finding, as ever, the snake's voice punctuating the politics of each make-believe, tottering government in these islands of the blessed: the Saints and the Virgins. In 1968 Walcott had asserted:

> from the arts, no challenge of authority through the mass media, which are almost wholly absentee-owned. Any group of artists must challenge the state's indifference to the growth of its culture (apart from the tourist-pleasing nightclub culture of calypso, limbo and steelband) must question the benefit of the Better Villages competition which has become a pastoral hallucination of handicraft and folk-dancing, rural concerts and country cuisine. ("Where Exuberance Triumphs")

By 1980, the poet's creative spirit and voice, inured now to three decades of indifference from public and State alike, assumes the guise of a sea-bird, hidden in the storm-clouds above the islands' tourist-hotelled beaches, [illegible] silence, but still barely audible and seeking once more the audience he has abandoned. If the Spoiler persona was both visible and audible and spoke an easily accessible dialect, now the bittern is more withdrawn from these hissing snake-pits of the archipelago, more isolated in his self-chosen solitude, quite invisible but still entreating islanders to listen to his auguries. The word "bittern" is particularly apt, since its sound suggests "bitter" which is the poet's mood and tone as he circles over the islands [illegible]

[illegible] from his high [illegible] – one recalls the circling aircraft of Chapter X, "Tales of the Islands" (*In A Green Night* (1962)) – is a darkening doom. The thundercloud in "A Sea Change" becomes now not a deliverer of [illegible] redemptive rain but [illegible] of Caliban's or Friday's darkening resentment and rage at the prospect of continued servitude in this new age.

all the dark-gathering rage
of a bruised electorate
tired of its billboard image

on the hotel-crusted reef
from Pigeon Point to Nassau
the sand's white, gritted teeth
it's "yes, sir" and "no sir"? (*The Fortunate Traveller*, p. 20)

Rejecting this crust of hotels, which, hovering from his vantage point high above the billboards, the bittern sees as pigeon droppings stretching from Tobago's Bucco Reef in the south to Nassau at the far north of the archipelago, the bittern foresees that the Jacksons and Man Fridays of the islands will one day soon cast off the role of [illegible] and contemplate rebellion. They will not, however, be able to move beyond simplistic external trappings, the Carnival costumes, uniforms and "green fatigues" of revolution. Ignorant of the soul-wearying ordeal ("green fatigues" in quite another sense) of maintaining the revolutionary dream, Caliban/Friday [illegible] revolution [illegible] solution to the region's deeply engrained problems.

Walcott, as steadfastly against a revolution based on class as he is against one based on race, warns against all violent revolt. Revolution, he concludes, is no way out of the islands' predicament. Nor is "Progress" which Shabine in "The Schooner *Flight*" dismisses as "history's dirty joke". Revolution is not a corrective to or reversal of History but rather the final manifestation of the burden of History, which the islands still pointlessly carry. The final irony of "A Sea Change" is the illumination that it offers – that nothing has changed, or will change; there will be no transformation [illegible] recrossing of the Middle Passage into imagined innocence.

III

"We read, we travel, we become" (p. 31) writes Walcott in *The Prodigal*, and "the poem as travelogue" or "the travelogue as poem" might be the title of a study of Walcott's poetry from the early 1980s into the twenty-first century. This essay will offer no more than an overview of Walcott's enormous output over those three decades where he moves from unillusioned bittern middle age towards the serenity and distance of his twilight years. It will focus on the themes of caretakership and love of islands in an era when the poet's mask has gradually changed from Crusoe, Adam, enraged prophet, sad encircling bittern to that of traveller, wanderer or pilgrim who views the islands and metropole from the air, or some moving vehicle; or from destinations such as hotels, guest-houses across Western Europe or apartment rooms in lower Manhattan and verandahs in Trinidad's slowly disappearing but still at times immortelle-festooned Santa Cruz Valley. Gone is the domestic serenity he enjoyed in 1968 or the trauma and paranoia of the dark seventies. Walcott's travelogue poems are meditatory sketches or fully-fledged portraits of the Hudson River, Switzerland, Italy, East Germany, Columbia and the islands, which have now become the termini of repeated revisitations.

The mission of caretakership is never abandoned. Walcott, rather, attempts a reconciliation of his Antillean and Eurocentric selves, via modes of seeing that portray the islands through the orange and yellow light of Europe's painters; and that simultaneously discover in Europe and America resemblances to the islands. The Wanderer comes to acknowledge a resistance to and love of all places, even as his perspectives are coloured by the illusory light and shade of distance and memory. Raw irascibility slowly weathers into impermeable hardness and indifference, or softens through profound aloneness into mellowness. Self-righteousness wears into self-acceptance, while loss of friends, his mother, his twin-brother Roderick, co-workers and builders of the Theatre Workshop – Wilbert Holder, Ermine Wright, Claude Reid, Charles Applewhaite – teaches him what he had from as early as "Steersman, My Brother" termed, "a need to simplify and to forgive" (*In a Green Night*, p. 40), beginning with self-forgiveness.

This movement towards "mellowness" and "ripeness" can be seen as early as "The Schooner *Flight*" in Shabine's metamorphosis from a guilt-ridden, foul-mouthed manic depressive, to a serene hermit whose prayer offers healing and benediction. It continues in *Midsummer* (1984) when a 54-year-old Walcott is in the middle of his Dantesque journey through circles of an oppressively hot inferno towards the gentler possibility of flowers and cool valleys. *Midsummer* characteristically begins in the air [illegible] Walcott, the returning wanderer, scans the coralline Caribbean Sea that he sees as busy and indifferent to the brief shadowy passage of the humans above it.

The Wanderer's return is beset by memories of Naipaul's *The Middle Passage* and Trollope's and Froude's travelogues of the nineteenth century in which Trinidad is represented as an island famous "for making nothing. Not even a people."[illegible] Yet Walcott, whose exile has taught him that "[illegible]" [illegible] Rome, a city of high culture visible in its statues, cathedrals and monasteries, is depicted as flaking, peeling in "midsummer's furnace"; its history of war, death and oppression still visible on imagined blood-stained togas and catacombs. This reductive portrait of Rome precedes the depressing ones that follow of Port of Spain

> with its one-eyed lighthouse, this damned sea of noise,
> this ochre harbour, mantled by its own scum, (*Midsummer* IV, p. 14)

its "crusted roofs," "river of clogged, circling traffic", its glass-and-concrete jungle of commercial buildings barely concealing an ancestral primitivity and barbarism. Walcott's portrait of Port of Spain hardly differs from Naipaul's portrait of the African town in *A Bend in the River*. Both authors locate their failed post-colonial backwaters in the context of Conrad's *Heart of Darkness*, though Walcott carefully hangs his portrait of Port of Spain between one of rusting Rome and another of New York's jungle of flea markets, "drugged dance of dealers", (*Midsummer* V, p. 15) and sinister, trigger-happy policemen.

The image of the infernal sun of midsummer dominates the portrayal of all of Walcott's interconnected worlds: urban or rural Trinidad, New York, Brixton, Boston, Rome and Athens. While Walcott, in the midst of all this grimness, concludes one of the Port of Spain portraits with: "I can understand/ Borges's blind love for Buenos Aires" (*Midsummer* VI, p. 16) it is not easy to locate Walcott's love for towns where "Our houses are one step from the gutter" (*Midsummer* VII, p. 17) and the cities that are [illegible] regress, literally or metaphorically to "the bush". Ultimately, however, the exile confesses that for all his wandering in space and reverie, he is bound to landscapes he has deserted.

> [illegible] step over the low wall if you should come to,
> recaptures a childhood whose vines fasten your [illegible]
> And this is the lot of all wanderers, this is their fate,
> that the more they wander, the more the world grows wide.
> (*Midsummer* VII, p. 17)

The image of entanglement suggests that one can never really escape from the trammels of one's childhood, and in this context it speaks of Walcott's memory of and dedication to a particular place and landscape.

Yet, the following two lines suggest that wanderers are doomed to be forever setting forth on journeys into ever-widening worlds that must inevitably take them away from the landscape of their childhood. Here Walcott seems to contradict his mentor, Baudelaire, who in "Le Voyage" writes of the shrivelling of the world as one's every new setting forth becomes a circling back to aboriginal tedium and ennui after each encounter with the unsurprising unknown.

For Walcott's Wanderer, movement becomes its own meaning, blurring the deeper and, maybe, ultimate reality of void that had challenged him in *The Castaway*, *The Gulf* and *Another Life*. Movement seems to help him cope with grief, regret and sometimes guilt at not having been able either through Art or loneliness adequately to bless, redeem or bestow meaning and illumination on the lives of the islands' simple folk. Walcott's journey after *Midsummer* is towards a reconciliation of all the myriad points of his physical and mental travelling. Hence *Omeros* (1990) marks a return to his earliest dream of reading the Caribbean via the mythology of the Mediterranean. In it Walcott reclaims St Lucia, fleshes out his "alphabet of the emaciated", and retraces the triangle of the Middle Passage: Europe, Africa, the Caribbean. This is something he had never really attempted before, preferring a mulattitude that excluded or marginalized its African component. *The Bounty* (1997) tempers the harshness of *Midsummer* with a gentler return to St Lucia and Santa Cruz, foreshadowing *The Prodigal* (2004) where compassion and resignation replace the Muse of middle age, Irascibility, a Muse whose demands on emotional energy are extreme and exhausting. There is, also, a kind of serenity that emerges after one submits to arthritis and diabetes and the threat of glaucoma.

The Prodigal, Walcott drily admits to himself, will be "an old man's book/ whenever you write it, whenever it comes out/ the age in your armpits in the pleats of your crotch" (*The Prodigal*, p. 8). Reading landscape through literature and painting, reading literature through landscape, juxtaposing vicarious with lived experience, the traveller's wandering eye records each place it visits with, at times, flat banal detachment. Walcott, seventy-four at the time of the book's publication, seems to have travelled beyond all causes. Yet on occasion, the world intrudes and demands his compassionate response. Such is the case with his portrait of Yugoslavian refugees, which begins imperceptibly with one of his sketches of a particular woman, one of those Muses of place that capture his imagination as he passes through each new landscape.

> a girl with jet hair, black as her skirt, red mouth
> and cheeks that were brightening now with the sun
> and the drying sand. The sky grew Caribbean. (*The Prodigal*, p. 18)

Here, the place is Pescana, a city on the Italian coast of the Adriatic Sea, whose sand and sky reconnect him in imagination with his remembered Caribbean.

But the young woman on the bus, pictured in the window's frame against pines, olives, castles, speaks softly of the war in Serbia and the [illegible] in Kosovo [illegible] on the [illegible]. [illegible] filled with sadness as the romanticized Andreuille's gaze in "Pays-Natal" (*In A Green Night*, p. 62), but her voice interrupts the Wanderer's pastoral reverie, redirecting [illegible] behind "the Province of Mercy,"

> where the only government is that of the apples
> and the only army the wide banners of barley. (*The Prodigal*, p. 20)

In other words, these are your farmers and peasants, the most universal of the world's workers, who Thomas Hardy says[32] will outlast dynasties, yet who everywhere are the victims of governments and armies and, as Walcott constantly reminds us, of Progress, History and the dead-march of Civilization.

A quietly reductive portrait of the whitewashed statue of Columbus in Genoa leads to a revisionary meditation on his former awe as a new world colonial, of statues which he then understood to be markers of historical and cultural achievement.

> "Envy of statues; this is how it grew."
> [...]
> I passed my rigid, immortal friend, the General,
> on his morose green horse, still there on weekends.
> The wars were over but he would not dismount
> [...]
> We had no such memorials on the island. (*The Prodigal*, p. [illegible])

Thirty-four years before in "What the Twilight Says: An Overture", Walcott had lamented this absence of memorials that seemed then to prove the inferiority of his colonial status:

> Slaves, the children of slaves, colonials, then pathetic, unpunctual nationalists, what have we to celebrate? First, we have not wholly sunk into our own landscapes, as one gets the feeling at funerals that our bodies make only light, unlasting impressions on our earth. It is not an earth that has been fed long with the minerals of cultures, with [illegible] nihilism, feudalism, monarchy, democracy, industrialization. Death, which lays us in the earth, [illegible] personal or heraldic, because no single corpse contributes to some [illegible] concept of a past. (pp. 20-21)

Looking back on such notions of the history-less and cultureless nature of post-colonial new world societies, Walcott now recognizes statues and memorials as no more than visible ossifications of history – concrete history, as it were, commemorating war and the never-ending tragedy and human waste of conquest propagated as civilization. It may, of course, be argued that Walcott had always been sceptical of statues, monuments and noble ruins. Poems such as "Ruins of a Great House"[33] and "Statues"[34] prove this. But Janus-faced on this issue as on others, Walcott had also partially accepted the myth of Levi-Straus's *Tristes, Tristes Tropiques* that saw in the absence of monuments and millennia-old structures, the fragility, historylessness and virtual insubstantiality of the New World.

Travel to Europe deepened the contradiction of his response: near-worship of Europe's art, thought, landscapes, literature, versus near-revulsion at the savagery "high" civilizations share with and habitually inflict on "low" ones. Thus Walcott writes of:

> the widening love of Italy growing stronger
> against my will with sunlight in Milan... (*The Prodigal*, p. 26)

But he also writes, after visiting "a cultural outpost in the old regime" in East Germany of "folded" echoes "of interrogation, of conspiracy" and concludes:

> For History here is the covering-over of corpses,
> not only in trenches of quicklime, but also
> the dandruff of pigeon-drops in the stone wigs of statues
> (*The Prodigal*, p. 38)

"History" also lies secreted in the now ominous landscape where the Wanderer hears:

> a fusillade of skylarks in the smoking sky
> and the screams of lilies harvested into a vase,
> a sky composed of bandages and cotton
> and the needles of sick spires (*The Prodigal*, p. 39)

Everything that used to signify culture, civilization, history, now reeks of torture, death, drug-addiction and sickness. "Sick spires" tell of the crisis of Christianity, its impotence in the face of the violent self-destruction of civilization.

Overexposure to Europe has bred in the Wanderer not only scepticism but a reawakened nostalgia for the Caribbean. From the window of his apartment overlooking the Hudson, Walcott, recently returned from Europe, sees a cruise ship:

> [...] magisterial, a white city gliding between buildings
> leaving the river for the Caribbean
> its cargo: my longing. A high immaculate ship (*The Prodigal*, p. 40)

The cruise ship closes a circle that began with, perhaps, Columbus. It is sinless, immaculate, like American imperialism, Christianity, progress, tourism and mercantilism, that are the islands' fate as they become more dependent on the "white city", Conrad's "whitened sepulchre" in *Heart of Darkness.*

After such knowledge how does Walcott now view his mission? As he reminisces at the death of his twin-brother, he asks:

> What was our [illegible]
> To save the salt light of the island
> to protect and exalt its small people (*The Prodigal*, p. 51)

[illegible] his island securely cradled in his heart, head and memory, missing his island as deeply as he once missed Andreuille, his first love who was for him the island. Thus Venato, a coastal Italian town, reminds him of "Gros Ilet, the sea and the village", "Unimportantly beautiful". Gros Ilet, like the remote Rampanalgas of *Another Life* is, by any conventional measure, outside of "history." There is

> […] no echo in the name Gros Ilet
> no literature, no history, at least until now. (*The Prodigal*, p. 28)

The love, the caretakership, the mission "to protect and exalt" are fulfilled through the act of writing the name Gros Ilet and thus beginning its history. Walcott's mission as writer, painter, playwright, teacher, poet, journalist and polemicist, has been to bring the archipelago into its own light and colour and thus into his own reconception of history and civilization. His personal achievement has been imaginatively to reconcile all the small or great places he has lived in, loved, dreamed and worded into visibility.

> I lived in two villages: Greenwich and Gros Ilet,
> and loved both almost equally. One had the sea,
> grey morning light along the waking water,
> the other a great river, and if they asked
> what country I was from I'd say, "The light
> of that tree-lined sunrise down the Via Venato." (*The Prodigal*, p. 29)

This essay ends itself as it began, with a consideration of Walcott's concern for West Indian cricket, a game that Walcott, a promising off-spinner by his own account, refused to pursue in school.[35] He was, however, always aware of West Indies' performance in the game as a symbol of Caribbean potential, and recognized the significance of the simultaneous emergence of West Indian cricket, democracy, literature and the concept of "islands of the heart" coming together to form "a federated Archipelago". In one of his *Trinidad Guardian* articles of 1964, Walcott commented on the consequences of the dissolution of the Federation and its replacement by separate island nations:

> The collapse of the power-space that was the first West Indian Federation deprived its artists of a common spiritual purpose. It also made the individual artist more pathetically isolated, although more important to his "nation."[36]

This "loss of a common spiritual purpose" that so deepened the isolation of the individual artist did not immediately affect the West Indies cricket team which for three decades would stamp its own style, aesthetic and authority on the game, before it began to show signs of disintegration and collapse in the latter half of the 1990s, when no player was certain any more which country or people he represented, or what spirit of what place fuelled his purpose.

Walcott's awareness of the common significance of the West Indies cricket team and the region's emerging writers first became evident in an article he wrote about the different styles of West Indian writers, in which he presented eleven of the most accomplished of these writers as if they were members of a West Indies test side of opening batsmen, middle order stroke-players, spinners, fast bowlers and so on. For each player Walcott wrote a brief, witty pen portrait highlighting that player's "style". Astonishingly, he did not include Derek Walcott in the main eleven, but in a concluding footnote wrote something like "Number 12, Derek Walcott: Water Boy."[37] Walcott had earlier reviewed C.L.R. James's seminal *Beyond a Boundary*[38] and in an article entitled "An Artist Interprets Cricket" mused on the possibilities for developing "a style of musical comedy that is based on calypso, sophisticated satire and dance. The pantomime as it is in Jamaica, is the place where it might evolve."[39]

Cricket for Walcott, as it was for James, was related to the idea of a Caribbean with a distinct aesthetic and "common spiritual purpose". It was a manifestation of regional style as distinctive as calypso, carnival or pantomime. Walcott, a survivor from the forty-five years of West Indies cricket between 1950 and 1995, when cricket was seen as a test of manhood and character, a symbol of growing democracy, of the dismantling of moribund feudal and racist plantation-society class structures and the germination of the larger idea of Caribbean regionalism, has in this new millennium been forced to contemplate the implications of more than a decade of decline in the performance of the West Indies cricket team. This decline reached what seemed to be its nadir during the summer of 2007 when the West Indies were mauled by England 3-0 in a four-Test series. The only batsman who showed some consistency was Shivnarine Chanderpaul, the single hero in a constantly foundering team. The general verdict after the Second Test, which the West Indies in the absence of Chanderpaul lost by an innings and 283 runs, the direst defeat in the team's eighty-year history, was that the West Indies were succumbing mildly, like lambs under the onslaught of lions.

Walcott, on June 26, 2007, wrote a poem in which he endeavoured both to lament the ruin and to anticipate the resurrection of West Indian cricket. The poem entitled "Lament and Triumph: for Shirley Kelsick"[40] was first presented at a charity function held at Lords in London on Wednesday June [illegible] 2007. The venue was significant because it was at Lords in the summer of 1950 that Lord Kitchener had led a gyrating chorus of Sam Selvon's lonely Londoners – West Indian immigrants – across until then sacred turf, singing a calypso that celebrated the West Indies' [illegible] the "MCC". That moment [illegible] Lord Beginner [illegible] in his *Victory Test Match*:

> At Lords was the scenery
> Bound to go down in history

was as much "history" as Walcott's writing of the name "Gros Ilet" while on a tour of Italy.

Fifty-seven years later the irony is glaringly obvious: The British commission one of the greatest poets in the world, a West Indian who has received "a sound colonial education", to reverse, erase or at the very least balance out Lord Kitchener's and Lord Beginner's inscriptive victory calypsos of 1950 with a poem that by the logic of things would need to lament West Indies' defeat or perhaps celebrate England's retributive victory. (England had in the summers of 1984 and 1986 lost ten Test matches in a row to West Indies' teams captained by Clive Lloyd and then Vivian Richards. So their rebirth between the latter days of the twentieth and first decade of the twenty-first centuries, deserved – so they must have felt – some sort of ritual marking or anointment beyond what the Barmy Army had yet produced.) Derek Walcott, straddled between this Caribbean of post-colonial regression and the English tongue he loves, undertook the composition of "Lament and Triumph", dedicating the poem to Shirley Kelsick, a former lawn tennis champion in Trinidad and Tobago, and a harshly fair critic of West Indies' cricket teams over the last two decades, whose concern has been with the quality of regional character as measured through excellence of performance on the international stage.

"Lament and Triumph" presents the contest between West Indian and English cricketers as a ritual confrontation of hunter and prey, warrior and young lion, both of whom are caught up in a timeless ceremonial, some contemporary version of an ancient male rite of passage. The language of the poem is that of old ceremonial with something of African oral tradition and something of Hebrew biblical lamentation. An allusion is made to David's lament over the deaths of Saul and Jonathan. "The beauty of Israel is slain in thy high places. How are the mighty fallen!"

"Lament and Triumph" begins with the image of the English fast bowlers as lions "loping, gathering speed to leap at the crease", and the West Indian batsmen as warriors who "flash their spear blades in vain", and reflects on the nature of honourable sportsmanship – those who would lose their "[illegible]" if the lions lost their lion nature and showed mercy. Then focusing on the position of the West Indian spectator, the poem makes a plea for the absence of self-pity and special pleading, asking whether it can be right to say to the opposition, or maybe the gods, "Our luck has grown dark. This isn't cricket! Play fair?"

Sport is portrayed as a gladiatorial contestation that is "beautiful", primal, feral. Cricket isn't "cricket", that gentleman's game, with more rules and mannered conventions than any of the region's national constitutions. Cricket, especially when its protagonists are former masters and liberated servants, is the feral contest of boarhound and boar, whose only rule is kill or be killed. Derek Walcott seems to be presenting the primal ritualized violence of sport as admirable and beautiful. One isn't sure.

Here the victory is for the imperial lions, while the warriors, "except Chanderpaul [...] who tires the lions", are all dying, flashing "their blades in vain". The sequence of questions – "all fallen? So fast? What about Gayle or Samuels?" suggesting the mystified, lamenting West Indian spectator who cannot believe this has come to pass. After all, the present team are the figurative "sons of the lion-killers" of the 1970s and 1980s. The defeat is given Biblical and Shakespearean resonances, not quite plagues of frogs, but the "beauty of Israel" is slain and "On every field in the islands dust hides the sun." It is the total nature of this collapse of what had seemed to be firmly rooted and deeply established that causes anguish. The isolated Hero, Lara in Sri Lanka in 2001, then Chanderpaul, becomes, for all his individual excellence, a tragic figure as series after series the team itself caves in.

Walcott finally queries the significance of the Hero in such times, salvaging from the Hero's exemplary resistance hope for some future resurrection of the fallen team. It takes some effort, this salvaging of hope from the jaws of melancholic despair, but Walcott as caretaker and pointer-man attempts it, like a Henry V at Agincourt, for if Chanderpaul could do it, "where were his band of brothers who once whitened the flag of St George to a bloody cross?", an allusion perhaps to the inversion of the whitewash, the "blackwash", that the West Indians inflicted on England in the ten consecutive Test match defeats between 1984-86.

There is, perhaps too, a witty inversion of the kind of consolation that England was renowned for giving itself, the consolation of the heroic loser – of the "beauty of defeat. The beauty of the great boxer going down". The poem ends: "Nothing is sadder than an unlucky streak, nothing is nobler than an unlucky hero. Our enemies are beautiful, the lions, but we are not weak."[42] One is unconvinced about the philosophy of "the beauty of defeat". Beauty? Pathos perhaps, tragedy maybe. The final line of the poem offers the faint hope that the archipelago, inured in the agony of defeat, will develop strength and toughness of spirit for future encounter. The Warriors will rebuild their ego and pride, while the Lions will continue to lick their chops and gloat.

[illegible] at least, is the faith of Walcott, a man who has, beyond doubt, loved these islands.

Endnotes

1. Derek Walcott, "Travelogue", *25 Poems* (Port of Spain: Guardian Commercial Printery, 1948), pp. 17-18.
2. D.A. Walcott, *Epitaph for the Young* (Barbados: Advocate Co., 1949), p. 9.
3. D.A. Walcott, *Poems* (Kingston: Jamaica City Printers, 1951), p. 26.
4. Derek Walcott, "Islands", *In a Green Night: Poems 1948-1960* (London: Jonathan Cape, 1962), p. 77.
5. Derek Walcott, "A Map of the Antilles," *In a Green Night*, p. 55.
6. Derek Walcott, "Leaving School", *Leaving School* London Magazine editions (London: Alan Ross Ltd., 1966), pp. 114-136, quotation from p. 130.
7. Derek Walcott, *The Prodigal* (New York: Farrar, Straus and Giroux, 2004), pp. 12-14.
8. Derek Walcott, "Leaving School", p. 135.
9. "Chapter IV, Tales of the Islands," *In a Green Night*, p. 27.
10. Derek Walcott, *Another Life: Fully Annotated*, with a critical essay and comprehensive notes by Edward Baugh and Colbert Nepaulsingh (London: Lynne Rienner Publishers Inc., 2004), p. 86. Originally published by Farrar, Straus and Giroux, New York, 1973, p. 86. Hereafter page references are given in the text, the original 1973 edition first, the 2004 annotated edition following.)
11. All published in *In A Green Night* (1962).
12. Bruce King, *Derek Walcott: A Caribbean Life* (New York: Oxford University Press, 2000), p. [illegible]
13. *Drums and Colours: An Epic Drama, Caribbean Quarterly*, 7: 1-2 (March 1961), pp. 1-104; and in *The Haitian Trilogy* (New York: Farrar, Straus and Giroux, 2002)
14. *Ti-Jean and His Brothers* in *Dream on Monkey Mountain and other Plays* (New York: Farrar, Straus and Giroux, 1970); first published as *Ti-Jean: A Play in One Act* (Jamaica: Extra Mural Department, 1957).
15. Derek Walcott, *Ti Jean and His Brothers* in *Dream on Monkey Mountain and Other Plays* (New York, Farrar, Straus and Giroux, 1970), p. 140.
16. Derek Walcott, "The Castaway", *The Castaway and Other Poems* (London: Jonathan Cape, 1965), p. 9.

17. Derek Walcott, "What the Twilight Says: An Overture", *Dream on Monkey Mountain and Other Plays* (New York, Farrar, Straus and Giroux, 1970), p. 34.
18. Derek Walcott, "The Figure of Crusoe: On the Theme of Isolation in West Indian Writing", *Critical Perspectives on Derek Walcott*, Ed. Robert D. Hamner (Boulder & London: Lynne Rienner Publishers, 1997), pp. 33-40. Originally a lecture delivered at the University of the West Indies, St Augustine, Trinidad & Tobago, 1965.
19. Phrase taken from "The Castaway", *The Castaway and Other Poems* (London: Jonathan Cape, 1965), p. 10, and adapted by Patricia Ismond for the title of *Abandoning Dead Metaphors*, her study of Walcott.
20. Derek Walcott, "A Georgetown Journal", *The Gulf and Other Poems* (London: Jonathan Cape, 1969), p. 45.
21. Victor Questel, "Ash Wednesday", in *Near Mourning Ground* (Port of Spain: The New Voices, 1979), p. 41.
22. Kamau Brathwaite, "Sam Lord", in *Mother Poem*, *Ancestors* (New York, New Directions, 2001), pp. 20-21; and in the original publication of *Mother Poem* (Oxford: OUP, 1977), pp. 8-9.
23. Dennis Scott, "Walcott on Walcott", *Caribbean Quarterly* Vol. 14, Nos. 1 & 2, (1968), 77-82 (Quotation from p. 79).
24. Nina Simone, "Why? (The King of Love Is Dead)", *'Nuff Said* (Stereo LSP. 4965, New York, RCA, 1968).
25. D.A. Walcott, "Travelogue", *25 Poems*, p. 18.
26. *Three Plays: The Last Carnival; Beef, No Chicken and A Branch of the Blue Nile* (New York: Farrar Straus and Giroux, 1986).
27. David Rudder, "Another Day in Paradise", *Lyrics Man* (Port of Spain: Lypsoland CR023, 1995).
28. Derek Walcott, "The Spoiler's Return", *The Fortunate Traveller* (New York: Farrar, Straus and Giroux, 1981), p. 60.
29. Derek Walcott, "Where Exuberance Triumphs", *The Times* , 8 Oct. 1968.
30. Derek Walcott, *The Star-Apple Kingdom* (London: Cape, 1980), p. 14
31. Derek Walcott, *Midsummer* (New York: Farrar, Straus and Giroux, 1984), p. 11.
32. Thomas Hardy, "In Time of 'The Breaking of Nations'", in *Collected Poems of Thomas Hardy* (New York, The MacMillan Company, 1925, (12th edn. 1968), p. 511. (Poem first written in 1915).
33. "Ruins of a Great House", *In a Green Night*, pp. 19-20.
34. "Statues", *The Castaway and Other Poems*, p. 40.
35. *Leaving School*, p. 118.
36. Derek Walcott, "Spiritual Purpose Lacking", *Sunday Guardian*, 5 Jan. 1964, p. 3.

37. Derek Walcott. "Where Do They Get Their Style?" *Trinidad Guardian*, 21 Apr. 1965. 5.
38. Derek Walcott. "The West Indian Attitude to Cricket". *Sunday Guardian*. 28 July 1963. 14.
39. Derek Walcott. "[illegible]." *Trinidad Guardian*. Wednesday, 1 Jan. 1964. 5.
40. Derek Walcott. "Lament and Triumph", for Shirley Kelsick. "Walcott [illegible]."
41. Lord Beginner. (Egbert Moore) "Victory Test Match", 1950.
42. "Lament and Triumph". The poem was presented in *The Express* as prose.

HAROLD N. McDERMOTT

THE MULATTO OF CRITICISM: WALCOTT AND LITERARY THEORY

Derek Walcott's pronouncements on literary theory and criticism have, on occasions, seemed absolute and definitive. For example, in "Caligula's Horse"[1] his denouncing of European contemporary literary theory as the "veneration of rot" would seem to suggest that post-structuralism or postmodernism are not, ipso facto, Caribbean and therefore not suitable conceptual paradigms to articulate what Antonio Benitez-Rojo terms "the complexity of the system we call Caribbeaness".[2] Further, Walcott's classification of the state of Caribbean literary criticism in a 1982 interview as "standpipe criticism"[3] is no less dismissive. The usefulness of either pronouncement to understanding Walcott's position on literary theory and criticism properly lies, perhaps, in the nexus each reveals between literary theory and cultural theorizing. Caribbean literary theory becomes an integral part of the wider agenda of theorizing Caribbean syncretic culture. The conceptual paradigms that constitute this critical endeavour must go beyond simply describing and differentiating the regional experience to include a recuperative dimension. This is a point Walcott underscores in *The Antilles: Fragments of Epic Memory*: "Antillean art is the restoration of our shattered histories, our shards of vocabulary, our archipelago becoming a synonym for pieces broken from the original continent."[4]

The task of describing and differentiating the Caribbean experience is a problematic undertaking, for the very reality to be classified and catalogued is unstable because of socio-cultural and ethnic differences and tensions within the region. Any theoretical model that would adequately define this protean reality must itself be malleable enough to contain the divergences and points of convergence contained within the region, within the individual self, between the self and the other and among various ethnic groups. A discussion of Derek Walcott's position on and attitude towards literary theoretical practice must begin with his acknowledgement of just such a socio-cultural dynamism which he attempts to accommodate in the often ambiguous and even paradoxical positioning and manoeuvres in his "mulatto of style" stance.

This paper argues that elements of Walcott's hybrid cultural and racial formation circumscribe the nature and manifestations of his aesthetic theorizing and create a model that is ultimately positional and contingent for two reasons. First, because his theoretical model should be capable of representing what Walcott terms, in "The Figure of Crusoe", "various problems organic to West Indian life", such problems involving issues of identity, agency, subject formation and attitudes to language. These were unresolved [illegible] time and place and [illegible]. Second, Walcott maintains in "The Muse of History" that such an approach, which involves assimilation of "the features of every ancestor",[6] is the only mature position for the sensitive mind to adopt. This suggests the evolution of a critical sensibility that seeks to synthesize two different and, at points, seemingly contradictory archives – the Classical European tradition and the African-inspired folk tradition which are competing yet complementary co-constructs of his vision of Caribbeaness.

Walcott's earliest theoretical essays reveal a liberal humanist orientation specifically influenced by Matthew Arnold, T.S. Eliot and F.R. Leavis. During the 1950s and 1960s, Walcott's theoretical formation was particularly susceptible to the ideological prescription of Arnold and Eliot as these relate to the centrality of the European literary tradition as filial, the ontological nature of art, the exclusion of autobiographical elements from the meaning of art and the view of the aesthetic realm as free from the taint of the socio-historical and political. Walcott articulated this position in some detail in "Necessity of Negritude".[7] In both "Society and the Artist"[8] and "History and Picong… in The Middle Passage"[9] Walcott emphasizes the Arnoldian liberal humanist idea that poetry "has its discipline and its formulae" and to disregard them is to "deprive the resulting work of any degree of permanence and beauty",[10] which are the qualities poetry seeks. These prescriptions are offered as necessary preconditions for the emergence of a West Indian literary and critical tradition.

Walcott's acceptance of the "discipline" and "formulae" of poetry is clearly influenced by T.S. Eliot's espousal of the synthesis between intellectual rigour and comprehensive knowledge of canonical standards of greatness; his insistence that "tradition" cannot be inherited but may only be obtained by hard work – the labour of knowing the work of one's literary ancestors through which they "assert their immortality most vigorously".[11] Nonetheless, there is a clearly discernible countervailing openness to the ideological orientation of the Romantic movement, despite his dictum in "History and Picong… In The Middle Passage" that "the benefit of style is that it can conceal emotion" (p. 19). Here the echo of Eliot's famous warning against emotion and individuality in artistic creation is unmistakable: "Poetry is not a turning loose of emotion, but an escape from emotion; it is not the expression of personality, but an escape from personality".[12]

Walcott's appropriation of Eliot's aesthetic prescriptions gives rise to, as I have argued elsewhere, a Classical/Romantic tension in his critical sensibility at this stage of his career.[13] On occasion, this tension is evident in the difference between his aesthetic theorizing about the figure of the poet and the nature of poetry, and conversely, his own practice of the poetic craft. On the one hand, in "The Figure of Crusoe", Walcott's acceptance of the role of the artist as the suffering soul and *isolato* in the process of becoming, his instinct towards emotional honesty in his early poetry, his signature self-referentiality in his poetry on the level of both theme and style, and the intense lyricism particularly of his earlier poetry have more in common with the Romantic tradition. His tendency, on the other hand, towards the prescriptive commitment to traditional and long-established theories and styles, particularly as he eschews individuality and originality in the name of tradition, his insistence on apprenticeship to and imitation of the canon, and the rigour and calculated craftsmanship he venerates regarding poetic form, are clearly part of a Classical tradition.

Charles Pollard offers one of the most insightful and helpful exegeses on Walcott's ironic and ambivalent appropriation of Eliot's European modernism, based on the claim that aspects of Eliot's modern aesthetic enable Walcott to understand and to better represent the experience of the Caribbean's postcolonial modernity. Pollard reasons that, like Eliot, Walcott subscribes to a constructivist's approach to the founding of a coherent and cohesive tradition from the region's fragmented experience of modernity that involves synthesizing fragments from diverse cultural domains.[14] Walcott's recasting of Eliot's concept of tradition is inspired by his desire to identify and evolve a tradition that simulates a cultural home in the sense that it controls, orders, and gives shape to the region's turbulent colonial history in which the public poet speaks for a unified cultural community. Pollard argues that Walcott reshapes Eliot's European modernist principles via a cross-cultural intertextuality that is at once contestatory and complementary. Indeed, Walcott strategically and selectively models the contingent nature of Eliot's modernism as a useful resource in refining his own thinking about the social function of poetry. For Walcott, Eliot's collocating method is particularly apt since it acknowledges cultural fragment but offers the rescuing synthesis of a potential or even imagined cultural unity.

Walcott's particular classicism is ironic since it presumes a provisional, if not imagined, cultural wholeness issuing from the diasporic cultures of Europe, Asia and Africa. It presumes that the New World experience becomes emblematic of the modern condition and that the processes of Caribbean creolisation offer an efficacious template for understanding the transculturation occurring in other parts of the world. The resultant implicit tension in Walcott's aesthetic, of simultaneously contesting and complementing canonical tradition, is a characteristic duality within

Walcott's critical sensibility, which is to persist into later stages of his poetic development. Pollard argues that correctly perceived, Walcott's commitment to tradition is not necessarily derivative of Eliot, but instead creates his own brand of New World modernism that augments, recalls and complements Eliot's European modernism and New World Modernist poetry. For Walcott, duality is not necessarily antithetical as he explains in "The Caribbean: Culture or Mimicry", for there can be "ambiguity without crisis".[15] This middle ground is possible only because his reconciliatory, synthesizing vision rescues him from crisis. His position here is not uncritical, however.

Walcott's commitment to the tradition of his literary ancestors in his conceptualizing of the "truly tough aesthetic of the New World" ("The Muse of History", p. 36) obliges him to posit the synchronic interrelationship between the cultural and conceptual paradigms of the imported and the local. In "Necessity of Negritude" he dismisses out of hand the notion that a nascent West Indian literary tradition can be a separatist one. Indeed, he here envisions a hybrid aesthetic tradition that combines the seemingly European and creolized Caribbean archives and speaks from a space where both spill into each other. But there is no equivalence between the hybrid and the parent tradition in this schema. This fusion is qualified by a hierarchical ordering that posits folk culture as instinctive, untutored, raw and requiring transformation by the rhetorical and formal modes of cognition that would ennoble and sanitize it via alignment with a pre-existing Western aesthetic tradition. This notion that the folk aesthetic is uncouth and awaiting refinement was first suggested in the poem "I with Legs Crossed Along the Daylight Watch"[16] and later expanded and codified in "What the Twilight Says: An Overture".[17]

At this stage, Walcott's linguistic model, English, (a concomitance of his artistic allegiance to the Great Tradition) is troubled by a duality implicit in his purpose. In his 1962 article, "Poetry – Enormously Complicated Art", he aimed at writing with "the flavour and inflection of contemporary speech" while avoiding "syntactical distortions and the inversions of alien language and earlier styles" ("Poetry – Enormously Complicated Art", p. 3). He further argues that at that time "poetry written in the West Indies by people like [himself] was still precocious and artificial [...] for a society which has not settled and whose language has a protean vitality that has not yet formalized its own grammar and accent" ("Poetry – Enormously Complicated Art", p. 3). There is an echo of Matthew Arnold's prescription (that poetry represents the best of that which is thought and said) in Walcott's reasoning here that the structural inadequacy of the vernacular, its protean vitality, disqualifies its written poetry from being "good poetry". Arnold's concern was against "ordinary popular literature" of his time that did not seek to promote "the best knowledge" and "the best ideas of [the] time" as a counterforce "to knowledge of all that was harsh, uncouth [and] difficult" in the hope of achieving "sweetness and light".[18] Walcott's argument that vernacular poetry is "crude poetry" because such works might be regionally popular but still would lack permanence for they compress and contract what he terms "the tribal experience"[19] is a by-product argument of Arnold's. By this logic, calypsos are accepted only as "accidental" or "song poems" ("Poetry – Enormously Complicated Art", p. 3). Later, in "What the Twilight Says: An Overture", Walcott is to dramatically recant his position on calypso poetry when he dismisses those who "apotheosized the folk form, insisting that calypsos were poems…". He further criticized those who wanted "politically to educate the peasant yet leave him intellectually unsoiled" (p. 35). A further qualified reversal was to follow in 1977 in an unpublished essay, "Calypso as Theatre" when he accepted "calypsos as verse–writing," but warned against the "dangers of teaching calypso as poetry".[20]

The decade of the 1970s is seminal to the refinement of Walcott's positions on a number of artistic and aesthetic principles that shaped his critical sensibility. The four major critical essays ("Meanings",[21] "What the Twilight Says: An Overture", "The Muse of History" and "The Caribbean: Culture or Mimicry?") produced during this period illustrate strategic revision and repositioning of his stances on critical issues such as the nature of language, the ontological nature of art, mimicry and the figure of the poet.

Perhaps no other engagement within Walcott' literary aesthetic is to prove more contentious than his theorizing about language. His revision of his position on the language of artistic discourse is in part motivated by two powerful drives. First is the internal contradiction within his stated purpose of imitating the canon while simultaneously achieving freshness of expression; what he calls in a 1977 interview, "a voice not inflected by influences" which is "both refinement of language and possible invention of a new language."[22] Second is the counterforce of Black Nationalism which accused him of mimicry and of denying the centrality of African influence in a regional aesthetic. In the Edward Hirsch interview, Walcott adjusted his linguistic strategy to call for a new hybrid language, "divorced from English and the vernacular", which would allow a West Indian and an Englishman alike to read a single poem, each with his own accent without either one feeling that it was written in dialect" (Hirsch "Interview", p. 53) These concessions did little to quiet the criticism by some of the idea of organic deficiency in folk culture inherent in his espousal of the poet's philosophical duty to "purify the dialect of the tribe" ("Poetry – Enormously Complicated Art", p. 3). Walcott was further criticised for the implied hierarchical high culture/ low culture dichotomy that justified his perceived need for aesthetic purification and refinement of vernacular culture. This hierarchical ordering of art is based on both Arnold and T.S.

Eliot for the "maintenance of an elite" who serve as the "vanguard to ensure that no segment of the community lags more than a generation behind".[illegible] In a 1982 interview he spelt out the dictum, "art is not democratic, art is hierarchical, and all artists know that" ([illegible] [1983], p. [illegible]).

In "The Caribbean: Culture or Mimicry?", Walcott expands on his theory of linguistic and cultural mimicry which he had earlier introduced [illegible] 1970s his justification is more self-conscious, if not more defensive. This is patently clear in the duality contained in his affirmation of the artistic influence of Africa in the region. He wrote, "…America is black… [and t]he most significant experience in America's recent past […] this revolution […] was designed by West Indians like Garvey, Césaire, Fanon, Padmore and Stokely" (p. 52). This was followed by a further statement in 1977 in which he insisted on the existence of Africa in all of us: in our music, speech and all the things that are organic to its way of life, which he says are African (Hirsch, "An interview", p. 56). Interestingly, in that same year, in an interview with Sharon Ciccarelli, he significantly modified the aesthetic implications of both confessions by positing the absence of an unbroken arc in the tradition of "the black arts" in the form of the Pan-African movement.[24] His denial here of an unbroken African aesthetic tradition echoes his previously held position in "Necessity of Negritude" where he asserted that, "for us, whose tribal memories have died, and who have begun again in the New World […], the assertion of the 'African personality' is of limited benefit" (p. 23). The upshot of this qualification is what he perceives as a generic aesthetic void in Caribbean folk culture. He rationalizes the presence of this void in his claim that in the New World situation of transplantation and exile from ancestral culture, there is an aesthetic imperative to connect linguistically with kindred spirits of other ages and cultures in the Caribbean cosmorama. The jusitification of this undertaking is found in his mantra of artistic purpose set out in "The Muse of History" as "assimilating the features of every ancestor" (p. [illegible]). In the wake of this perceived void, he reasons in a 19[illegible] interview that, "whatever tools you need[ed] to capture the experience were legitimate" (Hirsch, "An interview", p. 292).

Walcott's duality in acknowledging the centrality of Africa in the [illegible] American tradition and cultural history, while denying the continuity of an African inspired aesthetic tradition and what he calls the assertion of the "African personality", is perhaps an attempt to divest the aesthetic realm of the [illegible] of the socio-political, specifically [illegible]. This, ironically, [illegible] he was admitting the [illegible] (in "What the Twilight Says: An Overture") of his vision based on the [illegible] of his republic of art: "When twenty years ago we imagined cities devoted neither to power nor money but to art, one had the true vision" (p. 40). Walcott's tactical shift was coalescing around his transformed notion of the figure of the poet. His vision of the poet as *isolato* gradually veered during the 1970s towards that of the poet as public scourge. The strident tone of his denunciation of corrupt politicians and the politicization of the arts in *Sea Grapes* (1976) and "What the Twilight Says" is instructive, but this rage must be understood in the context of the statement issued at the start of the decade that "the future of West Indian militancy lies in art" ("What the Twilight Says", p. 18). Indeed, towards the end of the decade Walcott goes so far as to suggest a Marxist orientation to his critical sensibility by his bold assertion in the 1977 interview that "if the struggle is intense, the role of the artist is to pick up a gun like everybody else [...]; if there is an active struggle, the role of the artist is to involve himself physically in the struggle" (Ciccarelli, "Reflections", p. 41). The extent to which such a pronouncement represents a tactical retreat is best judged when set against his earlier mordant dismissal of the politics used as an interpretive lens for the arts. In "The Figure of Crusoe", he disparages this approach in what he calls the "fashionable, Marxist evolved method of analysing figures from literature as if they were guilty" (p. 36).

Walcott was simultaneously affirming allegiance to poetic tradition even as he was admitting changes, not so much fidelity to the abstract notion of tradition, but to the type of tradition to which he was committed. The affirmation, couched in unmistakably structuralist terms, posits that Caribbean folk literature shares deep structure commonalities with the literature of Europe: "The true folk tale conceals a structure as universal as the skeleton, the one armature from Br'er Anancy to King Lear" ("What the Twilight Says", p. 24). He further explains, in a deft stroke to quiet accusations of mimicry, "the apparent conservatism of West Indian fiction, whether in fiction or in theatre, is not an imitative respect for moulds, but a memory of that form" (p. 24). Claiming these common archetypal forms facilitated a dialectic of abrogation and reincorporation in the 1970s when he strategically distanced himself from the "Great Tradition" of English literature as the unique influence on his artistic sensibility and laid claims to a nascent literary fraternity which he called in the *Sunday Guardian Magazine* "the comradeship of Guillén, Borges and Neruda."[25] This appropriation of an alternate "American" tradition of influence is demonstrated during the 1970s in a deliberate movement towards orality as a viable stylistic vehicle in his poetry.

By the end of the 1970s, Walcott was confident enough of the development of his own aesthetic theorizing and critical practice to declare that he was outside the tradition of English literature:

> I think it is exciting to be outside English literature, in a hierarchic sense... Now most poets in a tradition have that kind of listlessness

> [illegible] something is going to happen, and eventually if they live long enough they will become part of some kind of club... In that way I'm completely free. I'm not part of the establishment. I'm not part of the gang. I'm not part of the club.[26]

In a seemingly radical departure from Eliot's prescription against individuality in the young artist, Walcott declares this new status as liberating, but such a liberation is not simply a rejection of apprenticeship but an admission of his [illegible] [illegible] ment in which he called a "recreated" sensibility forged in regional literatures. This arguably afforded him the security of person, to which he claimed to have aspired, before migrating to the United States early in the 1980s. But such a security was both problematic and contingent. The three collections of poems he produced during his first decade in America, *Midsummer*,[27] *The Fortunate Traveller*,[28] and *The Arkansas Testament*[29] illustrate that language, and in his specific case English, was the terrain in which aesthetic issues of artistic identity and sensibility were to be contested and resolved.

Midsummer treats with the issue of language as index of cross-cultural interweaving as Walcott anticipates leaving the Caribbean to teach in America. His claim to a "recreated" literary sensibility unmoored from the European tradition is echoed in statements like, "These poems I heaved// aren't linked to any tradition/ like a mossed cairn" ("L", p. 70). The collection reiterates his earlier preoccupations with clarifying and refining language – "[...] Ah, to have/ a tone colloquial and stiff,/ [...] all synthesis in one heraldic stroke [...]" ("IX", p. 19). In effect, linguistic purification meant amalgamating and fusing the different dialects of the region and beyond, thereby rejecting the notion of language as ethnographic or national differentiation – "Language never fits geography"(p. 19). There is anxiety to achieve an appropriate poetic language as the conduit to a syncretic literary and cultural ethos, where "all our differences fuse" ("XVI", p. 26).

Midsummer metaphorically represents a timeless epoch across cultures, races and climes characterized by a common language or poetic utterance. In a neo-Romantic flourish, Walcott suggests that nature is the muse imbued with this language and natural occurrences resonate with metalinguistic significance.[30] "the sea swift flew nameless in that wordless summer/ in the leafy silence before the first morning language", the [illegible] "crouched its own question and answer", "the light verb leapt like a fish from its element", "the tadpole wiggled like an eager comma", and "the snake coiled round its trunk in an ampersand" ("XXIV", p. 35). Later in *The Arkansas Testament*, Walcott posits the meta-literary resonances inherent in the landscape –

Raging, I'd skip a pebble
across the sea's page; it still
scanned its own syllable:
trochee, anapest, dactyl
("A Latin Primer", *The Arkansas Testament*, p. 22).

In *Midsummer*, Walcott restates a defence of his strategy of linguistic appropriation of English in questioning,

Have we changed sides
to the moustached sergeants and the horsy gentry
because we serve English, like a two-headed sentry
guarding its borders? ("LII", p. 72).

His response resonates the green imagery of fecundity and creativity associated with artistic calling and maturation found in his earlier collections such as *Epitaph for the Young*[30] and *In a Green Night*[31]. In *The Fortunate Traveller*, Walcott further develops the trope of vegetation as the index of cross-cultural linguistic interweaving and naturalization when he suggests that to become American is "to talk like birch or aspen confidently". His declaration of fealty to his new home in exile necessitates the seemingly painful articulatory adjustment of putting small pebbles "upon my tongue to learn her language".[32] But for Walcott, this adjustment is double-edged with a numinous dimension. In *The Arkansas Testament*, "It was such dispossession/ that made possession joy". His linguistic adjustment in America is cast in decidedly religious terms and likened to a "first communion/ there, with the English tongue". "Strict as Psalm or Lesson,/ I learnt your poetry" ("Eulogy to W.H. Auden", p. 64). This notion of English as a language which facilitates the growth and syncretizing of cultures and experiences is extended further in the trope of the tree of language. In "Cul de Sac Valley" the poet aspires to replicate the language of the St Lucian artisan class – specifically the carpenter working the raw and odorous wood from the tree of language – "consonants scroll/ off my shaving plane/ in the fragrant Creole/ of their native grain;" (p. 9). By his own admission, his desire here remains wish fulfilment, underscoring the difficulty of achieving the hybrid language he envisioned in his 1977 interview with Edward Hirsch. His "English, is a different tree", from theirs "with a French/ or West African root// from a dialect throng-/ ing, its leaves unread" (p. 9). Walcott's wistful desire for the language of the St Lucian folk here is dualistic and conflicted. Learning the language of America, in a sense eschews insular ethnographic differentiation because of the formal and stylistic benefits that a cosmopolitan English would confer on his craft. In "Gros-Ilet" his native English, described as "language soaked in salt water, garnished with conch shells", restricts "distinctions beyond the paradise/ of our horizon" and is a language of slaves. This perceived deficiency is helped in "A Latin Primer" by what he calls "the sand-crusted kelp/ of distant literatures" (*The Arkansas Testament*, p. 21). But the linguistic fusion of the local and the imported, implied here, is simultaneously the "privilege/ to have judged one's work by the glare of greater minds" (*Midsummer*, XXIX, p. 40) and the apprehension of moral superiority of entering an empire "the scale of [whose] conscience is too small for the size of the country". [illegible] point is the ethnocentric discrimination against the other that concerns the issue of language – since one's accent causes recoil "[illegible]" [illegible]

In the face of these limitations in American culture, Walcott affirms Caribbean cultural nationalism: "I prefer the salt freshness of that ignorance,/ as language crusts and blackens on the pots/ of this cooked culture, coming from a raw one" (*The Fortunate Traveller*, p. 15.) Walcott's allusion here to the structuralist anthropology of Claude Levi-Strauss's, *The Raw and the Cooked*[34] in which he designated Third World oral cultures as "raw" when compared to literate cultures of metropolitan societies which are "cooked", is not incidental. Up to *Another Life*[35] and even beyond, Walcott's attitude towards folk culture and the natural landscape as "raw and uncouth", in need of order and refinement by European conceptual and stylistic modes, represented a complicit postcoloniality. Now, there is an obvious shift in his position but it seems more visceral than cerebral. The pejorative implications of Levi-Straus's use of "raw" are perceived by Walcott as a centrist and ethnocentric attack on Caribbean culture, which he rejects on the grounds of a morally superior and enlightened view of cultural encounter that is not readily acknowledged in First World cultures.

The decade of the 1980s also saw a clearly discernible widening of Walcott's thematic and theoretical concerns as his focus pivoted from a predominantly Caribbean one to an American one during this phase of his career. This broadening of his focal length is illustrated in a number of critical essays which generally evaluate the geo-political and cultural impact of the twentieth century American empire on issues of diasporic identity, the nature of New World artistic sensibility and his place in a traditional "American" or new world poetic. His essay, "A Colonial's Eye View of Empire", for example, reflects on the role and nature of the poet's calling in the face of a homogenizing and hegemonic threat of empire. In his 1998 collection *What the Twilight Says: Essays* he brings together essays that critically examine the contributions of white British, American and Australian writers like Robert Lowell, Joseph Brodsky, Ted Hughes, Philip Larkin, Les Murray, Ernest Hemingway and Robert Frost whose works demonstrate characteristic features of a New World sensibility. In these essays and later in his Nobel Lecture Walcott returns to and expands his [illegible] [illegible] of literature and [illegible] America as unique and [illegible] the new world motifs of cross cultural synthesis. He seems to signal a strategic shift in artistic focus while keeping the Caribbean as his sounding board; three of the ten critical essays in this collection are dedicated to Caribbean writers: C.L.R. James, V.S. Naipaul and Patrick Chamoiseau. Central to his rationale for including these British, North American and Australian writers into his new found fellowship of American writers, is the New World aesthetic contiguity he posits between them and Caribbean writers. This claim of an organic linkage is not uncritical however.

Walcott's declared love for America in the poem "Upstate" (*The Fortunate Traveller*, p. 5) is an endorsement of cultural diversity and the submerged aesthetic linkages that require careful reconfiguring of the Caribbean poet's place therein. His process of "identity clarification" or more precisely what Stuart Hall[36] terms identity "positioning" in America is guided by both aesthetic and professional considerations. In "Magic Industry: Joseph Brodsky 1988", Walcott's comment about the Russian/American poet's living in and loving America is equally applicable to himself. The benefit of this "love of [the American] language expands the [poet's] spiritual biography, not with the hesitancy of the émigré, but with a startling exuberance."[37] His entry into this fellowship of the American literary tradition is motivated by personal reasons like this one articulated in a 1985 interview, "I am a Caribbean poet. I yearn for the company of better Caribbean poets, quite frankly. I feel a little lonely. I don't see what I thought might have happened – a stronger energy, a stronger discipline, and a stronger drive in Caribbean poetry" (Hirsch, "The Art of Poetry XXXVII, p. 106)

Walcott's proposal in "The Antilles: Fragments of Epic Memory"[38] that a Caribbean literary tradition represents shards of a universal continuity that transcends epochs and times stems from a modification of his position on tradition and history, first suggested in "The Muse of History" and further developed in *Midsummer* and beyond, as history-less simultaneity that fuses disparate times, cultures and locales. Walcott's identification with North American and European poets as he maps, constructs and locates himself in a wider global context, cannot simply be read as a generic lack or denial of his Caribbeanness, but as evidence of that very Caribbeanness if we accept Denis Williams's notion of the syncretic biological ancestor[39] and Walcott's own schema for the syncretic literary ancestor. But his belief in the synthesizing process of human brotherhood and the assimilation of the colonial subject into empire is neither unproblematic nor naïve. It necessitates shifts and adjustments in his previously articulated positions on the nature and function of art and the poet, on language and on mimicry.

Intellectual hybridity, a concomitant of the "startling exuberance" of loving America, is perhaps nowhere more clearly evident than in the formative influence that Lowell had on Walcott's own poetic development.

Walcott admits an "American" apprenticeship of sorts, to Lowell in which Lowell becomes the quintessential figure of the New World poet. In "On Robert Lowell", Walcott confesses: "I had practised imitation all my life, and I had given up hope of not sounding like Lowell."[40] Lowell's personage and practice of his craft are self-referenced in his poetic style and philosophy. Here, Walcott documents and expands a belief, earlier stated and a signature practice of his poetic craft, that there is an inseparable con- [illegible] poet's craft and [illegible] that the poet's life ended by the reader, for "the poet's life becomes a shadow cast by the reader" ("On Robert Lowell", p. 87)

In Lowell's case, poetry is a paradoxical calling which took its toll on his mind, resulting in mental exhaustion, even as its "sense of structure and of technical order was so strong it saved his mind and his work" (p. 103) from mental attacks. Thus empowered, Lowell was able to turn "paranoia into serenity" by "making honey from the bile of his illness" (p. 97). Walcott makes a similar claim for Robert Frost, stating that poetry provided the discipline his sorrow (a widower with a suicidal son) needed. His personal circumstances were troped in his poetry – "his scars seen in the devastation of his scansion but they did not break his metre or pitch it into a rant that broke his disciplined confinement." His poetry is read as a metaphor of protection and solace – "a door against foul weather [...] an old lamp, against even worse weather."[41]

Lowell's affable personal style aesthetically mirrors and approximates Walcott's syncretic mulatto style as it synthesizes sharp disparities and rejects a causal view of personal history. He writes of Lowell:

> He softened objects around him, blurred their outlines, made the everyday myopic, saw political systems as played out. History lived in his nerves, not as subject, but as irrational repetition. ("On Robert Lowell", p. 88).

There is a clear suggestion here that Lowell's success and stature as a poet is generated by his hybrid assimilation of all poetic styles and sensibilities. Like Walcott, his phenotype becomes the synecdoche for the fusion of disparate qualities: [illegible] in his work [...] all poetry was his. He had made the body of literature his body, all styles his style, every varying voice his voice" (p. 105). Hence, his poems themselves become a sort of *stigmata*, "raw as a flesh cut", within the poet's body and [illegible] through the tremors within his technique which are evident in "the halted fragments, the revisions, the compulsions". For the quintessential poet, the very practice of his craft is meta-poetic – "All his writing is about writing, all of his poetry is about the pain of making poems" (p. 89).

Indeed, Walcott goes beyond the overt practice of the craft to the [illegible] that casual and intimate interaction with the poet [illegible] significance – "In intimacy, their perceptions go by so rapidly that a few drinks with them are worth a book on poetics" (p. 92). To this end, Lowell's insistence on "casual elegance" in dress becomes for Walcott a metaphoric "moment's [technical] revelation of style". In his verse, Lowell wore his metre "loosely with ancestral hauteur", hence his poetry "had the casual symmetry of a jacket draped on a chair, genius in shirtsleeves" (p. 92). The "casual elegance" in language, which Walcott now lauds in Lowell, alludes to his earlier stated stylistic intention in *Epitaph for the Young* of "stripping speech of its tie and socks".[42] It involves what Walcott through experimentation in *Another Life* has achieved, the infusion of the language of poetry with ordinary banal details.

The characteristic features of the New World poet observed in Lowell are also self-imaged in Walcott, the poet, and there is interchangeability of the subject within the essay as the narrative voice pivots between the third person references to Lowell and the first person references to Walcott. This cross-identification with Lowell emphasizes points of confluence in aesthetic practice and sensibility such as a catholic openness to artistic influence which is termed "omnivorous", and an eclectic attitude towards imitation described as the "magpie" style of using other masters, ancient and modern (p. 93). Walcott's co-identification with Lowell also involves his adopting the Elizabethan notion of imitation as improvement and heightening of one's gift through the hands of the great dead (p. 97); participation in a nurturing tradition and fraternity of artists – making "the great his colleague" (p. 98), and a self-conscious self-referentiality and obsession with craft – refusing to let go of oneself and never taking time "off" as a poet. (p. 95) The image of the poet as suffering under the burden of his craft – "a writer worries and works away from his fate, and he becomes it" (p. 96) – divorced from the earlier proposed Romantic notion of the poet as *isolato* and the perception of poetry as an artisan ("stonemason") vocation achieved through effort and apprenticeship – "believ[ing] not in 'inspiration' but in labour" (p. 100) – are putative features of the New World poet which Walcott claims in common with Lowell.

In this continued reworking of his previously articulated criteria for the New World poet, Walcott has decidedly shifted from a vision of poetry as a uniquely hermetic craft to a fusion with the poet as social advocate. In "Caligula's Horse" (1988), he terms the result of this fusion "something of a public figure, but still I hope, a hermit, a hider, a protector of silences" (p. 142) On the face of it, the "public hermit" construct seems a contradiction of Eliot's warning against committed art, but Walcott locates the posture of the poet as social scourge within the practice of canonical writers. To validate his own emerging practice, he cites writers like Graves, Pound, Williams, Yeats and even Eliot who "buttress[ed their] poetry with polemic; with the politics of [their] literary platform" ("On Robert Lowell", p. 102). Lowell is placed within this pantheon of precursor poets as one who "never relented in his undertaking to be, even in private, the conscience of

America, of the twentieth-century mind" (p. 103). But this sense of public responsibility which Walcott deems a characteristic feature of American poetry, has what he calls "its manic alternative" manifest in, on the one hand, the [illegible] and, on the other, the [illegible] hybrid [illegible] and "the wildness" (p. 102) is unmistakably Walcott's own position which decries perceived social injustice but never to the point of becoming "*poète maudit*."[42]

A concomitant of Walcott's "public hermit" dialectic is a significant shift in his linguistic strategy to accept that language is not a *cordon sanitaire* insulating the aesthetic realm from incursions and infiltration from the socio-political. This adjustment has its clearest expression in *Midsummer*. As clarification of his maxim, "no language is neutral", he further argues in a 1987 interview that "when you enter a language, you enter a kind of choice which contains in it the political history of the language, the imperial width of the language, the fact that you are either subjugated by the language or you have had to dominate it." He continues, "language is not a place of retreat, it's not a place of escape, it's not a place of resolution. It is a place of struggle."[43] This is a sharp departure from the position he had adopted at the beginning of the 1980s in an interview with Ned Thomas. In that interview he claimed disinterest in "either dialect or standard English". He explains, "You see I no longer think in terms of a tool [...] if it works it works for the one or the other."[44] As the 1980s wore on it became clear that this explanation was not going to suffice. So further clarification was given, first to Leif Sjoberg, that the job of the poet is to "fuse the noble and the common language [...] in a tone that is true to his own voice, in which both accents are heard naturally."[45] Later he describes this fusion to J. P. White as "tonal English with a creole inflection."[46] What then is the nature of the struggle he identifies? He hints at the nature of this struggle to Rebekah Presson when he argues that being given another language during colonialism and migration results in the "erosion of identity and the desperation to preserve identity". He continues, "the experience of being American [involves a] "transference of whatever colour, or name or place."[47]

The poet as chameleon, an adjustment on his schema for artistic/linguistic mimicry, is Walcott's recommended trope of scaling the anxieties of repositioning identity in America. He explains to David Montenegro his commitment to the premise by claiming to be "barefoot in spirit", "becoming water with no colouring, no obvious source ... no frame" ("Interview" [1987], p. 145). Further, Walcott modifies his theory of linguistic imitation from the "endemic cunning" argument of the late 1970s to one in which "one's own [poetic voice] is an anthology of all the voices one has heard. As it is with children so with poets" (Sjoberg, "Interview" [1983], p. 83). But this stated notion of neutral identification is problematic precisely because it comes at a time when the rhetoric of his aesthetic theorizing was suggesting the very opposite. A clear example is his lingering tentativeness and irresolution regarding the potential generic lack in the vernacular. First, his 1987 explanation to Robert Lowell is illustrative: "...our thinking is not pitched on the level of dialect. I'm not saying that dialect is incapable of conveying intellectual subtleties; I'm saying that to be true to the interior tone of reflection you need to know the exact measure of the sound you are reflecting" ("On Robert Lowell", p. 130). Second, it is based on his idiosyncratic reading of the relationship between speech and writing. Countering the judgment of linguistic science that thought precedes speech and speech precedes writing, Walcott insists that formal structuring has its co-genesis with speech. He argues in "The Master of the Ordinary: Philip Larkin 1989":

> Oral composition is mental writing. Poetry is speech, but it is also writing. Words have shape. It is composition in verse before it is anything else. Metre precedes breath, shape foreshadows content. Melody indicates meaning. The rest comes afterwards.[48]

Walcott's position here is ironically similar to Derridean deconstruction of the binary opposition between speech and writing. He suggests that writing is both an addition to speech and a substitute for speech. His suggestion of the unstable and problematic relationship between speech and writing is ironic given his distaste for "theory" stated in "Caligula's Horse". However, he equates elegance and order exclusively with the standard code when he argues that it is "folly... to believe elegance is treachery, that it deceives the tribe."[49]

"Caligula's Horse", signals a discernible return to the Romantic and Post-Romantic notions of Shelley and Arnold on the poet's unique qualification to be critic as well. In earlier decades, Walcott had suggested that poets make the best literary critics, emphasizing the specialized knowledge which he believes critics must hold. This is a qualification which "create[s] criticism that is as relevant as the writing".[50] In the ideologically charged 1970s, Walcott's characterization of West Indian critics and criticism is polemical. He likens West Indian criticism then to "little household quarrels" that are "so sociological and so particular that it cannot apply universally."[51] In the 1980s he continued to emphasize the divisive and insular nature of local criticism, based on non-aesthetic considerations such as race and nationalism, by referring to it as the "village mentality" and "standpipe criticism" (Milne, "This Country is a Very Small Place", pp. 71-72).

"Caligula's Horse" expands Walcott's earlier concern as to the extent to which literary criticism has been made to serve political ends. He suggests an antithesis between prose (which is the discourse of politics) and poetry (which is accidental, contradictory and ultimately results in revelation). Given this contrast, he dismisses the Modern schools of literary criticism, which he thinks substitute political discourse for sublime illumination. He singles out the injurious relationship between French poetry and criticism: "When French poetry dies the dead fish of French criticism is sold to the suckers."[illegible] The trope of the market, used here in his dismissive treatment of the literary Academy, has previously been used by Walcott to characteristically denounce populist nationalist posturing on aesthetic matters, especially since his hierarchical perspectives on the nature of art equate [illegible] literary criticism [illegible] Walcott underscores the [illegible] criticism emanating from the "Academy" can have on the artistic imagination. He posits a dichotomy between reason and the imagination when he quips, "A historian dare not imagine, a poet dare not think" ("Magic Industry", p. 142). In sum, he dismisses the discourse of the "Academy" as the "intellectual veneration of rot" ("Magic Industry", p. 141).

The preceding arguments would seem to endorse an "anti-theory" stance, but this perception needs to be nuanced by his self-proclaimed and deliberate strategy of indeterminacy and even contradiction. In *Another Life* he acknowledges: "my sign is Janus,/ I saw with twin heads,/ and everything I say is contradicted" (p. 139). Despite his stated revulsion to theory, it is ironic that Walcott's argument against theory draws heavily on the theoretical arguments of Shelley, Arnold and Eliot. One is bound to suspect his seeming anti-theory stance when a number of his major critical essays make clear allusions to the seminal literary theories of Eliot. His "Society and the Artist" echoes and comments on Eliot's "Tradition and the Individual Talent" and "The Caribbean: Culture or Mimicry?" is an even more obvious engagement with Arnold's *Culture and Anarchy*. He has even cited theory from the "Academy" in defence of his linguistic theory as cited earlier when he used Derridean deconstruction to help justify his preference of the scribal over oral expressive modes. It is clear, through his conflicted attitude and use of theory, that Walcott's angst might be directed more against the theory-based practice of some critics who pontificate to the [illegible]. By the time he wrote "Caligula's Horse", Walcott had [illegible] from the notion that immortality and permanence may be secured through art and he dismisses this notion as "superficial" and a "prosaic idea of time."[53] In "The Road Taken: Robert Frost", he offers a possible explanation for his retreat from the notion of artistic immortality that is grounded in an altered view of historical linearity that positions the work of art outside of temporal phenomena. He explains, "poetry is its own realm and [...] a great poem is a state of raceless, sexless, timeless grace". He continues that poems do not obey linear time: "poems are the composition and [illegible] of time, not [illegible]" (p. 210).

In "Caligula's Horse", Walcott makes the startling assertion that the subject of critics is not literature but God or the gods; that poets should be judged by their approach to this subject which has as its emblem, *Dominus illuminatio mea,* Lord who art the light of my life (Caligula's Horse", p. 139). This statement, taken in context, represents the culmination of a trend toward an ambivalent affirmation of religious faith by the poet which is present in Walcott's oeuvre, but which began to gather momentum in the 1970s. Walcott's work in the 1980s is replete with the tropes, imagery and motifs of the Christian faith that buttress his ideological positions on the key issues of amnesia and ethno-cultural syncretism.[54] Paul Breslin attempts to account for this phenomenon by questioning whether Walcott's use of scriptural allusion in his poetry of the 1970s and 1980s is not a strategy to secularize the language of the sacred or to recover the sacred from the secular. He suggests that this might be part of the poet's longing for an earthly centre and "home".[55]

Walcott's "mulatto" approach to theorizing Caribbean literature and criticism teaches, if anything, the multiple determinisms of Caribbean subject formation and identity. It rejects a single teleological narrative and deterministic logic that has its own end already inscribed in its beginning. The historical reality to be explained has no known or determined end. Herein lies an opening for an inter-theoretical or trans-theoretical field of enquiry. The tactical shifts and strategic retreats within Walcott's aesthetic theorizing and critical sensibility posit that the Caribbean author produces works of literature by subjecting the self to the conventions and meanings of language, and the shifting circumstances of history and culture, without which, as a people, we could not have made ourselves. If indeed, the historical reality to be analysed and explained has no deterministic end then the conceptual and interpretive tools, and the perception of the role and nature of the author or the function of the text cannot be fixed either. Walcott's ideological and aesthetic manoeuvres in defining and clarifying Caribbean experience function as a "mulatto criticism" that underscores the contingent nature of aesthetic theorizing in a multi-ethnic, multicultural and polyglot context such as ours.

Endnotes

1. Derek Walcott, "Caligula's Horse", Opening address delivered at the Eighth Conference on West Indian Literature, Mona, Jamaica, May 1988. Pub. in Stephen Slemon and Helen Tiffin, Eds. *After Europe* (Mundelstrup: Dangaroo, 1989), pp. 138-142.
2. Antonio Benitez-Rojo, *The Repeating Island: The Caribbean and the Postmodern Perspective*, trans. J, Maraniss (Durham and London: Duke UP, 1997), p. 303.
3. Anthony Milne, Interview with Derek Walcott: "This Country Is

a Very Small Place", *Conversations with Derek Walcott*. Ed. William Baer (Jackson: University Press of Mississippi, 1996), p. 74.

4. Derek Walcott, "The Antilles: Fragments of Epic Memory", *What the Twilight Says: Essays* (New York: [illegible]), p. [illegible]
5. Derek Walcott, "The Figure of Crusoe" [1965], *Critical Perspectives on Derek Walcott*. Ed. Robert Hamner (Washington DC: Three Continents Press, [illegible]), p. [illegible]
6. Derek Walcott, "The Muse of History", in *Carifesta Forum*. Ed. John Hearne (Institute of Jamaica, 1976), p. 111. Reprinted in *What the Twilight Says: Essays*, p. 36. Page references from this source.
7. Derek Walcott, "Necessity of Negritude" [1964], *Critical Perspectives on Derek Walcott*, pp. 20-23.
8. Derek Walcott, "Society and the Artist" [1957], *Critical Perspectives on Derek Walcott*, pp. 15-17.
9. Derek Walcott, "History and picong… in the Middle Passage" [1962], *Critical Perspectives on Derek Walcott*, pp. 18-19.
10. Derek Walcott, "Poetry – Enormously Complicated Art", *The Trinidad Guardian*, 18 June 1962, p. 3.
11. T.S. Eliot, "Tradition and the Individual Talent" [1920], *Selected Essays*, 1932 (London: Faber and Faber, reprint, 1972).
12. T.S. Eliot, "Tradition and the Individual Talent", p. 51.
13. See Harold N. McDermott, "Ethnicity and the 'Mulatto of Style': Towards a theory of Theory of Caribbean Aesthetic in the Works of Derek Walcott 1940-1993" PhD Thesis Unpublished, (University of the West Indies, Mona, 2005).
14. Charles W. Pollard, *New World Modernisms: T.S. Eliot, Derek Walcott, and Kamau Brathwaite* (Charlottesville: University of Virginia Press, 2004), p. 10.
15. Derek Walcott, "The Caribbean: Culture or Mimicry?" [1974], *Critical Perspectives on Derek Walcott*, p. 51.
16. Derek Walcott, *25 Poems* (Port of Spain: Guardian Commercial Printery, 1948).
17. Derek Walcott, "What the Twilight says: an Overture", *Dream on Monkey Mountain and other Plays* (London: Jonathan Cape, 1972).
18. Matthew Arnold, *Culture and Anarchy*. Ed. J. Dover Wilson (Cambridge University Press, Cambridge, 1978), p. 70.
19. There is also a clearly discernible allusion here to Eliot's argument that the function of the poet's use of language is to "purify the dialect of the tribe" in order to give his or her audience a more refined language ("Little Gidding", *The Complete Poems and Plays, 1909–1950* (New York: Harcourt Brace Jovanovich, 1971), p. [illegible]). Charles Pollard (*New World Modernisms*, p. 11) offers some differentiation

between Walcott's and Eliot's use of key terms associated with language use when he opines that while Eliot speaks of purification as "developing" and "refining" common speech, Walcott aspires to contribute the sound of his own accent to the common, transnational, and interethnic language of the New World. In effect, Walcott's poetry "purifies" speech by amalgamating and fusing the different dialects of the region.

20. Derek Walcott, "Calypso as Theatre" [1977], unpublished. Held in Special Collection, University of the West Indies Library, St. Augustine, Trinidad, p. 4.
21. Derek Walcott, "Meanings" [1970], *Critical Perspectives on Derek Walcott*, pp. 45-50.
22. Edward Hirsch, "An interview with Derek Walcott" [1977], *Conversations with Derek Walcott*, p. 53.
23. T.S. Eliot, "The Social Function of Poetry", *On Poetry and Poets* (London: Faber and Faber, 1956), p. 21.
24. Sharon Ciccarelli, "Reflections Before and After Carnival" [1977], *Conversations with Derek Walcott,* p. 42.
25. Derek Walcott, "West Indian Art Today", *Sunday Guardian Magazine*, 8 May 1966, 8.
26. Ned Thomas, "Interview" [1980], *Conversations With Derek Walcott*, p. 68.
27. Derek Walcott, *Midsummer* (New York: Farrar, Straus and Giroux, 1984).
28. Derek Walcott, *The Fortunate Traveller* (New York: Farrar, Straus and Giroux, 1981).
29. Derek Walcott, *The Arkansas Testament* (London, Boston: Faber and Faber, 1987).
30. Derek Walcott, Derek, *Epitaph for the Young: XII Cantos* (Barbados: Advocate Co., 1949).
31. Derek Walcott, *In A Green Night: Poems 1948-1960*, (London: Jonathan Cape, 1962).
32. Derek Walcott, *The Fortunate Traveller*, p. 6.
33. Walcott, "A Colonial's Eye View of the Empire", *Tri-Quarterly* 65 (Winter 1986), 79.
34. Claude Lévi-Strauss, *The Raw and the Cooked: Mythologiques, Volume 1* (University of Chicago Press, 1983).
35. Derek Walcott, *Another Life* (London: Jonathan Cape, 1973).
36. Stuart Hall, "Cultural Identity and Diaspora", *Colonial Discourse and Postcolonial Theory: A Reader*, Eds. P. Williams and L. Chrisman (New York: Columbia University Press, 1994), p. 394.
37. Walcott, "Magic Industry: Joseph Brodsky", *What the Twilight Says*, p. 138.
38. Derek Walcott, "The Antilles: Fragments of Epic Memory", pp. 65-84.

39. Denis Williams, "The Concept of the Ancestor", *Image and Idea in the Arts of Guyana: The Edgar Mittelholzer Memorial Lectures*, 2nd Series, The National History and Arts Council (Ministry of Information, Georgetown Guyana, [illegible]).
40. Derek Walcott, "On Robert Lowell", *What the Twilight Says*, p. [illegible].
41. Derek Walcott, "The Road Taken: Robert Frost", *What the Twilight Says*, p. 212.
42. [illegible]
43. David Montenegro, "An interview with Derek Walcott" [1987], *Conversations With Derek Walcott*, p. 142.
44. Ned Thomas, "Interview" [1980], *Conversations With Derek Walcott*, p. 67.
45. Leif Sjöberg, "An interview with Derek Walcott" [1983], *Conversations with Derek Walcott*, p. 83.
46. J.P. White, "An Interview with Derek Walcott" [1990], *Conversations With Derek Walcott*, p. 152.
47. Rebekah Presson, "The Man Who Keeps the English Language Alive: An Interview with Derek Walcott" [1992], *Conversations with Derek Walcott*, p. 192.
48. Derek Walcott, "The Master of the Ordinary: Philip Larkin", *What the Twilight Says*, p. 163.
49. Derek Walcott, "A Letter to Chamoiseau", *What the Twilight Says*, p. 229.
50. Walcott's Romantic sensibility waxes and wanes during the course of his poetic career but never totally disappears. It is perhaps most evident in his conflicted attitude towards the danger posed by tourism and development to local culture.
51. Robert Hamner, "Conversation with Derek Walcott" [1975], *Conversations With Derek Walcott*, p. 27.
52. Derek Walcott, "Magic Industry: Joseph Brodsky", *What the Twilight Says*, p. 141.
53. Walcott, "Caligula's Horse", *After Europe*, p. 142.
54. Certain religious allusions are conspicuously deployed in Walcott's poetry during this period. For example, "The Light of the World" alludes to the gospels of Matthew and John and echoes its first deployment in *Another Life*.
55. Paul Breslin, *Nobody's Nation: Reading Derek Walcott* (Chicago: The University of Chicago Press, 2001), p. 235.

RACHEL D. FRIEDMAN

"GREEK CALYPSO": WALCOTT, HOMER, AND THE FIGURE OF THERSITES

Towards the end of *Omeros*, Walcott's poetic persona, after admitting to the figure of Omeros that he has never read his poems "all the way through", proclaims to him that he was the "freshest" of all of his readers.

"I have always heard
your voice in that sea, master, it was the same song
of the desert shaman, and when I was a boy

your name was as wide as a bay, as I walked along
the curled brow of the surf; the word 'Homer' meant joy,
joy in battle, in work, in death, then the numbered peace

of the surf's benedictions, it rose in the cedars,
in the *laurier-cannelles*, pages of rustling trees.
Master, I was the freshest of all your readers."[1]

For me, coming to Walcott as a classicist and after years of reading and studying the Homeric poems, the freshness of his readings was stunning and invigorating and has helped me to discover a Homer that I did not previously have access to.

Walcott has spoken often of the simultaneity of great art and of the damaging limitations imposed by readings based on chronology. He encourages us, instead, to listen to the *conversations* that emerge between him and the poets he has read. At a symposium at Duke University, for example, held in 1995, he spoke in a room filled with collages by Romare Bearden and used the occasion to reflect on Bearden's response to Homer in his *Odyssey* collages. He analogized Bearden's creative process to his own:

> And yet I think it is this whole freshness of experience that made me feel that my references to Homer, and to all the other writers I was indebted to in the book, were perfectly valid. And I knew it would lead to a kind of academic acclaim that I'm not very happy about – "Oh, so much is owed to so-and-so" – I hate that. It is a patronizing way of saying about, for instance, Romare's work: "Look at those black cutouts. They are

> like Greek vases.' Yes, they may be like Greek vases, but they are *simultaneous* concepts, not *chronological* concepts. The black cutout of a diving figure is no more historical than the silhouette of a Greek athlete on a vase. It's not a question of where you stop, since you then have to go from the Greek silhouette back to the Egyptian profile, et cetera. If you think of art merely in terms of chronology, you are going to be patronizing to certain cultures. But if you think of art as a simultaneity that is inevitable in terms of certain people, then Joyce is a contemporary of Homer (which Joyce knew).

Walcott's appeal to the work of Bearden to explore the nature of the relationship between two artists across the ages can provide us here with a fruitful starting point for considering the nature of Walcott's own collaboration with Homer in the 1993 *The Odyssey: A Stage Version* (henceforth *STO*), the focus of my attention here.

In the catalogue of a recent exhibit of the Bearden *Odyssey* collages at the DC Moore Gallery in New York, Robert G. O'Meally effectively compares this process of collaboration between Bearden and Homer to the kind of improvisation that happens between two jazz musicians playing together:

> But Bearden was also an improviser in the "Harlem" sense that that title implies collaboration. For like Charlie Parker, working so closely with Dizzy Gillespie that on records you can feel the two men breathing together as they create their exciting musical lines, Bearden in this series of collages gets close enough to *The Odyssey* of Homer that the two artists play together like section-mates in a jazz band. Just as Homer the writer/singer/(and perhaps dancer) of poetic lines depended on his audiences to complete the creative process (jazz people call this the swinging "call-response" pattern), Bearden's collages invite active viewers into the bright and shining space of improvised creation that includes the artist himself along with the ancient Greek bard, still speak-singing his lines.[4]

The language of jazz that O'Meally employs to speak of Bearden's improvised collaboration with Homer so that, as he says, "we can hear the two men breathing together" also gives us a wonderful model for thinking about Walcott's own Homeric collaborations. The kind of collaboration that O'Meally describes is enacted literally at the end of *Omeros*, just after the passage I cited above, when Walcott's persona and Omeros extemporaneously compose a praise song of St Lucia together:

> Then I saw the ebony of his lifted hand
>
> And Omeros nodded: "We will both praise it now."
> But I could not before him. My tongue was a stone
> at the bottom of the sea, my mouth a parted conch
>
> from which nothing sounded, and then I heard his own
> Greek calypso coming from the marble trunk,
> widening the sea with a blind man's anger:

> *"In the midst of the sea there is a horned island*
> *with deep green harbours where the Greek ships anchor"*
> and the waves were swaying to the stroke of his hand,
>
> as I heard my own thin voice riding on his praise
> the way a swift follows a crest, leaving its shore [...]
>
> [...] My voice was going
> under the strength of his voice, which carried so far
> that a black frigate heard it, steadying its wing. (*Omeros*, pp. 286–87)

The voice of the older poet carries the voice of the younger as they compose the song together.

The emergence of this "Greek calypso" in *Omeros* marks the culmination of a strain of thought that has long been present in Walcott's work, made particularly evident by his more theoretical comments in essays and interviews. In his importantly prescriptive 1974 essay "The Muse of History", Walcott lays out a crucial critical model for the writing of poetry in the New World that is based largely on his conviction that the New World poet must engage in this kind of conversation with the poets who have gone before him. Walcott celebrates "the great poets of the New World" like St-John Perse who are able to make such seamless connections with the past:

> Their vision of man in the New World is Adamic. In their exuberance he is still capable of enormous wonder. Yet he has paid his accounts to Greece and Rome and walks in a world without monuments and ruins. [...] Like Borges, too, the poet St.-John Perse conducts us from the mythology of the past to the present without a tremor of adjustment. [...] What Perse glorifies is not veneration but the perennial freedom; his hero remains the wanderer, the man who moves through the ruins of great civilizations with all his worldly goods by caravan or pack mule, the poet carrying entire cultures in his head, bitter perhaps, but unencumbered.[6]

Perse's hero is free and unencumbered, yet he "has paid his accounts to Greece and Rome" and "carries entire cultures in his head". Unlike poets who are imprisoned by chronology, the poets of "remorse and regret", Perse is emblematic for Walcott of the great New World poet who can move seamlessly from one era, and one world, to another.

Later on in "The Muse of History", Walcott connects this kind of poetic conversation across the ages to the process of oral composition, linking it both implicitly to the composition of the Homeric poems and, in his own ahistorical leap from one world to another, explicitly to the musical traditions that the African slaves brought with them to the New World. While he doesn't specifically reference jazz here, he appeals to the related genre of the blues to evoke a process similar to the one that O'Meally describes:

In an oral tradition the mode is simple, the response open-ended, so that each new poet can add his lines to the form, a process very much like weaving or the dance, based on the concept that the history of the tribe is endless. There is no dying fall, no egotistical signature of effect; in short, no pathos. The blues is not pathos, not the individual voice, it is tribal mode, and each new word poet can contribute his couplet, and this is based on the concept that the tribe, inured to despair, will also survive: there is no beginning but no end. The new poet enters a flux and withdraws, so the act is to continue the pattern, hand to hand and [illegible]

Many days of sorrow, many nights of woe,
Many days of sorrow, many nights of woe,
And a ball and chain, everywhere I go,

No history, but flux, and the only sustenance, myth:

Moses lived till he got old,
Where shall I be? ("Muse of History", pp. 47-48)

Walcott's poet "enters the flux and withdraws", continuing the song where the poet before him left off and then withdrawing to allow for the continuation of the song after him. His representation of the process of oral composition is, in fact, very close to what we now understand about the processes that led to the composition of the Homeric poems. Here though, in a move not unlike O'Meally's use of jazz as an analogy for Bearden's collaboration with Homer, he connects this "ancient mode", with the more modern mode of the blues singer. The blues that he sings are not the product of his "individual voice", but they emerge from the tribal memory and form a continuous song, with no beginning and no end. By way of example, Walcott quotes from two songs. The first, "Chain Gang Blues", was performed by Ma Rainey, called the "Mother of the Blues", in 1926, and the second, "Where Shall I Be", was a black spiritual from the American south. Both genres, the blues and the spiritual – which here reinterprets Old Testament myth – speak to the model of integrative and improvised poetic composition that Walcott sees as emblematic of the greatest poetry of the New World.[7]

The theoretical models that Walcott articulates in this essay, as well as the analogies that he suggests between ancient modes of poetic composition and the song traditions that emerged among the Africans transplanted to the New World, are both crucial for understanding his own turns to Homer in *Omeros* (1990) and the *Odyssey*, commissioned by the Royal Shakespeare Company, which followed shortly thereafter. If we take seriously Walcott's understanding of the role of the poet and of his situation within the collective epic poetic composition, then we are obliged to understand his works not as isolated poetic orphans, but as works that are in explicit conversation with the poems that have preceded them. In the remainder of this paper, I will first generally consider the ways that Walcott's *SVO* enacts on stage the kind of improvisatory collaboration that I have been discussing, and then I will narrow my focus to the figure of Thersites, a character that Walcott imports into his *Odyssey* from Homer's *Iliad*. My hope is that my focus on this one figure, a figure that can be seen as performing a metapoetic function in both Homer and Walcott, will serve as a way of illustrating that some of these theoretical concerns can be translated into a practice of reading Walcott's Homeric works. In this practice, our reading of one poet is enhanced by our reading of the other; Walcott, as I have said, opens up new readings of Homer, but so too does close consideration of the Homeric poems deepen our appreciation of Walcott's work.[8]

Unlike *Omeros*, where the Homeric echoes are clearly heard but emerge from the background of the poem, the *SVO* positions itself as a "version" of the *Odyssey* and conforms to the shape of Homer's poem quite closely. In the play, for the first time, Walcott puts the Greek material front and centre and uses it to shape the work, not implicitly, behind the scenes, but as an explicit pre-text around which the work is built.[9] The *SVO*, then, is a particularly interesting place to look for exploring the question of Walcott's relationship with Homer, not only because it is his most explicit and sustained engagement with the ancient poet to date, but also because of the particular form that this dramatic work takes. Particularly relevant to the discussion above is the fact that the whole play is presided over by a blues singer, Blind Billy Blue, who takes on the role of the play's bard and MC. As a blues singer he links the experiences of the play's creolized characters with the Homeric material on which the play is based; he becomes the voice of the tribe who can connect past to present.

The image of the poet joining his voice to the song and then retreating, which is conjured by Walcott in "The Muse of History", echoes almost literally in the opening lines of the *SVO* when Blind Billy Blue sings the first line of Homer's *Odyssey* in Greek and then reflects on the sea's movement back and forth over the line as he joins his voice to Homer's:

BILLY BLUE (*Sings*)
Gone sing 'bout that man because his stories please us,
Who saw trials and tempests for ten years after Troy.

I'm Blind Billy Blue, my main man's sea-smart Odysseus,
Who the God of the Sea drove crazy and tried to destroy.

Andra moi ennepe mousa polutropon hos mala polla...
The shuttle of the sea moves back and forth on this line,

All night, like the surf, she shuttles and doesn't fall
Asleep, then her rosy fingers at dawn unstitch the design.[10]

Walcott's figuring of his Homeric narrator/poet in the *SVO* as a blues musician directly echoes his appeal to the blues in "The Muse of History": in these opening lines, the blues singer, reciting the first line of the *Odyssey* in Greek and then using it as a riff for his own song, performs the kind of call and response across the ages that Walcott encourages in his theoretical discussion.

The prominent role given to the blues singer in the play can also be seen as intimately related to the particularly African nature of the form of the drama itself. I refer here to one of the play's most distinguishing features, namely the fact that the whole play is composed in stichomythia, the continuous back and forth exchange of single lines and half lines. With the exception of Billy Blue's songs and a few other passages, most of the play consists entirely of such exchanges. Of particular interest to me is the openness of this form; because of the play's complete avoidance of longer speeches, each utterance stands by itself seeming to invite a response, association, addition or embellishment. The dialogue thus spins itself out and has an improvisatory quality. Sometimes Walcott provides an actual exchange or conversation, but often the lines feel fragmentary and we are left to fill in the blanks ourselves. This is another kind of call and response that speaks not directly to the timelessness of the conversation between poets across the ages, but to another improvisatory feature of oral poetic traditions, namely, the active engagement between the poet and his audience.[11]

The play's dramatization of a fast-paced back and forth among the performers also evokes the *particularly Caribbean* form, evident especially in Trinidadian Calypso performances, of picong, which involves a call and response between the performer and the audience. Picong, like blues and jazz, is often seen as having its roots in the musical traditions that transplanted Africans brought to the New World.[12] This association, yet another way of linking back Walcott's own idiom with the poetic traditions that he has inherited, is one that Walcott himself has explicitly made:

> Here's this marvellous idea of Homer, and then every other, or the singer, who contains the history of the race: it's an oral history of the race that's being set, by this legend… there've been great blind blues singers, and the same thing is true of the calypsonian, who is untouchable as a figure, who contains the history of the race, who is a vessel for that. And I see absolutely no difference… The tribal sense is unified in the black man, in the blues singer…[13]

In the *SVO*, then, an adaptation of ancient Greek epic composed in one line exchanges and presided over by a blues singer, Walcott is foregrounding this intricate web of connections between the Homeric tradition, the transplanted poetic traditions of African Americans generally, and the particular idiom that these song traditions acquired in the Caribbean.

Central to the myth of the blues singer and to the traditions surrounding many of the performers that Walcott references is their positioning as outsiders, often itinerant, a status that enhances their ability to serve, as Walcott says, as the "voice of the tribe", and to offer cultural and political criticism to the communities in which they perform.[14] Billy Blue is this figure in the *SVO*. He is outside of the play's action and able to comment on it, but he is also outside of it temporally and culturally, with an identity that is definitively black and definitively American, in a play peopled otherwise almost exclusively with characters inhabiting the ancient Greek world of Homer's *Odyssey*, albeit a creolized version of it.

The other outsider in the play, though, is Thersites, who is literally an outsider to the *Odyssey* since, unlike all of Walcott's other ancient Greek characters, he does not appear in the ancient poem, but has been imported by Walcott from the *Iliad*. He is further made into an outsider by Walcott's figuring of him as a mercenary, a role he does not have in Homer. In the opening stage directions of Act I, Scene I, the "kings" Agamemnon, Menelaus, and Nestor are identified as such. Ajax, the famous warrior, is named without need for identification, and then attached to the end of this list is the surprise inclusion of "Thersites, the mercenary" (I.i. p. 2). While Walcott clearly marks him as an outsider among the other warriors at Troy he also simultaneously highlights his role by situating him so prominently in the play's opening scene.

Thersites is one of several Homeric characters, in both the *SVO* and *Omeros,* whom Walcott brings in from the edges of epic; they are characters who are curiously marginalized *within* the very tradition that they come from.[15] Walcott's focus on these characters picks up on a strange kind of marginalized but central role that they themselves play in the ancient epics. While it might be tempting to see Walcott's focus on these outcasts as a simple act of appropriation whereby those neglected by ancient epic are now appropriated and given a voice, in fact Walcott's promotion of these marginalized characters points us back to some of the obscure but crucial functions that they perform within their own tradition. In the case of Thersites, Walcott's shining of a spotlight on him helps us to recover some of the surprisingly intimate ways that he is connected to the heroes at the centre of the Homeric poems, Achilles and Odysseus, and to the figure of the poet himself.

The *SVO* opens at the end of the Trojan War while the Greek warriors are still at Troy, standing around Achilles' funeral pyre and preparing to sail back home. Thersites seems to be the only one not happy that the war is over:

AGAMEMNON
Through the length of war, home was our long desire.
MENELAUS
It was mine, Menelaus, whose wife was its cause.

AJAX
And mine, Ajax, the heir of Achilles' armour.
(ODYSSEUS *enters at a distance.*)
ODYSSEUS
What?
THERSITES
Not mine. Thersites. No wife, no son, no house. (*SVO*, I.i. p. 2)

Later on in the scene [illegible]

ODYSSEUS
You regret victory, Thersites. I know why.
THERSITES
Yeah? Then you make my dissatisfaction exact.
ODYSSEUS
After victory what?
THERSITES
Peace. Screw peace. No money.
ODYSSEUS
Peace ruins mercenaries. (*SVO*, I.i. p. 4)

While Thersites initially seems to be positioned as the outlier isolated from the others by his lack of interest in the idea of going home after the end of the long Greek campaign at Troy, it emerges that there is a curious affinity between him and Odysseus. After the other warriors leave the stage, Thersites and Odysseus are left alone, and Odysseus, reluctant to part from him, tries to convince him to come home to Ithaca with him.

ODYSSEUS
Come to Ithaca.
THERSITES
Can you promise me a war?
ODYSSEUS
No. Hang your sword on a hook.
THERSITES
What? Hang my own wife? (*SVO*, I.i. p. 5)

Further on in this [illegible] offers Thersites to rule next to him in Ithaca. He then bequeaths Thersites "Mt. Neriton's poplars", but Thersites declines derisively, saying that "Trees spread peace".

When we turn back to the *Iliad* with this scene from Walcott in mind, Walcott's Thersites initially seems to be unrelated to Homer's.[10] The Homeric Thersites is known to us from Book Two of the *Iliad* where he speaks out in the assembly against Agamemnon and is then beaten and reproached by Odysseus. Agamemnon, testing the Greek troops and trying to incite them to battle, suggests to them that they should all give up the fight for Troy and head home. This test, though, seems about to backfire when the Greeks start preparing to head for the ships. Athena quickly comes down from Olympus, speaks to Odysseus and repairs the damage so that the Greeks are now, once again, determined to fight. All of the Greeks acquiesce to this plan except for Thersites, who rails against Agamemnon and accuses him of wanting to stay only so that he may accumulate more women and gold.

He is an unusual, even exceptional, character in Homeric epic for several reasons. Homer tells us that he was the "ugliest man who came to Troy" and that his speech was all out of order; he then devotes another remarkable three lines to describing the details of Thersites' deformities:

> Now the rest had sat down, and were orderly in their places,
> but one man, Thersites, of the endless speech, still scolded,
> who knew within his head many words, but disorderly;
> vain, and without decency, to quarrel with the princes
> with any word he thought might be amusing to the Argives.
> This was the ugliest man who came beneath Ilion. He was
> bandy-legged and went lame of one foot, with shoulders
> stooped and drawn together over his chest, and above this
> his skull went up to a point with the wool grown sparsely upon it.
> Beyond all others Achilleus hated him, and Odysseus.
> These two he was forever abusing, but now at brilliant
> Agamemnon he clashed the shrill noise of his abuse. The Achaians
> were furiously angry with him, their minds resentful.[17]

The description is striking not only for its vividness but also because of its unusual place within Homeric epic; no one else in either of the Homeric poems gets such a lengthy physical description. Beyond this, though, Thersites is even more remarkable for being the only character in the *Iliad* for whom neither a patronymic nor place of origin is specified. Both his lack of physical beauty and his lack of distinguished ancestry, or any ancestry at all for that matter, put him in sharp contrast to heroes such as Achilles and Odysseus for whom both of these features play significant roles in defining their heroic identity.[18] Thersites is, in the *Iliad*, the ultimate outsider – not only ugly but even more importantly, without place and without history.

For a long time scholars tended to view Thersites only as the outlier within the Greek camp who serves to highlight the nobility of the other Greeks at Troy through all of his deviations from the heroic code. One scholar dismisses him as "rude, boorish" and "menial", and calls him a "nonentity among dynastic aristocrats", who "has no other dimension to his being than his physical appearance", and another says that he is "the aristocrat's image of a perfect plebeian, an ugly loudmouth and coward."[19] His primary poetic function in many readings of the scene has been as a marker of difference from the rest of the Greek heroes.

It is tempting, perhaps, to make the same move in Walcott's play too and to read Thersites the mercenary, who has no wife and no home to return to, simply as a foil to the play's homecoming hero. But Walcott's highlighting of Thersites' importance to Odysseus is not satisfactorily explained this way. After Odysseus fails to convince Thersites to come home with him to Ithaka, Odysseus doesn't let him depart until he admits love:

> ODYSSEUS: Open the gates of those locked teeth. Admit love, friend.
> THERSITES: I'll say it with grinding jaw. I loved you. Go on.
> (*They embrace, then exit in opposite directions….*) (I.i. p. 6)

The two might appear to make opposite choices, to go in opposite directions, but in fact throughout the play Walcott calls our attention to all of the dimensions of Odysseus that are Thersites-like. Their unique bond can be seen as a reflection of the way that Thersites becomes the only Greek warrior in the play who is able to voice the centrifugal side of Odysseus, an Odysseus who is, as are many of the Odysseus figures in Walcott's oeuvre, ambivalent about going home. This Odysseus is still drawn, like Thersites, who claims the sky as his roof, to the life of the wanderer at sea.[20] He must, finally, admit to Penelope, once he is back on Ithaca, that he will miss the sea (II.vi. p. 159).

Thersites' life of wandering ultimately connects him not only to Odysseus, but also to the play's poet(s), Homer/Billy Blue/Demodocus, to whom, of course, Odysseus the archetypal wanderer and storyteller is also connected. In the play's opening conversation between Thersites and Odysseus, when Odysseus is trying to convince him to come back with him to Ithaka, Odysseus tries, unsuccessfully, to appeal to the idea that everybody needs a shore to return to:

> ODYSSEUS
> Our ribbed bodies long for their original shore.
> THERSITES
> Except this body. That's found no shore to believe. (I.i. p. 5)

Next in the exchange, however, Thersites takes up and transforms Odysseus' image of a ribbed body. As Odysseus uses Thersites' sword to write his will in the sand, Thersites interjects: "My white ribs, a harp that the sea-crab's fingers pluck." In this line, where he plays with what Odysseus has said about "ribbed bodies longing for their original shore", he offers his own ribs not as a source of longing for natal place, for "an original shore", but as an instrument, a harp, plucked by the fingers of the sea-crab. His body, instead of longing for an original shore, becomes a vehicle for poetry. Plucked by an ocean creature, the rib harp is floating, out at sea and thus evocative of the production of a particular kind of poetry produced by an itinerant bard who composes his songs as he moves from place to place without connection to "original shores". The mercenary, along with Odysseus and the play's various bards, becomes another expression of the itinerant poet.

Associations between seafaring and poetry making can be felt right from the prologue where Billy Blue sings the opening line of the *Odyssey* in Greek and then continues:

> The shuttle of the sea moves back and forth on this line,
>
> All night, like the surf, she shuttles and doesn't fall
> Asleep, then her rosy fingers at dawn unstitch the design. (p. 1)

The pattern of the sea is identified with the pattern of the poem. Similarly, when Billy Blue appears in Ithaca as Demodocus, he is figured as a wandering islander:

> ODYSSEUS
> That's a strange dialect. What island are you from?
> DEMODOCUS
> A far archipelago. Blue seas. Just like yours.
> ODYSSEUS
> So you pick up various stories and you stitch them?
> DEMODOCUS
> The sea speaks the same language around the world's shores. (II.iv. p. 122)

In assigning to the wandering mercenary the imagery of the bard, Walcott makes it impossible to dismiss the perspective that he represents. Instead, Thersites, the itinerant mercenary whose ribbed body out at sea facilitates the production of poetry, becomes a double of Odysseus the poet-wanderer who is himself yet another iteration of the poet, whether Homer or Walcott himself.

When we go back to Homer with *this* Thersites in mind, Thersites the poet-wanderer and close friend of Odysseus, we become more sensitive to the ways that the *Iliad* too, takes interest in its outcast. We are also more open to seeing that Homer too subtly points to certain important affinities that Thersites shares with Odysseus, Achilles, and the Homeric poet himself.[21] While the Thersites of the *Iliad* appears to be a total outcast from the rest of the aristocratic warriors at Troy, significantly, in *non*-Homeric myth, Thersites is of stock as illustrious as Odysseus' or many of the other Greek heroes, and is ranked among the noble heroes who participated in the legendary Kaldonian boar hunt. Similarly, vase paintings survive which depict him without any of the ugly features attributed to him by Homer.[22] In another *Iliad* then, another version of this ever-changing orally composed poem, it is entirely feasible that he would not occupy the marginalized role he is given in Homer. Much as Walcott has transformed Thersites into a mercenary, Homer's *Iliad* has possibly deliberately suppressed Thersites' homeland and his patronymic and transformed him from an aristocrat into an ugly outcast. The non-Homeric evidence suggests that Homer was not necessarily working within an inherited tradition that portrays him as such.

Thersites' name, from a Greek word implying either boldness or [illegible] seems to begin to point the way to the particular nature of the role Homer has given him.[7] As the only hero in the poem without connections to ancestry or place, his role in Homer's *Iliad* is to be the anonymous speaker of truth who can say what no one else in the community can. As W.G. Thalmann has said, "His detached, ironic perspective also allows a peculiar clarity of vision, bringing into focus tensions and contradictions in society that otherwise would remain half concealed."[8] Thersites [illegible] introducing his alternative voice and building in, as it were, a critical perspective. In the description of Thersites from the *Iliad* cited above, the poet tells us that he was "forever abusing Odysseus and Achilles", and the form of the verb that the poet uses, an iterative imperfect, stresses that this was a frequent, ongoing phenomenon; the episode of the quarrel in Book Two is not to be seen as an isolated one.

In a fascinating new reading of Thersites' social function in the *Iliad*, J. Marks moves away from readings that have focused on Thersites' social class and suggests, instead, that Thersites, the anonymous and placeless figure who was "frequently" quarrelling with Achilles and Odysseus, should be understood as related to a version of the traditional figure of the *iambic poet* whose poetry seems to have consisted of a kind of ritual insult and scornful criticism. Marks thus makes Thersites' marginalized status a function of his role as a kind of poet who must be positioned outside of the community in order to critique it. By including him in the *Iliad* and transforming him from just another aristocratic warrior into a marginalized figure whose outsider perspective allows him to see the events unfolding in the epic through a different lens, the Homeric poet signals both his own interest in singing a song that complicates the portrayal of the heroes whose glory he sings and his understanding of his role as a poet as one who gives voice to these outsider/insider perspectives. Homer's Thersites, the ugly misfit and social outcast, becomes, then, much like Walcott's, a metapoetic figure through whom the poet can explore his own positioning in his society and the role that his poetry plays.

Thersites as poet is initially obvious neither in Homer nor in Walcott nor, in fact, are any of the connections between Walcott's treatment of him and Homer's immediately apparent. More, though, than pedantically insisting on the connections between them that I have been suggesting here, what I hope to have shown are some of the ways that exciting new readings are opened up when we put the two poets in conversation with each other. Walcott's promotion of Thersites to the inner circle of Greek warriors and his constructing of a close relationship between Thersites and Odysseus takes us back to Homer with new interest in the ways that the Homeric Thersites might also be more intimately connected to the poem's central heroes. When we follow that interest and discover non-Homeric traditions in which Thersites was as aristocratic as Odysseus and Achilles, we become more sensitive to the ways that Homer might have deliberately disfigured and marginalized him. Walcott's scenario of Thersites as close friend to Odysseus and mercenary at Troy suddenly takes on new meaning. This is the moment when we see "the bright and shining space of improvised creation" to return to the image from O'Meally with which I began, when we start seeing all kinds of synergies between Walcott and Homer and the poetic worlds that they inhabit. Walcott's archipelago becomes an extension of Homer's; we start to hear the two poets singing together and to grasp anew the expansiveness of each of their visions as the voice of one lends richness and depth to the voice of the other.

Endnotes

1. Derek Walcott, *Omeros* (New York: Farrar, Straus and Giroux, 1990), p. 283.
2. Derek Walcott, "Reflections on Omeros", *South Atlantic Quarterly* 96.2 (1997), 240–241.
3. Derek Walcott, *The Odyssey: A Stage Version* (New York: Farrar, Straus and Giroux,1993).
4. Robert O'Meally, *Romare Bearden: A Black Odyssey* (New York: DC Moore Gallery; distributed by D.A.P, 2007), pp. 22-23.
5. My thanks to Emily Greenwood for bringing this wonderful book to my attention. See also Emily Greenwood, "Re-Rooting the Classical Tradition: New Directions in Black Classicism", *Classical Receptions Journal*, 1.1 (2009), 87–103.
6. Derek Walcott, "The Muse of History" [1974], *What the Twilight Says* (New York: Farrar, Straus and Giroux, 1998), pp. 37–38.
7. Daniel Banks takes these ideas in interesting new directions in his discussion of Homer and Hip Hop in "From Homer to Hip Hop: Orature and Griots, Ancient and Present". *Classical World* 103.2 (2010) 238–45.
8. I am currently at work on a book length project that is based on a series of such backward and forward readings between Homer and Walcott. For a clear articulation of this newer model of classical reception studies, see Lorna Hardwick, *Reception Studies* (Oxford and New York: Oxford University Press, 2003), pp. 1–11. For an early response to *Omeros* that takes a similar approach, see Carol Dougherty, "Homer After *Omeros*: Reading a H/Omeric Text", *South Atlantic Quarterly* 96.2. (1997), pp. 335–57.

9. [illegible] the relationship between *Omeros* and the *SVO* and the different positions that they take towards their shared Homeric intertext, see Rachel D. Friedman, "Derek Walcott's Odysseys", *International Journal of the Classical Tradition* [illegible]
10. [illegible] References hereafter in the text will be to act, scene, and page number.
11. Greg Doran, who directed the *SVO* for the Royal Shakespeare Company has said that while the [illegible] performances as they were taking place by composing new stichomythia. See Paula Burnett, *Derek Walcott: Politics and Poetics*, (Gainesville: University Press of Florida, 2001), p. 155.
12. My thanks to Al Creighton who pointed out the connection between the stichomythia and picong. Richard Allsopp, s.v., defines picong as follows: "A spontaneous, verbal battle in rhymed song between two or more contending Calypsonians, in which the wit and humorous impact of a contender's improvisation determines his supremacy" (Richard Allsopp and Jeanette Allsopp, *Dictionary of Caribbean Usage* (Oxford: Oxford University Press, 1996), p. 439).
13. Derek Walcott, "Reflections on Omeros", *South Atlantic Quarterly* 96.2 (1997), 229–46.
14. On this feature of the traditions surrounding the ancient Greek poet/singer (*aoidos*), see, now, Richard Hunter and Ian Rutherford, *Wandering Poets in Ancient Greek Culture: Travel, Locality and Pan-Hellenism* (Cambridge and New York: Cambridge University Press, 2009).
15. I would also include in this category the figure of Philoctete(s) in *Omeros* and the figure of Elpenor in the *SVO*.
16. I should be clear that I think it is entirely possible that Walcott might not even know Homer's Thersites and might be familiar with him only through later intermediaries (for example, Shakespeare's *Troilus and Cressida*). My analysis is not based on a claim of direct influence but rather on my interest in seeing what [illegible] when we put Walcott and Homer into [illegible] conversation with each other.
17. The translation of Homer is from Richmond Lattimore, *The Iliad of Homer* (Chicago: University of Chicago Press, 1951), Bk. 2, ll. 211–223. See William G. Thalmann, "Thersites: Comedy, Scapegoats, and Heroic Ideology in the *Iliad*", *Transactions of the American Philological Association* 118 (1988), 1–28.
18. J. Marks, "The Ongoing Neikos: Thersites, Odysseus, and Achilleus", *American Journal of Philology* 126 (2005), 1-31; quote, p. 4.
19. N. Postlethwaite, "Thersites in the *Iliad*", *Greece and Rome* [illegible]
20. Rachel D. Friedman, "Derek Walcott's Odysseys", *International Journal of the Classical Tradition* 14.3/4 (2007), 455–80; quote, pp. 468-71

21. For discussions of Thersites' similarities with Odysseus and Achilles other than the ones I discuss here, see, on Odysseus, Andrea Kouklanakis, "Thersites, Odysseus, and the Social Order", in *Nine Essays on Homer*, edited by Miriam Carlisle and Olga Levaniouk (Lanham: Rowman and Littlefield, 1999), pp. 35–53 and on Achilles, Norman Postelthwaite, "Thersites in the Iliad", *Greek and Rome 35* (1988), p. 126 and William G. Thalmann, "Thersites: Comedy, Scapegoats, and Heroic Ideology in the *Iliad*", pp. 19-20.
22. J. Marks, "The Ongoing Neikos: Thersites, Odysseus, and Achilleus", pp. 2-3.
23. It seems to be a "speaking name" derived from the Aeolic adj. *thersos* (*tharsos* in Ionic). See G.S. Kirk, *The Iliad: A Commentary* (Cambridge: CUP, 1985), pp. 138-139.
24. William G. Thalmann, "Thersites: Comedy, Scapegoats, and Heroic Ideology in the *Iliad*", p. 17.

EDWARD BAUGH

WALCOTT'S ISLAND(S), WALCOTT'S WORLD(S): ON INHABITING DISPARATE, SHIFTING, OVERLAPPING SPACES

I have an island. (Walcott, *The Prodigal*)

My community, that of any twentieth-century artist, is the world.
(Walcott, interviewed by Leif Sjöberg)

Given the history of its emergence and the history out of which it emerged, Anglophone Caribbean literature has understandably been much involved in questions of definition and identity, questions of difference and relationship, the fixity or fluidity of the boundaries between itself and other literatures to which it may bear some relationship. Such questions may be cast in terms of Caribbean literature's distinguishing cultural and geographical spaces, and whether these are exclusive of the cultural and geographical spaces of other literatures. Given the key role of European colonialism and the slave-plantation system in the history of the Caribbean, the defining of Caribbean literature has necessarily foregrounded the question of its relationship to Europe, Africa and Asia, with the concomitant racial and ethnic issues that this involves. Inevitably too, the questions of definition, identity and difference have had to involve considering the Anglophone Caribbean in relation to the United States of America and Latin America, as well as to other "Commonwealth" or "Post-colonial" regions.

How the work of any given Anglophone Caribbean writer embodies or provokes consideration of such issues has been of central interest, whether explicitly or implicitly. The nature and degree of the Caribbeanness of each has been a matter of remark, and has been, in some cases, controversial. Walcott invites careful, thought-provoking interest in this regard. Further, to adopt an even more contemporary viewpoint, his work is productive ground for considering the global connections of Caribbean literature. Indeed, "Globalization" and its cognates are now in vogue, just at the time when Anglophone Caribbean literature is more inclined to look outward, beyond and across boundaries.

When West Indian literature, emerging out of a colonial history which sought to keep it a mere tributary of English literature, came to realize itself as a literature with its own distinctive identity, and a West Indian criticism began to emerge to define and theorize that literature, the dominant impulse was to close the doors to outside presences and influences, in response to an imperative to look into and at ourselves on our own ground and on our own terms, even if this impulse of necessity had something idealistic and reductive about it.

A defining moment of this period was the ACLALS (Association for Commonwealth Literature and Language Studies) Conference held at Mona in January 1971, which I said something about at the Conference on West Indian Literature held in Grenada in 2004, and which Laurence Breiner made, illuminatingly, the starting-point of his *Introduction to West Indian Poetry* (1998). He describes the conference as "the first comprehensive presentation of West Indian literature by West Indians that included fully articulated critical positions". Of Kamau Brathwaite's keynote address, which did indeed set the tone of the conference, Breiner observes that it "could literally provide the keynote for a discussion carried on by an audience of informed participants assembled from the entire Caribbean area".[1]

On the basis of these valid observations (except that "Caribbean area" should more properly read "Anglophone Caribbean area"), one might think, if one did not know otherwise, that the ACLALS Conference of 1971 was a West Indian conference on West Indian literature. It wasn't. It was a conference, as all the ACLALS conferences have been, on the literatures of the former colonies and dominions of Great Britain, including Australia and New Zealand, Canada, certain African countries, India and certain other Asian and South Pacific countries, as well as Guyana and the former British West Indian islands. There were papers from most of these places, and participants from them, as well as participants from England and Europe. Naturally, the literature of the country and region in which the conference is being held will enjoy particular visibility, but the 1971 conference turned out to be a special case. The West Indians and the eruption of a simmering quarrel about the "correct" view and self-definition of West Indian literature took over the conference. They locked the door, so to speak, closing and claiming their space to define their literature on their own terms, without much regard for "Out There", except by way of counter-discourse, implied and explicit, against the colonialist legacy, and by way of the affirmation of the African connection as definitive input into Caribbean culture and aesthetic.

It seems only natural, then, that when next an ACLALS conference was held in the Caribbean, again at Mona, twenty-one years later, there was none of the intense, inwardly turned West Indian heat and friction of 1971.

[illegible] in a different context from what had prevailed prior to 1971. Caribbean space could now more self-confidently engage with, and extend its curiosity and cordiality towards disparate non-Caribbean spaces. The Caribbean mind is now more willing to think in terms of interlocking basins of a global [illegible] overlapping mutually energizing spaces.

These generalizations oversimplify. On the one hand, Caribbean space can never close itself off from the world [illegible] the global reach of information is so instantaneous. On the other hand, even when Caribbean literary space comes to be more open to interacting with outside spaces, there remains an edgy, insecure self-protectiveness, a suspiciousness that is like a nightmare shadow of the deep-seated fear of colonial and metropolitan control. In any event, Caribbeanness is always in process, and Caribbean space is always being renegotiated, re-peopled, and reclaimed from different standpoints.

In this scenario, Walcott attracts attention. He has been noted for his openness to non-Caribbean spaces and influences, and controversially so, to the extent that he has not sought to distance himself from the Western tradition, whether in his life-long engagement with the Classics, or in his unapologetic openness to influence from, and creative dialogue with, First World writers. The extent to which he has been acclaimed by Western metropolitan readers has not been altogether to his benefit in some Caribbean eyes.

Long ago, West Indians greeted with something of an awkward silence the encomium accorded him by Robert Graves, which used to appear on the jackets of his early collections: "Derek Walcott handles English with a closer understanding of its inner magic than most (if not any) of his English-born contemporaries."[2] In an interview with Walcott in March 1982, Anthony Milne referred to an article about V.S. Naipaul, published in the *Sunday Express*, in which the "writer joined in the criticism of both Naipaul and [Walcott], apparently because [they didn't] always say the things a certain kind of person likes to hear. It seems [Milne continued] as though that type of person feels he must malign those who, by international standards, are the finest literary products of the region".[3] At the 1971 ACLALS conference, a notable absentee was Walcott, and a rumour was in circulation at the conference that he wasn't there because he was afraid of the flak that was likely to greet him. In other words, he wasn't Caribbean enough.

The fact that Walcott has made a point of explicitly identifying himself as a Caribbean poet may be a mark of his awareness that the identification sometimes comes up against West Indian doubts. In a 1977 interview with Edward Hirsch he spoke of his "determination to make sure [he] was valid in the place where [he] was born".[4] In 1985, speaking again to Hirsch, he insisted, "I am primarily, absolutely a Caribbean writer".[5] This was by way of answering Hirsch's question as to how the poet saw himself "in terms of the great tradition of poetry in the English language" (Hirsch, "The Art of Poetry", p. 105). Anxious to aver that his choosing to work in English (and, by implication, in traditional English forms and versification) did not compromise his Caribbeanness, he went on to say:

> The English language is nobody's special property. [...] I have never felt inhibited in trying to write as well as the greatest English poets. Now that has led to a lot of provincial criticism: the Caribbean critic may say, "You are trying to be English," and the English critic may say, "Welcome to the club." [...] It's not a matter of trying to be English. I am obviously a Caribbean poet." (Hirsch, "The Art of Poetry", p. 106)

In 1990, in an interview with J.P. White, he spoke of his ambition "to be a fulfilled West Indian artist", positing as the criterion for that achievement the ability to write in what he called the "ritualistic" spirit of calypso, "comic in its drive, even if you have a tragic content".[6] If it was to be argued that "The Schooner *Flight*" and "The Spoiler's Return" achieve this quality, it might then be asked, "Why hasn't he written more of this kind of poem?" Or, again, if a work like *Tiepolo's Hound* does not have this quality, is it any less the work of a Caribbean poet?

Running through Walcott's poetry is a drama played out between "Here" (his island, the islands, the Caribbean) and "Out There" (the world, a set of worlds, metropolitan spaces). The drama is enacted across multiple sets of spaces: geographical and climatic, temporal, ethno-cultural, artistic, linguistic, "material" spaces and spaces of the imagination. Within each set the sub-spaces compete, overlap and fuse, and the sets themselves also overlap. This drama, this fiction, reaches a climax and a resolution, albeit a problematic resolution, in his 2004 published volume of poetry, the book-length narrative poem, *The Prodigal*.

There is a quintessential moment in the poem when the Prodigal has returned to New York City from Italy and is greeted by a neighbour in the apartment building where he resides:

> "So, how was Italy?" My neighbour grinned.
> Trim-bearded, elegant. He was Italian.
> "Good. As usual. We were in Amalfi.
> Next to a picturesque port called Vertigo."
> He didn't get it. "Why didn't you stay longer?"
> I said: "I have an island." "And it was calling you."
> To say yes would be stupidness, but it was true.[7]

"Stupidness" provides a nice instance of the interplay and merging of linguistic spaces. When I first read that passage, something struck me about "stupidness". I thought, "A Standard English speaker would surely say 'stupidity'". "Stupidness" gives quite a different colour to the statement, [illegible] it occurred to me then that "stupidness" was a word I had grown up with (or, to speak "properly", with which I had grown up) as a very Jamaican word, although I had not consciously given any thought to it. But now I had to wonder, "Is it also a normal Standard English word?" So I went to the *Concise Oxford Dictionary*, almost hoping that I wouldn't find "stupidness" there.

Well, what I found was even more rewarding than what I could have imagined: [illegible] "stupidity" [illegible] (adverb) [illegible] last (and even the order of listing seemed significant), "stupidness" (noun), and, in brackets after "stupidness" the information "chiefly W. Indian". I said to myself, "A minor triumph for the West Indies!" I then went to Allsopp's *Dictionary of Caribbean English Usage*. There is a brief entry on "stupid", attributing to it a Caribbean-wide usage which was new to me, viz. "inconsequential, insignificant, small", and, by extension, "contemptible", "damned"; but there is a long entry on "stupidness" or "chupitness", identified as a word of Caribbean-wide usage. In the final analysis, "stupidness" is not simply a synonym for "stupidity".[8] If one was to try to translate "stupidness" as used in Walcott's line, one would appreciate the difficulty of the undertaking and the subtleties of difference.

The interplay between "stupidness" and "stupidity" is a small instance of the interplay between Walcott's "Here" and "Out There". It is a drama of competing allegiances, and of the simultaneous inhabiting of different, sometimes disparate spaces, a drama played out in the process of self-definition, the poet's articulation of his version of a Caribbean self. Near the end of the story, the Prodigal recalls,

> Then [illegible] rigid apprentice,
> to the horizontal sunrise, […]
> to the wrist of a cold spring between black rocks,
> and any road that lost its mind in the mountains,
> to the freight train of the millipede, to
> the dragonfly's biplane, and the eel's submarine
> [illegible], swearing not to leave them
> for real principalities in Berlin or Milan (*The Prodigal*, p. 94)

Incidentally, the metaphors of "freight train" and "biplane" and "submarine" for "millipede" and "dragonfly" and "eel" are also another instance of the creative merging of disparate spaces, on more than one level.

The vow recalled in *The Prodigal* had been recalled thirty years earlier, in *Another Life* (1973), where the poet wrote, remembering the youthful ambition of his painter-friend Gregorias (Dunstan St Omer) and himself,

> But drunkenly, or secretly, we swore […]
> that we would never leave the island
> until we had put down, in paint, in words,

as palmists learn the network of a hand,
all of its sunken, leaf-choked ravines,
every neglected, self-pitying inlet
muttering in brackish dialect [...][9]

"Drunkenly" and even "secretly" may suggest a suspicion that there was something foolhardy about the vow. Soon enough he was heading out for "Out There" – the wider Caribbean and, beyond it, the great world. Yet, in the moment of departure, the loving commitment to home is trenchantly, prayerfully stated:

Earth-heart, I prayed,
nerves of raw fibre,
uproot me, yet
let what I have sworn to love not feel betrayed
when I must go [...]

He prayed that his heart would be like

a ship within a
ship within a ship, a bottle
where this wharf, these
rotting roofs, this sea,
sail, sealed in glass. (*Another Life*, p. 108)

The image of a model ship in a bottle captures the paradox of motion in stasis, the situation of being rooted in one's native place even while responding to the call of the outside world, of "Here" and "Out There" sharing the one space. This idea was to be imaged much later, in *Tiepolo's Hound* (2000), in the figure of "moving trees [which, however,] must root somewhere", "in our attachment to the nurturing place/ of earth".[10]

The idea of betrayal by virtue of leaving the place in which he is so rooted has run through Walcott's poetry, culminating in *The Prodigal*. It is very much to the point that, on a return visit to St Lucia in 1985, when he was living in Boston, he should have said, "[T]he more I come back here the less I feel that I'm a prodigal or a castaway returning" (Hirsch "The Art of Poetry", p. 115). The idea of *The Prodigal* was already on his mind. He was replying then to Hirsch's question as to whether he still felt "the old tugs between home and abroad". The way in which he developed his reply was a carefully nuanced, almost paradoxical way of saying "yes". On the one hand, he says, "I've never felt that I belong anywhere else but in St Lucia. The geographical and spiritual fixity is there". At the same time, he couldn't deny the feeling of being fortunate at always having "the chance of taking a plane out", getting away from "those pathetically cruel circumstances in which people have found themselves following the devastations of colonialism" (Hirsch "The Art of Poetry", p. 115). There is an admirable honesty here, and it may be that he spoke for many a West Indian writer who has achieved international recognition. In any event, the tug between fixity and [illegible] tugging on an infinitely elastic umbilical cord, has been, as Hirsch recognized, a leitmotif of his poetry. Even as, in the early “As John to Patmos”, he prayed, “So I shall voyage no more from home; may I speak here”,[illegible] at the same time every boat passing by on the horizon, every “little sail in light [illegible] islands” [illegible].

An overarching theme of *The Prodigal* is travelling itself, the impulse to travel, the lure of new places, a compulsion made all the more compelling [illegible] the persona [illegible] himself, “Prodigal, what were your wanderings about?” The next line sums up, in an image of layered suggestiveness, a defining oscillation of his life: “The smoke of homecoming, the smoke of departure” (*The Prodigal*, p. 70). The [illegible] is in the wandering itself, in the seeming self-indulgence of it, but also in the suspicion of betraying home by succumbing to the seductions of “Out There”.

The poem moves on the trope of travelling. We are always reminded that the persona is “on the move”, by plane, by train, by bus, by car, by boat. His vantage point, his perspective is that of the traveller. He sees “through the plane window, meadows of snow/ on powdery precipices, the cantons of cumuli/ grumbling or closing” (*The Prodigal*, p. 9). Again, “We drove through the wet sunlight into Pescara” (p. 18). From hotel windows he sees “a train crawling up the mountain” (p. 10), “crawling impossibly like an insect/ across the drifts” (p. 13). He meets unforgettable travellers, like the beautiful young woman on the bus to Pescara, who “spoke softly . . . / of Serbia and its sorrow, of the horrors she had seen / on the sidewalks of Kosovo” (p. 19). (The theme of racism alluded to in this incident strikes a responsive chord in Caribbean history, providing another instance of overlapping spaces.)

When the poem opens, the persona is on a train to Pennsylvania. The poet’s “idea of America” (p. 4) is developed in his descriptions of Manhattan and Boston. We move with him from the United States to Europe (Switzerland, Italy, Spain, Germany), which is setting and subject of most of Part I, then back to New York. In Part II he is travelling in Mexico and Colombia, getting closer home. In Part III he is back on his island. Of all the locales of his wanderings, it is Europe which most seizes his imagination, with a complex interplay of admiration, awe, fear — [illegible] admiration for its literature and art, the awe of that History with which Walcott has argued throughout his career, and fear of an overpowering of his Caribbean sense of self. The appeal of Europe had, of course, made its mark on him from childhood, from his “sound colonial education”[13] to quote Shabine, from his reading of its literature, and from his seeing reproductions of the paintings of European Masters in books.

As Part III opens, he re-inhabits the landscape of home, in his characteristic, finely-crafted descriptions of it. However, one would be mistaken to expect that from this point on he has relegated to the back of his mind all the places in which he had travelled, that they were simply places through which he had passed.

At this point, before I go further into Walcott's wrestling with the idea of Europe in *The Prodigal*, I must digress for a while, to say something about Africa and Asia. The definition of Caribbean identity necessarily becomes involved with the question of the relative degree of focus and weight given to these three areas. I begin by taking as generally recognized (whatever one's own response to it may be), Walcott's ideal of multi-culturalism and hybridity, the idea of "the interlocking of the races", of the Port of Spain of his desire as "a city ideal in its commercial and human proportions" which

> would be so racially various that the cultures of the world – the Asiatic, the Mediterranean, the European, the African – would be represented in it [...] Its citizens would intermarry as they chose, from instinct, not tradition, until their children find it increasingly futile to trace their genealogy.[14]

I have thought it remarkable that from early Walcott sought to imagine himself into Indo-Caribbean mind-space, especially when we consider that the (East) Indian presence in St Lucia was very much a minority. I once heard the late Earl Warner say something about Walcott's play *The Sea at Dauphin* (1954)[15] which he was directing at the time, and what he said articulated what I had felt unconsciously. That play is dominated by the eloquently God-cursing, history-cursing Afa, but Warner said that it really became Hounakin's play, the tragedy of the old Indian Hounakin, who is the test of Afa's humanity. Walcott's compassion and respect for the Caribbean person of the Indian diaspora was developed in another play, *Franklin*, which has, regrettably, never been published. In his portrayal of Ramsingh and his daughter Maria, Walcott builds on his depiction of Hounakin. Ramsingh, too, is a tragic figure, unable to come to terms with the erosion of his cultural traditions. Then there is the poem "The Saddhu of Couva",[16] and the Mighty Spoiler's concern for the Indian field worker ("The Spoiler's Return"[17]) and the use, in the Nobel lecture, of the performance of the *Ramleela* at Felicity as the foundation-stone of the lecture, so to speak.

When we come to Africa, we are in uneasy terrain. Walcott has not been known for any desire to "inhabit" Africa. Harold McDermott has remarked his "seeming failure to accord the African the same privilege he does to the European in his work..."[18] Decades earlier, Maria Mootry, comparing the poetry of Brathwaite, Césaire and Walcott wrote: "As a man committed to 'West Indianness,' Derek Walcott tends to play down African influences and to insist on the West Indian's potential for creating a new world."[19] That was true enough, but later in the same piece she spoke of Walcott's "rejection of Africa" (p. 24).

[illegible] in his early poetry, such instances of African consciousness in the Caribbean as he essayed tended to be of the more questionable kind, as in "Chapter V" and "Chapter VI" of "Tales of the Islands", and in the story of Manoir, the island's "first black [illegible]" ([illegible] p. 29) [illegible]. The much-cited "A Far Cry from Africa" (*In a Green Night*, p. 18), while stating some allegiance to Africa, has its problems and has come in for some strong criticism. Walcott also emphasized [illegible] "gods that are not born again", seeking to turn this "deep, amnesiac blow"[20] to the advantage of his thought-provoking theory that this erasure of memory enabled Caribbean people to free themselves of the tyranny of history and to inscribe their presence on a "virginal, unpainted world" (*Another Life*, p. 152), to create a world like nothing the world had ever seen.

It is worth remembering that Walcott's position was, at the time, partly a reaction against the upsurge of Black African consciousness in the Anglophone Caribbean in the later 1960s and early 1970s, which he saw as being too much of "political nostalgia" (Hirsch "An Interview with Derek Walcott", p. 56) for "a kind of Eden-like grandeur" (Hirsch "The Art of Poetry XXXVII", p. 114). Hence the necessity of Makak's dream journey back to Africa to purge himself of his illusions, just as he had to kill, psychologically speaking, the ghost of the White Goddess who had held him in thrall.

At the same time, although, in an interview with Sharon Ciccarelli, he acknowledged that he didn't "think in the African mode",[21] he could say to Hirsch that "that is not to say one doesn't know who one is: our music, our speech – all the things that are organic in the way we live – are African" (Hirsch "An Interview with Derek Walcott", p. 56). Again, to Sjöberg "The African experience is historically remote, but spiritually ineradicable. Nothing has really been lost"[22] and, he comes to say in the Nobel lecture, "even the actions of surf on sand cannot erase the African memory ..." (*What the Twilight Says*, p. 81).

More to the point, though, is that Africa and reconnection with Africa eventually came to be represented in a major, regenerative, self-realizing way in Walcott's poetry, notably in *Omeros*. If I may quote myself: "If the poem brings to a head Walcott's long involvement with the classics, it is also his deepest, most unqualified acknowledgement to date of the African presence in the Caribbean."[23] Two crucial sequences are those in which Achille makes his dream-journey to Africa and Ma Kilman's journeys into the forest to find the lost African root that will heal Philoctete's wound, symbol of all the wounds of heart and history that the poem [illegible]. Achille's journey parallels but contrasts with and balances Makak's dream. It is a journey to complete himself, not, as with Makak, to discard a misguided part of himself. Similarly, Ma Kilman's journey into the forest revises the ironic "truth" enacted by the story of Manoir: that "One step beyond the city was the bush./ One step behind the churchdoor stood the devil" (*Another Life*, p. 25). Drawn by her subconscious African memory, she leaves her pew in church to go into the bush to find the healing herb.

In a recent interview, Walcott, telling the interviewer that he is "travelling [now] more than [he] ever did before", and that "seeing another place is always good", let on that he had recently been to Nigeria, "quite an experience", and that that was his first time in Africa. The interviewer, Dante Micheaux, then asked him what the experience of Nigeria was like. This was his reply:

> I don't want to summarise it in a sentence because there's bound to be a germ from the experience that I might use for writing. The one thing I would say is that it felt as if the years between Africa and the Caribbean, the 300 or 500 years, had vanished. A weird feeling.[24]

Perhaps there will be more to come on the matter of Walcott's inhabiting, or being inhabited by Africa.

But to return to *The Prodigal*. He returns to his island in pre-Easter drought, and notes that the ground dove, which "flew/ up from his path to settle in the sun-browned/ branches that were now barely twigs", coos with a "relentless ... tiring sound" that is "not like ... the flutes of Venus in frescoes". In his "scorched, barren acre", "he had the memory of rain/ carried in his head, the rain on Pescara's beach" (p. 59). The drought breaks, and the rain images the blessing and renewal of the return home, but it is now, as the poem draws to its close, even in the peace and fulfilment of "the enclosing harmony that we call home" (p. 82), that the dialogue between the Caribbean and Europe comes to a head in complex twists and turns, nuanced, subtilized, to a new level of self-conscious scrutiny of how "we have tortured ourselves/ with our conflicts of origins" (p. 75). The simultaneous inhabiting of disparate places is true, but conflicted.

The persona reaches the point where he asks himself, "So has it come to this, to have to choose?" To choose, that is to say, between the island and Italy, between Canaries and Venice, between "the marble miracles of the Villa Borghese" and "villages of absolutely no importance" (p. 78), with "streets untainted / by any history" (p. 99); between "a plank bridge" (p. 76) and Florence's fabled Ponte Vecchio. But, no, he says, "the point is not comparison or mimicry" (p. 75). "Both worlds are welded, they were seamed by delight" (p. 71). So the blending is enacted when

> [...] A crowd crosses a bridge
> from Canaries to the Ponte Vecchio, from
> Piaille to Pescara, and a volley of blackbirds
> fans over Venice or the broken pier of Choiseul,
> and love is as wide as the span of my open palm

> [illegible] country:
> one map of affection that closes around my pen. (pp. 65-66)

To inhabit, simultaneously, different, shifting, overlapping spaces is, to borrow a phrase from *Tiepolo's Hound*, [illegible] (*Tiepolo's Hound*, p. 11[illegible]), [illegible] than the maps of everyday, tactual use. While, in his right ear sounds "oak-echo, beech-echo, linden-echo" (*The Prodigal*, p. 62), his left hand writes "palms and wild sea-almond [illegible] (p. [illegible]) of the other. So, the stately Caribbean cabbage palm, the palmiste, stands beside "Doric and Corinthian" (p. 75) columns in the same line of verse, on equal terms. The palmistes speak, in their "correcting imprecations", saying to poet and reader,

> Listen, we have
> no envy of the white mountains [the Alps], or of the white horn [the Matterhorn]
> above the smothered inns, no envy of the olive
> or redoubtable oaks. We were never emblems. (p. 76)

In other words, they were and are only themselves, and that is everything.

In the final analysis, there is no resolution in the sense of accepting one place and rejecting the other. Europe will still have its place in the poet-Prodigal's head space, but he knows where his groundings are, he knows where is home. It is where he has the privilege of "mak[ing] each place"

> new again from naming it: the gaping view
> of the bay with its toy yachts at Marigot,
> and the plunge into the rich banana valley
> under the haze-blue ridges into Roseau. (p. 99)

Incidentally, the representation of home provides another instance of the simultaneous inhabiting of different places. Home is configured, in the most particular sense, as one would expect, in images of St Lucia, but at times it is also configured in images of Trinidad, "Sancta Trinidad" as he says (*The Prodigal*, p. 84), and more particularly the Santa Cruz valley, locale of the white egrets that will provide the title of his next collection of poems:

> Santa Cruz, in spring. Deep hills with blue clefts.
> I have come back for the white egrets
> [illegible] on the lawn, [illegible] their bills
> in that [illegible] stride, gawkily elegant,
> then suddenly but leisurely sailing
> to settle, but not too far off, like angels. (pp. 71-72)

Significantly enough, the poem ends imagining another land, another [illegible] of space, [illegible] another [illegible]. [illegible] the poet Prodigal is on a dolphin [illegible] boat ride, [illegible] between Martinique and St Vincent.

In a visionary, epiphanic close, the dolphins become the possibility of angels,

> And always certainly, steadily, on the bright rim
> of the world, getting no nearer or nearer, the more
> the bow's wedge shuddered towards it, prodigal,
> that line of light that shines from that other shore. (p. 105)

We may simultaneously inhabit worldly and other-worldly spaces.

Now, after all that, listen to this. In its list of "The Best Books of 2007", *Contemporary Poetry Review* (*CPR*) named, as "Best New and Selected Edition", Derek Walcott's *Selected Poems*. On the winner in each category, there was a comment. Here is the comment on Walcott:

> Yes, he won the Nobel Prize, but does Derek Walcott really get the respect he deserves from his fellow poets? His American colleagues tend to ignore him, while the Brits don't claim him as one of their own. "What are his politics? Who does he belong to? What group does his work represent?" You can just imagine the academics asking their reductive questions about him and shaking their heads in dismissal. Walcott is, however, one of the greatest poets alive in English – only Richard Wilbur, Seamus Heaney, and Geoffrey Hill are in his league.[25]

In other words, "Where does he belong, especially since acceptance and acclamation depend on our being able to place him, never mind that he has said, 'My community, that of any twentieth-century artist, is the world'?" (Sjöberg, "An Interview with Derek Walcott", p. 83) Interestingly enough, he has also said, "I think it's very exciting to be outside English literature, English literature in a hierarchic sense" (Ciccarelli, "Reflections", p. 47). And speaking of himself and his close Nobel laureate friends Joseph Brodsky and Seamus Heaney, he remarked, with an implicitly self-confident sense of place, "The three of us are outside of the American experience" (Hirsch "The Art of Poetry", p. 119). Haven't "the academics asking their reductive questions" ever heard of the Caribbean? What can we say: "Alas, poor Derek"? Or, better, following the *CPR* line, "More power to Walcott"? Perhaps *I* should say, "So much for all my wanderings and wonderings about the desire to inhabit different places simultaneously."

Endnotes

1. Laurence Breiner, *An Introduction to West Indian Poetry* (Cambridge: Cambridge University Press, 1998), p. 3.
2. Robert Graves, quoted on the dust jacket of *In a Green Night*, see *Critical Perspectives on Derek Walcott,* Ed. Robert D. Hamner (Boulder: Lynne Reiner, 1996).

3. [illegible] Milne, "This Country is a Very Small Place", *Conversations with Derek Walcott*, Ed. William Baer (Jackson: University of Mississippi Press, 1996), p. 73.
4. Edward Hirsch, "An Interview with Derek Walcott", in *Conversations with Derek Walcott*, pp. 50–63. Quotation, p. [illegible].
5. Edward Hirsch, "The Art of Poetry XXXVII: Derek Walcott", in *Conversations with Derek Walcott*, pp. 95–121.
6. [illegible], "[illegible] with Derek Walcott", in *Conversations with Derek Walcott*, pp. [illegible]–171. Quotation, p. 171.
7. Derek Walcott, *The Prodigal* (New York: Farrar, Straus and Giroux, 2004), p. 39.
8. Richard Allsopp, *Dictionary of Caribbean English Usage* (Oxford: Oxford University Press, 1996), p. 537 and p. 135.
9. Derek Walcott, *Another Life* (London: Jonathan Cape, 1973), p. 52.
10. Derek Walcott, *Tiepolo's Hound* (London: Faber and Faber, 2000), p. 160.
11. Derek Walcott, *In a Green Night: Poems 1948-1960* (London: Jonathan Cape, 1962), p. 12; and *Selected Poems*, (2007,) p. 4
12. Derek Walcott, "Sea Grapes", *Sea Grapes* (London: Jonathan Cape, 1976), p. 9; and *Selected Poems* (2007), p. 87.
13. Derek Walcott, "The Schooner *Flight*", *The Star-Apple Kingdom* (London: Jonathan Cape, 1980), p. 4; and *Selected Poems* (2007), p. 114.
14. Derek Walcott, "The Antilles: Fragments of Epic Memory", *What the Twilight Says: Essays* (London: Faber and Faber, 1998), p. 74.
15. *The Sea at Dauphin*, *Dream on Monkey Mountain and Other Plays* (New York: Farrar, Straus and Giroux, 1970), pp. 41-80.
16. "The Saddhu of Couva", *The Star-Apple Kingdom*, pp. [illegible].
17. "The Spoiler's Return", *The Fortunate Traveller* (London: Faber and Faber, 1982), pp. 53-60.
18. Funso Aiyejina and Paula Morgan, Eds., *Caribbean Literature in a Global Context* (St Augustine: UWI Faculty of Humanities and Education, and Lexicon Trinidad, [illegible]), p. [illegible].
19. Maria K. Mootry, "Three Caribbean Poets: Sea Imagery as an Index to their African Consciousness", *Pan Africanist* 1 no. 2 (1971), 22–27. Quotation, p. 23.
20. Derek Walcott, "Laventille", *The Castaway* (London: Jonathan Cape, [illegible]), p. [illegible].
21. Sharon Ciccarelli, "Reflections Before and After Carnival: An Interview with Derek Walcott", *Conversations with Derek Walcott*, pp. 34–49. Quotation, p. 47.
22. [illegible], "An Interview with Derek Walcott", *Conversations with Derek Walcott*, pp. 79–[illegible]; quotation, p. [illegible].

23. Edward Baugh, *Derek Walcott* (Cambridge: Cambridge University Press, 2006), p. 190.
24. Dante Micheaux, "The Wolf Interview: Derek Walcott", *The Wolf Magazine*, 2009. <http://www.wolfmagazine.co.uk/21_walcott.php>.
25. "The Best Books of 2007", Contemporary Poetry Review. Accessed 2007. <http://www.cprw.com/books07.htm>

RHONDA COBHAM-SANDER

"ANY ENEMY SO WAS A COMPLIMENT": WALCOTT, BRATHWAITE AND THE FORMAL POSSIBILITIES OF CREOLE

I

And this was the prayer that Achille could not utter:
"The spear that I give you, my friend, is only wood.

Vexation is past. I know how well you treat her.
You never know my admiration, when you stood
crossing the sun at the bow of the long canoe

with the plates of your chest like a shield; I would say
any enemy so was a compliment. 'Cause no
African ever hurled his wide seine at the bay

by which he was born with such beauty. You hear me? Men
did not know you like me. All right. Sleep good. Good night."[1]

To characterize the relationship between Brathwaite and Walcott as strained would be an understatement. Their many similarities in age, background, schooling and ambition give the smallest differences between the two men the dimensions of unbridgeable chasms. Although neither probably would admit it, they remain warily alert to each other's pronouncements, covert readers of each other's books and passionate rivals for their Caribbean readers' souls. Brathwaite can hardly be indifferent to the aesthetic validation that prestigious awards like the Nobel and MacArthur prizes have brought to Walcott. But Walcott, too, has remained irascible on the subject of Brathwaite, by turns, dismissive of or irritated by the lip service Brathwaite's cultural nationalist project elicits from ideological pundits who otherwise evince very little serious interest in poetry.

And yet, such covert animus is the least interesting aspect of this millennial rivalry. Brathwaite's work matters to Walcott because its popular appeal exposes Walcott's limits from the perspective of a regional audience, which clamours for accessibility and direct engagement from their writers;

qualities that have never come easily to Walcott. And the difficulty cannot be rationalized away by making distinctions between the "humanist" and socially committed "folk" visions of the two poets.[2] Rather, it signals an underlying tension within Walcott's oeuvre – between the effects it derives from the "universally" literary, and those it derives from the nationalist cultural milieu both he and Brathwaite helped inaugurate.

In *Omeros*, Walcott revisits several techniques Brathwaite first developed, resolving in the process perennial anxieties that have haunted his work. He relies most explicitly on Brathwaite for the images and arguments in Book III, where his protagonist, Achille, like the New World Negro in the *Masks* (1968) section of Brathwaite's *Arrivants* trilogy, makes his way back to Africa in a dream to confront his ancestors and the legacy of slavery.[3] I want to focus, however, on the more nuanced ways Brathwaite's influence can be divined. In its reliance on formal elements derived from Creole speech, *Omeros* augments a Caribbean epic tradition famously inaugurated in Aimé Césaire's *Cahier d'un retour au pays natal* (1939) and extended in Brathwaite's *Arrivants* (1973). *Cahier* became the manifesto of the négritude movement in the Caribbean, Europe and Africa during the 1940s and 1950s, while *The Arrivants* spawned a host of imitators at home and abroad during the "Black Power" era of the 1960s and 1970s. Such audiences seem remote from the elite circles in which *Omeros* often is championed, yet the poem's formal and linguistic virtuosity would not have been possible without those earlier works.

I used the word "irascible" earlier to characterize Walcott's response to Brathwaite, because Walcott often uses it to describe his own and other Caribbean artists' relationships to local audiences and fellow artists. Most notably, he uses the term in *Another Life* where, in response to the suicide of his mentor, Harry Simmons, he lashes out:

> Irascibility, muse of middle age.
> How often you have felt you have wasted your life
> among a people with no moral centre,
> to want to move from the contagion of too many friends
> the heart congealing into stone, [...][4]

In Walcott's public pronouncements, that irascibility occasions quick jabs directed at rivals or intimates, which the poet almost always hopes will cut but which, one suspects, he almost as quickly regrets when they do. It inspires the *picong* moment, too good to miss, in the BBC "Caribbean Nights" interview, broadcast in October 1986, when he deadpans a parody of the opening lines of Brathwaite's poem, "Negus" – "It / It / It / It is not / It is not a very good poem" – effectively deflecting the interviewer's pieties about orality's significance for Caribbean poets.[5] And few readers of Walcott's magnificent essay, "What the Twilight Says," can have failed to take note of moments where the essay's unsparing critical insights tip over into the vituperative.

Regrets aside, Walcott is unapologetic about his irascibility. In his poetry and public pronouncements it has become part of his [illegible] of the [illegible] of Caribbean writing. From Walcott's perspective, the essence of Caribbean experience is, precisely, its pettiness – the rhetorical passion the region's inhabitants expend on relatively insignificant events. Caribbean [illegible] the [illegible] of island existence, which reduce even the magnificent battles of the Gods – *Dies Irae* in the classical and liturgical precedents – to plain old irascibility; peevishness, swift spite and a touch of what West Indians would call "ignorance". Thus, having castigated Naipaul's nihilism in the essay "The Caribbean. Culture or Mimicry", Walcott backtracks to point out that "[t]he embittered despair of a New World writer like Naipaul is also part of that impatience and irascibility at the mere repetition of human error which passes for history, and that irascibility is also a belief in possibility."[6] In a slightly different register, in "Tribal Flutes", his 1967 *Trinidad Guardian* review, after critiquing what he considers an enervating melancholy in the tone of Brathwaite's *Rights* (1967), Walcott qualifies:

> It is very difficult for foreign readers to understand the vacuum at the core of West Indian sensibility, a kind of deadness that no exhortations about community and achievement can stir, one that is suspicious and uncertain.
>
> The wavering, querulous note that "Rights of Passage" sounds is right for us [...] The search for our own sadness is the progression of that sensibility towards being named.[7]

"Querulous" lacks the asperity of "irascibility," but in this context the source of its negative energy is the same. Even when it exasperates, Walcott divines in its timbre a genuine attempt at articulating the nothingness that remains the bane *and* possibility of creativity in the New World. *Omeros* may thus be read as an attempt at [illegible] with fellow practitioners like Brathwaite, which Walcott hopes will outlive present rivalries by bringing his own poetic "energy, [...] discipline, and [...] drive" to bear on the formal experiments and linguistic effects they pioneered.[8]

II

Irascibility, querulousness, suspicion, exasperation, uncertainty, shame. These qualities suffuse the exchanges between the St Lucian fishermen Hector and Achille, whose rivalry over the local beauty, Helen, provides one main narrative strand in *Omeros*.

> "*Touchez-i, encore: N'ai fendre choux-ous-ou, salope!*"
> "Touch it again, and I'll split your arse, you bitch!"
> "*Moi j'a dire – 'ous pas prêter un rien. 'Ous ni shallope,*
>
> *'ous ni seine, 'ous croire 'ous choeur campêche?*"
> "I told you, borrow nothing of mine. You have a canoe,
> and a net. Who you think you are? Logwood Heart?"
>
> "*'Ous croire 'ous c'est roi Gros Îlet? Voleur bomme!*"
> "You think you're king of Gros Îlet, you tin-stealer?"
> Then in English: "I go show you who is king! Come!" (*Omeros*, pp. 15-16)

In this, their first – and last – direct encounter in the poem, Hector and Achille sink below the level of Ajax, the "debased, bored" cart horse in *Another Life* who doubles as "a thoroughbred/ on race-days, once a year".[9] Their epic battle is over a rusted can even they know is not worth the trouble. Achille says as much a few lines later when he acknowledges that: "[t]he rage that he felt against Hector // was shame. To go crazy for an old bailing tin / crusted with rust!" (*Omeros*, p. 17).

And yet, the language of that eternal rivalry of men over their manhood cuts crisp and startlingly beautiful across the page, despite – or perhaps on account of – the reining in of its pace, necessitated by the alternating lines of French Creole and English Creole translation. Walcott stitches together rhymes across the two languages; for example, between "bitch" and "campêche" in the first two stanzas quoted, and between "bomme" and "come" in the next tercet. Patterns in one language also find their echo in the rhythms of the other. Thus, even though "You think you is king of Gros Îlet..." repeats a different vowel sound in English Creole than the French Creole "'Ous croire ous c'est roi Gros Îlet," the patterns of rhythm and assonance progress in tandem with each other. Walcott deploys similar techniques to splendid effect in another bilingual passage involving Ma Kilman and Philoctete:

> *Mais qui ça rivait-'ous, Philoctete?*
> "*Moin blessé.*"
> But what is wrong wif you, Philoctete?
> "I am blest
> wif this wound, Ma Kilman, *qui pas ka guérir pièce.*" (*Omeros*, p. 18)

Here, the poet connects the patois "blésse," meaning wounded, through an aural pun on the English "blest", with the patois "pièce". "Pièce" is also a sight rhyme with "piece" (as in pieced together) for the English reader, and, by extension, "peace," whose meaning also ties back to the Standard English "blest".

Walcott first uses Creole in his poetry in the early sonnet sequence, "Tales of the Islands", in which Anglophone Creole cadences stretch the sonnets' metrical patterns beyond their conventional limits, before redirecting their energy to invigorate the underlying iambic of Standard English diction. In the sixth sonnet, for instance, which starts "Poopa, da' was a fête!" the quatrain describing the [illegible] the more introspective [illegible] returns to standard English.[illegible] At the end of the second quatrain, where the sonnet turns, the poet clearly signals a philosophical and philological [illegible] of the drunk, who also muddles the rhyme scheme when he misquotes Shelley, "with 'Each/ Generation has its *angst*, but we has none'".[11] Although the term "native art" seems culturally remote from "Poopa, da' was a fête!" these modulations do not seem forced, since all the language registers Walcott introduces have their place in Caribbean speech. Indeed, most Creole speakers would agree that the language sounds inauthentic in literary contexts where it would not be used in "real life", just as the drunk in the poem sounds ridiculous when he attempts "textbook" English in a Caribbean oral context. But when the drunk lapses into Creole, he misses the ironies of his own angst, leaving us with the impression that the Creole speaker is less self-reflexive than either the English poet he misquotes or the Standard English-speaking reader. Here, as elsewhere, Walcott seems to imply that it is impossible to think in Creole – that is, to represent complex philosophical ideas in a language register other than the Standard English in which most educated West Indians, like Walcott, first encountered them.

One needs to be very careful when imputing such views to Walcott, whatever he himself may have said in an irascible moment. In fact, his position on language is a lot more complicated than a simple bracketing of Creole speech beyond rationality. In an interview with Anthony Milne, for example, he explains: "I don't think you can say that a thought is more subtle in an imperial language than it is in a colonial dialect. I know a feeling cannot be".[12] At one level Walcott is defending Creole's range here. Yet his claims for it as a language of reflection seem tentative in comparison to the categorical tone of his corresponding claim for Creole as a vehicle for conveying emotion. His qualifications challenge readers to complicate how we think about the uses to which writers put Creole on the page. Nevertheless, their equivocation reprises the theme and limiting condition of Walcott's early sonnet sequence.

In "Tribal Flutes", his 1967 review of Brathwaite's *Rights of Passage* (1967), Walcott comes close to engaging the possibilities of a different approach to Creole forms when he singles out the poem "The Dust" for its technical mastery. He [illegible] this poem, a conversation between [illegible] in a Barbados corner shop. [illegible] account of how the "May dust" blocked out the sun over Barbados after the St. Pierre volcano exploded in Martinique in 1902, becomes a metaphor for the imponderables of suffering in the women's experience and the region's catastrophic history.[13] Unlike the Creole monologues framed by Standard English commentary that both Walcott and Brathwaite favoured in their early poems, "The Dust" is made up almost entirely of Creole dialogue. Yet, it delivers all the registers of narrative suspense, comic relief and self-reflexivity the poet needs to convey. The dialogue first establishes the ambience of the social space in which the women interact, as well as the measure of their speech; its mostly anapaestic feet are interrupted by frequent line breaks, approximating the lurching gait of the women's Bajan speech patterns, without unduly constraining the narrative flow:

[...] How
you, Eveie, chile?
You tek dat Miraculous Bush
fuh de trouble you tell me about?

Hush!
Doan keep so much noise
in de white people shop! (*The Arrivants*, p. 62)

As the poem's tripartite folk-tale structure unfolds, the poet lingers over the minutiae of the women's everyday lives, which are bounded by the vicissitudes of their bodies, animals and crops, and the contours of the beaches and cane fields of the Barbadian landscape – what Walcott, writing decades later about Chamoiseau, describes as the *histoire* (with a small "h") "of a very small territory not seen in proportion to 'the great mutations of the world'".[14] Gradually, the onomatopoeia ("*brugg-a-lung-go*" (*The Arrivants*, p. 66) and the pithy folk aphorisms with which the women pepper their exchanges ("the body int dead"; "Mundee Dee Vee" (*The Arrivants* p. 62, 63) take on a choric function, drawing the reader into the world view of the women, so that we begin to interpret events within the framework of their cultural assumptions.

By the time we get to the poem's final movement, which opens by reprising the women's activities – "you does eat an' sleep/ an' try to fuhget [...]" – we are completely caught up in the rhythms of their lives (*The Arrivants*, p. 67). The May dust breaks that rhythm. Although the meter is still mostly anapaestic, end-stopped rhymes now replace the comfortably meandering enjambments. The abrupt stops take the ear by surprise, occasioning an auditory confusion that echoes the cosmic uncertainty the speaker describes:

An' then suddenly so
widdout rhyme
widdout reason

> [illegible] dark in the
> you can't even see the sun in the sky;
> an' suddenly so, without rhyme,
>
> without reason, all you hope gone
> ev'rything look like it comin' out wrong.
> Why is that? What it mean? (*The Arrivants*, pp. 68–9)

These closed-off lines, shaped as a plaint, bring the poem's drama to the point where the women converge in the arbitrariness of their suffering. Their insight into the contingent nature of an existence "widdout rhyme / widdout reason" comes to us, paradoxically, via the poem's most stylized ordering of language. Thus, even though the women may be helpless to stave off suffering or to rationalize injustice, their human capacity for reflection and awe provides them with the cultural resources to impose symbolic order on the chaos of their lives.

Our only indication that the poet may have arrived at his own philosophical insight by a different route than the women is the subtle modulation in the final lines, from the Creole "widdout" to the standard spelling of "without" in the second iteration of the phrase, "without rhyme, / without reason." The modulation distinguishes between the folk context within which the women operate and the poet's formal education. However, unlike the ironic tension in Walcott's "Tales of the Islands" between Shelley's purported axiom ("'Each/ generation has its *angst* […]'") and the drunk's grammatically distorted emendation ("'[…] but we has none'"), the tight rhymes connecting the Creole and Standard versions of the poem's insight suggest that the women's world view and that of the poet have, indeed, converged upon the same existential dilemma. The women work things out through a form of representation they control – an oral narrative, passed down from Gran to Pearlie. That process preserves the memory of a relatively remote historical event as myth, enabling Pearlie and her audience, as well as the reader and the formally educated poet, to achieve a shared response to life's exigencies.

Walcott in his 1967 review does not identify the myriad oral forms on which Brathwaite draws to create the mosaic of responses to displacement *Rights of Passage* attributes to the New World Negro. He focuses instead on Brathwaite's general indebtedness to "the poetic documentary" form, pioneered by T. S. Eliot, Ezra Pound, and Archibald MacLeish, and on his specific borrowings, in "Wings of a Dove" and "The Dust," from the Jamaican novelist Roger Mais's *Brother Man* and the Barbadian George Lamming's *In the Castle of My Skin*.[15] He commends Brathwaite's "wry, self-mocking, melancholic" tone, which he associates with Hart Crane, but finds *Rights of Passage* limited by the absence of a compelling personal narrative that could provide an internal rationale for the long poem's emotional and rhetorical range. Ever the consummate dramatist, he distrusts the overdetermined correspondences in Brathwaite's teleological world-view, looking instead for ways to motivate his characters within the stories he tells about them.

Walcott's 1973 adaptation for performance of both "Wings of a Dove" and "The Dust" allowed him to develop Brathwaite's archetypes into more fully rounded *dramatis personae* and, in an essay written to mark that occasion, he praises the trilogy's theatrical qualities: "compressed island dialect spoken, swift character delineation, music in speech rhythms".[16] As a poet, however, Walcott remained sceptical about the capacity of folk forms to function as the basis for modernist poetry, and in the essay "Meanings", he consigns the mimetic elements of song, dance, and storytelling to the side of his creative imagination dedicated to drama rather than poetry:

> I am a kind of split writer: I have one tradition inside me going in one way, and another tradition going another. The mimetic, the Narrative, and dance element is strong on one side, and the literary, the classical tradition is strong on the other.[17]

Although he has always utilized Creole language on the stage and he continues to see praising and naming as the primal function of poetry, Walcott, at this stage, seems genuinely unable to credit how Creole forms affect Brathwaite's poetry.

III

There remains one further crucial distinction between the ways Brathwaite and Walcott approach language and form. Walcott shares a French-based, rather than English-based Creole with his St Lucian community. More so, then, than for exclusively Anglophone writers, his every move in representing St Lucia involves, at the most literal level, an act of translation. Describing how he stumbles over the poetic possibilities of the French Creole while navigating the rigours of Latin scansion in the poem "A Latin Primer", he claims to have had "nothing against which/ to notch the growth of my work/ but the horizon".[18] Yet his path would have been equally indirect had he taken Brathwaite's route through Jamaican "Dread Talk" or the African American blues idiom. Those languages share lexical components with Standard English, which the *bois canot* and *bois campêche* trees in Walcott's "Cul de Sac Valley" already have rejected when they hiss: "[...] *What you wish/ from us will never be,/ your words is English,/ is a different tree*" (*Arkansas*, p. 10). Walcott acknowledges his dilemma when he points out that "[t]oday, still in many islands, the West Indian poet is faced with a language which he hears but cannot write because there are no symbols for such a language and because the closer he brings hand and word to the precise inflections of the inner language and to the subtlest accuracies of his ear, the more chaotic his symbols will appear on the page" (*What the Twilight Says*, p. 49). His attempts to manipulate the spelling [illegible] Brathwaite's [illegible]. Nevertheless, though he distrusts the politics behind Brathwaite's formal experiments, Walcott would not be the consummate artist he has become, had he not [illegible] to purify the language of the tribe" in much the same way that he continues to refine his classical models (*What the Twilight Says*, p. 8).

IV

By the mid-1970s, when Brathwaite's experiments with oral forms began to converge with other regional cultural developments, like "Dub" poetry, Walcott had started to expand his use of Creole in his poetry. Most critics associate this shift with Walcott's dramatic monologues, "The Spoiler's Return" (*The Fortunate Traveller*, 1981), and "The Schooner *Flight*" (*The Star-Apple Kingdom, 1979)*, both of which draw heavily on Anglophone Creole forms associated with Trinidad Calypso. But the real linguistic breakthrough comes earlier, in the 1976 *Sea Grapes* collection,[19] where the poet experiments with the French Creole folk forms of his St Lucian childhood. Here, Walcott engages Brathwaite's cultural project directly, arguing explicitly with the ideology behind Brathwaite's aesthetic choices even as he attempts to approximate their effects. In retrospect, we can read this volume as a way of preparing for the task of writing *Omeros*.

The poem "Sainte Lucie" in *Sea Grapes* introduces several characters and thematic elements that resurface in *Omeros*, while simultaneously grappling with formal and linguistic problems the later work resolves. At the core of the poem, in sections III and IV, Walcott retails two versions, one in French Creole, the other in English and English Creole, of a St Lucian *conte*, which he explains he once heard "on the back of an open truck travelling to Vieuxfort, some years ago" (*Sea Grapes*, p. 48; *Collected Poems*, p. 314). The poem incorporates fragments of songs about a character named for the region's black vulture, the corbeau, which often features as a kind of Everyman in Caribbean literature. One story line is about a shopkeeper called Ma Kilman who steals Corbeau's money. Another is about Corbeau's "horning" at the hands of Iona – "while you were in Curaçao,/ I made two little children, come and see if they're yours" (*Sea Grapes*, p. 50; *Collected Poems*, p. 315). A third describes how Corbeau [illegible] when he tries to make a living playing music. The themes of ambiguous paternity and the struggle to make a living, as well as Ma

Kilman's name and trade, all resurface in *Omeros*, but the poem's true function as epic prolegomenon resides in its experiments with language and form, similar in many respects to those essayed by Brathwaite. For a start, Walcott relies, as Brathwaite does in "Wings of a Dove", on a folk song to provide the core of the poem with its St Lucian rhythms – "Ma Kilman, Bon Dieu kai punir 'ous" (*Sea Grapes*, p. 48; *Collected Poems*, p. 314). He does not reproduce the St Lucian *conte* verbatim, but remains faithful to its tone and form. He also utilizes rhyming sentences that change subtly each time they return, in ways that intensify the narrative's ironies. When Corbeau checks to see whether Iona's children are his, he says "pour moi garder ces mamailles-la!" but when he realizes they are not and decides to mind them, all the same, his line is "moi kai soigner ces mamailles-la!" (*Sea Grapes*, p. 48; *Collected Poems*, p. 315).

The poet's decision to segregate the French Creole and English Creole versions of the *conte* throws the challenges of such bilingual composition into relief. The identical *double entendre* of the French Creole "corne" and the English Creole "horn," used as a noun to name a musical instrument and as a verb ("to cuckold"), allows him to translate "Corne-la qui cornait-a,/ c'est Iona ka cornait moin" in section III as "[t]hat horn you heard/ was Iona horning me" in Section IV, preserving the pun in both languages (*Sea Grapes*, pp. 50, 52; *Collected Poems,* p. 316, 318). But the English Creole version sacrifices the snappy tongue-twister effect the pun had in the original – a cost Brathwaite does not have to accommodate when he integrates Dread talk puns or Bajan onomatopoeia into his poems without translation. The whole process of lining up the two versions of the *conte* serially feels laboured after a while, even though each section, taken separately, has its distinctive feel and rhythm. Nevertheless, for the first time outside of his plays, Walcott commits St Lucian Creole forms to the page and experiments with techniques adapted from other Caribbean writers to manipulate them.

In section II of "Sainte Lucie", Walcott utilizes another of Brathwaite's signature forms – the short line, of which Walcott had observed earlier in his review of *Rights of Passage*: "The initial rhythm is faint, light, and studied. Read aloud, the poem subdues and arrests the onrush of its subject by closely packed rhymes, by the tautness of its short stresses".[20] Like Brathwaite, he arranges a variable number of syllables around two beats, rather than using metrical feet of equal length, thereby forcing the reader to focus exclusively on the rhythms inherent in the Creole words themselves:

Pomme arac,
otaheite apple,
pomme cythère,
pomme granate,
moubain,
z'ananas (*Sea Grapes*, pp. 43-44, *Collected Poems*, p. 310)

What begins here almost as a technical exercise in listening to the Creole names of Caribbean fruits, eventually flowers into verse. As the list ends, the poet's anguished outburst, "Come back to me,/ my language," represents that flowering, paradoxically, as a failure of memory: as if, in the move from pure sound to signification, the [illegible] inevitably loses some of its mnemonic power. But the outburst enables new forms of hybridity, as the list of names begins to blur the distinction between language registers, switching [illegible] [illegible] fairly short and arranged around two stresses, then frequent enjambment produces phrases of two or three lines that accumulate the familiar ten syllables of the pentameter, even though they do not quite yet revert to the iambic (my slashes mark out the ten-syllable phrases):

> Evening opens at
> a text of fireflies, /
> in the mountain huts
> ti cailles betassion /
> candles,
> candleflies
> the black night bending /
> cups in its hard palms
> cool thin water (*Sea Grapes*, p. 45; *Collected Poems*, p. 311)

The contrapuntal relationship between the short lines and the longer phrases preserves a residual tension between the sound patterns of the earlier Creole list of fruits and the more expansive reflective passages later in the poem: between the tautness Walcott attributes to Brathwaite's stresses, and his own more lush style. The poet heightens that tension when he intersperses Creole phrases like "ti cailles betassion" between the lines in Standard English. Thus, Walcott is able to vary pace and emotional intensity in the poem by combining the various formal elements the different language registers bring with them.

Beyond the Anglophone Creole elements in the stanzas encircling the French Creole version of the *conte*, "Sainte Lucie" still begins and ends with passages fully controlled by conventional English diction. Here, the language of the educated observer, tortured by an incommunicable passion for his island, remains unambiguously front and centre. In fact, his litany of Creole fruits comes after he admits in the poem's haunting opening section: "[...] I am growing no nearer/ to what secret eluded the children/ under the house-shade" (*Sea Grapes*, p. 43; *Collected Poems*, p. 309). For a brief moment, in the lead up to the *contes*, the poet achieves the full emotional intensity of passionate belonging by successfully blending Standard English, French Creole and English Creole:

> I'm [illegible] golden apple
> that will burst with love.

of you and your men,
those I never told enough
[...]
moi c'est gens Ste. Lucie.
C'est la moi sorti;
is there that I born. (*Sea Grapes*, p. 47; CP. p. 314)

Nevertheless, his is still a secret allegiance. By the end of the poem we are back at Dunstan St Omer's altarpiece in the Roseau Valley church, indulging a vision of St Lucia as the garden of Eden. But the vision can only exist in the absence of viewers, "from time to time, on Sundays// between adorations [...] if one were there, and not there" – like Walcott's poetry, which seems to serve his island best when it can no longer be heard or (mis)understood by the community it celebrates (*Sea Grapes*, p. 55; *Collected Poems*, p. 323).

The poems in *Sea Grapes* present Walcott's most direct concessions and challenges to Brathwaite's aesthetic project. Although they greedily incorporate many of the techniques *The Arrivants* trilogy pioneers, they also push back against what Walcott sees as Brathwaite's privileging of African aspects of the Caribbean aesthetic landscape. In the poem "Names" which he dedicates explicitly "for Edward Brathwaite" Walcott remonstrates:

Listen, my children, say:
moubain: the hogplum,
cerise: the wild cherry,
baie-la: the bay,
with the fresh green voices
they were once themselves
in the way the wind bends
our natural inflections. (*Sea Grapes*, p. 42; *Collected Poems*, p. 307)

Like Brathwaite, Walcott employs the cadences in the Creole names for New World objects to good effect. But he insists on respecting the European origins of many of these words, resisting Brathwaite's ideological preference for connecting the Caribbean, on the one hand, predominantly to its African past and, on the other, to a posture of resistance to all forms of European cultural hegemony. In Walcott's vision, the region's inhabitants appropriate and transform all their languages of origin, asserting the creativity as well as the humanity enslaved Africans and European masters ultimately share:

Being men, they could not live
except they first presumed
the right of everything to be a noun.
The African acquiesced,
repeated, and changed them (*Sea Grapes*, p. 42; *Collected Poems*, p. 307)

Despite these reservations, Brathwaite is the only Anglophone Caribbean poet whose formal concerns elicit a sustained literary response from

Walcott. Such direct engagement with the work of another Caribbean poet is a rare luxury for Walcott, who sees few of his peers as offering him the calibre of writing against which it is worth pushing back.

*

We can observe Brathwaite's formal influence in Walcott's successive drafts of *Omeros*' opening sequence. The published version gives the first lines to Philoctete, who delivers them in a stylized version of St Lucian English Creole. However, earlier drafts of the manuscript, preserved at the University of the West Indies' library in Trinidad, reveal that Walcott originally intended to open each book of the poem with a set piece about the landscape or action, written in Standard English diction and arranged in irregularly rhymed lines of iambic pentameter.[21] Manuscript item 0564:3:1, for instance, gives us this version of the opening sequence:

> This was how, in green sunrise, they chose the canoes.
> On a cold ridge, as the hazed sea was waking,
> they stood in dewy ferns. Now their gaze follows
> the masts of mossy trunks, the top leaves shaking
> in windy light like the noise of emerald shallows,
> with that identical noise. Also, the slow, creaking
> branches creaked like the screech of pulleys,
> so that the running hills, the fog-thinned valleys
> were to these fishermen, extensions of the sea's
> early sound, and they saw the wind agreeing
> with their rooted judgment, the axes in their eyes,
> that had already hacked and trimmed the cedars.
> Columns are brought down, and towering cultures
> from the root, from the speckled blight at the base
> of Troy, the way those cedars slowly leaned towards
> the ferns, with a long, sideways groan, leaving a space
> for the new sky, where no sky was before.
> The fishermen leapt back, then, like barbarians
> storming a breach, or a beach where a breaker
> surges between black rocks, the fallen giants
> of the cedars were hacked in the joyous war
> of pygmies, leaving them [illegible] (MS 0564:3:1)

In this early version, the narrator's elevated diction seems so remote from the characters it describes that the poet has difficulty attributing some of his more refined flights of fancy to the fishermen. When their "gaze follows/ the masts of mossy trunks", we know at once that the conceit is the narrator's, not the fishermen's, since all along, the narrator has been marking the land/sea substitutions in his own description. A few lines later, the connection becomes so attenuated that the poet has to signal explicitly "that the running hills, the fog-thinned valleys/ were *to these fishermen* extensions of the sea's early sound" (my emphasis).

The poet brushes aside such token nods towards the fishermen's imagination as he hurries on to Troy to connect the island scene to its epic model. His passive construction describing how "Columns are brought down, and towering cultures/ from the root," effectively cuts the fisherman out of all significant action, while his ornate metaphors reduce them further, to "barbarians/ storming a breach" stripping the trees in the "joyous war/ of pygmies." Both pygmies and barbarians have their literary precedents. However, the poem provides no organic link between St Lucian fishermen and these images, apart from the uncomfortable popular associations of both images with derogatory ways of describing black men. In a subsequent revision, Walcott crosses out the word barbarians and replaces it with *gommiers*, the French Creole name for gum trees as well as for the canoes made from their trunks (MS 0546:4:1). The revision conflates the fishermen's strength with that of the trees, making the men equals in a heroic struggle with nature, as opposed to uncivilized barbarians with no respect for the dignity of their foe. However, the move feels out of step in a train of images that stresses the unequal proportions of the men and the trees. Nor do the three equal stresses of the word *gommiers* succeed in breaking the stride of the iambic with the syncopated grace of the phrase "ti cailles betassion," inserted between lines of Standard English, in the poem "Sainte Lucie". The isolated substitution of *gommiers* for barbarians feels like too little, too late, and the poet abandons that line of development.

The next major reworking of the opening sequence is preserved three versions later in MS item 0546:2:1. By this point, Walcott has shifted the verse form to tercets and the line length to hexameter, borrowed from Dante but capable in the Caribbean poet's hands of suggesting the incessant, irregular heaving of the sea "from whose ground-swell the great hexameters come/ to the conclusions of the exhausted surf" ("Sea Grapes", *Sea Grapes*, p. 9 has "to finish up as Caribbean surf", and *Collected Poems*, p. 297). He also has given the narration, in the form of a dramatic monologue, to Philoctete, into whose Creole speech, however, the original narrator's metaphorical flights fit awkwardly:

> 'This is how, foreday morning, we make choose them canoes. –
> We stand in wet roots, while the ground mist was making
> just like a snake, thigh deep in fern. We watch the noise
>
> at the top of the tall trunks, their young leaves shaking
> in the (cold) emerald light, with the same noise that the shallows
> make in the sunrise. The smooth ones would be oars.
>
> The heights was cold, boy. The forest shaft its shadows,
> but our breath was smoke. We jam hands in our jacket
> and pass the white rum around. We heard the valleys

of banana below, and, when wind came back, it
was like standing in the very sea that feed us
all our life. (MS 0546:2:1)

[illegible] back with his literary antecedents. His Creole speech, in particular, remains in their thrall: "foreday morning", for example, is Walcott's translation for the French Creole of "*au bout de petit matin*". But in English, [illegible] inappropriate in a St Lucian context. "Boy" as a tag at the end of a sentence ("The heights was cold, boy") has pretty widespread usage in the Anglophone Caribbean. However, because Creole raconteurs often use it for comic effect, the term has become a clichéd marker of the burlesque, making its presence in this context confusingly jocular. Such random imports of Anglophone Creole literary conventions sound as jarring as the earlier draft's references to Troy. Walcott's most felicitous gesture towards St Lucian language registers is his use of the verb "to make" in the Creole manner as an intransitive verb – as in "the ground mist was making/ just like a snake, thigh-deep in fern." However, the land/sea simile he now transfers to Philoctete ("it was like standing in the very sea that feed us/ all our life") still seems laboured. The sound the Standard English "very" makes, as it jangles up against the uninflected Creole forms of "feed" and "life," is about as discordant to the West Indian ear as the green verb, "we has," sounds to a Standard English speaker listening to the drunk in "Tales of the Islands".

Walcott seems still to be struggling with the problems of translation he encountered in "Sainte Lucie" as he moves in his mind's ear between French and English Creoles as well as between both Creoles and Standard English; or between the classical precedents he hopes to embellish and conventions for representing Creole forms on the page he has picked up from other writers. But just as Brathwaite channels the conversational voices of the women in "The Dust" both by reading Eliot and Lamming, and by listening to the women in the corner shops of his childhood, Walcott finally gets his opening sequence right, by channelling Brathwaite's techniques and attending more closely to the formal properties of the language around him.

Walcott's most significant final change allows Philoctete to address a specific audience, rather than leaving his words to hover without context until the poet/narrator folds them into his larger rhetorical project. This is the same dialogic move that made Pearlie's voice in Brathwaite's "The Dust" come alive. The tourists listening to Philoctete were already there in at least one of the earlier drafts [illegible], but they were relegated to the end of Philoctete's monologue, where their presence reinforced the distancing effect of the Standard English narration:

> [...] The trees had to dead. The ferns said 'yes'
> the moment the axe of sunlight hit the cedars
>
> and we measure them with the axes in our eyes.
> And that first stroke wound the gommiers into canoes'.
> So, daily, Philo gives this spiel to the tourists
>
> who keep taking his soul with cyclops cameras
> squinting in the sun, while he grips a hull with wrists
> as gnarled as a sea-grape branch (MS 0565:5:1)

The idiomatic incongruity between the self-consciously folksy "the trees had to dead" and the Yiddish American colloquialism, "spiel", leaves Philoctete's soul at the mercy of the tourist's cameras as well as the poet's intrusive omniscient narration, so that the familiarity of calling him "Philo" sounds patronizing – who in this tale could possibly be on such intimate terms with a fisherman? Presenting Philo's "spiel" as spectacle also harkens back to Walcott's words of scorn in his "Muse of History" essay for those who celebrate any and everything folksy – "the critic-tourist [who] can only gasp at such naturalness [... but] wouldn't care to try it himself, really" (*What the Twilight Says*, p. 55). Moreover, the distance between the fisherman's language at one extreme and that of the narrator at the other, even after the tourists have gone, makes it difficult to discern who is agent and what is object in this tableau.

Once Walcott blocks in an interactive relationship on his poem's stage, between Philoctete, the narrator and the listening tourists, the poem can move freely between the abstract and the mimetic – between the part of his imagination Walcott usually reserves for poetry and the part devoted to drama. He can now place his entire repertoire of oral forms and dramatic techniques at his Creole speaker's disposal, without compromising the self-reflexivity of his opening sequence:

> "This is how, one sunrise, we cut down them canoes."
> Philoctete smiles for the tourists, who try taking
> his soul with their cameras. (*Omeros*, p. 3)

In this, the final published version, "sunrise" has replaced the anatopistic "foreday morning", and "cut" replaces "choose", "make" or the earlier passive "are brought down". Thus, the violent action of cutting down "them canoes" now fully belongs to the fishermen, as opposed to the narrator, or to the Greek warriors of Walcott's literary imagination. Philoctete's language also draws perceptibly closer to that of the narrator. Thus, a few stanzas later, the word "spiel" is gone, but "the trees had to dead" also has been replaced by the more standard "the trees have to die", leaving it to the line's rhythm to preserve its Creole intonation. That convergence of Creole and Standard English mirrors the narrative convergence of speaker and omniscient narrator through the mediation of free indirect discourse. Similarly, Philoctete's relationship to the tourists becomes less one-sided. Whereas, in the previous version, they "keep" taking his soul, now they can only "try" to do so, suggesting that the speaker, too, is an actor in this [illegible] [illegible] judgement [illegible]

The fishermen's relationship to their classical counterparts also has shifted. Like Pearlie and the other women in "The Dust", who understand [illegible] fishermen grasp the metaphysical implications of their battle with nature, not because they have read Homer, but because the task at hand is actually difficult and dangerous on its own terms – either the trees or the men are literally going to die. It is this mortal extremity, not the mere existence of a classic parallel, which gives an epic dimension to their struggle. The white rum, the shivering of the men and the leaves, the axes in the sun's rays reflected in the men's eyes, can now function both as vehicle and tenor for Walcott's complex metaphors.

When the images of pygmies and barbarians return several pages later, they do so in the context of the immense relief the fishermen experience after having conquered these towering, dangerous trees:

> Like barbarians striding columns they have brought down,
> the fishermen shouted. The gods were down at last.
>
> Like pygmies they hacked the trunks of wrinkled giants
> for paddles and oars. They were working with the same
> concentration as an army of fire-ants. (*Omeros*, pp. 6-7)

By allowing his barbarians to stride the tree trunk columns, Walcott refines his initially vague epic simile to hone in on a direct parallel between the historical barbarians sacking Rome's columned temples and the actual work the fisherman do to turn the logs into canoes. The rest of the opening sequence has already represented the forest grove as a temple of the fallen Aruac civilization. It is thus no longer a stretch to see the exuberance of the [illegible] who take down its columns [illegible] a sign of their ignorance about the civilization they are destroying, as well as a celebration of the vigour of a new race, which in turn will leave its own unique mark on this landscape. Rather than [illegible] Walcott's [illegible] about epic poetry [illegible] the classical allusion [illegible] Similarly, the reference [illegible] pygmies, rather than invoking some recondite connection to a "joyous war", now focuses solely on the contrast between the stature of the men and the massive size of the *gommiers*, before miniaturizing them even further into [illegible] fire-ants. This final image [illegible] effort will required [illegible] the logs [illegible] with the ants' [illegible] in breaking down fallen logs [illegible] vast, half-buried catacombs.

As he does in the second section of "Sainte Lucie", Walcott slips in the

French Creole, "*laurier-cannelles*", in *Omeros*' opening sequence to anchor his hexameter's rhythms in the cadences of French Creole speech. But he moves away from pedantic translation, inserting the English alternative, "cedars", only when it maintains the next line's meter. Translation in this context, therefore, is active rather than passive, pushing forward both the story and the rhythms of the poem. By the time Chapter III assaults us with the violent Creole exchange between Hector and Achille, ("*Touchez-i, encore: N'ai fendre choux-ous-ou, salope!*") we are fully versed in the multilingual properties of the St Lucian discursive landscape (*Omeros*, p. 15). Rather than hissing "*your words is English,/ is a different tree*" (*Arkansas Testament*, p. 10), the trees, here, "[utter] as one nation, [...teaching] their saplings: from the towering babble/ of the cedar to the green vowels of *bois-campêche*" (*Omeros*, p. 6). Like Brathwaite, Walcott now moves effortlessly between language registers within a single line. Not only does Achille express his anger in French and English Creoles, but the language through which we are given access to his reflections – "To go crazy for an old bailing tin/ crusted with rust!" – also retains an unmistakable Creole cadence (*Omeros*, p. 17). Walcott (or, at the very least, his narrator) is thinking in Creole!

Perhaps the most moving image of this perfected opening sequence is Philoctete's phrase "[d]ew was filling my eyes" (*Omeros*, p. 3). Walcott refines it from a French Creole expression, which describes dew or mist, like tears, as actively "falling" or "breaking". In Philoctete's phrase, the dew's action simultaneously reveals and obscures the emotions that well up in him as he approaches his grim task through the early morning mist. The fact that Walcott derives that image from an actual Creole expression excises any coyness in its usage here. We hear it first as a statement of fact, even as, on account of the tense beauty of the image, dew breaks in the eyes with which we contemplate the page.

VI

Walcott probably appropriates Brathwaite's formal techniques unconsciously. Perhaps that would have to be the case, since readers unfamiliar with Brathwaite's long association with such techniques are wont to credit Walcott with inventing them. Yet, without appreciating how *Omeros* echoes and refines Brathwaite's original experiment we risk losing much of the nuance and richness of Walcott's achievement. In a move of consummate cathexis, Walcott instructs his readers in how to measure his achievement in *Omeros* by drawing attention to how Patrick Chamoiseau uses similar techniques in *Texaco*.[22] Commenting on how classic folk tale structures inform Chamoiseau's opening, as well as the poetry of Aimé Césaire and the Guadeloupian St-John Perse, Walcott avers:

> Césaire's incantation in his poem invokes an island dawn, "*Au bout du petit matin*," just as Chamoiseau's "*Nous tait ka*" does. Join the three beginnings "In those days" (Perse in Guadeloupe), "At foreday morning" (Césaire in Martinique), and "We used to" (Chamoiseau), and you have the chant, Caribbean memory, as calm as smoke rising from blue hills. "In those days... at foreday morning... we used to..."
>
> That "*Noutaka*," that "We used to," of *Texaco* is the real history, the *histoire* seen for itself of a very small territory not seen in proportion to "the great mutations of the World" [illegible] and far from wars and changing empires. (*What The Twilight Says*, p. 219)

Extend the list of beginnings and Walcott might as well be writing his ideal reviewer's appreciation of the opening lines of *Omeros*: "This is how, one sunrise, we cut down them canoes." But the technique he commends in Chamoiseau is almost identical with the bounded "*histoire* [...] of a very small territory not seen in proportion to 'the great mutations of the world'" in Brathwaite's poem "The Dust", which also unfolds from the mist of an island dawn.

In his 1967 review of *Rights of Passage*, Walcott had rated Brathwaite just outside that charmed circle of Caribbean writers into which he now inducts Chamoiseau: "There is nothing in 'Rights of Passage' that equals the fan-poem [sic] 'Cahier d'un Retour Au Pays Natal', or the sustained ram's horn splendours of Perse's 'Eloges' and 'Pour Feter Un Enfance'. Wry, self mocking, melancholic, Brathwaite is at his best" (*Critical Perspectives*, p. 41). The review adequately appreciates the challenge Brathwaite mounts to Naipaul – pointing out that "[w]here Naipaul fumes with exasperation at the deracinated wreckage that makes every island a compost heap, Mr Brathwaite picks his way through the wreckage, selecting broken artifacts, unshaped memories" (*Critical Perspectives*, p. 42). It commends the "refined, anguished sensibility" of Brathwaite's tone, "bent on achieving not power, but grace, not grandeur but sharp, piercing truths" (*Critical Perspectives*, p. 45). It even urges aspiring West Indian poets to learn from *Rights of Passage*'s stylistic achievement. Nevertheless, his estimate of Brathwaite seems tepid when compared to Walcott's fervent praise for Chamoiseau:

> I would press this book into the hands of every West Indian as if it were a lost heirloom, even on those who cannot read. After that formality, I would run through the markets with vendors in the shade of huge umbrellas, past abandoned fountains, stopping traffic with an uplifted hand, entering dark retail stores selling fading ledgers and disintegrating chalks, preaching "You have to read this book, it is yours! It has come to reclaim you!" (*What The Twilight Says*, p. [illegible])

The language in this apparent tribute is deliberately hyperbolic, aiming, in homage to Chamoiseau, at a declamatory style that allows Walcott to be "impulsive, elliptical, to indulge in that simultaneity which you call 'opacity'" (*What The Twilight Says,* p. 214). Its almost sophomoric veneration has a lot to do with Walcott's anxiety that, to a Martiniquan ear, the less developed St Lucian French Creole probably sounds "cautious and awkward, enthusiastic, ungrammatical" (*What The Twilight Says,* p. 223). But, until now, he alone among the major Anglophone Caribbean writers has had to negotiate this linguistic tangle of English, French, English Creole and French Creole. And as he unravels it here, the poet also experiences a tremendous sense of vindication on discovering how many of the technical and linguistic choices he made in *Omeros* work as well as or better than those in *Texaco* or its English translation. Even as he fusses with Chamoiseau's decision to go with a phonetic spelling for "Noutéka" for "nous tait ka", or the translator's decision to replace the French Creole names for the trees with Standard English equivalents, we can sense his excitement at finally having a chance to wrangle with a fellow writer over this quadrupled linguistic challenge:

> The word *gommier*, for example, translated into "gum tree," is not only the tree itself but also the dugout canoe manufactured by the indigenous Caribs; and as the tree, its sound contains the activity of a light breeze in the gum tree's boughs or branches; "boughs," however, is archaic, containing a mild assonance – "*gommier,*" "boughs" – but it is so right a sound for the Carib canoe in its buoyancy and elegant length, its riding and shearing of water, the carved trunk of the floating tree and the blue echo around the word. (*What The Twilight Says,* p. 225)

Walcott's elation in such passages arises from more than having encountered, in Chamoiseau, a writer worthy of emulation. It is also a measure of his linguistic isolation, which keeps a very vital part of his literary identity separate from that of an Anglophone writer like Brathwaite. After all, fresh and expansive as he makes it sound, not even Walcott could sustain the hothouse Francophone rhetorical style he reproduces here, in emulation of Chamoiseau, for the length of an entire English novel or epic poem, without exasperating an Anglophone reader. That rhetorical affectation lies at the other extreme from the unadorned English style of the "poetic documentary", replete with "biblical conjunctions and liturgical responses" that Walcott identifies in Brathwaite's borrowings from Lamming, Mais, McLeish, Eliot and Crane. Chamoiseau indulges the "nostalgia for obscurity" by which Walcott confesses he often has been seduced, even as he disciplines his poetry to eschew its worst excesses. (Hirsch, "The Art of Poetry", p. 78). And yet, facets of the St Lucian French Creole heritage partake to a significant degree in this hyperbolic Gallic tradition. If Walcott discerns in the work of Chamoiseau, Césaire and Perse elements that he misses in his reading of Brathwaite, it may be because the linguistic culture that links St Lucia to its francophone neighbours is not wholly contiguous with the political histories that bind it to the former British West Indies. The burden of negotiating those competing traditions subtends many of the virtuoso effects Walcott achieves in *Omeros*.

It is tempting to see, in Walcott's expansive tribute to Chamoiseau rather than in his tempered praise for Brathwaite, a more intimate correspondence to Achille's eulogy for Hector:

[illegible]
[illegible] at the bow of the long canoe

with the plates of your chest like a shield; (*Omeros*, p. 233)

With one important exception: when Walcott celebrates Chamoiseau, he expresses reverence at a distance for a newly discovered hero, but the unspoken tribute Achille never quite offers to Hector (it is, after all, the prayer he "could not utter") acknowledges a long, intimate history of personal rivalry and mutual irritation that resembles Walcott's relationship to Brathwaite much more closely (*Omeros*, p. 233). Then, too, there is Achille's discomfiting awareness that he may have stolen his rival's "craft" – a word Walcott puns on throughout *Omeros* to connect the fisherman's boat, the poet's art and the Creole term for a sexually attractive woman. Achille considers himself the better man than Hector. After all, he has won "the craft" and survived to eulogize his compère. But he will never know if the child Helen is carrying is his or Hector's. And if Hector had not died, the two men probably would still be quarrelling over rusted tin cans in the bellies of leaking crafts.

Walcott may consider his writing to have "a stronger energy, a stronger discipline, and a stronger drive" than that of his Caribbean contemporary but he cannot know whether posterity will deem his appropriation of the formal effects Brathwaite pioneered in *Rights of Passage* legitimate or stolen; or whether, for that matter, anyone will care (Hirsch, "The Art of Poetry", p. 73). Already, their mutual anxieties about regional authenticity are being eclipsed by the preoccupations of a new generation of Caribbean writers who can take their linguistic and cultural hybridity for granted in ways nationalist writers of Walcott's and Brathwaite's generation, with their colonial educations and their insecurities about their relationship to the common folk, cannot. When Walcott offers his allegiance to Chamoiseau, he repays an old debt to Brathwaite even as he intimates a nagging anxiety that both he and Brathwaite may be battling merely over "an old bailing tin/ crusted with rust" (*Omeros*, p. 17).

Beyond their rivalry over Helen, Achille claims solidarity with his rival on account of Hector's mastery of the craft they both ply: "I swear no/ African ever hurled his wide seine at the bay// by which he was born with such beauty" (*Omeros*, p. 233). Despite his review's parsimonious praise for

Rights of Passage or his poetic refusal in *Sea Grapes* of the ideology behind *The Arrivants*, one senses in Walcott, too, a grudging admiration for his rival: for Brathwaite's technical prowess, his willingness to risk mockery and isolation in pursuit of his craft, and his loyalty to a regional literary fraternity, whatever its shortcomings. Although, like Achille, Walcott refuses the easy pieties of class or racial solidarity, he acknowledges those things he shares unequivocally with his West Indian compère: their passionate allegiance to their island homes – figured as Helen for Walcott, mother for Brathwaite – and their devotion to their craft. His unspoken accolade for his rival sustains a fervent hope for the possibility of a regional literary fraternity that can transcend insular boundaries and the ravages of time.

Endnotes

1. *Omeros* (London: Faber & Faber, 1990) p. 233.
2. The terms are Brathwaite's, introduced in one of his early critiques of Walcott, delivered at a seminar series at the University of the West Indies, in 1965 on "The State of the Arts". Mervyn Morris cites it and then defends Walcott from its attacks in "Walcott and the Audience for Poetry" [1968], *Critical Perspectives on Derek Walcott* (Boulder: Lynne Rienner, 1996, p. 177). See also Patricia Ismond's "Walcott versus Brathwaite" [1971], *Critical Perspectives,* pp. 220-238). Rohlehr addresses the controversy indirectly in "Withering Into Truth: A Review of Derek Walcott's *The Gulf and Other Poems*" [1969], *Critical Perspectives* pp. 212-219.
3. Walcott also appropriates Brathwaite's coral metaphor ("A yellow mote of sand dreams in the polyp's eye;/ the coral needs this pain./ Look closely:/ the pearl has limestone ridges, hills,/ out of it grows the sun/ and the fat valleys of Haiti [...] The coral killers crust my wall of bone" ("Coral", *Islands*, p. 75; *The Arrivants*, p. 232) as the basis for one of the most memorable images in *Omeros* ("strong as self healing coral, a quiet culture/ is branching from the white ribs of each ancestor,// deeper than it seems on the surface; slowly but sure/ it will change us with the fluent sculpture of Time" (p. 296)). Patricia Ismond, in *Abandoning Dead Metaphors* (Kingston: UWI Press, pp. 271-273), locates a similar series of appropriations, this time, from Brathwaite's *Mother Poem* in Walcott's long poem about Michael Manley's Jamaica, "The Star-Apple Kingdom", *Star-Apple Kingdom* (London: Jonathan Cape, 1980), pp. 46-58.
4. *Another Life* (London: Faber & Faber, 1973), pp. 122-123; and *Collected Poems 1948-1984* (London: Faber & Faber, 1986), pp. 264-65.
5. Bruce King in *Derek Walcott: A Caribbean Life* (Oxford: OUP, 2000), pp. 455-56, offers an extended version of this story.

6. Derek Walcott, "The Caribbean: Culture or Mimicry" [1974], *Critical Perspectives* p. 57.
7. Derek Walcott, "Tribal Flutes" [1967], *Critical Perspectives*, p. 44.
8. Edward Hirsch, "The Art of Poetry" [1986], *Critical Perspectives*, p. [illegible].
9. *Another Life*, pp. 16-17 and *Collected Poems*, pp. 158-59.
10. "Tales of the Islands", *In a Green Night* (London: Jonathan Cape, [illegible]) and *Collected Poems*, pp. [illegible].
11. Critics have discussed the sonnets exhaustively on account of their use of language. In "Walcott and the Audience for Poetry," (*Critical Perspectives* pp. 184-86), Mervyn Morris offers an analysis of their evolution from the time of their first appearance in *Bim* magazine to their publication, five years later in *In a Green Night*, which anticipates several of my arguments later in this chapter about the significance of Walcott's revisions to the opening sequence in *Omeros*.
12. Anthony Milne, "Derek Walcott" [1982], *Critical Perspectives*, p. 63.
13. Kamau Brathwaite, "The Dust", *The Arrivants* (Oxford: OUP, 1973), p. 65.
14. Derek Walcott, "A Letter to Chamoiseau" [1997], *What the Twilight Says: Essays* (London: Faber & Faber, 1998), p. 219.
15. Derek Walcott, "Tribal Flutes", *Critical Perspectives*, p. 41.
16. "'Rights of Passage', Drama in Itself", *Trinidad Guardian*, 25 Apr. 1973, p. 5; referenced in *Critical Perspectives*, p. 425.
17. Derek Walcott, "Meanings" [1970], *Critical Perspectives*, p. 48.
18. Derek Walcott, *The Arkansas Testament* (New York, Farrar, Straus and Giroux, 1987), p. 21.
19. *Sea Grapes* (London: Cape, 1976).
20. "Tribal Flutes", *Critical Perspectives*, p. 42.
21. In personal correspondence with me, Paul Breslin remarks that Walcott told him he initially thought of writing all of *Omeros* in St Lucian Creole. However, Breslin's studies of early drafts of "Tales of the Islands" and "The Schooner *Flight*" reveal that, in actual practice, Walcott usually revises "downwards" from Standard to Creole. Both his observations corroborate my argument here about the unique difficulties Walcott faces in moving between Standard English, English Creole and French Creole.
22. *Texaco* (Paris: Editions Gallimard, 1992), English translation (New York: Pantheon Books, 1997).

LOUIS REGIS

A HACK'S HIRED PROSE? WALCOTT'S ARTICLES ON THE CALYPSO

In 1959 Derek Walcott settled in Trinidad and initiated the weekly actor's studio which eventually became the Trinidad Theatre Workshop. For the seventeen years during which he was domiciled in Trinidad, he supplemented his earnings from the theatre and his publications of poetry with feature articles for the *Guardian* newspapers specializing in matters literary, artistic and cultural. "Codicil", published in *The Castaway and Other Poems* (1965), reflects the feelings of artistic dividedness, isolation and perpetual exile which were exacerbated by settling in Trinidad: "Schizophrenic, wrenched by two styles/one a hack's hired prose, I earn/my exile".[1] The phrase "a hack's hired prose" has resonated loudly and for long. Its presence in "Codicil" suggests Walcott's alarm at the possible deleterious effects on his creativity of having to yoke his literary abilities to the mundane work of journalism. The phrase, however, is conventionally read as Walcott's dismissal of his journalistic career in Trinidad 1959 to 1976.

In a doctoral dissertation which examines the contradictions, paradoxes, inconsistencies, ambivalences and their resolution in the work of Walcott from 1946 to 1976, Victor Questel warned,

> one must be aware of the danger of making too much of Walcott's statements in his reviews which are after all merely 'a hack's hired prose' in which much is said off the cuff, as it were, and when catalogued and examined, certainly do not add up to anything too remarkable, though their importance cannot be denied.[2]

Responding to Questel, although never naming him, Gordon Rohlehr, Questel's doctoral supervisor, argued that Walcott's newspaper articles on the calypso, carnival, and calypso drama manifest his (Walcott's) internal dialectics. Rohlehr dedicated a long section in the magisterial essay "The Problem of the Problem of Form" (1991) to discussing Walcott's wrestle with the oral paradigm.[3]

Walcott's sixteen *Guardian* articles on the calypso, written between 1960 and 1967, cannot and should not be dismissed casually as "a hack's hired prose". They are critical to any reconstruction of the calypso scene of the

1960s. Through them, Walcott reveals himself as a major theorist on the calypso and in particular on the calypso as a performance art form: he discusses the major calypso personalities, their songs and performance styles; and he analyses the issues involved in adjudicating the national calypso King competition. Further, and most importantly, Walcott turns the spotlight on The Mighty Sparrow, the phenomenon of the modern calypsonian who informs and links all of the concerns outlined above.

[illegible] severely tested", establishes the parameters for his subsequent affirmations and contradictions in relation to the calypso. He begins by suggesting limits to the calypsonian's role and function: "As an ephemeral poet no one is subjected to a severer test than the carnival balladeer". Walcott's classification of calypsonians as "ephemeral poets" is highly problematic. Read against the title of the article it suggests that he equates popular with ephemeral. He seems not to have realized that by 1960 some calypsonians regarded themselves as far more than mere "carnival balladeers". Most could not transcend the limited role of carnival entertainers, but a few functioned as poets and prophets for their social groups – if not for the larger society. As early as the 1930s, Atilla the Hun and others whipped up anti-colonial sentiment to the point that the British colonial administrators imposed a form of censorship to limit their appeal to the proto-nationalism they championed in their songs. Calypsonians continued extending this appeal and their audience so much so that political scientist, Gordon Lewis, in his discussion of the evolution of modern Trinidad, writes of "the slow transformation… of the calypsonian from being simply the court jester of the society, tolerated with bemused condescension for the period of Mardi Gras only, into the national hero of the new national feelings". Walcott's sweeping statement of 1960 ignores all of this and it may well be that he mistook the calypso tent activity and the national competition, two of the highlights of the Carnival season in that period, as the be-all and end-all of calypso.

A second Walcott statement from the article is also contestable: "No calypso succeeds which has not an exact rhythm with the topics of the time. The [illegible] concerning a personal problem or a protracted joke" ("Popular Poets", p. 7). This is a loose generalization based on a misapprehension that a calypso is an ephemeral song with no real life beyond the year of its first performance in the tent. Topicality is important in the reception of a calypso, especially at the tent, but many compositions based on personal problems and protracted jokes have achieved classic status and are in great demand at the out-of-season calypso concerts, [illegible] programmes. Conversely, some of the topical calypsos which were successful at the tent in their season, lose the appeal outside of their immediate contexts. Topicality, then, is just a variable in the popularity of a particular song and in the scheme of things ranks less than individual constants such as melody, rhythm, lyrical construction, use of humour and so on. The integration of these constants rather than topicality is responsible for the popularity of a calypso.

Walcott also presents as absolute truths other questionable statements: "Each song, by custom, contains the seed of its own death, since the final judges, the public, expect novelty, and any calypso which is ambitious in melody or in language, and which may prove a strain on the memory is regarded with suspicion".[6] This again can be demonstrated to be a false generalization. Many of Sparrow's classics, for example, are quite "ambitious in melody" (witness the difficulty steelbandsmen of the 1960s experienced adapting them for the road) but they live on in public memory especially when purists hark back to the golden age of the calypso.

This is not to say that Walcott was absolutely wrong in his theorizing on the calypso. In his introductory article he declared, "The calypso must seek the identity of its composer, not only his opinion but the sound of 'his very self and voice'" ("Popular Poets", p. 7). He reinforced this two years later: "the calypso remains a matter of original presentation, it contains the presence of its creator and it is still in its best place, the tent" ("Danger lurks in Tin Pan Alley", p. 23). This truism captures the essence of the folk tradition as it was (perceived) in the 1960s when the majority of calypsonians were composers and performers and the tent was the dominant space in the calypso industry.

The most intriguing section of Walcott's second calypso article, however, is the comparison of calypso and poetry:

> Songs like Melody's "Peddlers" can be read as poems without accompanying music, and so can most of Commander's or Mr Action; in fact Commander's ballad of last season on the paradox of crime and justice can stand by Germany's best poet of this generation, Bertolt Brecht, in its irony.[7]

It seems paradoxical that in one breath Walcott should rate calypsonians as ephemeral poets ("Popular Poets", p. 7) and in the very next breath compare some of their best work favourably against European masters. As the decade wore on, however, and the conditioned reflexes of pro-European bias reasserted themselves over the instinctive admiration for the folk art, he sought "to resolve the distinctions between Calypso and poem which had always existed in his mind" (Rohlehr, "The Problem of the Problem of Form", p. 32). This differentiation manifests in Walcott's critique of Sparrow's "Slave" (1963)[8] when he writes:

> One admires what Sparrow is after. A dignity and extension of the range of the calypso. But is seems to me to be making the same mistake of formal poets who try the calypso in poetry. The poetry has to be used; it does not belong to the poet but the public and must be danced. "The Slave", however daring in intention, is feeble in lyrics and sounds more right for the concert hall than for the open road.[9]

I suspect that Sparrow intended "Slave" for Queen's Hall, the premier concert hall in Port of Spain where some of his work was recorded for marketing, rather than the Queen's Park Savannah, the centre stage for the Trinidad Carnival. [illegible] intended [illegible] glory.

The following year, in a clear manifestation of his continuing internal [illegible] with the oral tradition, Walcott wrote:

> Nobody expects great poetry from calypsos but it is, after all, a poetic medium and it can come pretty close, no? Compare Eliot's meeting with a master in "Four Quartets"
>
> He left me, with a kind of valediction
> And faded on the blowing of the horn
>
> with Bomber's bidding farewell to Spoiler's ghost
>
> The break of day
> I don't know where he went
> But he went away [10]

Reading the articles against Walcott's creative work, especially his theatre, Rohlehr reasons that Walcott has felt "the irresistible force of the oral paradigm but he experiences it as something to be confronted, wrestled with until it is made to justify itself" ("The Problem of the Problem of Form", p. 31). Rohlehr sums up Walcott's contradiction and resolution in the words: "The law of dialectic, so crucial for an understanding of the aesthetic code-switching in the Caribbean, makes us confront our imagined opposite which in the process of trying to negate we come to resemble" ("The Problem", p. 39).

Reading Walcott by the light of Rohlehr's revelations it is easy to understand that Walcott's internal arguments are merely a prelude to resurrecting Spoiler's ghost to employ a traditional minor key verse to chastise Trinidad of the 1970s in his poem, "The Spoiler's Return".[11] Despite the reference to Spoiler and with due deference to Rohlehr's observation that Walcott resembles Spoiler in his employment of shadows, doubles, fantastical situations and so on ("The Problem", p. 40), I read Walcott's article "The Clown Prince of Calypso Drops a Bomb"[12] as the genesis of his own calypso-style poem. In this article Walcott examines the quality of Cypher's reductive satire which,

> lacerates statesman, clergyman and fool. In fact it makes no distinction. It's [illegible] to believe that we accept the world Cypher satirizes [illegible] without [illegible]. The title 'Clown Prince of Calypso' is belittling. Cypher has his own [illegible], [illegible] may strike him as ridiculous. But every politician should keep Cypher in his back pocket. There'd be less rhetorical rubbish. ("The Clown Prince", p. 4)

From this near anatomical image there is a simple step to the scatological one of the parasite "whose sting, between the cleft arse and its seat/ reminds Authority man is just meat" ("The Spoiler's Return", p. 55).

Walcott continues: "Cypher makes an ass of every little god we have, but it's not merciless, he just shows them up as pathetic idiots, the mockery purges the audience" ("The Clown Prince", p. 4). This anticipates the content and style of "The Spoiler's Return". The choice of Spoiler as narrating consciousness can be explained by Walcott's need for a distancing device endowed with the Tiresias-like omniscience and omnipresence of the immortal dead (Spoiler died on 24th December 1960). Walcott's genius invested the ghost of Spoiler, calypso's ultimate fantasist, with mordant wit sharpened by experiential bitterness.

While Walcott's theorizing on the calypso is flawed by the contradictory pulls of his internal dialectic, his analysis of the social psychology of the calypso-performing experience is clinically accurate:

> These performers face one of the toughest audiences in the world, because unlike the claques of La Scala what is being sung is national property and the contempt of a Trinidad audience, an indestructible optimism that immediately and finally understands failure and as immediately looks forward to "better dan dat", is paralysing.
>
> No audience can clap so cynically, and a calypsonian sells not only his composition but his whole personality.
>
> When they reject the song, they also reject the singer, and it takes a brave man to come back.[13]

This is a constant with Walcott: his publicly stated admiration for the public poets who enter the calypso *gayelle* and take the blows from an unpredictable audience. It informs his admiration for Sparrow, as will be discussed later.

In the last of his fourteen articles on the calypso, Walcott engages with the business of calypso judging in which he was involved for some time. He begins his reflections on the upcoming competition of 1967 with the confession, "I gave up the privilege only because I was afraid of being too conditioned, of developing reflexes instead of a true impartiality".[14] He then takes us backstage to a scenario of judges being "assaulted, overwhelmed or seduced by the obvious favouritism of disc jockeys, crowd reaction, the charisma of personalities and the faith in tradition" ("It's Our Own Kind of Artist Figure", p. 11). All of this prepares for his statement on the upcoming competition of 1967 which he expects to feature songs which at first he rates "poor", but then concedes that "the subliminal persistence of steelbands, TV and the radio have made ... sound the equal of any season". In closing he seeks to rationalize the inevitable conflict between conditioned reflexes and true impartiality: "These prejudgements are no different to when I played judge, but often the winner is so obvious that the work is easy and once the competition begins, all the favouritism dissolves in the heat of the contest" ("It's Our Own Kind of Artist Figure", p. 11). All of this is remarkable because it is the first – if not the only – time that a calypso judge has discussed the psychology of his profession so openly and so rationally. That curious phrase "when I played judge" strikes me as being Walcott's attempt to place emotional distance between himself and the practice of an art form for which he cared deeply.

[illegible] contribution to Calypso research. One of the most remarkable truths about the scholarship on the modern calypso is that, to the best of my knowledge, no one has attempted a full-length study on the Sparrow. Any such project must [illegible] the Sparrow's discography against his biography and against the critical commentary of Gordon Rohlehr,[15] C.L.R. James,[16] Earl Lovelace,[17] Derek Walcott and a host of media practitioners. Like the other commentators named, Walcott saw The Birdie in full flight and he commented on this phenomenon with an attentiveness and a sensitivity which rebukes his self-deprecating dismissal as "a hack's hired prose". Whoever the calypsonian introduced as the subject of the *Guardian* articles, whatever the issue to introduce the discussion, Walcott returns automatically to Sparrow.

Walcott pays Sparrow the supreme compliment by crediting him with "the invention of calypsonian as a citizen, not a human ruin revived for a Carnival season" ("Alas! The Last Minute Road March Is Gone").[15] What prevents us from accepting Walcott's endorsement without reservation is the memory of the earlier achievements of Atilla the Hun who was, at various points of his career, major recording artiste, international kaisonian, political swordsman of calypso, tent manager, deputy mayor of Port of Spain and calypso historian.[18]

Curiously, Walcott failed to recognize that over the years Sparrow was exceeding his (Walcott's) constricting definition of the calypsonian as carnival balladeer. I have noted that Walcott faults Sparrow's "Slave" on the grounds that it seemed made for the concert hall rather than the road ("Alas! The Last Minute Road March Is Gone"). In that very article Walcott noted that the mood of the Original Young Brigade was "confident" and "commercial" and that the tent was acclaimed as the [illegible]. Two years later he regretted the change in The Birdie's presentation style: "I miss the feather ruffling, the old arrogance, the sudden electrifying appearances (always exactly delayed) of a couple of years ago. The Birdie is now efficient and managerial, starting the show on time, toning down on the rudeness and establishing discipline" ("Efficient 'Birdie', Minus the Feather Ruffling", p. 5). Clearly Sparrow of [illegible] was upgrading his tent practice in favour of the efficiency required of the concert hall. Middle-class production values were superseding the folk casualness and roughness of the traditional tent as The Birdie had progressed beyond mere flight and was clearly seeking lift off into a new orbit. Two years after this Walcott noted that the "OYB is courtly to tourists. The atmosphere is benign, no picong, no insults". Noting the abrupt disc jockey manner of the masters of ceremony, he concludes wryly, "everybody's getting bourgeois" ("The Clown Prince of Calypso Drops a Bomb", p. 4).

Walcott begins his examination of Sparrow with comments on his musicianship. He notes that Sparrow shows versatility in his range of theme and that he "knows the effect of flattened ending, both verbally and musically for comic effect".[19] In the article "Calypsonians! Danger Lurks in Tin Pan Alley" which warns against the growing tendency on the part of calypsonians to string words haphazardly "to introduce a bang-up chorus", he remarks that Sparrow, like Melody, can write well [and] escape the "crosseyedness of others" (p. 23). My only reservation about this is that Sparrow, although a gifted writer, was even then employing ghost writers. This saddles researchers with the task of identifying compositions, declaring them authentic Sparrow, and then proceeding to make statements about Sparrow's skill as songwriter.

Walcott did not dwell much on Sparrow as songwriter, however; he preferred to examine Sparrow's performance style, which he did with the trained eyes of a professional dramatist: "Sparrow has now progressed from a lyrical to a dramatic intensity that hardly bothers to frame the words. You supply these. He is in danger like all good actors of letting technique replace emotion".[20] To his mind, then, Sparrow is not merely a singer but a performer whose medium is calypso, for which he enacts a performance script, which materializes the potential of the calypso as an integration of word, song and performance.

In 1965, Walcott commented thus on Sparrow's performance of "Congo Man", a song whose lyrics he described as feeble:

> Doing superb imitations of orchestra instruments, drum beats and jungle noises, miming, growling, leaping and howling like a Congo cannibal, Sparrow demonstrated again that as a performer he is unsurpassable. In fact he is now better than the songs he sings. It's the problem the finest artists face. There are moments in their career when they are superior to the material they have to hand ("Efficient 'Birdie', Minus the Feather Ruffling" p. 5).

In 1966 he reported on Sparrow's tent performance of "Melda" aka "Obeah Wedding", which what would later be acclaimed road march:

> Sparrow, the non-competing king whose theory of heredity and the divine right is confirmed this year by "Melda", is performing with all the authority of a man who knows he does not have to win. His success is so assured that he can lean towards the crowd and make them sing with him, something which is hardly ever heard in the tent nowadays. The last time I heard

> it and it was not repeated with such force either, was in Kitchener's tent in the year of "Love in the Cemetery". Perhaps nothing since "Jean and Dinah" has been sung so loudly and for so long in the king's tent.[21]

As with "Congo Man" [illegible] performance technique distinguishes Walcott's commentary on Sparrow from that on Kitchener, Cypher, Terror or Bomber.

[illegible] the immense courage demonstrated by the then Calypso King of the World. Walcott confesses his admiration for the very act of performing in public:

> When I first came to Trinidad, I had an isolated respect for calypsonians. In other words, I could stand back, I could look at the calypsonians, admire them tremendously and what they stood for and what they were doing and all that because they were working as poets in a public auditorium with public approval and public booing and that sort of thing.[22]

Sparrow is the supreme example of the singer who enters the *gayelle*, takes and gives his blows, persists and prevails. In the 1965 article cited above, in which Walcott remarked the cynicism of audience applause and the paralysing effect of audience rejection, he added, "When they reject the song, they also reject the singer, and it takes a brave man to come back" ("Efficient Birdie minus the feather ruffling" p. 5). It is almost certain that Walcott was referring particularly to Sparrow.

It is a well-known fact that Sparrow took up the challenge of engaging and defying a society with which he maintained a love-hate relationship for most of his career. Part of this is manifested in the content of his songs as he deliberately answered criticism with increasingly outrageous material. Walcott's undisguised admiration for Sparrow is that of the rebel for his soul brother, the isolate challenging the collective that demands that he validate himself annually.

Walcott begins his magnificent 1965 tribute to Sparrow's unsurpassed performing abilities by recalling the then current street gossip that "Sparrow boil down" and "Sparrow in trouble". Sparrow's response in 1965 to this kind of reductive gossip, which persecuted him for most of his career, was an unforgettable performance of "Congo Man". In 1967 Walcott returned to the phenomenon of Sparrow as performer:

> Every year the myth totters, every season our lips begin to curl as we wait for the phenomenon. Sparrow has a fierce authority that defies challenge and sometimes when it is really threatened he would take it to excess from fear but one supposes that it's the kind of fear... not of defeat but of failure. This drove him to a pitch where you are overwhelmed that anyone should take a song as seriously as if his life depended on your liking him. It's now important to distinguish [sic] the personality from the performer, the performer from the song. ("The Clown Prince of Calypso Drops a Bomb", p. 4)

There is no doubt that Walcott was fascinated by the calypso and the calypsonian. He confesses this even while in the process of differentiating the calypso from the poem: "It's an indescribable art form, all right, since it depends directly on immediate exposure tuning itself finely to popular feeling, precariously balanced between making an out, or catching you where you weren't looking" ("Efficient 'Birdie', Minus the Feather Ruffling", p. 5). In a 1973 interview with Raoul Pantin, Walcott reinforced this perception:

> I think that a lot of West Indian writers should experience this society, especially poets. First of all this is a society that is very verbal... Apart from its music there is a strong sense of composition... The dialect for instance, even if it borrows a little too much from the States now and it's got tired in terms of its own originality, is always being refreshed... Now from the time I was a boy in St Lucia, Trinidad expressions were popular all up the Eastern Caribbean... ("We Are Still Being Betrayed", p. 14)

Walcott was quite sincere when he compared Commander to Brecht and Bomber to Eliot. Apparently, his praises emerged out of an appreciation of the high quality of good calypsos, which he differentiated from bad calypsos, as he admitted, "you come to realise how many bad calypsos there are, you get tired of hearing the same type of calypso and so on" ("We are Still Being Betrayed"). This explains his interest in Kitchener among others, and his deeper interest in Sparrow. It also explains why he wrote only sixteen articles on the Calypso in seventeen years.

In the 10 January 1967 edition of the *Trinidad Guardian* there appears, under the nom de plume "Kaiso man", a report of the tent show at the Original Young Brigade [OYB] over which Sparrow presided. This article entitled "Laro 'Holes' Them at the OYB" begins with an analysis of the difference between the failed calypso and the failed calypsonian apropos of what the writer perceived as the early failure of Sparrow's tent presentation. According to Kaiso Man:

> ...the failed calypsonian is a dismal man to watch and hear. The audience realizes that he should not be in the business at all, that he will never make the grade because he simply hasn't got the talent, the gift, the style, the panache and whatever it takes. A good calypso gets an immediate, overwhelming, almost frightening success. The good calypsonian's poor calypso is listened to attentively and politely but the poor or failed calypsonian is given short shrift.[23]

Kaiso Man then proceeds to account for the success of Laro ["Hole"], Cypher ["Last Elections" and "If the Priest Could Play"] and Duke ["Soft Candle"] against the failure of Sparrow ["Education"] and of the Guyana-born, King Fighter. Kaiso Man opines that Sparrow tried too hard to impose on the calypso tent a didactic face while Fighter "showed the buffoon's face with a bitter personal anti-jest", which the crowd sensed and rejected. Kaiso Man does not further engage Sparrow's failure because he knows that this was the failure of a calypso not of the calypsonian. He has a special word for Fighter, however:

> Fighter had happier days and sweeter songs as we can remember only too well. Perhaps he will have the strength to [illegible] nourish his roots. Exile and disillusionment make the calypsonian, like anyone else, sick and weary of the world, and damages [sic] his soul. ([illegible])

At this point the mask, which was always transparent, and perhaps deliberately so, slips completely and Kaiso Man reveals himself as the writer of "Codicil".

In "Codicil", Walcott's phrase "a hack's hired prose" refers disparagingly to the journalese demanded of his survivalist excursions into media reporting. While his journalese is necessarily diametrically opposed to his metaphor-centred poetry and his poetry-based drama, it does not differ qualitatively from many of the passages in some of his published essays. In any event, Walcott's articles transform journalese both in content and style.

In conclusion, then, this paper challenges the phrase "a hack's hired prose", as applied to Walcott's articles on the calypso. While it seems foolhardy to challenge Walcott's self-designation, an analysis of his articles written for newspapers provides compelling evidence for that challenge: a hired hack would write basic journalistic reports of tent shows providing skeletal summaries of tent performances and how they were received. I know of no hack's single report that attempts the several things Walcott essayed in any one article. With respect to Walcott's articles, a hack may have commented on the changes in management style as Walcott does in "Efficient Birdie minus the feather ruffling". But no hack in the same article, or in any other, would reflect upon the quality of audience appreciation and the effect of negative audience reception on singers. No hack would advance a theory of calypso, include analyses of performances and offer serious reflections on the psychology of judging the finals of the national Calypso King show. Above all, no mere hack would have gifted us with the remarkable insights into the psychology and performing style of the Mighty Sparrow. For all of this we must consider ourselves blessed that Walcott practised as a journalist during the golden age of the calypso era when Sparrow ruled the roost.

Endnotes

1. Derek Walcott, "Codicil", *The Castaway and Other Poems* (London: Jonathan Cape, 1965), p. 61.
2. Victor Questel, "Derek Walcott: Contradiction and Resolution – Paradox, Inconsistency, Ambivalence and their Resolution in Derek Walcott's Writings 1946-76", Diss. UWI, St Augustine, 1979, p. 560.
3. Gordon Rohlehr, "The Problem of the Problem of Form", *The Shape of That Hurt and Other Essays* (Port of Spain: Longman, 1991), pp. 1-65. On Walcott's wrestle, see pp. 31-43.
4. Derek Walcott, "Popular Poets Are Now Being Severely Tested", *Sunday Guardian* (Trinidad), 14 Feb. 1960, 7.
5. Gordon Lewis, *The Growth of the Modern West Indies* (New York: Monthly Review Press, 1968), p. 221.
6. Derek Walcott, "Calypsonians! Danger Lurks in Tin Pan Alley", *Sunday Guardian* (Trinidad), 25 Feb. 1962, 23.
7. Derek Walcott, "Sparrow Shows Versatility in Range of Theme", *Sunday Guardian* (Trinidad), 26 Feb. 1960, 16.
8. The Mighty Sparrow, *The Slave,* LP National Calypso, NLP-4188, 1965.
9. Derek Walcott, "Alas! The Last Minute Road March is Gone", *Sunday Guardian* (Trinidad), 3 Feb. 1963, 4.
10. Derek Walcott, "Cheers For an Insincere Clown", *Sunday Guardian* (Trinidad), 30 Jan. 1964, p. 5.
11. "The Spoiler's Return", *The Fortunate Traveller* (London: Jonathan Cape, 1981), pp. 53-60; and in *Collected Poems 1948-1984* (New York: Farrar, Straus & Giroux, 1986), pp. 432-438.
12. Derek Walcott, "Every Politician Should Have a Cypher in his Back Pocket... The Clown Prince of Calypso Drops a Bomb", *Sunday Guardian* (Trinidad), 15 Jan. 1967, 4.
13. "Efficient 'Birdie', Minus the Feather Ruffling", *Guardian* (Trinidad), 6 Jan. 1965, 5.
14. "Its Our Own Kind of Artist Figure in the Panmen, the Steelbandman, the Calypsonian", *Sunday Guardian* (Trinidad), 5 Feb. 1967, 11.
15. See Gordon Rohlehr passim *A Scuffling of Islands: Essays on Calypso* (San Juan: Lexicon Trinidad, 2004), and on "Congo Mañ" in "Carnival Cannibalised or Cannibal Carnivalised: Contextualising the Cannibal Joke in Calypso and Literature", *Transgression, Transition, Transformation: Essays in Caribbean Culture* (San Juan: Lexicon Trinidad, 2004), pp. 50-81.
16. See C.L.R. James, "The Mighty Sparrow", *The Future in the Present* (London: Allison & Busby, 1977), pp. 191-201. Originally published in *Party Politics in the West Indies* (Port of Spain: Vedic Enterprises, (1962).

17. See Earl Lovelace, "Watch, Your Freedom is in Jeopardy" (1968), *Growing in the Dark; Selected Essays*. Ed. Funso Aiyejina (San Juan: Lexicon Trinidad, 2003), pp 65-67.
18. Raymond Quevedo, *Atilla's Kaiso: a Short History of Trinidad Calypso* (Trinidad: University of the West Indies, St. Augustine, [illegible]).
19. "Sparrow Shows Versatility in Range of Theme", *Sunday Guardian* (Trinidad), 26 Feb. 1960, 16.
20. [illegible], *Sunday Guardian* (Trinidad), [illegible] 1964, 13.
21. "Vintage Year for Calypso", *Sunday Guardian* (Trinidad), 16 Feb. 1966, 6.
22. "We Are Still Being Betrayed", Interview with Raoul Pantin, *Caribbean Contact*, 17 July 1973, 14.
23. Kaiso Man, "Laro 'Holes' Them at the OYB", *Guardian* (Trinidad), 10 Jan. 1967, 4.

Other articles by Walcott on Calypso

"A Fracas of Words and Music When Giants Meet", *Sunday Guardian* (Trinidad), 27 Jan. 1963, 4.
"Curious Mishmash of Style", *Guardian* (Trinidad), 12 Feb. 1964, 5.
"Dark Horses" *Sunday Guardian Magazine* (Trinidad), 29 Jan. 1967, 4.
"The Mighty Terror – A Great Matador – With a Cape and a Hangover", *Sunday Guardian* (Trinidad), 17 Jan. 1965, 3.
"Our Poetry in Song", *Sunday Guardian* (Trinidad), 9 Feb. 1964, 13.

JEAN ANTOINE DUNNE

"OVERTONES OF THE VISUAL IMAGINATION": OR "JUST LIKE THE MOVIES"

> For the territory upon which the poet visualizes a drama of consciousness is a slow revelation or unravelling of obscurity – revelation or illumination within oneself; whereas the territory of the dancer remains actually obscure to him within his trance whatever revelation or illumination his limbs may articulate in their involuntary theme. The 'vision' of the poet (when one comprehends it from the opposite pole of 'dance') possesses a 'spatial' logic or 'convertible' property of imagination. Herein lies the essential humility of a certain kind of self-consciousness within which occurs the partial erasure, if nothing more, of the habitual boundaries of prejudice.[1]

Wilson Harris's articulation of a "convertible" "spatial logic" of the imagination is a profoundly important idea for Caribbean art. His sense of overlapping forms, of fugitive spaces and sounds and the involuntary expression of secret knowledge and intuitions through exteriorization in space is one that has engaged writers of the Caribbean as a whole and may in fact, in some of its reverberations, account for the increasing tendency of our writers, including Brodber, Brathwaite, Walcott, and Harris himself to use Magic Realist forms. Harris is speaking here of the essential vision of the artist, but he is also speaking of Caribbean arts as existing on the threshold of body and spirit, mind and sense in a quite particular way. This "limbo" state is for Harris of particular relevance because of our history of fracture – and limbo in itself, in his writing, becomes an unconscious exteriorization of the Middle Passage and the god Anancy.

Harris is of course referring, in the passage quoted, to the process of re-membering in space via the movement of the body or through the creation of portals of experience. Exteriorisation in space enables an image of concrete reality, which opens the way to such re-membering and connection. Harris is also describing a problem of art and of the artistic imagination and its relation, on the one hand, to thought or abstraction and, on the other, to the need to figure artistic knowledge (secret and at times as in Harris barely fathomable) as a thing that is transmittable as a concrete image to the perceiver.[2]

In the mapping of space as a visual image of unconscious knowledge, the artist is creating a bridge between sensibilities, which is the creation of a form of relation between self and other that bypasses verbal language and the complication that often defies understanding. This depiction of [illegible] reverberations. These imagistic overtones use the body as a vehicle or channel of meaning and comprehension. I am interested in the creation of [illegible] forms, in particular film forms. Walcott's poetry is arguably dense, and the use of film forms enables a direct connection between poet and reader through the mobilisation of various sense projections that bypass cerebral thought. *Omeros*, through Seven Seas, articulates the poet's desire to transmit this visceral effect in the writing of a poem. Seven Seas sees "with his ears".[3] In him the senses become reversed or perhaps, more accurately, engender identical responses in the body; sound, touch, smell generate vibrations that are equal to and identical with sight. Through him Walcott describes a unity between man and nature, primarily through similes that further the concreteness of the projected idea. So, the blind Seven Seas feels "the sunlight creeping over his wrists" as "The sunlight moved like a cat along the palings/ of a sandy street" (*Omeros*, p. 12). Walcott will develop this mutuality and responsiveness of the body to nature more precisely through various means. Philoctete

> [...] felt the village through his back, heard the sea-hum
> of transports below. The sea-swift was watching him.
> Then it twittered seaward, swallowed in the cloud-foam. (*Omeros*, p. 22)

The projection of an idea through all the senses – sound, sight and tactility and even a sixth sense (the Caribbean idea that knowledge of a thing is felt along the body and makes the blood "creep") – shores up in the reader's mind the notion that the entire body is a vehicle of meaning in this work. The image of the wound, for example, that reverberates throughout the poem is echoed in the very shape of the poem's name, O-mer-os, and the various encircling Os that emanate from the mouths of Greek girl, Helen, and ground dove.

The use of the body as a purveyor of meaning may be found in many of Walcott's works, in his use of dance, in the metaphors and motifs of painting, drawing and hieroglyphs and in the sonic devices such as the conch shell. But what takes precedence in Walcott's later poetry is movement. Here movement becomes the vehicle for the production or release of subconscious levels of knowledge and experience, and counter-ideas that merge with the reality of the present moment of perception. This movement [illegible] to connect thought and memory and then the fugitive nature of art of which Harris speaks.

In movement, images of space create "bridges" between inner and outer reality, between past and present and between poetic and social concerns. They act as spatialised memory because the reader follows the tracks of remembering and the process of excavation. The history of the Caribbean is not something that can be accessed from easily available myths, but lies broken and submerged and the writer must excavate, very much like an archaeologist, to find these fragments.[4] In re-membering these fragments, the writer, the artist, creates a new architecture of the word as Harris intuits. For Walcott, in particular from *The Fortunate Traveller* onward and most clearly evident in *Omeros*, *Tiepolo's Hound* and *The Prodigal*, this reconstruction is a graphing through spatial imagery of the contours of Antillean experience.

The idea of space, therefore, is crucial to the understanding of the connections between Walcott and Harris. Space takes several forms. It may be imagined as a spiral. In this Walcott is seeking to give shape to his conception of the web of connections that exist over time. These spirals attach themselves to images, most of which derive from earlier work, such as the faeces of a dog which become transformed into the cruciform shape of the coral in *Omeros*. Walcott's account of how Philoctete's story is transmitted is the most cogent example of the development of this practice. Philoctete refuses to tell his tale to the tourist because it "worth more than a dollar" (*Omeros*, p. 4). So in the poem:

> He has left it to a garrulous waterfall
> to pour out his secret down La Sorcière, since
> the tall laurels fell, for the ground-dove's mating call
>
> to pass on its note to the blue, tacit mountains
> whose talkative brooks, carrying it to the sea,
> turn into idle pools where the clear minnows shoot
>
> and an egret stalks the reeds with one rusted cry
> as it stabs and stabs the mud with one lifting foot.
> Then silence is sawn in half by a dragonfly (*Omeros*, p. 4)

In these verses if we read them to the end, we have the development of a moving line that maps the contours of Antillean history and landscape and traces the social history of the place, its loss, its submerged memories and the history to be found in the very landscape and sounds of a place. The process is similar to the movement of fragments in the opening sequence of the film script version of this poem (Fisher Library, Ms. 1995) where the camera stitches together in a line the place, the action, the language of a particular memory of the past and, in so doing, evokes a specific multi-dimensional sensuous apprehension of what that part of history signified and how it impacted on the psyche of the poet as young boy.

The verses of the poem are seeking to map the landscape and merge that map with an actual hidden history and to make that mapping in itself the vehicle through which the various silent and submerged lives and experi- [illegible] [illegible] brooks and the sea and the "O" of the ground dove. The stabbing feet of the egret trace the event and if we look closely we see that these verses, as an [illegible] process of the entire poem.[5] *Omeros* seeks to bring repressed and silenced memories of a particular place to the surface and to demonstrate that the body carries such memories in its responses. The body of the black women of St Lucia are primary images of such cultural memory in their dignified carriage and in the memories they evoke in the poet of resilience and contained suffering. The script for the as yet unmade film version significantly places the images of black St Lucian women climbing up the steps of the ships with coal balanced on their heads at the very beginning of the action.

In the opening shot of the film script, the rhythmic movement of the camera across the landscape is linked to the movement of women. This rhythmic movement unites the narrator's history, the history of the women and the history of the island:

> (EXT. Sunrise. The island. Sepia. Close in on the PITONS, then its valleys and mountains. Travel the coastline.
> CUT
> (EXT. From the coaling ship: a view of the town, circa 1938, the women working. Pan to take in the roofs, the hills. The figures in white drill of tally clerks.
> CUT
> (EXT. A chant. Drummer and WOMEN'S VOICES. Sepia monochrome. Day. Close-up. The bare feet of women, sometimes showing under dingy skirts, crusted with coal-dust, climbing a gangway to a chant that sometimes breaks off from exhaustion.
> CUT
> (EXT. Long shot. A huge mound of anthracite coal close to the gang-plank. Another structure along which the women walk, balancing the filled baskets which they empty into the hold of the ship.)
> CUT
> (Ext. Montage of moving, ascending feet.
> Faces calmly straining under the weight.
> Descending feet.) Their rhythm.[6]

One needs to note the musical accompaniment to the visual, and the actual movements in the breaks and the timing and the tempo of the shots as well as the rhythm of the moving feet.

This opening movement echoes Walcott's statement in *Omeros* that he is seeking to mimic the form and the memory of the black women of St

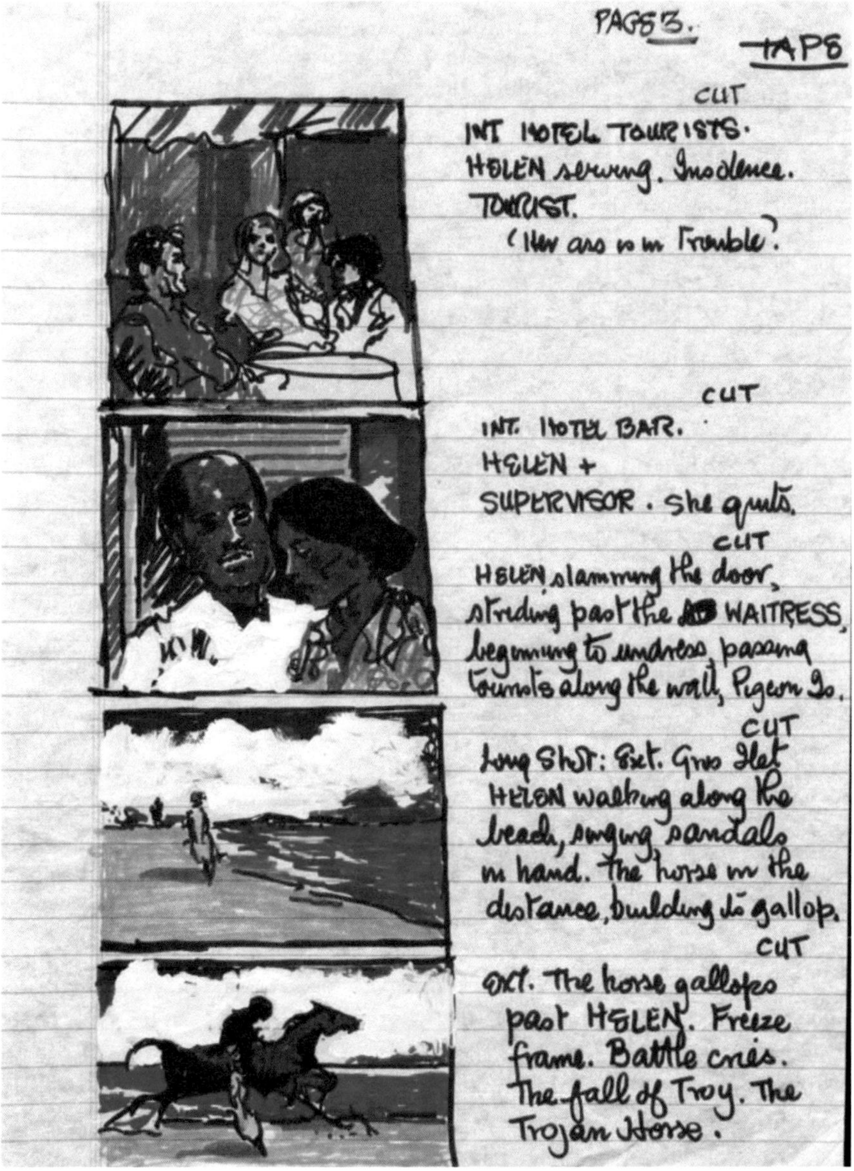
PAGE 3.
CUT
INT HOTEL TOURISTS.
HELEN serving. Insolence.
TOURIST.
CUT
INT. HOTEL BAR.
HELEN +
SUPERVISOR. She quits.
CUT
HELEN slamming the door, striding past the WAITRESS, beginning to undress, passing tourists along the wall, Pigeon Is.
CUT
Long Shot: Ext. Gros Ilet
HELEN walking along the beach, swinging sandals in hand. The horse in the distance, building to gallop.
CUT
EXT. The horse gallops past HELEN. Freeze frame. Battle cries. The fall of Troy. The Trojan Horse.

Lucia in the creation of this work. One can say that his desire in "Cul de Sac Valley" to "echo this settlement" and recreate the asymmetrical shape of the shacks and to enable the resonant creole to "curl at my foot"[7] finds resolution here:

[illegible]
and walk up that coal ladder as they do in time,
one bare foot after the next in ancestral rhyme.

[illegible]
shielding a candle's tongue, it is the language's
desire to enclose the loved world in its arms;

or heft a coal-basket; only by its stages
like those groaning women will you achieve that height
whose wooden planks in couplets lift your pages
[…]
[…]They walk, you write; (*Omeros*, p. 75)

The film script creates a specific rhythm through the movement of the camera and the movement of the edited pieces and shapes a spiral that graphs time and memory as a circling back and a movement forward. The oscillations in time within the poem, *Omeros*, create a similar tracking of events from the recent past (Philoctete's cure), the distant past (African enslavement and ensnarement and the death of the Sioux Indians) as well as the ancient past (the siege of Troy). The caesuras are very significant here. They are spelt out at specific times as in the transitional section which begins, "Change burns at the beach's end" (*Omeros*, p. 34) and that includes "[…] In that pause/ that divides the smoke with a sword, white Helen died; / in that space between the lines of two lifted oars, / her shadow ambles" (p. 34). These caesuras mark the leaps from one dimension of time to another and also act as visual metaphors to suggest the gaps in memory that need to be bridged. These six lines of Ch. VI. 11 (p. 34) bring all these moments of time together as successive leaps – the continuing oppression of the black St Lucian through tourism, Helen's refusal to take "shit from white people and some of them tourist" (p. 33) that becomes a rebellion; the merging of that leap with the transformation into myth that aligns black Helen with the Greek Helen and also resonates with Yeats's use of Helen to depict Maud Gonne in "No Second Troy".[8] The smoke that divides also brings to this spatialisation of the past the buried memory of the native Indian and recalls the Sioux, the Caribs, the Aruacs and all those who once inhabited this space and have "gone up like smoke". This recurring image of the original peoples as ephemeral presence is part of that evocation of a buried series of pasts that [illegible] and that suggest [illegible] of history. The word "change", therefore, suggests a kinetic power that enacts a leap out of a closed cycle through imaginative recreation.

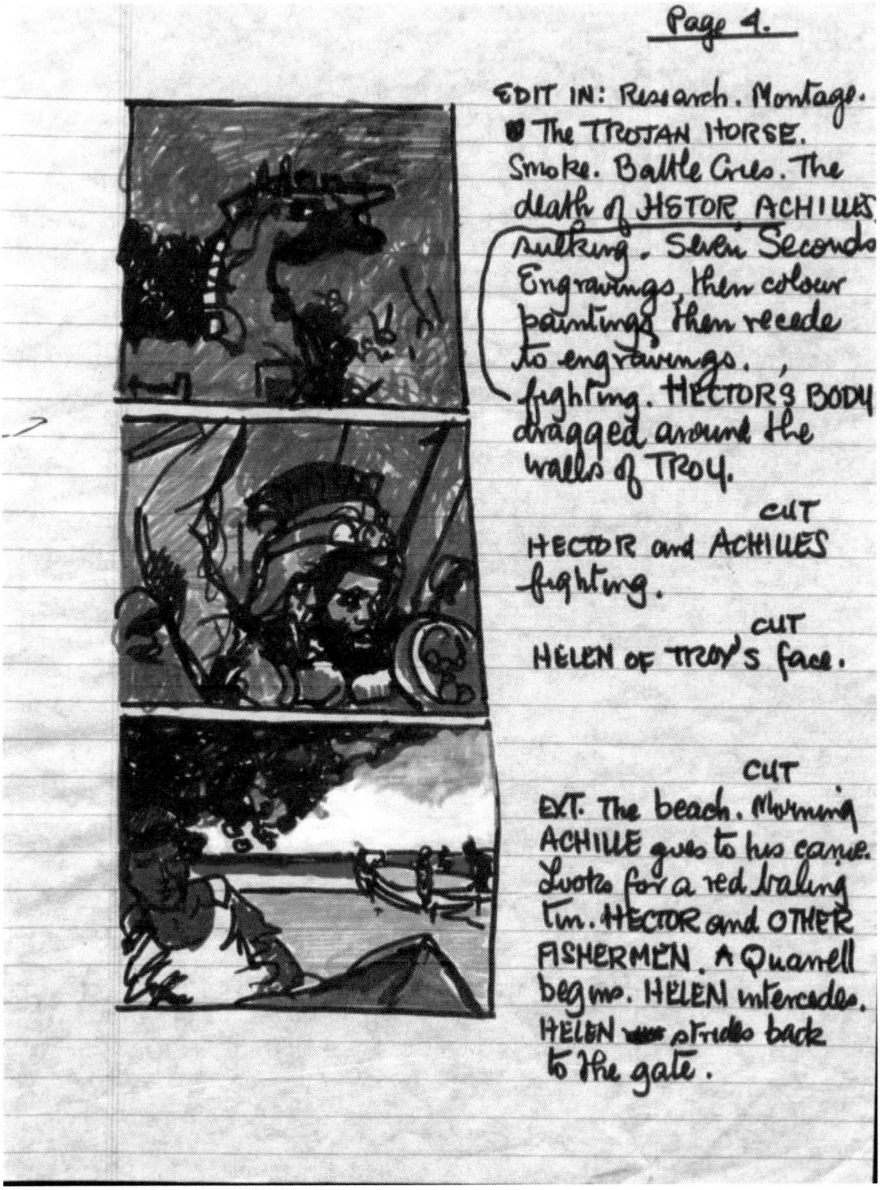
Page 4.
EDIT IN: Research. Montage.
The TROJAN HORSE.
Smoke. Battle Cries. The
death of HECTOR. ACHILLES
sulking. Seven Seconds
Engravings, then colour
paintings then recede
to engravings.
fighting. HECTOR'S BODY
dragged around the
walls of TROY.
CUT
HECTOR and ACHILLES
fighting.
CUT
HELEN OF TROY'S face.
CUT
EXT. The beach. Morning
ACHILLE goes to his canoe.
Looks for a red bailing
tin. HECTOR and OTHER
FISHERMEN. A Quarrell
begins. HELEN intercedes.
HELEN strides back
to the gate.

The movement of the various sequences of the work *Omeros*, the telling of the tale, the showing of the wounds of history, the cure, the various re-windings of the past as mirage or shadow, the parallel stories, the lines of colour, the many voices and the constant play of sound from the sound of [illegible] virtue of the fact that they shape a spiral. Through a process of intercutting and the creation of a particular ideational line, these verses elicit a number of responses at many levels on the reader – in particular on the level of seeing and hearing. They create overtones. What I mean by overtones is the multiplicity of meaning and evocation that takes on a life of its own and seems to call to other meanings. The use of echoes in this work is both a structuring idea and an image. It is based on the principle of association where images call to other images and is a key technique in classical cinema. The poem by the use of concrete imagery aligned to sound, by its utilisation of sense apparatus to generate reverberations in the psyche, beckons to the past and makes it emerge in the present space of the poem and the imagination. This past includes the past of the poet, his past works and the collective or communal past.

The closest analogy to what Walcott is seeking to do here may be found in Beckett whose *Not I*,[9] for example, emits a similar form of resounding echoes through the juxtaposition of vision and sound (sound emerging through the mouth as the externalisation of an "inner scream"[10] and the visual receiver in the auditor). Here the play or conflict of sound and the visual sets up a resonance in the seer/auditor. This effect is a direct result of the rhythm and pace of the utterance of mouth and the structure of the visuals. What Beckett is doing is transmitting the pain of the woman's desire to communicate through the interplay of sight and sound. This is emphasised in the monologue through the oppositions of the words "buzzing" and "beam". The buzzing as discordant sound is concretised in the actual movement of the mouth as it is shrouded in darkness and isolated in its light and in its projection of a state of intense suffering and agitation. The sound that emerges from mouth is also a form of "buzzing" because of the pace and the clipped expression. This suggests that words mean nothing – it is the emotion that matters and that must be transmitted to the audience. The beam of light is then the signifying mechanism as in *Play*. What emerges is a sense of the particular impact of the whole as it triggers a series of memories or perceptions both within the protagonist and in the viewer who is made to experience the actual pain of the breakdown of communication. Or again this process may be seen in a very graphic play such as *Breath*[11] where the whole of the human condition is traced in the movement of a spiral on stage through which humanity's rubbish is figured. Beckett traces a complete graph of time, a spiral and organic movement and death, life beginning and ending, from birth to dust (or the detritus that litters our passage). Indeed Beckett's *Trilogy*[12] provides a good entry into the successive movements of Walcott's late poem *The Prodigal*[13] since both can be graphed as a series of circles in search of origin or the "Worm" of being and that map parallel movements.

In *The Unnamable* Beckett's search is for silence that goes beyond reason and beyond words. The movement traced by the I narrator here is in a circle towards a perception of self beyond words and beyond reason. And this narrator is in accord with Molloy who recognises that "when a man in a forest thinks he is going forward in a straight line, in reality he is going in a circle" so that he does his "best to go in a circle, hoping in this way to go in a straight line. For I stopped being half-witted and became sly, whenever I took the trouble. And my head was a storehouse of useful knowledge. And if I did not go in a rigorously straight line, with my system of going in a circle, at least I did not go in a circle, and that was something" (*Molloy,* in *Three Novels*, p. 85). All this, of course, in *Molloy* in search of his mother whose androgynous figure equates with those other bodies that generate patterns in *Watt*[14] or *Murphy*[15] or in many of the prose pieces and plays such as *Footfalls*[16] and *Quad.*[17] This quest as in *Play*[18] goes beyond death and beyond the body, an idea repeated over and over again in the three novels of *The Trilogy* and that culminates in:

> Perhaps Mahood will emerge from his urn and make his way towards Montmartre, on his belly, singing, I come, I come, my heart's delight. Or Worm, good old Worm, perhaps he won't be able to bear any more, of not being able, of not being able to bear any more, it would be a pity to miss that (p. 371).

Movement is constant and goes beyond the grave, though the characters and the events while moving also repeat themselves and form a pattern that is a graphic mapping of a particular human condition and in particular an articulation and interrogation of the relationship between the solipsistic self and those whom he encounters. Part of the process of many of Beckett's works and Walcott's *The Prodigal* is, then, the creation of a series of patterns that suggests the similarity with, or the parallel nature of events over time. Ultimately life is a series of repeated events, shaped by the incapacity to see more clearly than "visibility permits" (*The Unnamable,* p. 297). The question then arises as to whether time, old age or history can ever change the relationships between human beings. But neither Walcott nor Beckett end in despair, nor do they suggest a closed circle. Part of the process of interrogating such human concerns and transgressing the traditional limits of art is to be found in the incorporation of lessons learnt from film.

It would seem that from the 1970s onwards, perhaps due to the aborted projects of *Vangelo Nero*[19] and the rather unsuccessful filming of *The Rig*[20] and *The Haytian Earth,*[21] Walcott has been occupied with the problem of evoking the multiple effects of history and the competing influences on language and literature in Caribbean writing through a quite specific use of visual and more exactly filmic forms in poetry itself. *The Fortunate Traveller* as a collection articulates these problems in a particularly lucid way and the [illegible] [illegible] pretty much sums up Walcott's problem as an artist and would-be film-maker in the cynical voice of the producer: "and we can keep all the/ [illegible] on keeping it tend-/ er, I can see it. But things must get rough/ pretty damn fast, or else you lose them, pally".[23] The emotions and the self reflection generated by poetry appear here to be antithetical to the dramatic requirements of film. The poet opposes the lonesome figure of the protagonist to the demands of an external audience and exoticised images of the islands and identifies the ways in which the islands have been seen, commodified and exploited by foreign image makers. Filmmaking as a process of selecting particular elements to "sell" an idea is linked to tourism and the tourist gaze. The poet plays on the notion of movement, in this way setting up an idea that film is essentially an art of the moving image. Movement here, however, is cause for suspicion and connected to "that tired artifice called history,/ which in its motion is as false as fiction" (*The Fortunate Traveller*, p. 38; *Collected Poems*, p. 421). But this caustic critique of the filmic here provides only one viewpoint; Walcott will later and in other works exploit the capacity of film to generate emotion in quite complex and direct ways, through the utilisation of the combined impact of sound and visual as a vehicle for creating new and potent images.

Tiepolo's Hound,[25] interestingly enough, explores the relationship between sound and the visual through an exploration of painting and the thrall of museums and books on painting, and in many ways is an elaboration of *Another Life*.[24] But something different happens in *Tiepolo* since Walcott by 2000 had already experimented quite substantially in film. *Tiepolo's Hound* relates painting to writing and seeks to map what Walcott perceives as the tropical spirit through the figure of a loping black mongrel "A mongrel follows them, black as its shadow,/ nosing their shadows, scuttling when the bells// exult with pardon" (*Tiepolo's Hound*, p. 4). This black figure is simplified in a manner similar to the black ants in women walking with loads of coal on their heads in *Omeros* and indeed in *Another Life* and shows the entire journey from the Caribbean to Europe (St Thomas to Paris) and from Trinidad to the museums of the world.

More pertinently, *Tiepolo's Hound* enables a specific play of light and shadow through the image (among others) of the white hound, the search for a flash of pink on a hound's thigh and the juxtaposition of the shadow of this black mongrel. *Tiepolo's Hound* engages in audio-visual play by making light the source of movement. This play of light and shadow elicits profound commentaries about the nature of the artist's relationship to European art and to classical traditions. As light it is reminiscent of the passage of phantasmal light in "The Season of Phantasmal Peace" that lifts the shadows of the world[25] – but it also generates phantoms: first the poet through self-doubt goes in search of a spectral white hound and a flash of light; a search that leads to the recognition of the exclusion of the black from metropolitan art, but that also emphasises his endurance and service as a dedicated poet. This artistic fortitude has effected a change in the recognition bestowed on those who originate in these islands and in Walcott himself.[26]

The use of light also enables an illusionary force field through which the poet can be translated into a newly freed slave in the St Thomas of the nineteenth century. This trick of light and its phantom leap creates several connections. As a vehicle of fiction it underlines the fictional nature of the quest for the white hound and suggests that the poet never took this quest seriously anyway. His return as a ghost to St Thomas becomes a form of imaginative reparation, one might say, but also a way of forging a connection with the past as memory, destiny and prophesy. He is, therefore, through his transformation into a phantom, at one with that slave and can now chastise Pissarro with a kind of self-righteous virtue and berate him for his doubt and failure to do what he, Walcott, still seeks to do: to record and write the Antilles.

Finally, the return to St Thomas asserts the falsity of a certain light or way of seeing the self. The play of light and the search for that flash of pink have yielded a truth – that we carry our light with us, that our perceptions shape how we see, that Pissarro (true or not) taught the Old World to see through his light, despite the fact that he never really had faith in himself as an Antillean artist. The use of light is then a mechanism for generating echoes. These reverberate and enable the flow of past and present time. They work in tandem with the overarching structure of time as a circle generating not a closed end but the possibility of a new beginning.

In the poem *Omeros* this light is refracted in several ways and moves the poet and his alter ego, Achille, to Africa to reconsider problems of origin and in particular the centrality of African tradition. In the telling of several tales, Walcott suggests that history itself must be seen in a new light. The world of nature is given a particular dominance from the onset of the work through the dawn that acts as an opening and a way of seeing. The darkness that envelops Achille, as he succumbs to a form of erasure or death at sea in the hurricane, is a movement into the darkness of the cavern of history. His emergence is into light that is a metaphor for a new beginning, and a new culture evoked through dance and the rituals of carnival.

The use of light suggests that the multiple events of the past have led to a form of synthesis and the emergence of a syncretic culture. In the tale told of the gods having a fete (*Omeros*, pp. 51–54) the natural elements merge and the folktale that results is a combination of African and Greek myth within a context that evolves from Caribbean encounters with nature. The elemental here refers us back to Walcott's approval and mimicking of John Millington Synge's *Riders to the Sea*, and the idea that life lived at the edge and in constant confrontation with the elements, in particular the sea, leads to the creation of something that is sublime and of the stuff of myth. What [illegible] Ogun, Lightning, Ma Kaln, Erzulie, Neptune and Damballa" is its unification of *Omeros* as a whole, in that the hurricane brings a "freshness" that resonates on several levels: a fresh people; a fresh land; a fresh fable. Walcott's use of the folk fable, traditionally recited in skeleton form to most Caribbean children when thunder and lightning occur, seeks to convey an idea that the land and its people share common memories and effects and these memories, as stories, emerge out of the confrontation with the elements and are shaped as stories by the historic encounter of different cultures and belief systems. This idea is repeated throughout the text as a whole. Its repetition in various forms underlines the significance of the filmic dimension of this work, since Walcott's use of film montage hinges on his understanding of the impact of the resonance of repeated lines and images throughout a work, and the impact that such recurring patterns induce in the body of the reader or the viewer. The multifaceted events of the past and the variegated versions of history are echoing patterns in the New World psyche and these influences add up to a peculiar type of movement, one that is accessed at an unconscious level by the artist. The poem *Omeros* suggests that all of these forces lead to the transformation of culture or, to put it another way, shape a "moving" island and a "moving" people. There is no stasis but perpetual changes that affect both the recipient of culture and the facets of culture that have been absorbed by those who live in the Caribbean and the Americas as a whole.

Walcott's film version of Achille's movement back to Africa led by the swift, which the poem repeats "the size of an hourglass, every twitter an accent from which a horizon climbed in the upturned vase" (*Omeros*, p. 189), illuminates this in quite specific ways. In one version of the film script (Fisher Library Ms 1995) Hector's death is intercut with a multi-dimensional re-winding of history. The film script superimposes Hector onto the dead slaves killed by Achille in Africa (*Omeros* Ms, p. [illegible]). This is [illegible] layering of processes of African enslavement over what Walcott considers to be neo-enslavement, that is tourism. This seems in opposition to the poem, *Omeros*, where Hector's death is intercut with images of African [illegible] and imperialism, as well as images of the Trojan war. These images must also be viewed, however, as echoes of neo-enslavement as well as neo-colonialism as the poem cuts to scenes familiar to tourists:

> Cut to a leopard galloping on a dry plain
> across Serengeti. Cut to the spraying fans
> drummed by a riderless stallion, its wild mane
>
> scaring the Scamander. (*Omeros*, p. 230).

Hector becomes "the double" (Omeros Ms 1995 p. 166) of a slave trader in the film script and is slain by Achille:

> CUT
>
> (EXT. Day. Smoke, a burning wall. A chariot racing with ACHILLES driving, and HECTOR's body being dragged around the walls. ACHILLES screams up to the Trojans. The voices are doubled, the images superimposed on the black ACHILLE and the Greek ACHILLES. To drums now African, now Greek.) (*Omeros* TS, 1995, p. 167).

The artist here achieves a quite overt sense of the simultaneity of Greek, African and Antillean history and myth through the use of superimposition which allows the viewer to see events from three eras happening at the same time (out of time). These become equivalent because the actions that lead to death are born of similar passions: anger, lust, betrayal. The film script enables this impact of the carnal nature of human existence in a way that the poem gestures towards. The narrator in the poem says that a girl smells sweeter than a book; he does not mean to say that St Lucia is like Greece, but rather that people in St Lucia and Greece share the same human carnal nature and it is from this carnality that myth springs. What the film script does is to graph these passions onto the concrete world that is being denoted and to suggest that there are deep resemblances, but also differences. These differences are to be found in the re-membering or re-construction of the particles that are on "show". A pattern of similarities and differences begins to emerge through which a particular visual line full of contradictory meanings and associations gives off multiple resonances to the reader or the viewer. The movement of Achille back to Africa in the film script takes on the beat of memory through the incursion of various lines of memory from different pasts, of myth and of buried history. So that the actual movement of the shots, their oscillation, repeats the pulsations of a painful and fitful recall of the past made complex by other memories that are superimposed on the memory of Africa and of being sold by slave traders.

This pattern of cyclical atrocity we also find in Harris's and in Brathwaite's work, where repetition reveals that enslavement is a manifestation of human evil and that from the point of view of history, European and African and New World individuals share memories of such shameful encounters. The patterns that unfold in *Omeros*, as poem and as film, are a form of mapping in space for it is through the visualization of these experiences, their realization on the screen, that we see such patterns emerging, and a new concept of history that refuses either revenge or remorse occurs.

In creating these filmic sequences (and I have chosen them because in [illegible] Walcott is not simply attaching the rhythm of film to the poem, but engaging with certain philosophical ideas that film theorists have worked with for the past [illegible] for both Beckett and Walcott, who have been each in their individual way caught up in the sense of the mundane and the repetitive. For Beckett life is burdened by the accretions of history; language is dulled by the meanings that have accrued through usage. For Walcott the mere fact of his indebtedness to old civilisations is baggage that he must on the one hand seek to jettison, yet must of necessity embrace. Repetition, the revolving of it all, is a fact of Caribbean art; the Caribbean cannot escape its constant fingering of the past for it is burdened by the received notion that it has no true core of being and is merely a copy or mimic. Film endows the idea of repetition and reproduction with a new potential. It suggests that in the clash of [poetic] images and in the patterning that can be imposed on language there is a capacity for the new and a possibility of illuminating the past by making it visible from new perspectives.

This re-volving of time is also inextricably linked in Walcott's work to the cross of intersection. This emerges as an image – and structuring principle – in the repeated crosses and cruciform shapes in the poem. The cross is of course mathematically the beginnings of a graph of a spiral and the spiral is the graph of organic growth and transformation. The whole poem moves to this idea of change emerging as a developmental or evolutionary process that enables new life to emerge from the darkness of death and nothingness. The O as graph of this hollowness, which is nothing and plenitude (both nothing and everything), enables Walcott to suggest that the Caribbean as denuded space can begin anew. This O is an opening, a cavern, or a place within which echoes emerge (the OOOOs of the dove). It is passage and mouth and grave. It signifies the spiral of filmic discourse whereby in placing two opposing fragments in a montage line, and by repeating this pattern, the film artist enables a leap to the new.

Pattern as Revolution

The O as nothing and everything is the chasm or hole that unleashes the revolutionary potential of poetry through its refusal of the very idea of emptiness or void. How can there be nothing? What is the vacuum that cannot be filled? What are the holes in the eyes of the beggar in *The Mask of the Beggar* (2005)[40] but spaces through which the poet inserts himself and like Ulysses escapes the monodic eye of the Cyclops? This revolutionary movement is, as Harris says, both circular and linear.

In a filmic sense, every projection by its passage in time becomes new: new meanings are shaped through the individual experiences and memories of the individual viewer. The very structure of filmic montage is a revolutionary process since it generates a change in how we perceive any specific image or event. The fact of bringing events from different times and places into the present of perception, as in the various lines of images in *Omeros*, or *Steel*,[29] to name two obvious examples from Walcott's work, means that the spectator can attain a revolutionary perception of these events through their enactment or re-volution in space. The idea of transformative vision or revolution is therefore a central concern in Walcott's use of the principle of montage. Walcott examines the idea of revolution as social transformation in *Omeros* and in a film script entitled *To Die for Grenada*.[30] Here he interrogates the idea of revolution through a spatial linear journey through Greece, Trinidad, New York and Grenada. He is seeking correspondences in an attempt to understand the impulse of revolution that he seems on the one hand to admire, while also conscious of the dangers of revolutionary processes. In the script which chronicles the betrayals that led to the murder of Maurice Bishop and the American invasion in Grenada, Bishop's congeniality appears to be a mask and as a revolutionary leader he seems to have become frozen in attitudes of comradeship by the very fact of the success of his revolutionary position. The attempt to find a correspondence with the 1970 Black Power Revolution in Trinidad yields a form of prophecy that goes beyond mere similarities. Max/Hanif the Muslim lawyer is a friend of Maurice Bishop and he heads a coup in Trinidad (this is written between 1983 and 1987 and the 1990 attempted coup, led by the Jamaat al-Muslimeen, in Trinidad and Tobago had not yet happened). Max is beheaded. Bishop is executed and burnt. Their mutual fate links them in a spiral of death that releases the ambivalence to death and revolution that one also finds in "The Star-Apple Kingdom"[31] in the Woman of Revolution.

In *The Prodigal* this revolutionary fervour breeds death in the woman who is a soldier. It evokes the continuity of historic atrocity and equally allows the possibility of twin realities, which may be their opposites. So angels fall along the slopes of the Alps, but are part of the heavenly bliss of Santa Cruz and the excited cries of children. Of course the re-volving nature of Walcott's encounter with death in *The Prodigal* is part of that confrontation with death as an inevitable passage. This we know is part of his mourning for his brother Roddy. What the conflicting images of death unleash – as a small city in my head; as an act of atrocity that I read about in the papers; or as a stench beneath the calm majestic beauty of European landscapes and cities – is an idea of life as a journey to somewhere else: a trip to heaven or a leap to a form of spiritual encounter that while mediated through the brilliance of colour and sound is, nonetheless, a transcendence of the actual. It is also a leap from quantity to quality and from concrete image to concept.

Tunnels

The Prodigal yields another form of patterning. It begins with a filmic image where the book and reading signal movement within the [illegible]. He [illegible] that the [illegible] is carried in "calm parallels" (*The Prodigal*, p. 3) and is linked to a European tradition of textuality. By the second stanza of that section that tradition is inexorably yoked to "Nothing" and "Nobody" the words that begin that stanza – in this way creating connections with the play of nobodies and nothings that have been part of Walcott's repertoire (and conversation with Naipaul) for many decades. Most specifically, it links his work to *The Arkansas Testament* when his identification with the plight of the African American Black leads to his self-recognition that "I was still nothing. A cipher/ in its bubbling black zeros, here"[15] which, by the end of that work, has opened the way to a light that potentially contains a new way of seeing. In *Omeros* that O/0 has multiple contradictory meanings that reverberate in their chiming to access the deep reverberations that shape his relationship with places like Ireland with its echoing glens and lakes, but which he none the less acknowledges in *Omeros* hide the atrocity of civil war.

What he foregrounds in the very first two stanzas of *The Prodigal* is the tunnel vision that has shaped this conception of the Caribbean as nothing. I use the word shape because there is a [illegible] occurring across the work that uses the filmic as a vehicle for two contradictory impulses: one of parallelism leading to the empty space between two lines and the other a movement leading to tunnels or holes. There are several moving lines in *The Prodigal*: the river, the moving train, the movement of time and the movement of language. As this movement proceeds and as the book "sleeps", a tunnel overwhelms the perception of reader and seer. These moving lines or parallels shape that tunnel. The lines depict the tunnel vision of the eye of those who appear and see themselves as quite separate from the "he" whose black skin [illegible] a form of tunnelling (*The Prodigal*, p. 3) "through which" "they entered the idea of America" (*The Prodigal*, p. 3). Within this tunnel (real and ideological) [illegible] glide as "un" familiar spirits locked in thought, serene though "gripped", a word substitute for "clenched" that yields intention and therefore culpability already associated in this burgeoning line of images that lead one into the other, (carefully chosen for their ideational content), to the "[illegible]" and the "toothless" (*The Prodigal*, p. 4) both signifying as in *The Fortunate Traveller* the ideogrammatical nature of Walcott's imagery.

Writing ZERO

The whole of *The Prodigal* is of course a journeying through the tunnel of time, forcing movement to give up echoes that meet other echoes and create new images and ideas. The repetition of "no" ensures the negative response of the reader and also demands that this "no" is part of "seeing": "Look at that man looking from the stalled window" (*The Prodigal*, p. 4). It is seeing on its own without availing of the other acute ways of gaining knowledge, as is demonstrated in *Omeros*, that leads to monodic perception or to put it more aptly to "tunnel vision".

This flow of lost time now emerges as synonymous with another form of "gliding" already conjoined to ghostly presences. The accumulation of echoes through the tunnel of time as a narrow passage entered into and moving enables the leap to "terror" or the sublime. Through the idea of a passage over "the levelled surface of elegiac earth" (*The Prodigal*, p. 4) (no coincidence that the "levelling" evokes destruction) the accumulated echoes merge or more accurately cause a superimposition of childhood images. The important idea is contained in this "sentence" of the third stanza that lasts fifteen lines and has the identical effect of the non-differentiated flow of images in Joyce's *Ulysses*,[33] when Molly Bloom in her nocturnal thoughts remembers her lovers. Images flow one after the other, each linked by an identical idea of lost time each shaping the tunnel movement of echoing memory and thereby emitting overtones into the mind and body.

It is an evocation of "a child's delight in motion,/ the lines and parallels and smoky arches/ of unread famous novels" (*The Prodigal*, p. 5). But what the poem is setting up is movement that allows the literary influences, childhood memory and received ideas of Europe to move in parallel lines towards a particular effect. Moving in time that is no longer the present tense yields a number of negatives or fictions. The negative is linked to the subject's childhood so that having none of the visions or visual artefacts of Europe has led to *his* tunnel vision, despite the fairy tales of memory; but what the traveller now dreams has already been undermined by sadness, alienation (no one waves) and a history of imperial and colonial savagery. Other memories or prior knowledge constitute a line in the development of the narrative, but these also become prophetic in terms of the images that are echoed later on in the poem.

By page sixty-two, that concretization of experience has led to a definitive statement of what is happening in the poem. Here "The blank page grows a visionary wood" where a "whole province" stands where "it has always stood" on "the right-hand margin of the page" where deep echoes rooted in time proceed through the "tunnel of the right ear", but also contradictorily on "my left hand another vegetation/ but not their opposite or their enemy,/ palms and wild fern and praising them, the sea" (*The Prodigal*, pp. 62-63). Of course, one needs to remember that in *The Fortunate* [illegible] the blank page is a space of inscription after the poet has yanked the putrid tooth of language and released the possibility of a hieroglyphic language where he can write "the sound for sea and the sign for 'sun'".[illegible] The landscape itself in *The Prodigal* [illegible] that he too should jettison the smoke of comparison, as in *Omeros*: "Why not see Helen//as the sun saw her, with no Homeric shadow,/swinging her [illegible] smoke a door!" (*Omeros*, p. 271).

The prodigal returning to claim his inheritance, having spent his fortune and perhaps having wasted his time and talent (in the service of international reputation), is still faced ultimately with a choice: to claim here or elsewhere. To place the Caribbean as second to some grand image or figure or, alternatively, see it for what it is. More pertinently, should one be satisfied with being here and not give in to the desire or yearning to be elsewhere? Interestingly the dramatization of this argument (*The Prodigal*, p. 78) is conceived as a play of sight and sound not unlike the visual play of say the death of Hector in *Omeros*:

> "I see."
> "No, you don't see, you're being stubborn."
> "Maybe when I get there I'll see."
> "It will change your life."
> "I like my life."
> 'You think here is enough?"
> "For me it is."
> "Fine."
> "Anyway I can see Martinique from here."
> (*The Prodigal*, pp. 78–79)

The outcome of this argument is completely filmic – a reproduction or a print that actually can move and therefore opposes the fixity of the photographic already implicit at the very start of *Omeros*.

> [...] O prodigal
> your momentary statue made by a traffic light
> on that sunlit corner across from the newspaper kiosk
> where the glass bank prints your transient reflection,
> [illegible] (*The Prodigal*, p. [illegible])

This is an assertion of the transience of Caribbean art and a celebration of the O that throughout the poetry as a whole is suggestive of the lack of a written or permanent art that in the dawning of *Omeros* opens the reader to the potential of perpetual new beginnings. It harks back to that moment with which the poem opens, an oral tale that reverberates across space, and that is uttered with an awareness of the need to hold back something from the fixing gaze of tourist and coloniser, what

Glissant has called "opacity".[35] This refusal (or perhaps inability to be fixed) is the result of multiple influences, but also a resistance strategy as in the art of carnival. Being recorded in books, as Harris suggests in *Mask of the Beggar*, can be a type of death. The "O" represented as an opening through which echoes emerge, as a representation of nothing and everything (the aperture as beginning; the yawning gap, in particular of the Middle Passage and the History of the Caribbean, as emptiness), enables the two sides of possibility and impossibility to emerge – both equally viable. But in this rewriting of Antillean history that is *Omeros*, the transient elements of the Caribbean aesthetic become reflections of the constantly moving nature of the Caribbean – its refusal of stasis. *Omeros* is an inscription of the changing nature of our relationships with each other, and an inscription that can only be mapped via the route of the visual and the sonic in accord with each other. For it is in the use of all senses and in the deployment of memory stored in oral narratives and forms alongside other modes of production, that memory in all its manifest forms can be engaged. Film, in its capacity to bring together past and present, to spatialise thought and emotion and to make ideas concrete, provides the structuring principle upon which Walcott builds an image of the Antilles in its unfixed and constantly transforming reality.

In summation, the idea of filmic movement provides a new conception of the ways in which the visual can become more than itself in its plasticity; for it is only when things move that they attain a malleability that allows both a real and an imagined world to exist simultaneously. What film does ultimately and effectively is to provide a form and a language through which Walcott's early recognition of the importance of myth and the transformation of history and experience into myth is realized. Cinematic form accessed as movement or moving images and lines enables that illusionary journeying in space and time and the reformulation of events across time and space so that multiple stories, truths and realities appear on the surface of space. In so doing space takes on the magic of evocation: ghosts, alternative histories, buried knowledge. These become "the territory upon which the poet visualizes a drama of consciousness [as] a slow revelation or unravelling of obscurity – revelation or illumination within [the self]".[36]

Endnotes

1. Wilson Harris, *Tradition, the Writer and Society* [1967] (London: New Beacon, 1970), p. 52.
2. Mary Lou Emery, *Modernism and the Visual in Caribbean Literature* (Cambridge: Cambridge University Press, 2007).

3. Derek Walcott, *Omeros* (London: Faber and Faber, 1990), p. 11.
4. See Wilson Harris, *Tradition the Writer and Society*.
5. See "Derek Walcott in Conversation with Jean Antoine", *Poetry Ireland Review* 34 (Spring 1992): 72-85.
6. [illegible] revisions and inserts throughout. The Thomas Fisher Library, The University of Toronto, p. 1.
7. [illegible] 1987), p. 9.
8. William Butler Yeats, "No Second Troy", *Collected Poems* (London: MacMillan & Co., Second Edition, reprinted 1967), p. 101.
9. Samuel Beckett, "Not I", *Collected Shorter Plays* (London: Faber and Faber), pp. 213-223.
10. Billie Whitelaw, "A Wake for Sam", YouTube, accessed 9 March 2013.
11. Samuel Beckett, "Breath", *Collected Shorter Plays* (London: Faber and Faber), pp. 209-11.
12. Samuel Beckett, *Three Novels. Molloy, Malone Dies, The Unnamable* [1951 & 1953] (New York: Grove Press, 1991).
13. Derek Walcott, *The Prodigal* (New York: Farrar, Straus and Giroux, 2004).
14. *Watt* [1953] (London: John Calder, 1998).
15. *Murphy* [1938] (London: Picador, 1973).
16. "Footfalls", *The Complete Dramatic Works* [1986] (London: Faber & Faber, 1990), pp. 397-403.
17. "Quad", *The Complete Dramatic Works*, pp. 449-454.
18. "Play", *The Complete Dramatic Works*, pp. 305-320.
19. Derek Walcott, *Vangelo Nero*. Ms. Film script, 1972. West Indiana Library, The University of the West Indies, St Augustine.
20. Derek Walcott, *The Rig*, 1984.
21. Derek Walcott, *The Haitian Earth*, *The Haitian Trilogy* (New York: Farrar, Straus and Giroux, 2002).
22. Derek Walcott, *The Fortunate Traveller* (New York: Farrar, Straus and Giroux, 1982, p. 39, and *Collected Poems* (New York: Farrar, Straus and Giroux, 1986), p. [illegible].
23. Derek Walcott, *Tiepolo's Hound* (New York: Farrar, Straus and Giroux, 2000).
24. Derek Walcott, *Another Life* (London: Jonathan Cape, 1973).
25. Walcott, "The Season of Phantasmal Peace", *The Fortunate Traveller*, pp. 98-99, and *Collected Poems 1948-84*, pp. 464-465.
26. See *Tiepolo's Hound*, [illegible], p. 157.
27. John Millington Synge, *Riders to the Sea* [1904] *Four Plays and the Aran Islands*, Ed. Robin Skelton (London: Oxford University Press, 1962).

28. Wilson Harris, *The Mask of the Beggar* (London: Faber and Faber, 2003).
29. *Steel* – A Musical by Derek Walcott & Galt MacDermot, premiered in Trinidad, 2005. Not yet published.
30. Derek Walcott, "To Die For Grenada", Ms. Coll. 136, Boxes 38-42, film script; storyboard in Box 67, 1983-1987. Thomas Fisher Library, Toronto.
31. Derek Walcott, "The Star-Apple Kingdom", *The Star-Apple Kingdom* (London: Jonathan Cape, 1980), pp. 46-58, and in *Collected Poems 1948-84*, pp. 383-395.
32. Walcott, *The Arkansas Testament* (London: Faber and Faber, 1987), p. 110.
33. James Joyce, *Ulysses*, Ed. Seamus Deane (Penguin, [1922] 1992).
34. Derek Walcott, *The Fortunate Traveller*, p. 36.
35. Édouard Glissant, *Poetics of Relation* [1997], Trans. Betty Wing (Ann Arbor: The University of Michigan Press, 2010).
36. Wilson Harris, *Tradition, the Writer and Society*, p. 52.

O Babylon!
Trinidad Theatre Workshop World Premiere, Little Carib Theatre

O Babylon!
4th King, Finale, Kiskadee Theatre 1979

O Babylon!
Selassie

O Babylon!
Stage Sketches

O Babylon!
Sufferer and Virgie, Act I.

O Babylon!
Priscilla

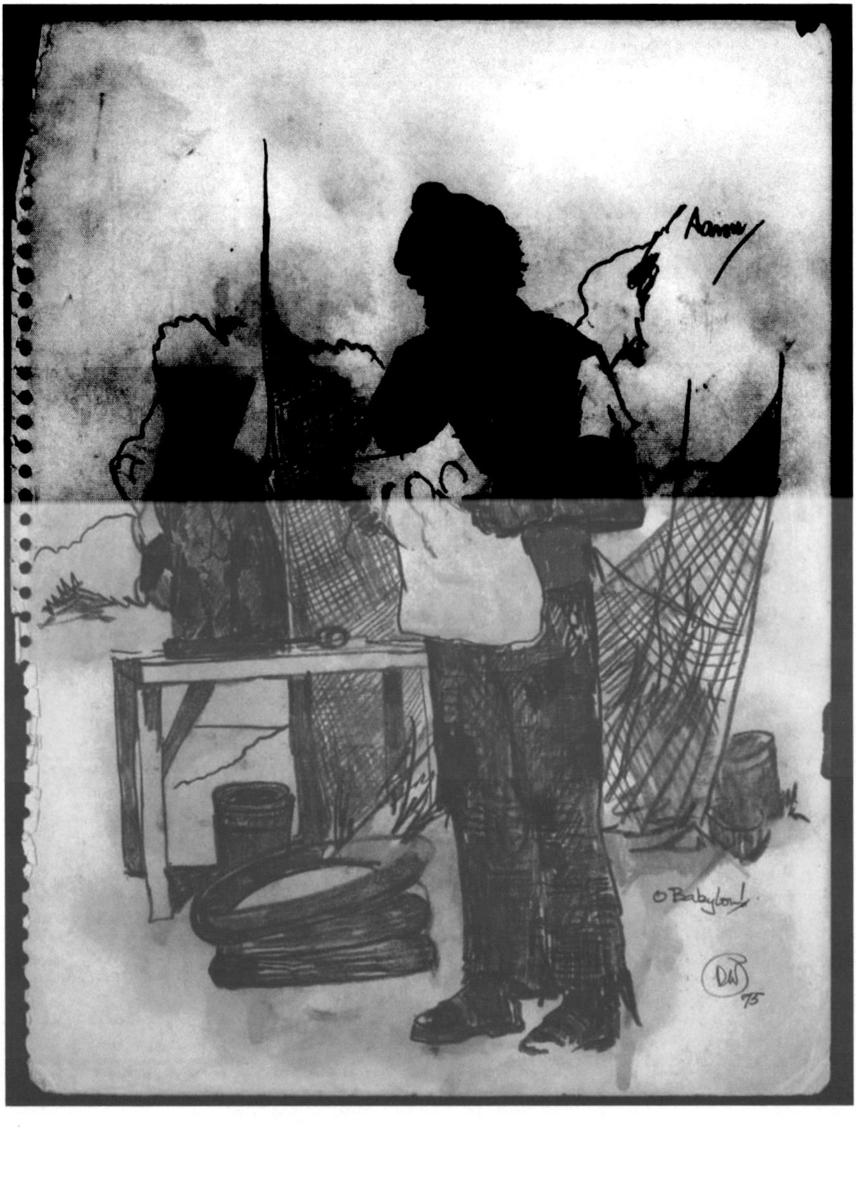

O Babylon!
Aaron

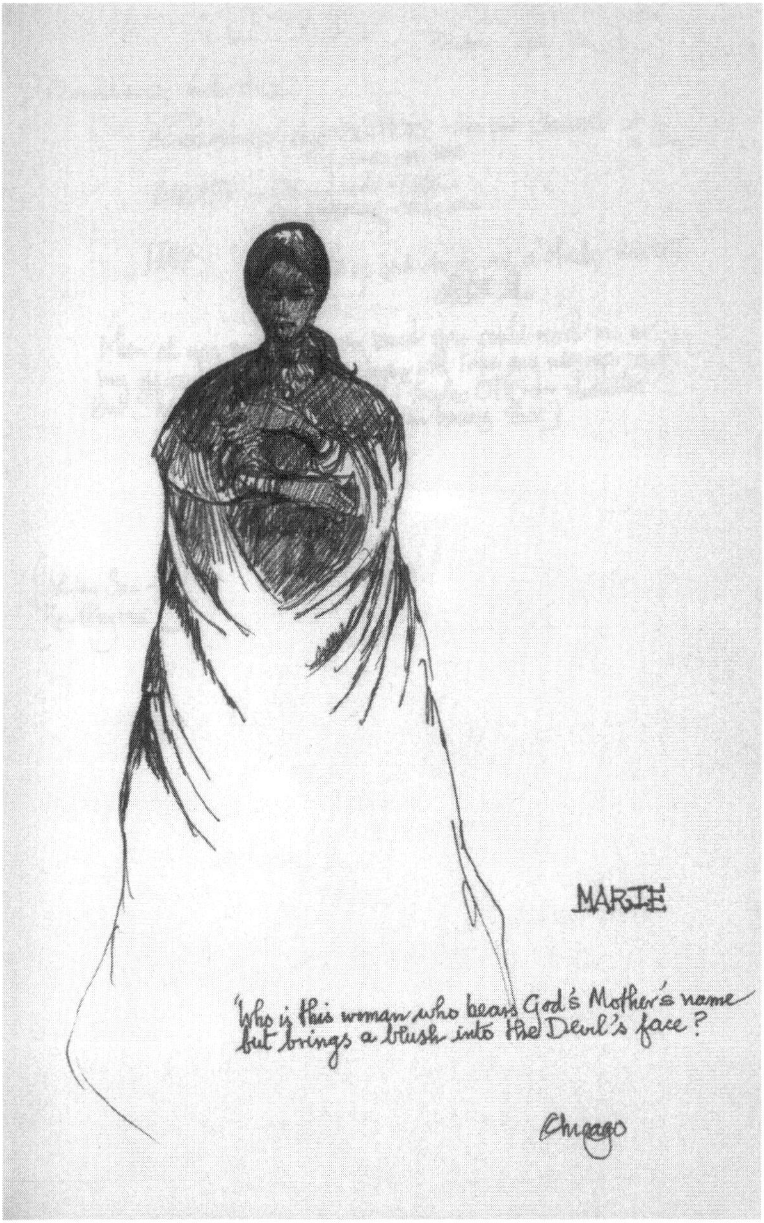

Marie Laveau
Marie

Marie Laveau
Mourners

Marie Laveau
Dancer: Bamboula

Marie Laveau: Participants

Marie Laveau: Aborzor "Zumba", Ex Haitian Slave, Drummer

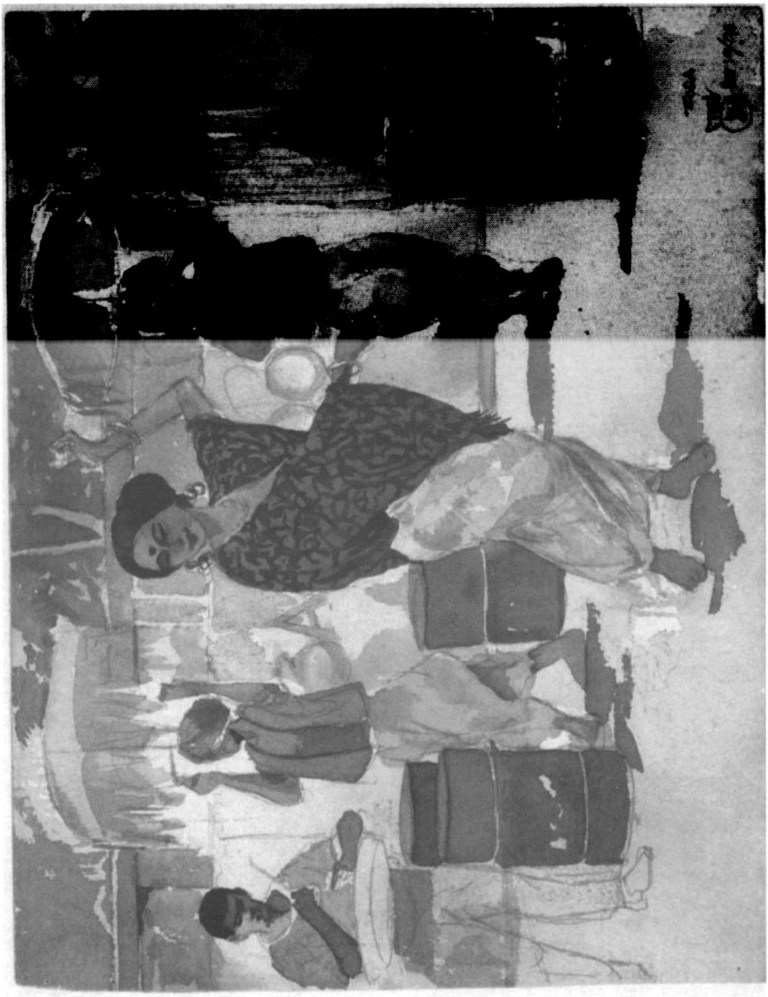

Steel: Zora

Steel: Kingdowm of the Night, Arenkian as Pluto

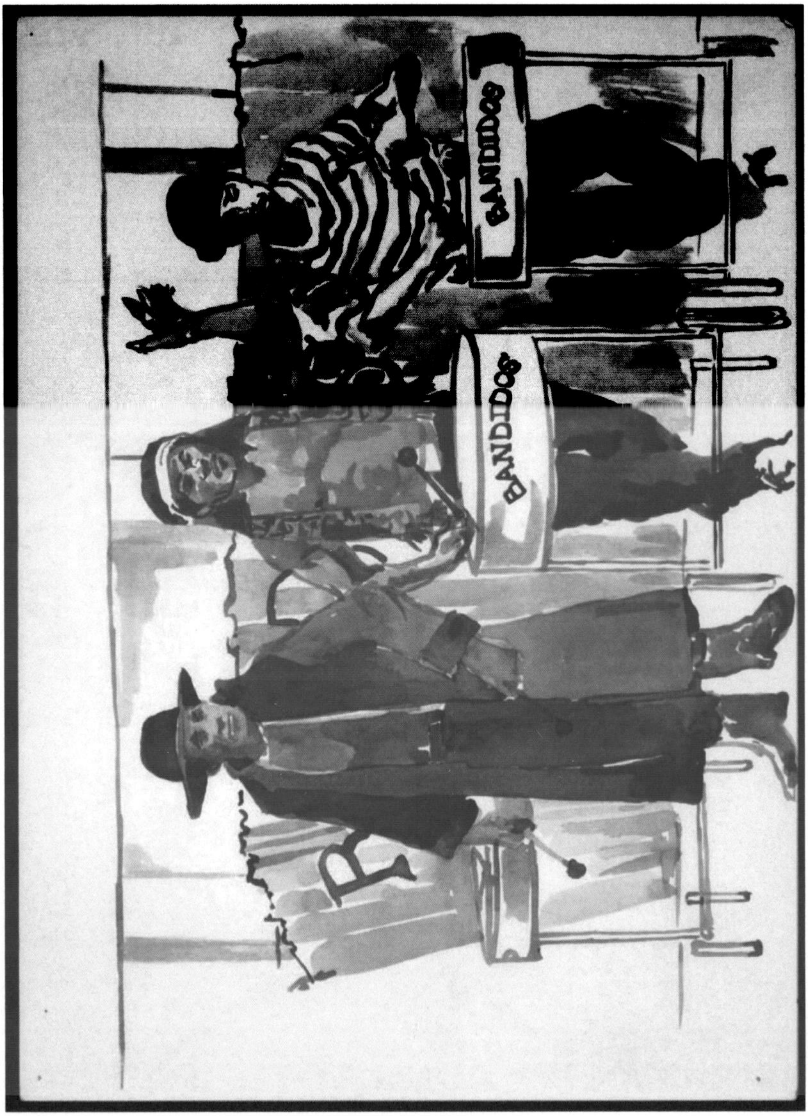

Steel: Steel Pan Drummers, Bandidos

Steel: Were You There

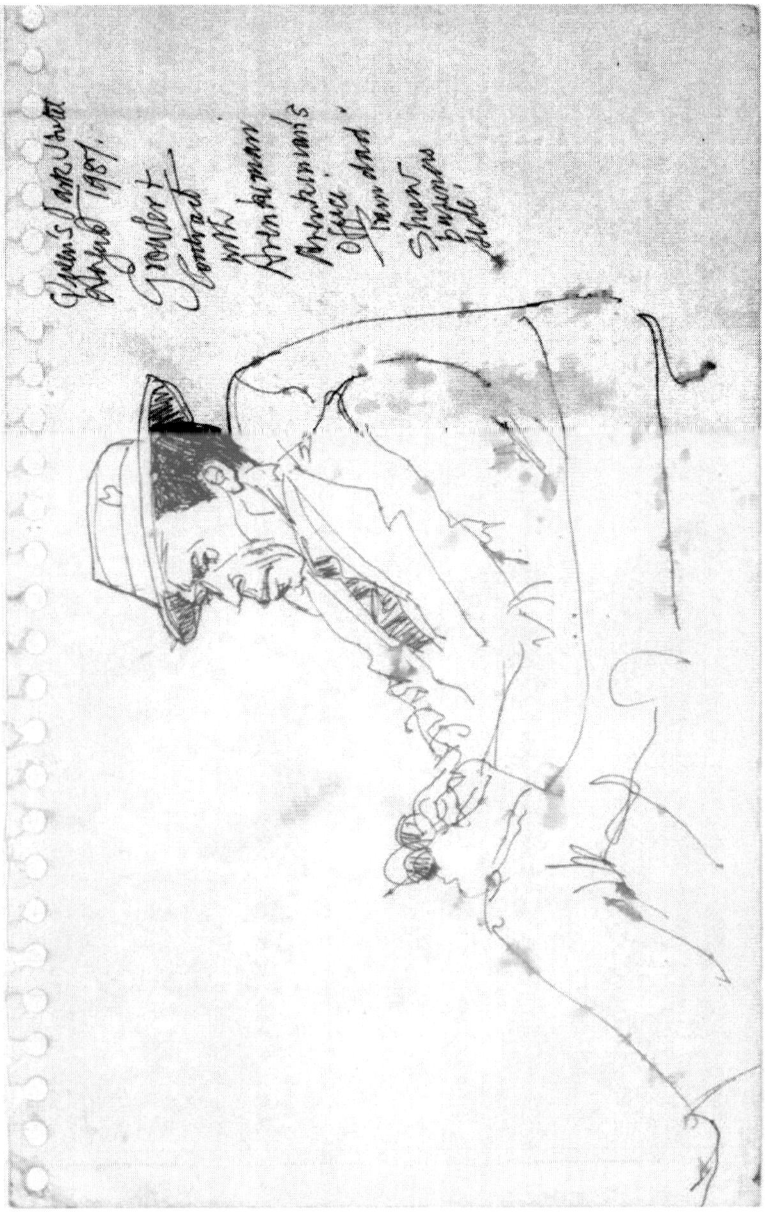

Steel: Growler

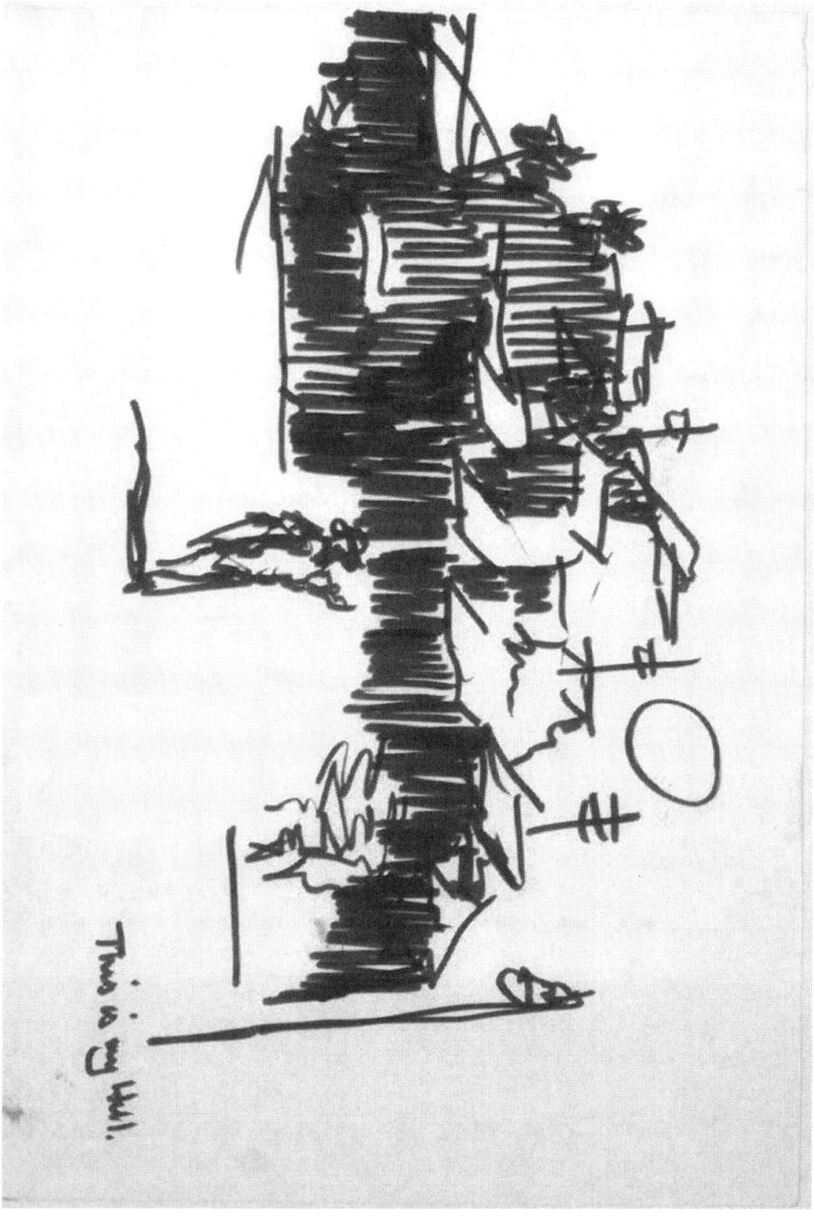

Steel: This is My Hill

J. EDWARD CHAMBERLIN AND JENNIFER TOEWS

DEREK WALCOTT LIFE AND WORK[1]

J. Edward Chamberlin

I first met Derek Walcott in 1989, when I went with his old friend Ron Bryden to the first production of Derek's play about the Ghost Dance of the Plains Sioux at Hartwick College in upstate New York. But I had been writing about his poetry since the 1970s, and was in his native St Lucia when it celebrated independence in 1979. I remember reviewing *Sea Grapes* for *The Hudson Review* around that time, a book in which he brought together in a refreshingly new way the ancient figures of the poet as maker, shaping ideal worlds, and as diviner, locating sources of inspiration in the everyday. But there was something more there, something that gave his people's suffering an island sanctity; and for over six decades he has sung a praisesong to their struggle, and to his own, in the soaked-in-salt languages of the West Indies. This exhibition bears witness to that achievement.

In 1993, after helping to arrange his visit as the Northrop Frye professor in the Centre for Comparative Literature and taking a line of his poetry as the title of my book, *Come Back To Me My Language: Poetry and the West Indies*,[2] I wrote – with a cheerful "good luck" from Richard Landon and Carole Moore – to ask whether he would consider making his manuscripts and other literary material available for purchase by the University of Toronto. To our delight, he was interested. The reputation of the Fisher Library and the University of Toronto figured largely in this, as did the enthusiastic West Indian community in Toronto and, old-fashioned though it might seem, the shared imperial and commonwealth histories of Canada and the West Indies. The question of whether it was appropriate to bring such an important archive out of the West Indies was much on our minds, reinforced by a first refusal that had been given by Derek earlier to the University of the West Indies, which already held some of his work in libraries on the Mona and St. Augustine campuses. But their resources, both financial and custodial, were limited; and we all knew that if something did not happen at either the University of the West Indies or the University of Toronto, the Walcott papers would go to one of the major American Universities, which were already tripping over each other to get the collection of the latest Nobel laureate in literature.

Sir Alister McIntyre, at the time Vice-Chancellor of the University of the West Indies, was involved in discussions from the beginning, and although he would have dearly loved to bring the material home, he realized that was not going to happen. He was particularly anxious that Derek not lose an opportunity for the financial returns that he both deserved and needed from his career. So with considerable flak from his academic and librarian colleagues, as well as from his university's lawyers, he supported our initiative by waiving the University of the West Indies' rights to Derek's material in favour of the University of Toronto. Without Sir Alister's decision to do so, and the eventual support of his disappointed colleagues (including Edward Baugh, still the most important scholar of Derek's work), this could not have happened; and it should be noted that when his successor, the late Rex Nettleford, came to Toronto in November, 1999, for the formal announcement and opening of the collection, he too was enormously generous in his praise of the Fisher library and the University of Toronto for keeping the collection within the wider West Indian family. Accordingly, it was described from the beginning as the University of Toronto / University of the West Indies collection, with that formality accompanied by a commitment to make material available to colleagues in the West Indies on a priority basis. And there was a good framework for this. The University of Toronto and the University of the West Indies had a formal agreement, negotiated and signed in 1993, which sponsored a very wide range of collaborations and exchanges to take advantage of academic strengths on both sides, and that certainly helped. Finally, early financial support from the McLean Foundation, from Avie and Bev Bennett, and from other individuals and organizations, was crucial, as was the word of Ron Bryden, who encouraged Derek to do the deal, and of Carole Moore, who agreed to it. But at the end of the day, as with so much at the Fisher Library, it could not have come to pass without Richard Landon. The actual dealing involved him and me and a trip to New York, where in the living room of his apartment in Greenwich Village, on 18 October 1997, after intense negotiations that took up all the time it takes to drink a cup of tea, Derek handwrote his agreement. He had never met anyone quite like Richard. Nobody has. The deal was done. It is worth noting that acquisition of the Walcott collection has brought important new material to the Fisher Library, including the complete archive of the Trinidad Theatre workshop, arguably the most important cultural institution of the last half century in the Caribbean, which Derek founded and which came to the Fisher though his intercession; and the literary manuscripts of Lorna Goodison. But back to the Walcott collection. The details were quickly worked out; all that was left was to get the existing material to Toronto.

This deal included all future material, so it is still coming, thanks to the scrupulous and scholarly custodial work of Derek's partner, Sigrid Nama. The Irish say that scholars and poets at their best are fellow travellers; and so are Derek and Sigrid, bless them both. By the spring of 1998, Derek and Sigrid were back in Boston, where he was teaching at Boston University. Some material was still in St Lucia, but the bulk of it was with them in Boston. I suggested, in a moment of cavalier bravado, that I would drive down and pick it up, since Richard and I were anxious about entrusting it to FedEx, good though that company is. What made me think that I and my Subaru sedan would be a better bet is beyond me now. But I did; and I drove to Boston, stayed overnight with Derek and Sigrid, and at six the next morning we began loading the car. By the time we were finished the trunk was full, the back seat was packed to the top, and so was the passenger seat, so much that I didn't have use of the handbrake and had to juggle a box every time I shifted into high gear.

Fortunately, on the interstate, that did not happen too often, for I drove nonstop from Boston to Buffalo. I was nervous about fire. Don't ask me how many times you see a car on fire on the interstate, but I did have a bad dream the day before I left for Boston, and I took along a small fire extinguisher, one just big enough, I realized later, for a small campfire. I stopped once for gas at a self-serve, so I could put out the flames myself, picked up a take-out snack, which I balanced on the little space there was still on the dashboard, and was off to the border. I was really nervous, with more justification, about the border. I knew that eventually the material would be allowed into Canada, but I did not want to leave the car in bond, since that would defeat the whole purpose of my trip. So I rehearsed my script for the eight hours of the drive. I didn't want to say anything that wasn't true; but I also had in mind a line of Seamus Heaney's from the troubles in Northern Ireland: what ever you say, say nothing.

There was very little traffic when I arrived at the border in early afternoon, and I drove straight up to the open booth, thankfully not having to wait in queue for a half hour, worrying about whether I had chosen the right line. The Canadian border agent leaned out, looked at me, and looked in the car. A live one, he must have thought. "What do you have in there?", he asked, pointed to the twenty or so boxes in the back and front seats (with ten or twelve more he couldn't see in the trunk). "Papers," I said (leaving out the fact that there were books, storyboards, watercolour paintings, and a whole bunch of valuable, but unclassifiable (except by Jennifer Toews!) odds and ends. (With my fallback script memorized, I didn't say there weren't any of those things.) "What are they for?" he asked. "For research," I said. "I work on them" (which was sort of true). "You work on all those?" he said, with a look that brought to mind the Unabomber. I said nothing. "Open that box right beside you," he demanded. I saw his right hand go down to what I assume was a red button as I twisted in my seat and slipped off the cover of the closest box, having no idea what was inside. I prayed it was just papers. It was, at least down a few inches, which was all he could see. He got out of the booth feeling safer, I presume, because both my hands were in sight, pulling out papers with manic delight and he looked at a couple of manuscript papers, drafts of *O Babylon!*. Then he slipped back to his booth, mumbling, "They're all like that?" and then once again, with feeling, "You work on those?" and then, "Get out of here. Quickly, please." Finally, as I turned the key in the ignition, he said with a kind of gracious sadness, "You know you're crazy, don't you?" I drove faster than I should have out of the terminal, up the road, and onto the loading docks at the Robarts Library.

So the material arrived into the safe hands of Richard Landon and Anne Dondertman. But then the real work of organizing and describing the collection began, undertaken with exceptional grace and rare skill by Jennifer Toews, who has provided us all with new insight into the work of one of the world's great writers. This exhibition, with its extraordinary range and rigorous discipline, is a testament to her achievement, as well as to Derek Walcott's.

HOW BEAUTIFUL MY BRETHREN AND SISTREN: DEREK WALCOTT, LIFE AND WORK

Jennifer Toews

The University of Toronto and the University of the West Indies have enjoyed a long-standing relationship, involving exchanges of students, faculty and ideas. The Fisher Library acquired the first significant portion of the Derek Walcott papers in 1997, as the result of a complex effort on the part of Richard Landon, the director of the Fisher Library, Carole Moore, Chief Librarian at the University of Toronto (recently retired), Professor J. Edward Chamberlin, Professor of English and Comparative Literature, J. Robert S. Prichard, President of the University of Toronto (at the time), the McLean foundation, the Jessie Ball DuPont fund, Sir Alister McIntyre, Vice Chancellor of the University of the West Indies, Mona, Jamaica and, of course, Derek Walcott.

The Thomas Fisher Rare Book Library is honoured to hold the papers of Derek Walcott, which are consulted by scholars from all over the world, as well as by local students, faculty and other researchers. The papers include drafts of his poetry, prose, plays, critical works, drawings, paintings, sketches, storyboards, correspondence, and a variety of other material related to his life and work. The bulk of the material centres around work created in the 1980s and 1990s, with some from the 1970s and some more recent work. The other significant portion of his archival papers is held as part of the special collections of the Alma Jordan Library at the University of the West Indies, St Augustine, Trinidad and Tobago, and at the UWI Library at Mona, Jamaica. Some of Walcott's earliest archival material may be found there.

The Fisher Library also holds the papers of the Trinidad Theatre Workshop, founded by Derek Walcott in 1959.

Arguably the most famous citizen of St Lucia, Derek Alton Walcott is internationally known for his poetry, plays and prose.

Born to parents Warwick and Alix Walcott, on January 23, 1930, in Castries, St Lucia, Derek Walcott is one of two Nobel prize recipients from the island, the other being economist Sir William Arthur Lewis (1915-1991). Walcott received the Nobel Prize for literature in 1992 for his entire body of work and specifically for his epic poem *Omeros*.

As a youth, Walcott was trained in painting and drawing by Harold Simmons (1914-1966). Simmons is widely recognized as mentor to a generation of St Lucian artists, writers and musicians, including Derek Walcott, painter and muralist Dunstan St Omer (1927-), photographer Leo St Helene, folksinger Marie Selipha "Sesenne" Descartes (1914-2010), and composer Charles Cadet. The most celebrated St Lucian artist of his time, Simmons invited Walcott, Dunstan St Omer, Leo "Spa" St Helene, and others, to his studio and the surrounding countryside on Saturdays to paint and draw, in an effort to encourage them to absorb and learn about their native land though their artwork. These Saturday sessions were very important for the development of the young people, and contributed to St Omer becoming the most famous painter in St Lucia, and one of the Caribbean's leading muralists, developing his own unique style and vision, dubbed "Prismism" by Walcott. St Omer become known for transforming the sacred icons of the Roman Catholic Church into recognizably Saint Lucian figures, including a native Madonna, and as the designer of the national flag. Leo St Helene became an athlete and photographer, and Derek Walcott an internationally acclaimed poet and playwright.

Walcott's father, Warwick, was also a painter and poet and had been a mentor and inspiration to Harold Simmons as a younger man. Warwick Walcott's untimely death from mastoiditis at the age of thirty-one left the young Derek without paternal guidance and support, and Simmons proved vitally important in the development of his creative talents. Walcott's highly visual approach to his poetry and prose no doubt developed, in part, from these early experiences.

Walcott was educated at St Mary's College in Castries, later becoming the first St Lucian to be awarded a colonial development and welfare scholarship to study at the University College of the West Indies in Kingston, Jamaica, where he studied English, French and Latin, among other subjects. He then moved to Trinidad in 1953 to take up work as a teacher and writer. In 1959, Walcott established the Little Carib Theatre Workshop in Trinidad, his home for twenty-two years, which would later become the Trinidad Theatre Workshop. The Rockefeller Foundation awarded him a fellowship to study American theatre in New York City in 1957. He is the recipient of numerous awards for his work, including a Cholmondeley Award in 1969, an O'Neill Foundation-Wesleyan University Fellowship for Playwrights (1969), an Obie Award for *Dream on Monkey Mountain* in 1971, the Queen's Gold Medal for poetry in 1988, a five-year MacArthur Foundation "genius" award in 1981 (part of the proceeds from this award he used to start the Boston Playwrights Theatre), a Royal Society of Literature award, the 1992 Nobel prize, the St Lucia Medal of Honour in 2000, the 2011 T.S. Eliot prize for *White Egrets*, the inaugural 2011 OCM Bocas Prize for Caribbean literature – also for *White Egrets*, and many others.

Walcott describes his family background as being mostly made up of his mother, Alix Walcott, though he also had a twin brother "Roddy" (Roderick Aldon Walcott, 1930-2000) to whom he was very close, sister Pamela and his father's sisters. The Walcotts were English-speaking Methodists, a minority in St Lucia. While English is the official language of the island, some 95% speak Kweyol, or Creole, based on French, African languages and Carib, and are predominantly Catholic. The Walcott home was one filled with poetry, music and art, with mother Alix often to be found quoting poetry and singing about the house. Alix was a teacher in Castries, and though not wealthy by any standard, she managed as a single parent to raise the children through teaching and sewing, while being fully supportive of their talents and dreams. According to Walcott, the presence of his father, Warwick, could be felt throughout the house despite his untimely death, as his mother spoke continually about him for the rest of her life. Many of his watercolours were on view and his poetry was always to hand in their home. The Walcott household contained a number of books by such authors as Dickens, Walter Scott, and a great deal of poetry, as well as many classical musical recordings. Derek and Roddy regularly used to put on short plays with and for each other as children. Walcott remembers a self-portrait in watercolour by his father which was displayed next to an oil painting of Alix, also by him. He was always very aware of his mother's grief over the loss of his father, and also her pride in him. Walcott describes his early life as giving him a strong sense of continuity in his art and writing, and of the responsibility of carrying on a tradition.

In a draft version of *Tiepolo's Hound*, Walcott writes of Warwick:

> Without ever knowing my father it seems to me now
> (I thought I saw him pause in the parenthesis
>
> of our stairs once), from the blank unfurrowed brow
> of his self-portrait, that he embodied the tenderness
> of water, his preferred medium, its English reticence
> but also its fragile delight, like a prediction
>
> of his own passing, its tinted mist and essence,
> and the verse that made him my precocious fiction…[3]

When he was ten years old, the headmaster of his school asked permission to read out one of his poems at a school function. Walcott's first published poem, "1944",[4] was printed in *The Voice of St. Lucia* when he was fourteen years old. Written from a Methodist point of view, in blank verse, elements of the religious subject matter of the poem raised the ire of a local Catholic priest who wrote to the newspaper in verse, condemning the poem as blasphemous. The young Walcott was rather surprised by this reaction to his poetry – perhaps his first, but certainly not his last experience with controversy in his life.

In 1948, at the age of eighteen, Walcott self-published his first book of poetry, *25 Poems*, initially funded by his mother at a cost of two hundred dollars. *25 Poems* was favourably reviewed by Harold Simmons in the local newspaper, *The Voice of St Lucia*. With solid support from his mother, Harold Simmons, Frank Collymore, the Barbadian writer and editor of *Bim* (1893-1980), and others, Walcott continued to write and publish with increasing confidence. Following *25 Poems*, he published *Epitaph for the Young: XII Cantos*, and *Poems. In a Green Night: Poems, 1948-60*, published in 1962 by Jonathan Cape in the UK, brought much greater attention to his work in the English-speaking world and came to be considered as the book that helped give him his "break" into the literary world outside St Lucia and the Caribbean. Following the success of *In a Green Night*, Walcott produced numerous books of poetry though the next decades, including *The Castaway and Other Poems* in 1965; *The Gulf and Other Poems* in 1969; the autobiographical *Another Life* in 1973 featuring the characters "Harry", based on Harold Simmons, and "Gregorias", modelled on Dunstan St Omer; *Sea Grapes* (1976); *The Star-Apple Kingdom* (1979); *The Fortunate Traveller* (1981); *Midsummer* (1984); *The Arkansas Testament* (1987); the much-lauded *Omeros* (1990); *The Prodigal* (2004) also autobiographical, focusing on travels and reaching late middle-age, combined with his memories and grief surrounding the death of his twin brother, Roddy; *The Bounty* in 1997 and *White Egrets* in 2010. *White Egrets* continues to win awards and praise, including the 2011 Eugenio Montale literary prize in Milan, Italy.

Omeros[5] is a brilliantly conceived epic poem combining elements of classical Greek myth woven into a St Lucian context with St Lucian characters. Written in terza rima, *Omeros* focuses on a group of fishermen (a favourite character type of Walcott's), the young woman Helen, the white couple for whom Helen works, the Plunketts, and a cast of locals. The blind guide Omeros and the blind fisherman Seven Seas are both representative of a deeper type of guidance, both spiritual and psychic.

Here, Seven Seas begins his day and thinks of the change in his senses since he lost his vision:

> [...] Then he heard the first breeze
> washing the sea-almond's wares; last night there had been
> a full moon white as his plate. He saw with his ears.
> [...]
> and an inward darkness grew where the moon and sun
> indistinctly altered – he moved by a sixth sense,
> like the moon without an hour or second hand... (*Omeros*, pp. 11-12)

Later, Walcott describes the community healer and spiritual leader, Ma Kilman:

> [...] the obeah-woman, in the swell
> of the huge white satin belly, the dark gust that bent her

limbs till she was a tree of snakes, the spidery sibyl

hanging in a sack from the cave at Cumae, the obeah
that possessed her that the priests considered evil
in their white satin frocks [...] (*Omeros*, p. 245):

Walcott has described the creation of *Omeros* as "an act of gratitude for St Lucia, the people, the weather, the life I have lived there." And mindful of the ongoing difficulties faced by the majority of writers, in regard to money and protected time to write, Walcott founded the Rat Island Foundation as an international writers' retreat with some of his Nobel prize money in the 1990s, on an island off the coast of St Lucia.

In his 1992 Nobel address, *The Antilles: Fragments of Epic Memory*, Walcott speaks about the future of the Caribbean:

> [...] How quickly it could all disappear! And how it is beginning to drive us further into where we hope are impenetrable places, green secrets at the end of bad roads, headlands where the next view is not of a hotel but of some long beach without a figure and the hanging question of some fisherman's smoke at its far end. The Caribbean is not an idyll, not to its natives. They draw their working strength from it organically, like trees, like the sea almond or the spice laurel of the heights. Its peasantry and its fisherman are not there to be loved or even photographed; they are trees who sweat, and whose bark is filmed with salt, but every day on some island, rootless trees in suits are signing favourable tax breaks with entrepreneurs, poisoning the sea almond and the spice laurel of the mountains to their roots. A morning could come in which governments might ask what happened not merely to the forests and the bays but to a whole people.[6]

Tiepolo's Hound,[7] published in 2000, tells the life story of the painter Camille Pissarro (1830-1903) from his birth and upbringing in St Thomas, Danish West Indies (U.S. Virgin Islands), to his emigration to Paris, France, and subsequent life and career among the French Impressionists and Neo-Impressionists. Cleverly counterbalanced with Pissarro's story is the story of Walcott's quest to locate and catch a second glimpse of a mysterious hound in a painting by Tiepolo:

Then I caught a slash of pink on the inner thigh
of a white hound entering the cave of a table,

so exact in its lucency at *The Feast of Levi*,
I felt my heart halt [...] (p. 7)

And he allows the reader to travel with him as he searches from St Lucia to New York City. The experience for the reader of travelling with Walcott on a quest or journey is a recurring device in much of his work. There is a constant sense of "we" as one reads through his poetry, prose and plays. Generously illustrated throughout with Walcott's own paintings, Walcott presents Pissarro as the first West Indian painter.

He weaves the two stories together, including their mutual love of painting, a multisensory approach to their work and their common beginnings in the richness of Caribbean life. The influence of the Caribbean landscape, its fecundity, variety and the unique quality of light Walcott sees in Pissarro's later French Impressionist paintings:

> a tune he cannot shake from his head,
> that sings like gnats around the drying picture,
>
> the delight in light remains unaffected,
> till even his greys have joy, his indigo,
>
> all of that muted bliss contained in a red
> rusting roof, an ochre wall, patches of snow. (p. 62)

Later, in dealing with Pissarro's failure, his flight from seeing the Caribbean as worthy of art, Walcott doubts his quest for the hound as a metaphor for the fragility of all art and his own failings:

> ... One dawn I woke up to the gradual terror
> that all I had written of the hound was false.
>
> I had pursued a melody of error,
> my craft seduced by the twin siren calls
>
> of Memory changing to Imagination,
> of Reason into Rhyme. [...]
>
> [...] the hound, now a chained Cerberus, growled
> and lunged its treble heads at Accuracy. (p. 134)

From almost as early as his first poems, Derek Walcott was writing plays. His first play, *Henri Christophe: a Chronicle in Seven Scenes*, privately printed in 1948 and performed in 1950, following the suggestion of his brother Roderick, was the first part of *The Haitian Trilogy*,[8] which would include *Drums and Colours* (commissioned for the opening of the first Federal Parliament of the West Indies, April 23rd, 1958) and *The Haytian Earth*. *Henri Christophe* follows the struggle between Jean Jacques Dessalines (1743-1806), and Henri Christophe (1767-1820) in the power vacuum following the deportation and imprisonment of the revolutionary hero, Toussaint L'Ouverture, in France. Walcott writes:

> [...] the Haitian revolution, as sordidly tyrannical as so many of its subsequent regimes tragically became was an upheaval, a necessary rejection of the debasements endured under a civilized empire, that achieved independence. The revolution is as central to the plays as it is to the history of the islands.[9]

Also in 1950, Derek Walcott, Roderick, and others founded the St Lucia Arts Guild to develop local and international drama. The Guild performed *Henri Christophe* that same year. After Derek left St Lucia for university in Jamaica, and later to live and work in Trinidad, Roderick took over to act as leader of the Guild from 1951-1967, but many of Derek Walcott's earlier plays were premiered in St Lucia, including *Ti-Jean and his Brothers*, published in 1958, which tells the story of a battle between three brothers and the devil, being told by a bird, a cricket, a firefly and a frog.

As a playwright, Derek Walcott began to attract international critical attention with *Dream on Monkey Mountain*, which won an Obie award in 1971 and is considered by some to be his most powerful play. *Dream on Monkey Mountain*[10] was commissioned in 1967 by the Royal Shakespeare Company and first performed in Trinidad. The main character, Makak, has a dream that suggests he should leave his home and travel to Africa – an exploit he attempts with his friend, Moustique – a quest that is thwarted. In this magical realist tale, Walcott explores the themes of colonial and post-colonial struggles – a common theme in his work, as are exile and return, seers and visionaries – especially in the guise of everyday people, i.e. fisherman, peddlers, and the like who often have the best and most important roles. Walcott is careful to distinguish his approach:

> The people I honour and glorify from simplicity, not from a Marxist or political viewpoint, rather say from a Whitmanesque one, are my heroes. Fishermen. Working men, isolated artists. Makak, the main figure in *Dream on Monkey Mountain* is a man who is tempted into being such a hero.
>
> When he awakens from his dream, his wisdom is that he has refused the opportunity.
>
> He is himself, not what others would make of him.[11]

The performance of *Dream on Monkey Mountain* was one of the high points of the Trinidad Theatre Workshop, which was founded in 1959 by Derek Walcott, Roderick Walcott, and a number of well-known performers such as Beryl McBurnie, Errol Jones, Fred Hope, and Joya Gomes-Ryan. Walcott says that he is not the creator of theatre in Trinidad, but rather: "there is a very sophisticated culture in the Caribbean that people don't know. To say that I began theatre in Trinidad is not true. The only thing I innovated was to form a company and to pay the actors."[11] The veteran actor Albert Laveau recalls Walcott paying him ten dollars for an early performance. The mission of the Workshop was to train, develop and produce theatre and actors in the Caribbean to the highest possible standard. Through the Theatre in Education programme, actors, dancers, singers, and others from the workshop offered theatre training to young people, especially those who might not otherwise have been able to afford it. The Trinidad Theatre Workshop travelled all over the Caribbean and the world, performing works by Walcott and many others, including *The Blacks*, by Jean Genet (1910-1986), *Belle Fanto*, by Eric Roach (1915-1974), and *The Road* by 1986 Nobel laureate Wole Soyinka (1934-). Since its inception, the Workshop has produced some of the best actors and performers in Trinidad and Tobago. Workshop members from the earliest days recall long days, evenings, weekends, and holidays spent rehearsing and performing. Nearly all these performers had day jobs and family responsibilities and were very dedicated to their craft, and with little or no income worked purely for the pleasure and satisfaction of being part of something great put on for the community.

Later, Derek Walcott's activities as a playwright became more international in scope. Drama critic and writer, Ronald Bryden (1927-2004), later professor of Drama at the University of Toronto, became the dramaturge for the Royal Shakespeare Company in London during the early 1970s. Bryden himself was born in Port of Spain, Trinidad and was a dear friend of Walcott's. Bryden was known for his sharp instincts regarding emerging playwrights, being credited with "discovering" Tom Stoppard with his very positive and insightful review of Stoppard's *Rosencrantz and Guildenstern are Dead*. Bryden could not be said to have discovered Walcott, but he was certainly a strong supporter and honest critic of his work. During the development of the musical *Steel*, Bryden and Walcott wrote long, in-depth letters to each other discussing its strengths and weaknesses. A letter from Bryden in 1991 discusses his ideas about *Steel* in frank detail:

> ... Anyway, I loved Steel. It was three hours of pure pleasure for me. Galt's score, like the score for the Joker, is a marvel – the flow of new melody never stops, all of it gold. The memories of Port-of-Spain, and climbing to the top of Laventille to explore the old Martello tower up there, were painfully gorgeous – Richard got the sense of those houses exactly... But what's to be done with it? It's too much – too much plot, too many characters, more songs than I can carry in my head, more subjects than a sunny Sunday at Speaker's Corner in London. Watching it in that tiny theatre, my instinct was to cut it down ruthlessly – reduce the cast by a third, throw out the piano-teacher get rid of Roger, forget all those quests for fathers and simplify, simplify, simplify...[12]

While at the Royal Shakespeare Company, Bryden commissioned Derek Walcott to write a "Caribbeanised" version of the Don Juan story, which became *The Joker of Seville*. As a result of budget problems at the RSC, the play was not performed there as originally planned, premiering instead in Port of Spain in 1974, performed by the Trinidad Theatre Workshop.

The affectionate, joking nature of the friendship is evident in a 1965 letter from Walcott to Bryden:

> Hello, Dryden.
>
> Bryden, is it? Got you mixed up with the other chap. Used to do crits

> for the Elder Statesman back in Annus Mirabilis. Provincial. Never made it. Must have met him... Who writes all that stuff for you? I mean you surely couldn't have READ ALL of Shaw's plays could you. Saw the volume in town. Would break any model's neck carrying that... [Ronald Bryden papers, Ms. Coll. 548, Box 1].

Another close colleague was the Canadian composer Galt MacDermot (1928-) who wrote the music for *The Joker of Seville*, the first of several collaborations with Walcott, which would also include *Steel*, *Marie Laveau*, *Walker* and *O Babylon!* MacDermot is probably best known as the composer of the award-winning 1967 musical *Hair*. When asked why he would choose to work with someone like MacDermot, Walcott answered that "any composer who loves Kitchener is fine by me."[13] Lord Kitchener, also known as Aldwyn Roberts (1922-2000), originally from Arima, Trinidad, was one of the most famous calypsonians, especially popular among the expatriate Caribbean communities of the 1950s, known for many songs, including "Cricket, lovely Cricket", "Mama dis is Mas" and "Jump in Line", and for developing younger artists like David Rudder. In an October 10th, 1992 letter to Walcott, in which he congratulates him on winning the Nobel Prize, MacDermot discusses *Steel*:

> [...] You have to face the fact that it is really the story of your life but transposed to a pan playing composer. Now that you've won top honors you can admit that as an artist you have tried to be a literate but at the same time a street artist and that it works... Forget the social problems like corruption. That's old news but to create art using all your faculties and not being afraid to do it is unheard of except in certain Nobel prize winning types of which I only know one [...][14]

Walcott has always avidly supported Caribbean actors in particular, though he loves actors in general. At various times throughout his career he has used his own money and resources to support local theatre groups and actors. He wrote at least some of his plays with particular Caribbean actors in mind. He has said that some of the finest Shakespeare he has ever experienced has been performed by Caribbean actors. He credits this in part to the classical training and education they receive in the Caribbean, as well as the theatrical tradition and love of rhetoric, combined with a unique sensitivity to language. "My society loves rhetoric, performance, panache, melodrama, carnival, dressing up, playing roles. Thank God I was born into it, which made me love life and artificial theatre."[15]

O Babylon!,[16] published in 1976 and first performed the same year by the Trinidad Theatre Workshop in Port of Spain, was directed by Walcott with music by Galt MacDermot. *O Babylon!* was later staged in 1988 in London, England. The story centres around events that took place during the 1966 visit of the Emperor Haile Selassie I of Ethiopia to the Rastafarian community in Jamaica. Storylines include a battle with developers trying to force the community from their land to build a luxury tourist hotel, and the conversion of a former criminal, Rufus Johnson, to Rastafarianism, after being treated kindly in a time of need. When Rufus is shot in the back by other drug dealers, he is rescued by Sufferer, Priscilla and other members of the community and nursed back to health. He later becomes known as Ras Aaron or Brother Aaron and Priscilla becomes his girlfriend:

> [...] A Rasta-man called Sufferer,
> an old-bottle collector,
> limp into the alley, with
> four next Rasta-man,
> saying: 'I-and-I shall hide him
> where the Babylon can't find him.
> Priscilla, stand bedside him.'
> And them take him in a van [...] (*O Babylon!*, p. 162)

Later Sufferer describes Rufus/ Aaron's transformation from dealer to artist (p. 168):

> The razor shall be turned to a chisel, so
> follow your true calling, which is to carve.
> Give him the chisel, and the cap with three colors
> Of holy Ethiopia [...] (p. 168)

Walcott's dramatic work in the United States brought him into contact with the wider American theatre scene, including the opportunity to work with a number of well-known actors at the start of their careers. These include Angela Bassett (1958-) as Drusilla Douglas in *Beef, no Chicken*, Joan Van Ark (1943-) in *In a Fine Castle* (later reworked and published in 1986, titled *The Last Carnival*) and Frances McDormand (1957-), all at the Yale Repertory Theatre in the early 1980s. McDormand, probably best known for her film work with the Coen brothers, had her first professional acting roles following her time at Yale with the Trinidad Theatre Workshop in Trinidad during the 1980s, starring in plays by Walcott.

In 1981, Walcott founded the Boston Playwrights' Theatre during the time he spent teaching at Boston University. The way Walcott's theatre ranged the New World in theme and performance is further shown in the play, *Marie Laveau*, first performed at St Thomas, U.S. Virgin Islands in 1979 and at the New Federal Theater in New York in 2009. Excerpts from the play were published in the *Trinidad and Tobago Review* in 1979.[17] *Marie Laveau* is a musical based on the story of a New Orleans religious leader, who was known for leading large gatherings in the practice of Voudou, especially on St John's Eve, June 23rd, on the shores of Lake Pontchartrain. The historic Marie Laveau (1794-1891) was known for her skill in healing, herbalism, divination, counselling and all manner of religious administration, particularly matters dealing with the care of the soul. She was also known to sit with prisoners awaiting their death sentences. Walcott's play incorporates many aspects of the complex multiracial society of New Orleans at this time, including the lives of former African slaves, many of whom were devotees of Marie Laveau. For example, Walcott creates scenes containing the dance known as Bamboula, brought to New Orleans by Africans.

Walcott has written two other plays which reflect events specific to American history, *Walker* and *The Ghost Dance*. *Walker* is about the black abolitionist David Walker (1785-1830), author of *Walker's Appeal* (1829), which urged slaves to resort to violence to obtain their freedom if necessary. *The Ghost Dance* revisits the historical events of the Wounded Knee Massacre of 1890 involving Sitting Bull and the Lakota Sioux attempting to resist the United States Army in the Dakotas. The Ghost Dance was an aboriginal religious movement which was believed to have contributed to the resistance of 1890 and which was banned by the government out of fear of uprisings.

It is evident that Walcott has never been reluctant to engage in potentially risky subjects. There was the original 1998 production of the highly controversial and financially unsuccessful Broadway musical written by Paul Simon, with lyrics by Derek Walcott, *The Capeman*. *The Capeman* garnered Tony Award nominations for Best Original Score, best Orchestrations and best scenic Design, but it opened to poor reviews and much controversy from the public, and closed after only sixty-eight performances. Hampered by production difficulties, excess expense, delays, differences of opinion, and perhaps Simon's inexperience in creating a Broadway musical, *The Capeman* was one of the least financially successful Broadway shows in recent history. For differing reasons, the public found the plot objectionable, with some people picketing the theatre. The story focuses on the 1959 New York City murder of two boys by a teenage member of a Latino street gang known as the Vampires. The attacker was sixteen years old at the time of the murder, becoming the youngest person ever sentenced to death in the State of New York. For some New Yorkers the murders were still a sensitive subject and not one to be set to music on Broadway. Some members of the Latino community were disappointed that a high-profile musical featuring Latino actors and storyline had to focus on gangs and murder, while others supported the production.

In 1998, Walcott was involved in rewriting parts of the script, originally written by David McKenna (1968-), for the controversial U.S. film *American History X*. The director Tony Kaye (1952-) turned to Walcott for help and flew to St Lucia to consult with him after encountering problems with the script. They spent several weeks together working on new dialogue and scenes. A film about racism, neo-Nazis and racial conflict, the project was plagued with difficulties, but it eventually proved a great box office success.

By the 1980s, Walcott was showing an increasing interest in film. For instance, after his play, *To Die for Grenada*, which deals with the United

States led invasion of Grenada in October 1983, was briefly and not very successfully performed in Cleveland, Walcott began revising it as a film script, and his papers contain a number of panels and storyboards. He has also written about the invasion of Grenada in his essay, "Good Old Heart of Darkness".[18] This interest in film was taken further in a film version of *The Haytian Earth* (1984), made in St Lucia with his participation as producer. He also narrated and wrote a documentary film for the *Voices and Visions* series on Hart Crane for the New York Centre for Visual History in 1995 and appears in another film made by the New York Centre for Visual History, *A Maddening Space* (1999), in conversation with his dear friend, Russian-American poet Joseph Brodsky (1940-1996).

Alongside these new directions, there were also returns to recurring, almost obsessional themes, for example, the connection between the Caribbean and Ancient Greece. So, after *Omeros* in 1990, Walcott wrote a stage version of the Odyssey.[19] This was performed by the Royal Shakespeare Company in 1992 with sold-out London audiences. *The Odyssey* was also very successfully staged at the 2007 Stratford Festival in Stratford, Ontario, starring Walter Borden, Allegra Fulton, Nigel Shawn Williams and Jeremiah Sparks, with direction by Peter Hinton.

After *Omeros*, Walcott's love of everyday people and the way he tries to honour them in his work was further shown in his play, *Steel*, first performed in 1991 in Cambridge, Massachusetts, at the American Repertory Theatre's New Stages series. The Trinidad Theatre Workshop also mounted a major production of *Steel* in 2005. *Steel*, dedicated to Roddy, and the Turks Steel Band, is the story of two competing steelbands, the Bandidos and the Desperados,[20] from the Port of Spain neighbourhood known as Laventille.

Settled by freed African slaves in the 1800s, Laventille was historically considered as the spiritual home of steel pan, and known for the excellence of its bands and musicians. It was and is also a very poor neighbourhood, with a history of violence and conflict with police stretching to the present day. Violence between bands was not unknown, especially in pan's early days. Walcott had already written about Laventille in a poem of that name in the 1965 collection, *The Castaway and other Poems*. In this he stresses more heavily how Laventille is a place where:

> The middle passage never guessed its end.
> This is the height of poverty
> for the desperate and black;
> climbing, we could look back
> with widening memory
> on the hot, corrugated-iron sea
> whose horrors we all shared.[21]

In *Steel*, the emphasis is much more strongly on the hill's creativity:

The hill
The hill
Sundays so sweet on the hill
a steel pan practicing one
tune/over
and over
down in the yard
While pigeon flocks
Wheel overhead
Come back Africa
Bring me peace of mind

The story of *Steel* is set during the 1930s and 1940s and traces the experiences of a musician who turns from the piano to steel pan, an obvious metaphor for the colonial/post-colonial experience, set against a backdrop of World War II. The Walcott papers include numerous sketches, drawings and watercolours illustrating his visual conceptions of the play, as well as scripts and drafts. Below, the lyrics to the song, "Were You There?", as sung by the calypsonian character Growler (played by Albert Laveau in the 2005 Trinidad Theatre Workshop production), narrates the early development of steel pan music:

Were you there?
Were you there
The night that peace declare?
Were you there
Were you there
On the night that peace declare?
Adolf Hitler gone
Mussolini bawl
And Hirohito hiding in the hospital
It was down in Belmont Eli heard a bugle
People running, screaming that 'Peace declare!
Three cheers for the American Eagle
The British Lion and the Russian Bear,'
He was heading for the docks on the graveyard shift
When he heard a noise down Observatory Street,
Fellers beating old iron, well, Eli lift
A dustbin cover and he start to beat.
No tune, just percussion, so he dent the pan,
He hammer two notes and them notes sound sweet
And is from that melody that steel began,
So that Pan victory was Japan defeat.'

Later in the play, during a calypso competition, Growler laments his waning fame as a performer:

I send a suit to the tailor
About a month in advance
You know he send me the jacket
But he hold on to the pants

In the days of my glory
It just wasn't so
It was a different story
When I was King of Calypso
Those days it was: Growler's
Monarch's Melody.
Tonight, where me trousers?
They in custody [...][22]

If Walcott has been married and divorced three times – to Fay Moston, Margaret Maillard, and Norline Metivier – he has come to rest, since 1987, with his partner Sigrid Nama, a Danish-American art dealer. He has three children, Peter, Elizabeth and Anna. And if his biography displays its share of quarrels and fallings out, Derek Walcott has many good friends in the United States and the rest of the world, including poets, editors, artists and musicians. One of the features of his later life has been a number of particularly deep friendships, mostly made during his time in the USA. One of his great friendships was with the Russian-American poet Joseph Brodsky.[23] Walcott and Brodsky met at the American poet Robert Lowell's funeral in 1977, with whom both had been friends separately. Brodsky was supposed to meet and travel to the Lowell funeral in Boston with Walcott, author Susan Sontag (1933-2004), and Roger Straus (1917-2004) of Farrar, Straus and Giroux.

The three waited for Brodsky at the airport but he did not appear. Walcott says that Brodsky sat down next to him at the funeral in the same pew and that later they formally met, forming the beginnings of an intimate and important friendship. While he often speaks of exile, he describes himself as not a true exile, saying that someone like Joseph Brodsky is a true exile since he could never return to his homeland whereas he, Walcott, is more of an "economic" exile, who can return home at any time he has sufficient money. Walcott's poem, "Forest of Europe", dedicated to Joseph Brodsky, explores some of the convergencies of their different paths:

There is a Gulag Archipelago
under this ice, where the salt, mineral spring
of the long Trail of Tears runnels these plains
as hard and open as a herdsman's face
sun-cracked and stubbled with unshaven snow.

[...]

The tourist archipelagoes of my South
are prisons too, corruptible, and though
there is no harder prison than writing verse,
what's poetry, if it is worth its salt,
but a phrase men can pass from hand to mouth?

From hand to mouth, across the centuries,
the bread that lasts when systems have decayed,
when, in his forest of barbed-wire branches,
a prisoner circles, chewing the one phrase
whose music will last longer than the leaves,[24]

Brodsky credits Walcott with the translation of his poem, "Letters from the Ming Dynasty", published in *The New Yorker* in 1980 and read by Walcott at *The New Yorker* festival. Walcott has said that this was typical of Brodsky's overly generous nature to share credit, and that he worked with Brodsky and a Russian translator on the poem.

... Wind blows us westward like the yellow tares
from a dried pod, there where the Wall towers.
Against it man's figure is ugly and stiff as a frightening hieroglyph,
As any illegible scripture at which one stares.
This pull in one direction only has made
Me something elongated, like a horse's head,
And all the body should do is spent by its shadow
Rustling across the wild barley's withered blade.[25]

Brodsky wrote of Walcott: "For almost forty years his throbbing and relentless lines kept arriving in the English language like tidal waves, coagulating into an archipelago of poems without which the map of modern literature would effectively match wallpaper. He gives us more than himself or 'a world'; he gives us a sense of infinity embodied in the language."[26] Brodsky died in 1996 in New York and Walcott was one of the readers at his funeral, along with other close friends such as Czeslaw Milosz and Mikhail Barishnikov (1948-).

A third poet was added to this incredible friendship in New York City in the form of Irish poet, Seamus Heaney (1939-). Walcott says that he became friends with Heaney following the appearance of a nasty review of Heaney's work. Walcott was outraged and sent Heaney a soothing note – "with a little obscenity" – through his publisher to support him. They became good friends. The essay, "Heaney in Ireland" is about Walcott's visit to Ireland and an homage to the life and work of his friend.

The peace of Ireland was passing by on the drive, and what was centrally contained in Seamus' poetry was also passing through and permanent, the window-glass. The tight coil of his lines, on which the words cluster like berries eaten one at a time, and along which there is a close-leaved thickening that, stripped like a rod would still show a live and pliant branch, the small walled fields, the morning rain on the grey lake, the tight cottages and the old trees of the dipping road to Derry were confirming the verse. The verse and the voice itself.[27]

Walcott, Brodsky and Heaney all lived in New York for a time within a short distance of one another and would frequently get together for long sessions. All three were Nobel laureates, poets, exiles of one type or another, and good friends. The three collaborated on the book, *Homage to Robert Frost*, in 1997. Walcott describes the trio as being outside the American experience:

> [...] Seamus is Irish, Joseph is Russian, I'm West Indian. We don't get embroiled in the controversies about who's a soft poet, who's a hard poet, who's a free-verse poet, who's not a poet, and all of that. It's good to be on the rim of that quarrelling. We're on the perimeter of the American literary scene [...] [28]

Walcott says that he began as an admirer of Robert Lowell and Elizabeth Hardwick (1916-2007), founders of *The New York Review of Books*, later becoming close friends with both. Lowell once told him that "he should put more of himself in his poems".

Walcott wrote of his appreciation for Hardwick following her death in 2007:

> Distance requires formality, but I cannot be distant writing about Lizzie Hardwick since everything has come alarmingly closer – the curls, the infectious chuckle, the drawl like poured-out honey, the privilege of sharing her astute delight, and the benign devastations of her wit. Because she hated pomposity she was more fun than any American writer I have known... You felt that she wrote for you, you hoped that those brilliant monologues of the best prose writer in America would not ever reach a period but you also knew that she would outlast it.[29]

Some other close American friends of Walcott's include Charles Simic (1938-), poetry editor at *The Paris Review* and poet laureate to the library of Congress in 2007; Jonathan Galassi (1949-), President and Publisher of Farrar, Straus and Giroux; Polish new wave poet Adam Zagajewski (1945-); editor Pat Strachan (formerly of Farrar, Straus and Giroux) and Alice Quinn of *The New Yorker*. He has also many dear friends in the Caribbean, Canada, and the rest of the world, including Professors J. Edward "Ted" Chamberlin (1943-) and Edward Baugh (1936-), who together nominated him for the Nobel Prize; Jamaican poet and artist Lorna Goodison (1947-), and the late Rex Nettleford (1933-2010).

Walcott has written numerous essays, reviews, critiques and appreciations of other writers, including a tribute to Arthur Miller (1915-2005); a review of the work of Cuban-American writer Guillermo Cabrera Infante (1929-2005), as well as essays on Ernest Hemingway (1899-1961) and Ted Hughes (1930-1998).[30]

Walcott has had a long and complex relationship with Trinidadian writer and 2001 Nobel laureate V.S. Naipaul (1932-), much of it in the public eye. He dedicated his 1965 poem "Laventille" to Naipaul and during their early days appeared to be on generally friendly terms. In a 1965 letter to Ronald Bryden, Walcott comments on Naipaul, "last saw him at a dinner given by him at his sister's house, where he had held forth, quite high. I like the little runt, but O Gord he over-bearing sometimes. Maiden aunt, accent on maiden..." and further on he jokes about being in Naipaul's next book,

> An Area of Light: Petit Valley Revisited: Being Conversations and Reminiscences With Derek Walcott, as distorted though my fiendish Oriental Gaze, With an appendix and thorax on Ronald Bryden, Critic and Snubber of Dinner Invitations (Andre Deutsch: 18 Guineas with photographs by Lilo Raymond [...][31]

Over the years, enmity and public animosity increased, with Walcott launching attacks on Naipaul though verse, sometimes vicious, sometimes humorous – his character V.S. Nightfall is a thinly veiled Naipaul in the poem "The Spoiler's Return" in *The Fortunate Traveller*, and the vitriolic "The Mongoose", which Walcott performed orally in Jamaica. He takes issue with Naipaul's harsh and pessimistic view of Trinidad and the Caribbean in general, as well as his overly positive attitude towards the former colonial powers, and his lack of support and respect for the place where he was born.

The pathos evident in all of Walcott's work is the basis for his inspiration. His work reflects the experience of himself and those around him, always celebrating the simple, everyday person. Clearly, Walcott is motivated by agape, or love, for the people around him – love of culture, self, place, and language.

Endnotes

1. Jennifer Toews. Foreword by Richard Landon. Preface by Ted Chamberlin, *How Beautiful My Brethren and Sistren: Derek Walcott, Life and Work*, Exhibition Catalogue, October 2011-April 2012, The Thomas Fisher Rare Book Library, University of Toronto.
2. Edward Chamberlin, *Come Back to Me My Language: Poetry and the West Indies* (Champaign: University of Illinois Press, 1993).
3. Ts. *Tiepolo's Hound*, 2000, Several drafts, Derek Walcott papers, Ms. Coll. 348, Boxes 12, 14 and item 15. The Thomas Fisher Rare Book Library.
4. The poem, entitled "1944", was originally published in *The Voice of St. Lucia* on 5 Aug. 1944. It and Friar C. Jesse's reply was reprinted in *Crusader Nobel Laureates Supplement* on 22 Jan. 2000, p. 3.
5. *Omeros* (New York: Farrar, Straus and Giroux, 1990).
6. *The Antilles: Fragments of Epic Memory* (New York: Farrar, Straus, and Giroux, 1993), np.; and in *What the Twilight Says: Essays* (New York: Farrar, Straus, and Giroux, 1998), p. 83.
7. *Tiepolo's Hound* (New York: Farrar, Straus, and Giroux, 2000).

8. "Foreword", *Henri Christophe*, *Drums and Colours* and *The Haytian Earth*: *The Haitian Trilogy* (New York: Farrar, Straus, and Giroux, 2000), pp. VI-VII.
9. On the significance of Haiti. Draft notes for the Haitian Bicentenary, Derek Walcott papers, Ms. Coll. 504, Box 6, The Thomas Fisher Rare Book Library.
10. *Dream on Monkey Mountain* (New York: Farrar, Straus, and Giroux, 1970).
11. Leif Sjöberg, *Conversations with Derek Walcott*, Ed. William Baer (Jackson: University of Mississippi Press, 1996) pp. 79-80.
12. Correspondence with Derek Walcott, Ronald Bryden papers, Ms. Coll. 548, Box 1. The Thomas Fisher Rare Book Library.
13. Patti Hartigan, "The Passions of Derek Walcott", *The Boston Globe*, 25 Apr. 1993.
14. Galt MacDermot letter to Derek Walcott, Derek Walcott papers, Ms. Coll. 136, Box 48, The Thomas Fisher Rare Book Library.
15. Derek Walcott, "The Art of Poetry No. XXXVII", Edward Hirsch interview with Derek Walcott in *The Paris Review,* reprinted in *Critical Perspectives on Derek Walcott*, Ed. Robert D. Hamner (Boulder: Lynne Reiner Publishers, 1997).
16. *O Babylon!* (New York: Farrar, Straus, and Giroux, 1978).
17. "Extracts from 'Marie Laveau'", *Trinidad and Tobago Review*, 3.6 (1979).
18. "Good Old Heart of Darkness", drafts of essay on Grenada, Derek Walcott papers, Ms. Coll. 136, Box 1, The Thomas Fisher Rare Book Library.
19. *The Odyssey: A Stage Version* (New York: Farrar, Straus, and Giroux, 1993).
20. There is a real steel pan band from Laventille called the Desperadoes Steel Orchestra, or Despers, for short. The real life Desperadoes took their name from a Glenn Ford movie that was playing at the time.
21. "Laventille", *The Castaway & Other Poems* (London: Jonathan Cape, 1965), p. 32.
22. *Steel*. Various drafts. Derek Walcott, papers, Ms. Coll. 136, Boxes 28-33, The Thomas Fisher Rare Book Library.
23. Joseph Brodsky was exiled from Russia to New York City in 1972, having been expelled by the government as a subversive, following years of incarceration in mental hospitals and prisons for political reasons. Russian friends say that Brodsky was one of the most apolitical poets they knew. He was a close friend of Anna Akhmatova's as a young man and pallbearer at her funeral. She was instrumental in securing his release from prison shortly before her death in 1966 and his exile to the United States.

24. "Forest of Europe", *The Star-Apple Kingdom* (New York: Farrar, Straus, and Giroux, 1979), p. 38.
25. Joseph Brodsky, "Letters from the Ming Dynasty", *The New Yorker*, 28 Jan., 1980.
26. Joseph Brodsky, "On Derek Walcott", *New York Review of Books*, 30.17 (10 Nov. 1983), pp. 39-41.
27. Derek Walcott, essay drafts "Heaney in Ireland", Derek Walcott papers, Ms. Coll. 136, Box 1. The Thomas Fisher Rare Book Library.
28. Derek Walcott, "The Art of Poetry No. 37", Edward Hirsch interview, p. 16.
29. "Tribute to Elizabeth Hardwick", *New York Review of Books*, 17 Jan. 2008. Draft, Derek Walcott papers, 2009 accession, The Thomas Fisher Rare Book Library.
30. Essay drafts for Arthur Miller Tribute, Derek Walcott papers, Ms. Coll. 504, Box 6, The Thomas Fisher Rare Book Library; Guillermo Cabrera Infante review draft of "The Great Exile" for *The New York Review of Books*, 28 Mar. 2002, Derek Walcott papers, Ms. Coll. 504, Box 1. The Thomas Fisher Rare Book Library; "On Hemingway", *What the Twilight Says: Essays*, pp. 107-114; and "Ted Hughes", *What the Twilight Says: Essays*, pp. 176-181.
31. Correspondence with Derek Walcott, Ronald Bryden papers, Ms. Coll. 548, Box 1.

KENNETH RAMCHAND

WALCOTT AND RAMLILA

"Felicity is a village in Trinidad on the edge of the Caroni plain, the wide central plain that still grows sugar and to which indentured cane cutters were brought after emancipation..."[1] Thus did Nobel Laureate Derek Walcott begin his Lecture at the Prize Award Ceremony in Stockholm on 7 December 1992.

A few years earlier the poet had journeyed to the village on a Saturday afternoon to witness the action on and around the ceremonial field of the First Felicity Ramlila and Cultural Group. The final movement in the Ramlila (a ten-day enactment of the epic life of Lord Rama) was in progress. The climax (due to be carried out on the Sunday as is the convenient practice in Trinidad) was going to be the burning to the ground of a towering, larger-than-life effigy of the vanquished demon King Ravan.

It was a moment of discovery. Walcott admits at once that he had "never seen *Ramleela*, and had never seen this theatre, an open field with village children as warriors, princes, and gods". And he had no idea "what the epic story was, who its hero was, what enemies he fought" (p. 66). He reproves himself and non-Indians in Trinidad for having this impoverishing bias in a country of such inviting cultural diversity. He had recently adapted *The Odyssey* for a theatre in England and he took their familiarity with the Greek epic as a given;[2] but he laments his own not knowing of the Indian epic or the Ramlila enactment, and is critical of his society's casual, almost proud, ignorance: they would tell him, as if it did not matter, that nobody knew any more than he did about the epic or about the Hindu Gods and personages who figured in it, "apart from the Indians". Nobody "apart from the Indians" (p. 66). The phrase spoke to him of the gulf that has been allowed to exist between the ethnicities in Trinidad and Tobago.

The speech drew the world's attention to the Trinidad Ramlila and it made Trinidadians of Indian origin feel proud that something they were living and enacting had been made visible to the world, not as a quaint or exotic "Indian" thing on the fringes of Trinidad culture and society, but as a living evolving presence that now belonged to the place as much as they themselves did. It was as natural a growth as the flora and fauna of the country. The speech by the Nobel Laureate on such a grand stage was validation. To some extent it affected those who had been "leaving it to the Indians" as it were; and it brought additional levels of meaning to followers and practitioners of Ramlila themselves.

Walcott's discovery of Ramlila at Felicity, and his acceptance of it as part of his heritage as a Caribbean person allow him to use it in a larger argument about the nature and possibilities of the Caribbean implicit in the Lecture's title "The Antilles: Fragments of Epic Memory". The argument rejects the view that the region is limited because of its fragmented nature, and it strenuously opposes the notion articulated by the English historian James Anthony Froude (1888) that there are no people in these islands in the true sense of the word.[3]

The Nobel Laureate elaborates a conviction, indeed, that "the gathering of broken pieces is the care and pain of the Antilles". He sees this purpose and process in Ramlila, and he sees it as identical with the making and remaking that is poetry and other forms of artistic creation: "Antillean art is this restoration of our shattered histories, our shards of vocabulary, our archipelago becoming a synonym for pieces broken off from the original continent" (p. 69).

The central argument of the Lecture is an argument that involves the overlapping terms "hybridity", "cross-culturality" or "creoleness". What these terms are intended to propose is a process of indigenization and the existence of a wholeness that has been shaping itself in spite of ideologies of exclusion, the making or remaking of a Caribbean that respects and pays homage to ancestral legacies, penetrates to the unity in our diversity, and joyfully takes unto itself elements of all the different ethnic cultures in the region. Walcott wants to make room for, take delight in, and learn from all our ethnicities. He also wants to project the startling life and energy of the nascent Caribbean (and Trinidad) as a unique product of a historical and ongoing process of the meeting of cultures and peoples. It is crucial to the process that it takes place at the same time that the different groups are bonding with their present and particular landscape:

> There is a force of exultation, a celebration of luck, when a writer finds himself a witness to the early morning of a culture that is defining itself, branch by branch, leaf by leaf, in that self-defining dawn, which is why, especially at the edge of the sea, it is good to make a ritual of the sunrise. Then the noun, the "Antilles" ripples like brightening water, and the sounds of leaves, palm fronds, and birds are the sounds of a fresh dialect, the native tongue. The personal vocabulary, the individual melody whose metre is one's biography, joins in that sound, with any luck, and the body moves like a walking, a waking island.
>
> This is the benediction that is celebrated, a fresh language and a fresh people, and this is the frightening duty owed. (p. 70)

In his collection of essays *The Unfinished Genesis of the Imagination*, Wilson Harris argues that "within the gulfs that divide cultures [...] there exists [...] a storage of creative possibility" that could energise "the unfinished genesis of imagination" and give access to "eclipsed bridges and potential bridges between divorced or separated or closed orders and worlds".[4] It is the same transforming liberation from closed identities, the same discovering of creative possibility and newness that Walcott's Lecture pursues.

The speech also projects the city of Port of Spain as a city whose original architecture and polyglot streets might have led to the creation of a city of our own more akin to the city states of Greece than to Paris, New York or London. This city, silhouettes of whose built heritage are "idealizations of the craftsman's handiwork, not of concrete and glass" would have broken down the historically-biased and biasing distinctions between port and plantation, and between cultures and peoples:

> A surrounding, accessible countryside with leafy suburbs, and if the city is lucky, behind it, spacious plains. Behind it, fine mountains; before it, an indigo sea. [...] Its docks would not be obscured by smoke or deafened by too much machinery, and above all, it would be so racially various that the cultures of the world – the Asiatic, the Mediterranean, the European, the African – would be represented in it, its humane variety more exciting than Joyce's Dublin. Its citizens would intermarry as they chose, from instinct, not tradition, until their children find it increasingly futile to trace their genealogy. (p. 74)

The Nobel Lecture is another foray in what one critic has called Walcott's quarrel with history (particularly, the view of our history as degrading and maiming); another attempt to celebrate the positives and the immense possibilities waiting to be released in our gathering of peoples and cultures; and a celebration of the transformative powers of the arts of the imagination and cultural expression.

My purpose is to acknowledge that Walcott's discussion of Ramlila is part of a larger argument and to make sure that neither this dimension nor Ramlila's implication in it are too far in the background as I focus on the dialogue between Walcott and the Ramlila. I want to consider aspects of the Ramlila and Walcott's visit to it in order to draw out some of the implications for the performing arts and for our attitude to the sacred. Two key statements in the lecture provide a focus. The first is: "I was seeing the Ramleela at Felicity as theatre when it was faith" (p. 66). The second relates to Walcott's misgivings about attempting to use conventional terms to classify the performers/participants in the Ramlila: "There was no theatrical term to define them" (p. 67).

The Ramlila referred to in Derek Walcott's Nobel Lecture is the Trinidad Ramlila which takes place every year in many parts of the island during the period September/October (the lunar month of Ashvin in the

Hindu calendar). It is an enactment of major events in the life of Lord Rama, seventh incarnation of the Supreme Protector Vishnu, who came to earth to annihilate the evil forces of the age. This "lila" or play of the Gods is called "avatar lila" because Ram, an avatar of Vishnu is playing at being a man on the earth. It is a divine play whose motive is the adoration of Sri Rama but it also purports to be a play about someone, a King, involved in struggles a mortal man might face. Which is why he is such a lovelorn human being when Sita is abducted and he is moving around in a frenzy trying to find out "where she gone, where she gone?" But he can no more than Jesus come over as anything less than an avatar.

The Rama story includes:

i. The birth and early life of Rama in Ayodhya up to his marriage with Sita;
ii. Rama's departure into exile from Ayodhya, accompanied by his brother Lakshmana and his wife Sita;
iii. Ram's sojourn in the forest and the abduction of Sita by Rawan who carries her off to Lanka;
iv. The search for Sita and preparations with the help of the Monkey God Hanuman for the crossing of the ocean to Lanka;
v. Hanuman's advance foray into Lanka and Ram's securing of the cooperation of the Ocean;
vi. The Epic Battle in Lanka and the defeat of Rawan; and
vii. The return in triumph to Ayodhya where Ramraj the blessed kingdom is established and the supreme emotion of peace (shanta-rasa) settles the audience and the participants.

Since the 1880s, Ramlila groups in Trinidad have enacted the story in the sequence given above, dramatizing selected events from each "kand".

The Trinidad Ramlila is based upon the *Ramacaritamanasa*, an epic poem written during 1574-1577 by Tulsidas (1532-1623).[5] It is an adaptation and a rendering in popular language of the Sanskrit Ramayana of Valmiki. Tulsidas's nationalist effort was the first "local" variant in a regional language of this sacred text. Hindus could now "hear" and remember it in the language they spoke. Through readings, the religious storytelling of "*kathas*", and Ramlila enactments, which proliferated in the Hindu heartland following the creation of the *Ramacaritamanasa*, it passed rapidly into popular consciousness and popular speech. It became a source of sayings and teachings and a powerful religious and ethical influence on millions who never read it. It came to Trinidad in the heads of the indentureds as religion and faith.

Some kind of Ramlila would have been performed on the estates and in locations where groups of Indians who had served out their indentures were living. The practice would have become stronger with the formation of communities and villages and the establishment of places of communal worship variously called "siwala", "kutia", "temple" and "mandir". We can speculate that enactments before the 1880s would not have lasted for nine or ten days as today, and would not have attempted to cover all the seven movements or "kands".

In the early years, Ramlila-type activities including street processions would have been based largely upon the worship of Ram, memories of Ramlila in India, and material picked up from gatherings, such as this one described in 1868 by the pioneer Canadian Missionary John Morton, in which "their Brahmans or priests... read to them from their sacred books the wonderful and questionable exploits attributed to their gods".[6] The "wonderful and questionable exploits" the disbelieving Morton mentions were very likely the heroic actions of Ram and one of the sacred books would have been the *Ramacaritamanasa*.

Before the wide establishment of the kinds of places of worship listed above, there were outdoor locations for communal worship and other gatherings in houses and barrack rooms. Morton's diary entry for 18 April 1868 describes private worship in a Hindu dwelling: "An altar with flowers all round it, a candle in a bottle on each side; a sacred book in the middle; three babujies [or priests]; heaps of cocoanut cut up, bêtel, sugar etc. They said it was their church same as ours."[7]

Interestingly, in the entry for Sunday 3 May 1868, Morton records a procession on the road that suggests the existence of some kind of street enactment that included the main Ramlila figures:

> In the afternoon, some men came down the street carrying on poles a canopy with four idols; three sitting up in a row, and one lying down in the corner. The canopy was painted with figures of men, fish, etc. One was Ram as might be expected; another was Seeta, the wife of Ram; the other they called Lakshmana, and said he was the son of Ram but others said he was Ram's brother. Seeta had a large ring in her nose as many of the Hindoo women wear. They were gaudily painted – red, and blue and green. The one lying in a corner was an ugly grinning creature; they called him Haldhar, and said he was a monkey. His body was covered with a light crop of wool. They set down their burden that I might see, and a crowd gathered round. (Morton, p. 53-54)

Such activities were undoubtedly connected with the strong tradition of devotion to Ram that came from India with the indentureds.

By the late nineteenth century, perhaps because memory was being supported by access to the Tulsidas text, all the "kands" or sections were beginning to be represented in order, over ten days. The Dow Village Ramlila and Cultural Group claims to have performed, in 1880, the first ten day Ramlila in Trinidad. From about that time, Ramlilas began to proliferate. Early accounts suggest that there was not any opposition felt between theatre and faith.

In October 1931 (this is one of many references in the newspapers) the *Trinidad Guardian*'s Chaguanas correspondent recognized both "theatre" and religion when he wrote about a Ramlila performance under the title "Open-Air Theatre in Caroni". He emphasizes the spectacular final battle ("theatre"?) which raged from midday to sunset in the Woodford Lodge Savannah while passages were read from the *Ramayana* ("faith") by a pundit. In the same issue, the paper's Carapichaima Correspondent calls Ramlila a play, entitling his piece "Ramlila Play Climax". He describes the fall of King Rawan "whose effigy stands many feet high, with ten hands and ten heads painted in black". He was "shot at with bow and arrows" and "ultimately burnt to ashes". This report also sees no contradiction between the "play" and the faith. The reporter makes sure to tell us that the "ceremonies were being conducted by Deo Pundit with K. Persad assisting, under the supervision of Mr Raju Singh."[8]

The centre of the Ramlila was Ram. Tulsidas portrays Ram as a man – ideal son, father, husband, brother, friend and leader – but every "kand" of "this very elegant composition relating in common parlance the story of the Lord of the Raghus" is suffused with devotion and worship to Shri Rama. His incomparable power and beauty are declared again and again by the untiring poet: "I adore Lord Hari, known by the name of Sri Rama, who is superior to and lies beyond all causes, whose Maya (illusive power) holds sway over the entire Universe including gods from Brahma (the Creator) downwards, and demons... Rama whose feet are the only bark for those who are eager to cross the ocean of mundane existence".[9]

Technically, the traditional audience and the performers of the play are taking part in a play, but all their acts are acts of devotion to Ram. They are participating in a "yagna" ("prayers") in open air (open to earth, air, water). They are involved in an increasingly ecstatic adoration of Ram, a puja that brings them into heightened consciousness and enables them to receive "darshan" or visions of the divine. This mental/emotional state or "rasa" is called "bhakti rasa" because it is an intense emotion arising from spiritual devotion.

There is a happy complication, a complementarity, to be noted because it suggests gender balance and because it intensifies the "rasa". The Ramlila which focuses on Ram occurs at the same time as the Maha ("Great") Navratri, a nine-night festival dedicated to Shakti, the feminine divine force. In this *navratri*, Shakti or Devi is worshipped in various forms that include Saraswati, Lakshmi and Durga. The day after the nine nights of *navratri* is the festival of "dussehra" which marks the triumph of the warrior goddess Durga over the buffalo demon Mahishasura, a victory on the tenth day ("dus" = ten) which symbolizes the annihilation ("har" = annihilation) of evil by good. But it was on this day also that Lord Rama defeated the once-shining King Rawan who had abducted Rama's wife Sita and taken her off to his stronghold in Lanka.

The strong link between the two sets of religious activities taking place in the same season is that Ram's victory over Rawan is an analogue of Durga's victory over the demon Mahishasura, both Maha Navratri and Ram Lila thus culminating in the "dussehra", celebrating the triumph of good over evil. The coinciding of the two sets of activities, with many celebrants involved in or sympathetic to both, would have served to intensify the emotion or "rasa".

Throughout the enactment we find in different moments the other nine rasas of the aesthetic theory, but the structuring of the Ramlila whose climax was happening around the time of Walcott's visit may be considered a device, an aesthetic means of stimulating "bhakti rasa" and "shanta rasa".

The ground that Walcott visited that Saturday is one of over thirty-five places in Trinidad where the ten-day Ramlila is celebrated. As noted, he knew next to nothing about Ramlila and he had never been to a performance before, and he left the ground early because he had to make his way through the Caroni swamp by boat to see the flocks of scarlet ibis returning home at dusk. So what elements of the Ramlila did he see? And what reflections were triggered by what he saw?

He saw "a field strung with different-coloured flags, like a new gas station". He saw Indian boys in red and black "aiming arrows haphazardly into the afternoon light" (p. 65). Images of the boys in scarlet, the red flags, and the flight of the arrows were in his mind's eye as he took in the ibises heading for the trees; and the colour and movement of the Ramlila scene fuse with the colour and movement of the birds. Both movements were natural, both part of the landscape, both proclaiming a space transcending the cares imposed by history, the visual delight of both leading the poet to "see" the unseen (a kind of "darshan"):

> In a performance as natural as those of the actors of the *Ramleela* we watched the flocks come in as bright as the scarlet of the boy archers, as the red flags, and cover an islet until it turned into a flowering tree, an anchored immortelle. The sigh of History meant nothing here. These two visions, the *Ramleela* and the arrowing flocks of scarlet ibises, blent into a single gasp of gratitude. (p. 68)

Later in the lecture Walcott elaborates on how the making of the Ramlila is not nostalgia or cultural incest, but a characteristic poetic act of the Antilles, the labour of the Antillean imagination "rebuilding its gods from bamboo frames, phrase by phrase" (p. 82).

He didn't just see parts of the Ramlila. He saw things *in* the Ramlila. One of the things Walcott saw in the Ramlila was an act of creation and possession defying the history of genocide, slavery, colonialism and the benign blights of tourism and "progress":

> Before it is all gone, before only a few valleys are left, pockets of an older life, before development turns every artist into an anthropologist or folklorist, there are still cherishable places, little valleys that do not echo with ideas, a simplicity of rebeginnings, not yet corrupted by the dangers of change. Not nostalgic sites but occluded sanctities as common and simple as their sunlight" (p. 82).

The second answer to the question "So what did Walcott see?" relates to the figure of Ravan. In the *Ramacaritamanas*, it is said by Ravan's principal spouse that the compassionate Ram has absorbed the dead King in his own being. Ram instructs Vibhisana to perform the funeral rites, and the text drily announces that it is done "strictly observing the scriptural ordinance" (*Ramacaritamanas,* Descent Six "Lanka Kanda", p. 925). Tulsidas does not mention cremation. But James Prinsep's *Banaras Illustrated*, is documentary evidence that the burning of a Ravan effigy had begun by 1831 and probably earlier.[10]

The practice came to Trinidad with indentured Indian labourers. It is a major feature of the Ramlila and the most spectacular one. On this day, in many parts of Trinidad and India, huge effigies of a larger than life Ravan, painted black, are set on fire to mark the victory of Ram over the demon king. To the exultant crowd it is a celebration of the victory of righteousness over unrighteousness. But the burning of the Rawan effigy has another dimension. It is a sad and chastening spectacle, the cremation and purification of a bright King who had fallen from grace. The participants identify with the process of purification: the burning out of evil in the external world is also a burning out of evil in the hearts of all living men and women.

As Walcott looked about him that day in Felicity, his eyes were drawn to an open shed on the edge of the field where "two huge armatures of bamboo that looked like cages" (p. 65) were lying on the ground. The "armature" here is the "skeletal framework" to support the papier-mache used in fleshing out the figure of Ravan. Although Walcott mistakenly refers to the demon King as a god and turns on the power of another sense of "armature" (the rotating coil or coils of a dynamo or electric motor) later to suggest the re-constitution of a god, he knew that the parts he was seeing on the ground would be put together to make a gigantic effigy of Ravan to be burnt as a conclusion to the epic.

With no knowledge of Ravan or Ramlila but with a poetic feel for archetypes, he understands what many celebrants tend to play down in the burning festivities, namely that the burning of Ravan is an act of forgiveness and an act of purification before the possibility of rebirth. Near to the body parts, Walcott saw the drummers warming the skins of their tassas in the heat of a makeshift fire and this is what he apprehends:

> "The saffron flames, the bright grass, and the hand-woven armatures of the fragmented god who would be burnt were not in any desert where

imperial power had finally toppled but were part of a ritual, evergreen season that, like the cane-burning harvest, is annually repeated, the point of such sacrifice being its repetition, the point of the destruction being renewal through fire" (p. 66).

Walcott does not get everything right. He noticed the different coloured flags strung in the field but he does not mention the main jhandi reaching up to the sky, at the foot of which is the bedi or altar on which are placed the *Ramacaritamanasa* and holy pictures as murtis. He does not know that the jhandi turns the Ramlila ground into a sacred space. Nevertheless, the third answer I propose to give to the question "What did Walcott see" is to describe a higher form of "seeing", his remarkable and apparently spontaneous entering into the spirit of the Ramlila. Only because he entered into the spirit was Walcott able to intellectualise the Ramlila and relate it to his thinking about the nature of Caribbean society and to confirm the store of growing resources in indigenous artistic and cultural expression.

The children gambolling on the field in this lila, and the handsome boys shooting arrows into the sunlight were gods at play with the gods. "Princes and gods, I supposed" (p. 66), not knowing he was supposing right. Tulsidas belonged to the tradition of Vishnaiva poets devoted to Ram: he goes so far as to assert that the name "Rama" is bigger than Rama, and is a mantra, a sound, the repetition of which can lead to the devotee's being transported into a higher state. Walcott did not know any of this. But for a man who did not know too much, Walcott felt a lot.

Walcott was in a tropical evening's cloud of unknowing. He was struck by the boys aiming arrows into the afternoon light just as he was struck by the confident beauty of the place: "Low blue mountains on the horizon, bright grass, clouds that would gather colour before the light went. Felicity!" (p. 65). He felt the ecstasy which was "the pitch of the sinuous drumming in the loudspeakers." He felt the joy of the celebrants. There was "elation, delight in the boys' screams, in the sweet-stalls, in more and more costumed characters appearing…" (p. 67).

He had come expecting that "the Ramayana would be poorly performed in this ocean of cane" (p. 66) by amateur actors from a village. And here it was now, the action was unfolding contrary to what his head had arranged. The people he saw on the sacred ground and stage were devotees who had been calling the name of Ram for days and had reached the point of being transported into a higher state. They were gods. They were experiencing "bhakti rasa" as they would have done on previous days.

From the account we can see that Walcott had picked up enough to understand, if someone had said it to him, that the Ramlila is a ritual for invoking the gods and an artistic device that includes song, dance, recitation, reading and mime for evoking an emotional response in the audience.

While it might be going too far to say that Walcott experienced "bhakti rasa", the poet was by disposition attuned to receive the powerful emotion evoked by the Ramlila and only that intensity could have inspired the collected exercise of mind that is the Nobel Lecture:

> I was seeing the *Ramleela* at Felicity as theatre when it was faith [...]
> They were not Amateurs but believers. There was no theatrical term to define them. They did not have to psych themselves up to play their roles. Their acting would probably be as buoyant and as natural as those bamboo arrows crisscrossing the afternoon pasture. They believed in what they were playing, in the sacredness of the text, the validity of India, while I, out of the writer's habit, searched for some sense of elegy, of loss, even of degenerative mimicry in the happy faces of the boy-warriors or the heraldic profiles of the village princes. I was polluting the afternoon with doubt... (pp. 66–67)

Walcott's reflections on the Ramlila are a call for a more joyful and imaginative acceptance of our cultural diversity. His declaration that the Ramlila was faith not theatre offers an insight but it is not a resolution. And far from bringing closure, the statement that "there was no theatrical term to define them" (p. 67) is a challenge to scholars and practitioners in Caribbean theatre. The questions raised for Caribbean theatre by Walcott's Lecture call for the exploration of another area of ignorance. The mandate for a national theatre further indicates the commencement of practice-oriented studies of Indian aesthetic theory. We have a lot more to learn from this, and from a similar approach to African performance culture, than from regurgitations of the hand-me-downs from Anglo-American Graduate schools.

Endnotes

1. Derek Walcott, *The Antilles: Fragments of Epic Memory. The Nobel Lecture* (New York: Farrar, Straus and Giroux, 1993), not paginated. References are given to the reprint in *What the Twilight Says: Essays* (London: Faber & Faber, 1998), p. 65.
2. Derek Walcott, *The Odyssey: A Stage Version* (New York: Farrar, Straus and Giroux, 1993).
3. James Anthony Froude, *The English in the West Indies* (London: Longmans Green and Co., 1888).
4. Wilson Harris, *The Unfinished Genesis of the Imagination* (New York: Routledge, 1992), p. 239.
5. Tulsidas, *Sri Ramacaritamanasa: with Hindi Text and English Translation*

(A Romanised Edition) (Gorakpur, India: Gita Press, No Date, but based on a 1968 edition, original text in Nagari with an English translation).

6. *John Morton of Trinidad: Journals, Letters and Papers,* Ed. Sarah E. Morton (Toronto: Westminster Company, 1916), p. 52.
7. *John Morton*, p. 53.
8. *Trinidad Guardian*, Wednesday 21 Oct. 1931, 9.
9. *Sri Ramacaritamanasa,* Descent One: "Bala Kanda", p. 2.
10. James Prinsep, *Banaras Illustrated* (Calcutta: Baptist Mission Press, 1831).

ANTONIA MACDONALD

STUDENTS, I PRESENT... THE YOUNG POET, DEREK WALCOTT

> [...] until after a while there was nothing left of him
> except this: a name cut on a wall that soon
> from the grime of indifference became indecipherable.[1]

Typically, the St Lucian student approaches Derek Walcott's poetry with respect and trepidation. After all, Mr Walcott's reputation as the greatest Caribbean poet has preceded him and St Lucia repeatedly attests to pride in having produced this son of the soil, a man who is also an excellent playwright and a competent watercolourist. Undeniably, Walcott, recipient of the St Lucia Cross, the nation's highest honour, is a great poet. There is international recognition of that claim because in 1992 Derek Walcott was awarded the Nobel Prize for Literature, the first person from the English-speaking Caribbean to be thus honoured.[2] Every January in this student's lifetime, the St Lucian media have devoted their attention to Nobel Laureate week – seven days of celebrating the accomplishments of Derek Walcott and Sir Arthur Lewis – proud that this two hundred and thirty eight square mile island can boast two Nobel laureates. It makes mileage of the coincidence of both Walcott and Lewis being born on January 23rd. It capitalizes on the opportunity for promoting tourism around the fact that these great men were born in St Lucia. Yearly, Mr Walcott, the living laureate, is put on parade. Public lectures are delivered in his honour and his artistic contributions are widely showcased. The St Lucian student watches, listens, applauds and admires without, for the most part, really knowing what makes Mr Walcott's poetry such celebrated writing. Many, having understood very little of what they have read, uncertain whether the parts they did understand were enjoyable, nonetheless are proud to stand shoulder to shoulder with all the other loud enthusiasts and testify to Derek Walcott's poetic greatness.

Honest admission will reveal that the typical St Lucian student has found Walcott's poems difficult to understand; that they had to depend on a dictionary as a companion, and this reliance detracted from the reading experience. Many of the words in the poems are unfamiliar: not words that appear in the schoolbooks being studied; not found in the local media; and not words used by the man in the street. The man in the street often speaks *kweyol*;[3] there is very little *kweyol* in Derek Walcott's poetry. Having been taught that a poem must mean something, that the poem is a code that must be cracked, the student cannot accept that a poem is a performance, that a poem can just be, that sometimes what is being said is not as important as how it is being said. Perplexed, the student wonders: "What is the poem about? Why am I not getting it?" Additionally, while the student has a good working knowledge of poetic devices, reading Walcott's poetry brings the student face to face with a bewildering number of allusions, ones that make the uninformed reader repeatedly ask: "What does this mean? Why is it included in the poem?"

While few will admit it, understanding Walcott's poetry is often a tenuous affair; you get the idea, or at least you think you get it, then suddenly meaning quickly escapes your reach, leaving you exhausted after having chased so many apparently conflicting and complex images. Harold Simmons, in his review of Walcott's first collection of poetry, *25 Poems*, provided the following telling assessment of the poet and his reader:

> When these lines [are] being written, images, words, ideas, dance in the mind, jostling, coming and going: the poet chooses, rejects, concentrates, accepting a rejected phrase or image. The reader too also experiences the dance of thoughts that originally jostled the poet's mind, flickering on the fringe of understanding, or fading into thoughts newly found by the reader. "It is a mistake to ask the poet what he means by an obscure phrase in a poem, as he may mean one thing or several things..."[4]

Derek Walcott's fondness for the musicality of words and his fascination with the capacity of metaphor to name things differently, creatively and transformatively are characteristics that have made his poetry outstanding. His ability to rework in his poems the influences of the many other poems he has studied has made Walcott's poetry multicultural. These characteristics are also the stumbling blocks that uninitiated readers face: complexity, denseness, richness. These ambiguous labels are both bane and blessing. The reader who is skilled in negotiating the thickets of language will receive those descriptors as a challenge. But what is the experience of the common reader? The young teller who serves Mr Walcott in the bank, the woman who owns the bar in Gros Islet where Mr Walcott stops in to buy cigarettes, the architect who designed the house in Cap Estate where Mr Walcott currently resides, students at Sir Arthur Lewis Community College who have had the pleasure of seeing Mr Walcott on their campus, and persons who have been to the UWI Open Campus and have heard Kendel

Hippolyte, another renowned St Lucian poet, talk about Walcott's poetic contribution to St Lucia: for them words like "complex" and "dense" mean, "Leave it alone. It is not for you!"

What, then, are the consequences of having a major contributor to St Lucian literature, a Nobel Laureate, who is unread? If we do not analyse his poetry, how can we accept the claims of his literary greatness as true, and offer others proof of that greatness? How do we ensure that his poems live on for the coming generations? How can we use Walcott as an advertisement for St Lucia yet at the same time fail to promote his poetry to our visitors? When do we get to post "I like Derek Walcott's poetry!" on Facebook or Twitter? With these questions in mind, I would like to reintroduce the St Lucian student to Mr Derek Walcott: poet. I have chosen to focus on the student because as a teacher I have too often heard frustrated students exclaim: "Derek Walcott's poetry is too hard" – or for those who are unwilling to admit to having difficulty understanding it, the dismissive comment, "Derek Walcott's poetry is boring." I believe that the study of poetry is important to one's intellectual and aesthetic development. I am convinced that if Derek Walcott is not read and understood by this generation of young people, he will in time become like the novels he describes in *The Prodigal* as the "unread famous…"[5] Accordingly, I offer this introductory essay in the hope that it will help to facilitate understanding and appreciation of Walcott's poetry amongst St Lucia's students.

I hope that Derek Walcott will become an often read, often cited poet, in much the same way that our parents and grandparents happily quoted memorable lines from the Romantic poets. While for many Caribbean people in the 1950s–1960s, the introduction to poetry came via that colonial textbook, *The Nelson Royal Reader*[6], what was important about those literary encounters were the pedagogical strategies implemented by educators in ensuring understanding and retention, while at the same time promoting poetry as a something to be enjoyed, respected and treasured. Although the subject matter of those poems – the much abused daffodils, London's urban landscape, nature in temperate lands – was not part of the lived Caribbean experience, readers were offered detailed annotations of the poems that allowed a thorough grounding in the world of the poem, delineating that British context so painstakingly that it sometimes became more real than the Caribbean space in which readers daily engaged. Walcott has been constantly praised for his unusual and memorable poetic lines. The hope must be that his verses come to be quoted from memory, so that his lines come to articulate the wonders of the Caribbean landscape, as the reader experiences them.

But this essay, whilst offered as a learning aid, in the first instance, to St Lucian and Caribbean students, so that they recognize him as the finest mentor any would-be poet can have, is also offered to international students whose encounter with Walcott's poetry may be made more fruitful by seeing it in its St Lucian context of time and place. The commentaries are not intended as the definitive or sole interpretation, but are proposed as keys to unlocking the magic of the poems and creating a discursive space that invites the reader's personal response. With repeated readings of the poems – and I encourage reading aloud because this best captures their musicality – new insights will be gained.

The still growing body of Derek Walcott's poetry is an extensive one. It includes the epic, *Omeros*, long poems such as *The Prodigal*, the verse memoir, *Another Life*, dramatic poetry such as *Henri Christophe*, extended meditations, medium-length narrative poems, lyrical sequences, sonnets and short poems. In twenty-first century Caribbean society, searching the worldwide web has become the first help-source for any student wanting to learn something about Walcott's poetry. "A City's Death by Fire" is among the most frequently listed. This poem was written in commemoration of the 1948 Castries fire, and was first published in 1948 in *25 Poems*. While it was not the most cited poem in that collection, "A City's Death by Fire" drew attention to itself because of its subject – an irrevocable change in the urban landscape of Castries[7] – and because it was the first poem written by a St Lucian about a subject that had provoked poetic renditions from persons throughout the Caribbean.[8] I will offer a close reading of "A City's Death by Fire", not only because it has been frequently anthologized, but also because of the boldness with which a young Walcott handled poetic form and structure in depicting this national tragedy. I will also analyse "Prelude", a poem that is not often referenced by critics, but one to which I believe students can relate, because it explores the teenage Walcott's contemplation of his future as a poet. "Prelude" was also published in *25 Poems*, but entitled, "I With Legs Crossed Along the Daylight Watch."[9]

Interviewed by Charles H. Rowell in 1988, Walcott provides a lengthy explanation of the context of "Prelude."

> I think I wrote that poem when I was probably sixteen or seventeen […] when we were boys at college, we felt that we were part of the heritage of the British Empire – its language, its history, and so on. We were quite aware of the fact that the background of the Caribbean was a background of slavery. But my generation was not schizophrenic about the heritage of the Empire and the heritage of the Caribbean. It was a double rather than a split thing. In other words, we had an interior life, the life of education.[10]

Walcott's admission that this may be one of his very early poems – in the sense that although it was published when he was eighteen, it may have been written the year or so before – is important. For critics who divide Walcott's poetry into periods – juvenilia, mature, etc. – this poem rightfully belongs to his *early* juvenilia period and must be analysed in that context.

But the placement of this poem as the first poem in his subsequent collection, *In a Green Night*, and the change of the poem's title to "Prelude" are indications of the importance Walcott himself gave to this poem. Indeed, though it disappears from Walcott's first American collection, *Selected Poems* (1964), it is restored to the *Collected Poems* of 1986,[11] suggesting that even in his maturity, Walcott considered this poem as the introductory note (to borrow a musical metaphor) to his *magnum opus*. The title suggests that the poem will introduce what is to follow – a revelation of Walcott's vocation as poet, his intention to make a difference to Caribbean *belles lettres*, his awareness that no West Indian before him had declared themselves as "poet" even though there were writers of poetry.[12]

Together "A City's Death by Fire" and "Prelude" explore such themes as coming of age in a rapidly changing world, defining one's place in that world, and anxieties about the kind of person one will grow into. Walcott's angst-ridden teenage voice will resonate with students who are beset by similar anxieties, and this creates a space for empathy and fellowship with these two poems. Moreover, these poems provide examples of Walcott's ambivalent responses to his St Lucian landscape – his sense of himself as a part of, yet apart from, what is happening around him, to the geography of the island as well as to how people interact with each other, their way of being. Both poems depict an island in the process of change and flux – a representation with which the St Lucian student can identify.

It is important to contextualize Walcott at this point at the start of his poetic career, when he was preoccupied with finding his poetic voice, in order to make him more pertinent to the student. As a Caribbean student interested in mapping out his future as poet in a colonial world, Walcott took directions from all possible sources. Today the would-be poet has the option of attending poetry workshops, but at the time Walcott was producing his first poems, he had no such opportunity. So he created his own version of a workshop, reading those he considered to be master poets and, like any good apprentice, he set about using what he had learnt to create poems that reflected his own way of thinking and the St Lucian space within which he was operating. His education and the collections he borrowed from libraries exposed him to poems written by British and American poets. These were his models. Believing that art is eternal, that certain truths are not restricted to race, place or time, Walcott also used his knowledge of the classics – Sophocles and Homer – to make links between the ancient world and his yet unexplored St Lucian one.

In the same way that young twenty-first century reggae or soca artistes listen to all musical genres and then create songs that borrow from these, while at the same time improvising in such a way that the sound produced has echoes of, yet is different from the original, the young Walcott was not so much copying what he had read but trying to capture a feeling similar to that conveyed in the poems he liked. The teenage Walcott was not a copier, but an experimenter, creating out of his reading experience poems that were original in their portrayal of the Caribbean world and distinctive in their language. St Lucia and St Lucians were not the subjects of the books he had read. Now he made those his subjects, and in so doing gradually produced poems that outdid those he had modelled himself on.

It is also important in any analysis of Walcott's poetry to recognize that the subject of the poem is usually Walcott, and that the poems make public the issues that concerned him at that time. In his book *Derek Walcott*, Edward Baugh has this to say: "Walcott's work as a whole... may be regarded then, as one continuing fiction, a story whose protagonist is the poet-person, a "character" who is gradually being discovered and created through various metamorphoses, contradictions and continuities."[13]

These two poems, published by a young black man from a little-known, pre-independent Caribbean island, are the work of a divided colonial who is beset by contradictions. He is anxious to prove his worth as a poet and feels that mastery of English poetic models will ensure his success. At the same time he is surrounded by the natural beauty of a tropical island that seems to demand from him a poetic response for which he has no models. This situation makes him feel like Adam in the Garden of Eden, starting from nothing, building his own images, naming his own world. Where he modelled himself on others, he made no attempt to disguise it. Later he said: "Young poets should have no individuality. They should be total apprentices, if they want to be masters."[14] He was always engaged in improving his artistic skills. From 1950 onwards he became heavily involved in dramatic productions and, along with his twin brother Roddy, organized his friends in the St Lucia Arts Guild. Approaching fifty, Walcott looked back on this creative phase and commented, "I knew I was copying and imitating and learning, and when I was criticized for writing like Dylan Thomas it didn't bother me at all because I knew what I was doing. I knew I had to absorb everything in order to discover what I was eventually trying to sound like."[15] In the absence of local or regional mentors he drew artistic guidance from the poets he was reading: W.H. Auden, T.S. Eliot, Walt Whitman and Dylan Thomas. He would be D. A. Walcott: creative, confident and complicated.

That he was able to self-publish a collection of poetry at the tender age of eighteen is indeed phenomenal, and for this remarkable feat, many dubbed him a prodigy.[16] But the act of producing enough poems for a thirty-five page collection, in a year when most people were recovering emotionally and financially from a devastating fire, is one that speaks to the young poet's sense of vocation, while the high quality of the poems is proof of his commitment to masterful execution, regardless of social or national context. More importantly, Walcott believed that what he had to share with the world was as important as poems published in the metropolis. He was confident enough to set about promoting himself, undaunted by his race, his age, the scarcity of publishing opportunities or his circumscribed economic status. In recounting the circumstances of the publication of *25 Poems*, Walcott foregrounds the pivotal role played by his mother, Alix Walcott, a school teacher and part-time seamstress. A widow (her husband died when her sons were two years old), "Teacher Alix" was strongly supportive of her son's talent and gave him the $200 which he paid to the *Trinidad Guardian* printery. This was a large sum of money in support of a venture that was neither popular nor profitable, and with no locally-known precedents.[17]

Publisher and now marketer, Walcott dedicated himself to the business of selling copies to friends and supporters. Harold Simmons, family friend and mentor, also helped promote the collection and wrote to Frank Collymore in Barbados asking him to review it in the local newspapers. At a time when communication between Caribbean people was largely by mail, occasionally by telephone, regional and international publicity for Walcott's first collection of poetry came primarily through referrals in the small but growing Caribbean artistic community. Frank Collymore offered the following prophetic tribute in what was an unusually lengthy notice for the work of a young poet:

> Derek Walcott is a poet of whom any community might well be proud. Let us hope that this significant voice in West Indian literature may continue to be heard often in the many years to come.[18]

The success of the first print run of *25 Poems* allowed for a second reprinting in April 1949 in Bridgetown, Barbados. Very much in the style of contemporary social networking, friends referred friends to Derek Walcott's poetry and his reputation as a poet began to spread beyond the Caribbean. While reviews continued to be enthusiastically generous, some critics noted the heavy influence of certain British and American poets on Walcott's poetic voice. It was obvious that the title that he had selected for his collection echoed Dylan Thomas's *Twenty Five Poems*,[19] and he chose to open his collection with " Inspire Modesty by Means of Nightly Verses", a poem that bears a strong stylistic resemblance to W. H. Auden's "Petition".[20] The theme of poetry as an important vocation is present in many of the poems in this collection. This corresponds to T.S. Eliot's preoccupation with the role of art in imposing order on reality, on the remaking of language in illuminating and enriching one's world. Influences notwithstanding, Derek Walcott, through the act of publishing, felt he had joined a literary fellowship that extended back beyond his contemporary influences to such great poets as Marlowe and Milton. He had produced a collection of poetry which, he believed, not only looked professional, but reflected his own sense of style, of grandeur even: "a large gesture" from a young man who grew up in a place that is "not inhibited by flourish."[21] As he reflected ironically in *Another Life*, some twenty years later:

> [...] The dream
> of reason had produced its monster:
> a prodigy of the wrong age and colour.[22]

"Prelude": Falling Dramatically in Love with Art

"Prelude" opens with the poetic persona sitting crosslegged, looking up at the sky, watching the landscape, noticing the ships out on the horizon and thinking that his homeland may be considered by others to be backward, "lost", as not important or big enough to have cities, as existing merely for the pleasure of tourists who believe island people to be happy natives without a care in the world.[23] This view of the island is not one that the persona altogether disagrees with. Perhaps the education he has received has supported this notion of St Lucia as a place where nothing significant happens. The persona then segues into a philosophical consideration of himself and of his future. He is hardly the patient, carefree islander. Although for the cosmopolitan outsider time stands still on the tropical island, for Walcott, time is passing by, albeit slowly and imperceptibly: "Time creeps over the patient who are too long patient". Having made poetry his vocation, he is anxious to embark on the life he imagines that poets live: one of isolation and discipline, one devoted to perfecting his poetic craft:

> And my life [...]
> [...] must not be made public
> until I have learnt to suffer
> In accurate iambics. ("Prelude", p. 11)

Nurturing the creative imagination requires fixity of purpose and the poet now considers, with a note of self-irony, how to prepare for this phase of his life: "straighten my tie and fix important jaws". The poem then moves to the various postures of grown-up behaviour and, as he considers that women are undoubtedly part of his future, notes the "living images/ Of flesh that saunter through the eye". This general meditation on women then brings him to the consideration of a special current love, one he describes as "Reluctant leopard of the slow eyes." We remain uncertain as to whether this love is a woman or, given the earlier consideration of his vocation as poet, the source of inspiration, his muse.

Encapsulated in these twenty-six lines are many of the themes that will recur in Walcott's later poetry: his ambivalent response to the St Lucian landscape, the relentless passage of time, love, the postcolonial condition, the development of the artist. These themes are also the subject of his prose writing and his essay, "Leaving School", written in 1965, provides in crisp yet poetic detail the autobiographical context that informs this poem. There he talks about how he spent his vacations, his leaving Castries to sojourn in the St Lucian countryside, "en betassion", where he would write one or two poems a day, preparing himself for the poetic life he had chosen. This single-minded dedication, this desire to become important and complicated, are noteworthy cues. In an interview some twenty years later, Walcott will admit to Dennis Scott his fear that he is becoming plainer as a poet and his wish that he could return to the angst-ridden complicatedness of his youth.[24] The anxiety about being taken seriously in the metropolis, by people in cities who do not believe that people from the islands can produce anything of merit, is introduced here and this will be a constant in Walcott's life. It will resurface in his essay, "What the Twilight Says". There he describes his efforts to create a Caribbean aesthetics, the challenges, the lack of support, the sense of isolation: "all we could successfully enact was a dance of doubt."[25] This essay is also an instance where he laments the provincialism of his island, where he has absorbed the prejudices of those who see small islands as inconsequential, as a place of "malarial enervation".[26] This conflicted response to home is one which Walcott will rehearse repeatedly, and with every iteration his position on the value of home will be slightly modified. Accordingly, some twenty years later, standing on the podium in Stockholm delivering his Nobel laureate lecture, Walcott references the prejudicial perceptions that many – writers included – have held about the Caribbean: a place to visit but not a place to live, a place of stasis, of elegiac pathos, a place where one cannot be productive. Standing there, he is a visible proof of the fallacy of this perception.

In "Prelude", the cynicism has not yet corrupted him; even while he chooses words such as "uncouth", "prone", "lost" to depict the island, there is the sense here that he is being careful to establish that these opinions are not his, and that he is merely reporting the impression of others. In lines five and six of the poem, Walcott experiments successfully with lineation. The visual impact of "Us lost" and "Found only" standing separate from each other reinforces the two distinctly different opinions of the island. Those who do not live on it have one impression. Those who reside there have a contrary position. The line break between "Us lost" and "Found only" becomes an indication of this layering of perceptions. At the same time it is an extension of the division mentioned in the previous line, "steamers which divide horizons". While he is making the point that his island home is objectified as a paradise island, Walcott is himself dehumanizing those who gaze on him. Through his use of metonym, he reduces them to "blue reflection of eyes". The false impressions of the outsider are further reinforced by the balancing of the word "known" with the uncertainty embedded in "think". The poem then returns to the "I", except this "I" is different from the spectator "I" in the first stanza. Here he is hopeful, energized by the optimism that he will, in spite of these prejudices, remain devoted to his art.

Considering that this poem is written by a teenager, the ironic tone that is threaded through it is impressive. The young rarely have learnt how to be self-deprecating. Usually it is in hindsight that one can laugh at one's posturing, and one's sense of self-importance, that one can recognize that the ego of one's youth was often inflated. That the teenage Walcott persona was able to stand back and look at himself critically, "making a holiday of situations" supports the claim made by many of his reviewers about *25 Poems*: "The most interesting poet so far from the Caribbean, a voice matured beyond its years."[27]

In terms of its use of symbolism, it is significant that the poem opens with a portrait of dawn. The vividness of the image of "variegated fists of clouds" reminds the reader that Walcott's involvement with painting began early. In this evocative word picture he is able to convey the different colours – the reds, oranges and yellow – that streak the early morning sky. At the same time the phrase "fists of clouds" conveys the texture of the puffy blotches of clouds decorating the sky. The tightness of the line, that ability to simultaneously convey colour and shape is an impressive example of the complexity of language for which Walcott has so often been praised. The symbolism of the early morning is also important in conveying newness, the sense of possibility, of life about to start. "For every poet it is always morning in the world." This claim, made in his Nobel laureate lecture, is relevant here. Walcott is seeing himself as an Adamic figure, naming his world, reimagining his landscape in a poetic language that he is creating. The phrase "legs crossed" is an evocative one. It supports the notion of relaxed observation, but also suggests a cross-legged meditative pose, where one is looking inward rather than outward. This play between observation and meditation continues throughout the poem.

Various poetic influences are evident in this poem, chief among them T. S. Eliot. As mentioned earlier, Walcott has always admitted to and defended those influences: "one's own voice is an anthology of all the sounds one has heard..."[28] There are echoes of Eliot's "Love Song of J. Alfred Prufrock", of Prufrock demonstrating his self-consciousness, sensitivity to the opinions of others and his fear of rejection:

> Do I dare
> disturb the universe?
> in a minute there is time
> for decisions and revisions which a minute will reverse.[29]

Similarly, Walcott is concerned about how he is perceived by various "publics": the local/island public and the international public, symbolised in the image of the blue-eyed tourist. Where Eliot creates a poetic persona who is isolated, intellectual, unsociable, Walcott, while sharing the intellectualism and isolation, is not stymied by the Prufrockian paralysis and the tone of "Prelude" is less pessimistic than "The Love Song of J. Alfred Prufrock". Unlike Eliot's Prufrock, Walcott has made his "*one* choice" (emphasis mine) to pursue a career as a poet and is considering how to realize this decision, regardless of the critical or unsupportive gaze of others. There is an interesting paradox that makes this poem such a wonderful one – and this inconsistency of thought and representation will later become a Walcottian characteristic. Even as Walcott rehearses his anxieties about his poetic future, he seems to be standing back and looking, in something close to amusement, at this worried self. Prufrock is never able to achieve this detachment. In "Prelude" the self-mocking tone is further demonstrated by the repetition of "of course". This anticlimactic phrase suggests that Walcott is able to recognize that he is making too much of this decision, and that the over-elaborateness of his preparation turns it into play-acting, "a holiday", rather than something that should be taken seriously. Even while he is impatient to launch into life, he knows that he is still a callow, posturing youth, too young to be smoking, too young to be staying out late, too young for the company of ladies of the night. He knows, too, that to be a poet requires hard work and dedication, the suffering in "accurate iambics". Play-acting aside, the threat of failure is real. Underlining this performance of bravado is the knowledge that he is young and black and, he believes, without Caribbean examples to inspire and encourage him.

The ending of the poem in its evocation of "leopard" as muse is nonetheless a hopeful one. The reader remains uncertain as to the poetic association that Walcott is making here. It may well be that "the reluctant leopard with slow eyes" is a girl with whom he is in love and that girl is also the guiding spirit that gives him the resolve to pursue life as a poet. In his autobiographical poem, *Another Life*, Walcott describes Andreuille Alcee, the young woman with whom he was passionately in love, and the way in which she was able to energise him to the heights of poetic excellence. Renaming her Anna in that poem, he talks about her as his first great love and of the potency of feeling that he experienced when he was in her company:

> They are moving towards each other.
> His head roars with hunger and poems.
> His hand is trembling to recite her name. (*Another Life*, p. 45).

In "Prelude", this love is similarly young and fresh and overwhelming. Walcott abandons the seriousness of the earlier lines and is now just a boy thinking about a girl, imagining her in the grandiose way of the young. The choice of the word "leopard" will capture the honey-brown tones of her hair and skin; it will evoke the amber that is poetically associated with Andreuille so that even while it seems that he is making a grand statement about poetic inspiration, on a more prosaic level it could be a statement on how important this girl is to him, how easily he is caught in "her slow eyes". The phrase "slow eyes" allows for metaphoric transferral: her eyes are being depicted in terms of the slow sinuous movement of the leopard while "reluctant" as a qualifier to "leopard" suggests that while the young woman entraps him she does so unconsciously. If we go with the alternate reading of "leopard" solely as poetic muse, rather than as person, then both "reluctant" and "slow" suggest that inspiration may not come as easily and as quickly as the poet hopes. This reading will extend the anxiety running through the earlier lines of the poem that time is passing by quickly and that the poet needs to grow up ("my boyhood has gone over") and start on his poetic career. That the poem "Prelude" can support a host of different readings is part of the pleasure of poetry. This early poem is experimental in language and in style and is an appropriate overture for a teenage poet committed to creating his own distinct voice, a teenager who has yet to learn "the noble treachery of art" (*Another Life*, p. 94). The ambivalences, both in meaning and in style, will continue to be an integral part of Walcott's poetry.

Chronicling Faith: "A City's Death by Fire"

In "A City's Death by Fire", the destruction of the poet's home town becomes the occasion for him to write about how the city can be regenerated through faith. Using his experience of walking through the burnt-out town, observing the widespread destruction of man-made structures, noting the loss of faith that has come with the loss of material possessions, the poet tells of his spiritual comfort in nature. The durability of the green hills that encircle his town reminds him of the importance of faith and of the need to move beyond sorrow. The poem ends with the poet's perception of the fire as both death-bringing and life-giving.[30]

Walcott's choice of the word "gospeller" as a metaphor to describe the fire provides an important guiding image in the poem. A gospeller is one who reads and teaches the Gospel, usually travelling from place to place to evangelize. Similarly, the fire, spreading through the town, teaches those who experience it the importance of faith. This religious reference can be traced through the poem. The "sea where Christ walks" evokes the biblical story of Jesus walking on the seas towards his disciples, reassuring them that their faith in him would keep them safe, would make them strong. The references to "wooden" and to "dead as nails" suggests the crucified Jesus who is nailed to the wooden cross but whose death offers mankind baptism into new life.

In the claim that the fire levelled all but the "churched sky", suggesting that only churches were left unscathed by the fire, Walcott takes poetic licence with the historical facts of the fire. Although the damage wrought to the town of Castries was immense, (by today's estimate, millions of dollars of real estate and invaluable print material), other buildings as well as the churches were spared. While the fire destroyed eighty percent of the town, it left the Power Station, the Telephone Exchange, the St Joseph's Convent and St Mary's College still standing. Nevertheless, the damage to the Carnegie Library, haunt of all young St Lucian readers (later renamed as the Central Library), may have impelled Walcott to the hyperbolic description of the loss as total and cataclysmic. Moreover, the choice of the word "levelled" suggests that the fire had been democratic in its destruction, and indeed the rich and poor, the near-whites and the blacks, the government and its citizenry all suffered loss, but the group that seemed least affected was the Catholic laity, hence, perhaps, the reference to "churched". Later in the poem, Walcott connects the adjective "churched" to the loss of faith that many people experienced. So, ironically, although the church may have survived as a building, it was not as a repository of faith. Moreover, faith was not the only thing levelled. In the weeks following the fire, the infrastructural damage to the town meant widespread discomfort to all, no matter what race, colour or creed. Temporary housing was set up in the barracks at Vigie and at Morne Fortune, and more than two thousand persons of all classes were forced to share the same living space in the shelters. Food was scare. Desolation and hopelessness were abundant. In his essay, "Leaving School", Walcott gives an account of life in Castries in the aftermath of this fire:

> Now all those people had moved to the Romanesque barracks on the Vigie headland... In fact Vigie was temporarily the new town, and when evening came those of us whose houses had survived preferred to go out there than to on that depressing, scorched plain where most of the City had been.[31]

In *Another Life,* Walcott will return to a portrayal of this historic event, describing its aftermath as:

> [...] haphazard tents,
> lives casually tangled like unsorted laundry [...]
> [...]
> A landscape of burnt stones and broken arches... (p. 84)

In his later essays and interviews he will describe on several occasions how the 1948 fire changed his life. These biographical chronicles are not necessarily historically accurate; they are what Walcott describes as "re-essentialized..., given more of an essence... made more focal."[32]

Walcott details the activity of writing his poem by candle light, "I wrote the tale by tallow" as both literal and performative. Because of the fire, the electric poles were destroyed; power cuts became the order of the day and candles were once more a household necessity. Describing the light of the candle as an eye, both in terms of the shape of the flame and because it is the light that allows him, like an eye, to see, Walcott captures the pathos of the act of chronicling this sad event. The smoke of the candle causes the eye to involuntarily produce tears; the horror of the damage done by the fire, also brings the poet/narrator and recorder to tears of sorrow. The hot wax that flows slowly down the side of the candle is similar to the tears that roll down the narrator's cheeks as he records this national tragedy. The sadness of the persona is a national one; the destruction of the fire has shaken the faith of many. Many feel God has abandoned them. In using the plural form of the noun "faith", Walcott conveys the widespread loss of faith in the possibilities of renewal, showing how fragile faith can be, as easily snapped by the fire as the electric wires that once connected the town. Walking through the town in the post-fire days ("all day I walked abroad among the rubbled tales"), Walcott describes the walls that survived the fury of the fire as "liars" because they do not depict the truth of the totality of the damage; his shock that these walls were not, like everything else, reduced to rubble functions symbolically to bring him to the realisation that the fire, while it has destroyed material things, has not destroyed his faith in renewal, in the possibility of surviving and transcending this adversity.

As witness to the looting that is going on, Walcott contrasts the damage being perpetrated by man to the clouds in the sky, which he compares to the bales that looters have torn open. Yet these clouds remain white in spite of the smoke that permeates everything – including the sea. This reminds us that destruction is never total. And looking up at the green hills of Morne Fortune, or the Vigie peninsula, the poet gains strength from their greenness. The echoes of Psalm 121 are loud: "I will lift my eyes unto the hills, from whence cometh my help."[33] In depicting the hills in the wonderful wordplay of "flock of faiths" Walcott connects this image to two earlier ones: that of the "bird-rocked sky" and to the loss of faith that people were experiencing. "Flock" anticipates the word "birds", but instead we have "faith". In comparing "faith" to "birds" Walcott makes this metaphor come alive to the reader. We imagine the way faith can take flight when life becomes trying. We imagine, too, that in the same way that birds come to roost in hills, the looming green hills become a collective place for regained faith where all are renewed. By this point in the poem, the word "rebuilding" works at multiple levels, from the physical rebuilding of the town, to the rebuilding of broken spirits. In actuality, the wooden buildings, very much in the current style of La Place Careenage, were replaced by concrete structures that many people saw as having very little architectural merit. A way of life was gone, destroyed by that fire. A new historical era was being ushered in. In the rebuilding of Castries after that fire, the William Peter

Castries after the fire, 1948

Boulevard – now a major centrepiece – was created. Bridge Street was transformed from a roadway decorated by wooden houses into a street lined by impersonal steel and concrete structures. Walcott's "rebuilding" refers to the resurgent love the persona experiences for place and perhaps for the people. In spite of its ruination, he continues to love his town. The poem achieves a wonderful unity in its concluding phrase "baptism by fire". Not only does the reference to fire connect back to the opening image of "hot gospeller", but the phrase, in echoing Matthew 3:11 ("I indeed baptize you with water unto repentance: but he that cometh after me is mightier than I, whose shoes I am not worthy to bear: he shall baptize you with the Holy Ghost, and with fire")[34] both links back to "gospeller" and reinforces the pentecostal overtones of the poem.

Written by a boy of "nineteen, an elate, exuberant poet madly in love with English",[35] "A City's Death by Fire" is by no means a flawless poem – few early poems are. In trying to make the 1948 fire symbolic, Walcott produces a poem which could have been about a fire in any country. A reader outside of St Lucia, unaware of the historical fire that inspired it, will interpret this poem as an extended metaphor on the importance of faith, which, like a phoenix, is regenerated through adversity. The devastating socio-economic effect of this fire on a small and impoverished island is never foregrounded – perhaps because other poets had already done so. This poem, in its generalization of a local catastrophe, provides a different and unexpected kind of relief – one which offers the balm of faith.

Patricia Ismond in her book, *Abandoning Dead Metaphors*, has commented on the heavy influence of Dylan Thomas on the young Walcott, noting that "Walcott has closely adapted Thomas's technique of extracting and combining the multiple associations and figurations of word as image."[36] It is this very close adaptation that sometimes makes the poem too rich, like a dish overlaid by too much cream, a dish that would taste just as good if it had been prepared in a simpler style. In particular, it is the interconnectivity of images that make for this "too richness". Walcott painstakingly teases out each image so that by the end of the poem, we are aware of a dense network of references: smoking candles become "smoking sea", candle wax becomes man's tears, "rubbled tales" become narrative proof that the wooden world fails. The act of recording becomes a way of surviving the trauma of the fire, a way of renewal. At the start of the poem, the choice of the word "wanted" suggests intentionality; the poet sets out to write about the loss of faith. But the act of walking, of surveying the damage, moves him beyond the impersonal chronicling of loss, to a personal testimony of hope.

While I have proposed a religious reading of the poem, one may approach it not so much as specifically Christian but as more broadly spiritual. The experience of the fire animates the persona into the recognition that material things are perishable. Durability comes from nature, from the green hills that breathe hope into man and allow him to endure. "Each leaf was a green breath" is a wonderful metaphor, one of the many complex metaphors that proliferate in the poem. Here Walcott is doing two things. He is comparing the leaf to a breath and at the same time he is describing the breath as having a colour (green). Since breath is colourless, its descriptor "green" is a surprising but effective collocation. We are reminded of the phrase "breath of fresh air" since "green" evokes life and youth, and being alive. In comparing the leaf to breath the poet allows the reader to connect the leaves on the trees that populate the hill and the new hope that the boy feels when he looks up at the hills. The desolation of a paper-strewn town is contrasted with the promise of the hills. There is, however, an earlier mention of leaves: "in town, leaves were paper." This metaphoric line is somewhat troubling. Leaves are being compared to paper. That is not a difficult comparison to understand. Paper can look like dry leaves, but where we would have expected the line to say "in town paper were leaves", we have an inversion with "leaves" being the subject. However, it is more likely that the town would be populated with the paper of burnt documents and that these would be scattered about with the same abundance of fallen leaves. What then do we make of this inversion? Are we to consider the leaves of the town and compare them to the green leaf in the line that follows? That way we can assume that the poet is leading the reader to consider that in each space leaves are functioning differently. In town there is dryness and death; in the hills there is life. The leaf image connects and compares town and hill. The difference is further strengthened by the conjunction "but". While the town is a place of hopelessness and lost faith, the hill is the home of hope, the place where life is renewed.

No matter what reading we apply to it, "A City's Death by Fire", in spite of its title, is not a gloomy poem. The themes of hope, faith and rejuvenation help to make this poem inspirational. Additionally, there is a lightness produced by the musicality of alliterative phrases such as "tale by tallow" or "flock of faith." The repetition of the consonant sound [t] in "tale" and "tallow" evokes the intermittent light of the candle, while the alliteration in [f] suggests the forceful noise of birds' wings, in turn conveying the power of faith. Experimental in its style and in its reworking of the sonnet form, "A City's Death by Fire" is a good example of the teenage poet's efforts to chronicle in verse, the history and culture of his island. This teenager will grow into a Nobel Laureate, a West Indian who will attest to the world that "Antillean art is [the] restoration of our shattered histories, our shards of vocabulary..."[37] At the same time he remains a St Lucian who as "a boy opened an exercise book and within the discipline of its margins, framed stanzas that might contain the lights of the hills on an island blest by obscurity..."[38]

Conclusion

In *Poetics*, the Greek philosopher, Aristotle claimed that "in any mode of poetic diction... the greatest thing by far to have is a command of metaphor... it is a mark of genius – for to make good metaphors implies an eye for resemblances."[39] As I have shown in my exposition of "Prelude" and "A City's Death by Fire", Derek Walcott is a master of metaphor. His early poems heralded his capacity to borrow and rework western ways of representing the world around us. Unusual, unexpected, the language of Walcott's poetry does more than communicate; it draws attention to the act of creative expression. The Russian poet, Joseph Brodsky, friend and admirer of Derek Walcott, describes the Nobel Laureate's poems in the following way:

> For almost forty years his throbbing and relentless lines kept arriving in the English language like tidal waves, coagulating into an archipelago of poems without which the map of modern literature would effectively match wallpaper. He gives us more than himself or "a world"; he gives us a sense of infinity embodied in the language.[40]

Here Brodsky references two aspects of Walcott's poetry: his careful yet powerful use of the English language and the way he uses poetry to express personal feeling – to explain himself in the world. In describing Walcott's production of poem as "archipelago", Brodsky is also locating Walcott's prodigious Caribbean roots: the fact that the St Lucian-born Walcott gained a university education in Jamaica, an island geographically located at the top of the archipelago of Caribbean islands, worked in Grenada and then in Trinidad, the southern-most island of the archipelago, where he made his home for many years. Unlike many Caribbean writers, Derek Walcott chose to remain in the region while so many sought the ease of diaspora. He has been unparalleled in his production of poetry, plays and essays. He has remained faithful to his first love – poetry – and with the familiarity of an old married couple, can affectionately curse it: "Poetry I think is the toughest bloody art in the world."[41] But poetry is also what made his soul sing, is what continues to animate him so that today when we chance to catch him walking across the street, hear him read his poetry on YouTube or in a public library, we can still see in him the boy of "nineteen, an elate, exuberant poet madly in love with English."[42] Perhaps now we will be able to smile in admiration at how he made successful use of his love of English, using it to fashion himself a distinct Caribbean identity. The exuberance that characterized the young Walcott remains; old age has not dampened it, and the poet at eighty is no less dedicated to his craft than the teenage boy had been. In his latest collection, *White Egrets*, he mourns: "so much to do still, all of it praise."[43] Walcott's poetry is his praisesong, and his bread of life. And if poetry is like bread – something that everybody shares and is nourished by, then an appreciative understanding of a Derek Walcott poem moves us one step closer to participating in his poetic exuberance.

Endnotes

1. Derek Walcott, *The Prodigal* (New York: Farrar, Straus and Giroux, 2004), p. 102.
2. When the president of the United States won the elections in 2008, national news media carried a picture of him toting Derek Walcott's *Collected Poems*. Significantly, immediately after the United States elected its first black president, Walcott wrote and published in the *Times* online website, "Forty Acres", a poem dedicated to Barack Obama.
3. *Kweyol* is the French-based Creole spoken by many St Lucians.
4. Harold Simmons, "A West Indian Poet Fulfils his Promise", *Critical Perspectives on Derek Walcott*, Ed. Robert D. Hamner (Boulder and London: Lynne Rienner Publishers, 1997), p. 97.
5. Derek Walcott, *The Prodigal,* p. 5.
6. The Nelson Royal Readers was a series of English textbooks produced in the 1880s. They were used to teach literacy in the colonies. The collection ranged from grade 1 through to 6 and included lessons on vocabulary building, punctuation, pronunciation, letter-writing and rhetoric. They provided information on the human body, the history of Rome and England, and lessons on English flora and fauna.
7. The St Lucia City Council's website is an excellent historical source on the widespread damage wrought by the fire.
8. Bruce King, in *Derek Walcott: A Caribbean Life* (Oxford: Oxford University Press, 2000), writes about Castries fire-themed poems submitted by poets from Barbados, St Vincent, Tobago, and Jamaica, and published in local newspapers in St Lucia. He also mentions the ongoing expectation that the newspapers would soon be carrying a poem by Derek Walcott. That expectation remained unfulfilled. Walcott's poem on the fire first appeared in print as part of *25 Poems* (Castries, 1948), pp. 51-52.
9. Both poems are readily available online.
10. Charles H. Rowell, "An interview with Derek Walcott" [1987], *Conversations with Derek Walcott*, Ed. William Baer (Jackson: University of Mississippi Press, 1996), p. 123.
11. Derek Walcott, *Collected Poems 1948 – 1984* (New York: Farrar, Straus and Giroux, 1986).

12. Later, Walcott was to acknowledge the importance of the Jamaican poet, George Campbell's *First Poems* (Kingston, 1945) as an example to him of a "modern" Caribbean voice. See Walcott's poem, "George Campbell" introducing the 1981 reprint of Campbell's poems. The poem is available in Peepal Tree Press's Caribbean Modern Classics edition of *First Poems* (Leeds, 2012). There was also the work of the Tobagonian poet Eric Roach, whose poems, appearing in *Bim*, *Kyk-over-Al* and on the *Caribbean Voices* programme, could have provided Walcott with another genuinely contemporary and authentically Caribbean example. Indeed, there are significant parallels of image and mood between Roach and earlier Walcott well worth exploring.
13. Edward Baugh, *Derek Walcott* (Cambridge: Cambridge University Press, 2006), pp. 5-6.
14. Robert D. Hamner "Conversation with Derek Walcott", *Conversations with Derek Walcott*, p. 32.
15. Edward Hirsch, "An Interview with Derek Walcott", *Conversations with Derek Walcott*, p. 53.
16. Much like the child who believes himself to be wonderful after being repeatedly told so, perhaps Walcott saw himself as a prodigy; in his autobiographical poem, *Another Life* (London: Cape, 1973), he describes himself as such (p. 3).
17. For more information on per capita GDP for OECS countries in the late fifties, see Delisle Worrell, Don Marshall and Nicole Smith, "The Political economy of Exchange Rate Policy in the Caribbean", Inter-American Development Bank, Research Network Working Paper # R- 401, June 2000. p.7. http://198.62.77.13/res/laresnetwork/files/pr72finaldraft.pdf.
18. Frank Collymore, "An Introduction to the Poetry of Derek Walcott", *Bim* 3:10 (June 1949), 125-132.
19. Both Dylan Thomas and Derek Walcott wrote numerous poems in their teenage years and had published collections by the age of nineteen.
20. W.H. Auden, "Sir, No Man's Enemy", *The English Auden* (London: Faber, 1977), p. 36; from *Poems 1927-1931*.
21. Edward Hirsch, "The Art of Poetry XXXVII: Derek Walcott", *Conversations with Derek Walcott*, p. 104.
22. Derek Walcott, *Another Life*, p. 3.
23. Derek Walcott, "Prelude", *In a Green Light*, (London: Jonathan Cape, 1962), p. 11, and *Collected Poems 1948-1984*, (New York: Farrar, Straus and Giroux, 1986), pp. 3-4.
24. Dennis Scott, "Walcott on Walcott", *Conversations with Derek Walcott*, p. 11.

25. Derek Walcott, *What the Twilight Says: Essays* (New York: Farrar, Straus and Giroux, 1998), p. 8.
26. Ibid, p. 5.
27. Bruce King, *Derek Walcott: A Caribbean Life*, p. 63.
28. Leif Sjöberg, "An Interview with Derek Walcott", *Conversations with Derek Walcott*, p. 83.
29. T. S. Eliot, *Selected Poems*, (London: Faber, 2009), pp. 12-13.
30. Derek Walcott, "A City's Death By Fire", *In a Green Night*, p. 14, and *Collected Poems 1948–1984*, p. 6.
31. Derek Walcott, "Leaving School", *Critical Perspectives on Derek Walcott*. Ed. Robert D. Hamner (Boulder and London: Lynne Rienner Publishers, 1997), p. 27.
32. Robert D. Hamner "Conversation with Derek Walcott", p. 23.
33. Psalm 121, verse 1, King James Bible.
34. Ibid.
35. Derek Walcott, *What the Twilight Says*, p. 10.
36. Patricia Ismond, *Abandoning Dead Metaphors: The Caribbean Phase of Derek Walcott's Poetry* (Barbados, Jamaica, Trinidad and Tobago: University of The West Indies Press, 2001), p. 28.
37. Derek Walcott, *What the Twilight Says*, p. 69.
38. Derek Walcott, *What the Twilight Says*, p. 84.
39. Aristotle, *Poetics* (Harmondsworth: Penguin, 1996).
40. Joseph Brodsky, "http://www.poets.org/poet.php/prmPID/220. Retrieved January 16, 2012.
41. Carl Jacobs, "There is No Bitterness in Our Literature", *Critical Perspectives on Derek Walcott*, p. 5.
42. Derek Walcott, *What the Twilight Says: Essays*, p. 10.
43. Derek Walcott, *White Egrets* (New York: Farrar, Straus and Giroux, 2010), p. 83

GEORGE B. HANDLEY

WALCOTT'S METAPHYSICS OF NATURE

As Rainer Maria Rilke once powerfully articulated in his *Duino Elegies*, our humanness manifests itself precisely in the activity of our conscious mind, our fleeting and changing memories, and the ways in which we experience our biological existence as if from a distance of distracted observation. Rilke says that we always "find ourselves in the attitude/ of someone going away." "So we live," he writes, "forever taking our leave".[1] Thus, our consciousness and our agency can never be determined or confined by our ecological context. He compares the shifts of nature that move through seasons with the way our peripatetic mind is always looking back or anticipating what is to come:

> O trees of life, when does your winter come?
> We're not in accord. Not attuned, like
> the migrating birds. Overtaken and late
> we abruptly crowd ourselves on a wind
> and come down on some uncaring pond.
> We're conscious of blossoming and withering both at
> once....
>
> But we, giving ourselves to one thing,
> feel it's at the expense of another. Conflict
> is our nature. (*The Essential Rilke*, p. 99)

For Rilke, this awareness of separation is the by-product of the play of the conscious mind which stands over and against the roiling chaos and the indifferent abyss of the universe that remind us of our own impending death. The result of a direct confrontation with the mortal facts of human existence is the hope of his poetry and its deeper attachment to life and to transient beauty. Of course, the sense that the world is imbued with immanence – that "being here is glorious", as he puts it – is facilitated by his imagination of what the disembodied dead might now see as they look back upon us (*The Essential Rilke,* p. 119). In other words, this deeper, more ecologically-oriented appreciation of life is generated by a willingness to imagine death, the end of physical existence, and to imagine the persistence of consciousness after death; it is to imagine that one can "praise this world to the Angel", that is, to write as if in communion with the dead and in defiance of the finality of death. Rilke's paradox is thus: to speak of the earth is to talk of our strangeness on it. Or, in other words, to awake to the reality of the physical is to inhabit the metaphysical.

Despite environmentalism's call for a more biocentric imagination, poetry has always made use of the discord of our consciousness with the rhythms of biology and remains rather obstinately anthropocentric, even or especially when it is particularly focused on the environment. With the example of Derek Walcott, whose poetics extends Rilke's existentialist metaphysics to important environmental values, I wish to suggest that poetry's capacity to invoke and imaginatively inhabit a metaphysical space that lies above and beyond this earth is precisely its environmental advantage.

In our postmodern age, we seem to have dropped the romantic and sometimes modernist idea that the priest and the poet share similar occupations and have instead come to assume that the word of man describes the earthly, physical reality of existence, while the Word of God describes the heavenly, metaphysical reality of existence. In a world endangered by our indifference and fragmented by our rich diversity of values, we need imaginations capable of resisting the balkanizations of postmodernity and of fostering what philosopher of science Michel Serres calls a "collective ethics in the face of the world's fragility".[2] Intolerance for competing worldviews and for competing metaphysics will not do, of course, but neither will nihilism or a wholesale rejection of the idea of sacred space. Serres calls for a "diligent religion of the world", a refurbishing of cosmology, of the human place within the universe that does not sacrifice the life of the earth and the life of the body in the interest of what might come after death but instead combines the devotional fortitude and universalist reach of religion with the presentist ethics of environmentalism (Serres, *The Natural Contract*, p. 47). This is a call that resonates with the work done by the majority of the world's ecotheologians, all of whom have suggested that the key to such an ethics begins with a deep concern with language and practices of reading. But more specifically, theologians such as John Haught, Catherine Keller and William Brown have provided strong arguments for why metaphysical concerns are not only consistent with values we place on the earth and earthly concerns but are vital to a deeper appreciation of physical existence. Haught, for example, argues that the sacramental tradition in Christianity, specifically as it relates to sacred space, can be extended to thinking about the earth as sacred ground deserving of special care. This is of specific relevance to Walcott. Christianity has been criticized for its indifference toward nature, especially as a result of its eschatology, but Haught suggests that Christian eschatology is more likely to inspire care than indifference when it includes the hope of divine fulfilment for all of physical life. He writes of Christianity's "vision of nature as promise. A biblical perspective invites us to root ecology in eschatology. It reads in cosmic and sacramental reality an intense straining for the future. It obliges us to keep the cosmos in the foreground of our theology without removing the restlessness forced on the present by a sense of the yet-to-come".[3]

Ecotheology avoids the divorce of man's word from the Word and returns the sense of the sacred to the places we inhabit or, to borrow the language of William Blake, that seeks a marriage of heaven and hell. As Blake argued, poetry can offer a more earthly theology, one that does not force a choice between the holiness of heaven and the holiness of the world, but instead calls us "To See the World in a Grain of Sand, and a Heaven in a Wild Flower".[4]

In his recent collection, *White Egrets*, Walcott recalls with a touch of nostalgia the loss of Blake's earthly theology. He writes that the beauty of fields of sunflowers in Italy "are poems we recite to ourselves, metaphors/ of our brief glory, a light we cannot avoid/ that was called heaven in Blake's time, but not since".[5] Indeed, one way to understand Walcott's poetics is as a postmodern attempt to recover this kind of earthly theology. Although hesitant, maybe even embarrassed at times, to express hope in the promise of life's continuity, he also cannot bring himself to announce his decisive break with Christian faith. As a result, his poetry explores the world free of any obligation to declare sacramental presence, but also free to invent the reasons to see holiness in the ordinary circumstances of his island home. The attachment to physical life and the hunger for physical beauty we find throughout his poetry are not mere symptoms of a lustful pursuit of selfish pleasure. Indeed, for the mature Walcott looking back on a life of mistakes, such pleasures, typical of unthinking youth, are in the end "treacherous" (*White Egrets*, p. 28). What can transform the pleasures of the senses into spiritual ecstasies, as we see in Blake and Rilke, is a profound awareness that we seem restless, inhabiting an elsewhere or a state of mind apart from or above the physical world. In this way our earthly passions, when fuelled by our awareness of mortality, resist but also make meaningful the finality of death. In Walcott's poetry, we are always inhabiting this earth, these bodies, even at the same time that we seem to be otherworldly. As Walcott describes the motions of the conscious mind, we are never perfectly coincident with our moment in time and space: "we are never where we are," he writes, "but somewhere else,/ even in Italy" (*White Egrets*, p. 29).

While experience is always conditioned by the entrapments of physical circumstance, as Rilke had similarly articulated, the imagination remains perpetually free and apart, even more so in old age as it has an ever larger storehouse of memories and experiences and places to visit. Memory as time passes beckons to images that increasingly bring with them the idea of death. And Walcott seems to agree with Wallace Stevens' famous dictum that "death is the mother of beauty". He understands the paradox, explored by Stevens in his poem "Sunday Morning",[6] that only by understanding the perpetual death of all things can we imbue each instantiation of a presence with holy meaning. For Walcott, the imminence of death and change only deepens the ambiguity of physical experience, since he can never be sure if death bestows such pleasure as a gift or if pleasure merely makes it treacherous. He uses poetry's use of metaphor to bridge the gap between the physical and the spiritual and between the subjectivity of the word and the objectivity of the world in order to avoid the conclusion that we are only biology; and yet precisely because of the peripatetic nature of metaphor, his bridges move both ways, carrying him away from direct metaphysical assertions.

Postcolonial critics and ecocritics alike assert a certain secular faith in literature's capacity to shape the moral imagination. We teach certain books and certain authors because we believe that worldviews matter and that they are informed by stories, by metaphors, by the imagination. What is perhaps not recognized is that this secular faith, as a wager of meaning, is not entirely unlike metaphysical faith. This, of course, has nothing to do with whether or not a work of literature concerns itself thematically with metaphysics. It is a matter of understanding how it is that we come to trust the process whereby meaning emerges from literature. As Giles Gunn has written: "no serious literature is neutral either to the question of belief or to the question of the relationship between belief and understanding".[7] Gunn notes that "in attempting to assess the actual in light of its full potential for comprehension, we thereby re-enact one of the chief functions of culture, if not religion" (*The Interpretation of Otherness...*, p. 124). George Steiner similarly argues that "to read the poem responsibly ('respondingly'), to be answerable to form, is to wager on a reinsurance of sense. It is to wager on a relationship – tragic, turbulent, incommensurable, even sardonic – between word and world, but on a relationship precisely bounded by that which reinsures it".[8]

In its persistent meditation on the world and its tender elegies regarding its transience, we can read Walcott's poetry as a probing of the very meaning of mortality and thus as retaining the structure of faith. Of course, Walcott's faith is distinct from sectarian definitions because it is an expression of hope in a sacred cosmos that transcends the many divisive identitarian claims of the Caribbean's various ethnic and religious cultures. Although speaking of narrative literature, Mario Vargas Llosa recently asserted this implicit trans-sectarian hope of literature in his recent Nobel Speech:

> Good literature erects bridges between different peoples, and by having us enjoy, suffer, or feel surprise, unites us beneath the languages, beliefs, habits, customs, and prejudices that separate us... Literature creates a fraternity within human diversity and eclipses the frontiers erected among men and women by ignorance, ideologies, religions, languages, and stupidity.[9]

Walcott similarly writes, of course, within a context of racial, religious, ideological, and linguistic diversity, and he is always vigilant about marking those differences. However, his poetics seeks to subsume these divisions into a broader cosmos. Indeed, as he argues in "The Muse of History" the "truly tough aesthetic of the New World neither explains nor forgives history", but instead turns to praising the world's beauty, not as an escape from the divisions of history but rather the means of forging new possibility.[10] Nature, in other words, is the cosmic kingdom of this world, and the dead do more than haunt the edges of the newly integrated cosmos his poetry projects; they are the very stuff of what he calls in "The Bounty" the "vegetal fury" of the earth.[11] In the back and forth of his metaphors, we can never be sure if the stuff of earth is just a stand-in for metaphysical reality or if metaphysical reality stands in for what we thought was our merely material existence. Either way, this world is strange and thus strangely sacred.

In "The Bounty" Walcott notes that awareness of death and change heightens the experience of beauty.[12] It is worth revisiting a few passages from the poem:

> No, there is grief, there will always be, but it must not madden,
>
> like Clare, who wept for a beetle's loss, for the weight
> of the world in a bead of dew on clematis or vetch (*The Bounty*, p. 5).

In other words, as our awe in the ordinary grows, as it did for the nineteenth-century poet John Clare, the more frightful and yet precious natural process becomes because its only story seems to be that of perpetual death and finitude. However, Walcott implies that the evanescent natural world begins to resemble the eternal light of God, as is evident in his invocation in the second part of the poem, of the figure of Dante whose poetry seeks to witness that light. While the dead serve various functions in his poetry and often suggest the ghosts of the Caribbean past, in the instances of his own family members they present the more immediate question of metaphysics and faith, a theme that I am suggesting provides special insight into his earthly poetics. One can hardly miss how persistently questions of faith, the afterlife, and the nature of death pervade his poetry, and while often linked to cultural questions of identity and sectarianism in the Caribbean by critics, these themes also suggest an intensely personal meditation in his poetry, one that helps us to understand his recourse to the ambiguities of nature. Walcott cannot reject the notion that his own mother, for whom this poem functions as an elegy, is no longer present in some form after her death. At the same time, however, he cannot accept the idea that his poetry can somehow claim her, or claim to know of her afterlife. So he remains agnostic: "But can she or can she not read this? Can you read this,/ Mamma, or hear it?" (*The Bounty*, p. 9). Although he admits uncertainty in his expectation that he will see her again ("I half-expect to see you no longer, then more than half,/ almost never, or never then – there I have said it", p. 12), he knows that something greater than language and mourning remains:

> but felt something less than final at the edge of your grave,
> some other something somewhere, equally dreaded,
> since the fear of the infinite is the same as death,
>
> unendurable brightness, the substantial dreading
> its own substance, dissolving to gases and vapours, (*The Bounty*, p. 12)

He implies that existential atheism makes the same mistake as dogmatic sectarian belief since both respond to what cannot be known with equal certainty.

Because its metaphors are like and unlike the dead whom it seeks to name, elegaic poetry, on the other hand, must admit the possibility of transcendence *and* finitude. He feels that his poetic deliberations about his mother are inherently treacherous because his metaphors only seem to make more evident the immateriality of that to which they refer. For that reason he remarks that "Faith grows mutinous" (*The Bounty*, p. 9) and asks for pardon, "as I watch these lines grow and the art of poetry harden me// into sorrow as measured as this, to draw the veiled figure/ of Mamma entering the standard elegiac" (*The Bounty*, p. 5). If Walcott has frequently imagined that poetry can transform the object of praise (and do so at the risk of betrayal), the question of what it can do to his mother's dead body becomes the ultimate existential test of poetry's faith. Instead of resurrecting her invisible body, his poetry only makes his own materiality more evident. The self-consciousness of his own measured lines constitutes his betrayal. But is this a betrayal of his mother or of the finality of his own mortality? If poetry fails to commemorate that which it mourns because it always turns back on itself in self-referentiality, it also then cannot name the end of human life definitively. The poet's faith is then to make the newness of the physical world itself the new emblem of the missing dead who are now "part of earth's vegetal fury". And since even nature itself is always dying and transforming itself before his eyes, metaphors are perpetually necessary and necessarily metaphysical. The poet can't escape the need for faith.

Walcott's suspicion that the eternal and the temporal were not the oppositions his colonial education might have taught him began early in his life. We find evidence of a neo-romantic longing to find God in the woods in his very first poem:

> Thus would my wanderings among the quiet woods
> Be my first lesson from the Holy book.

And while I wondered of the free creation,
The pure conception of a Hand behind it all,
Should be my subsequency to the other verses.
Oh! In what happy state I would then be
As an acknowledged friend to bird or beast
As our first father was – alive and free.[13]

Not the greatest of his poems, but not bad either for a 14 year old. And certainly better than the poem the Catholic priest wrote in response to reprimand him for his hedonistic faith in nature:

Youth here is wrong, for God's own Word
Was passed to men, to fill men's dearth
Moses, Prophets, Paul of the Sword,
Have been God's messengers to earth;
And Christ the Lord his church did found
His truth forever to expound.[14]

The priest's sectarian chauvinism and his erroneous and unfortunate divorce between the word of man and the Word of God and between nature and church is an example of why environmentalists have accused religion of contributing to our human indifference to environmental degradation. We see here an ethics insistent on an otherworldly focus, away from the beauty, transience, and fate of the physical world. Its triumphalism notwithstanding, this is a theology of despair.[15]

What is important for my purposes here is to suggest that many of the concepts in Walcott's poem – the notion of finding God in nature, of using nature as his own church, the implicit anti-sectarianism and broad universalism, and perhaps most importantly, the need for a sense of ultimacy against which to test the actuality of this world – all of these become important trajectories during his career. Later in the same adolescent poem he intuits that subjection to this God of Nature is deeply holy work and a prerequisite for poetry. Nevertheless, as he discovers in this poem and throughout his career as a poet, when the idea of God expands, language runs the risk of becoming too narrow or too literal. As the examples below begin to demonstrate, to avoid this risk of literature becoming merely a sermon, his poetry finds greater recourse to metaphor as the preferred representation of this discovered holiness. Even at this early stage of his career, the young poet wrote of his hesitancy to name God: "Yet, fearing to pray out,/ That by his speech the wrong name he would call/ And bring strong retribution from his Benefactor." ("1944")

If not defiantly resistant, Walcott remains at least reluctant to invoke the name or idea of deity in order to justify the inspiration of his poetry. When asked by Edward Hirsch in 1985 to explain the significance of the epiphanic experience described in *Another Life* that gave birth to his poetry and that was likely the inspiration for this adolescent poem, Walcott said: "There are some things people avoid saying in interviews because they sound pompous or sentimental or too mystical. I have never separated the writing of poetry from prayer. I have grown up believing it is a vocation, a religious vocation".[16] He has made similar claims on several occasions, and it is not uncommon to find AMGD – ad majorem gloria dei – written on the bottom of the page in his notebooks.

Indeed, not all forms of sectarianism were as painful to the young Walcott as the reproving priest's. Walcott's own mother's faith always drew his respect, and he admired, albeit with some ambivalence, Dunstan St. Omer's Catholic faith. He continued to assert, however, that nature was his alternative to sectarian faith and the walls of the Cathedral of the Immaculate Conception that called to Dunstan. In an unpublished essay from 1987, "Inside the Cathedral", Walcott explained his admiration for Dunstan's faith but his reasons for parting from such sectarianism:

> I had this to believe in: light and nature. We lived on an island with a light that had never been painted, and I had for my freedom, my universality, a larger cathedral than any St. Omer could enter, the sky and the moving floor of the sea. My unpainted walls were not the bored stones of the cathedral, but the virgin zinc of huge clouds, sunsets larger than Tiepolo's.[17]

For Walcott, becoming an artist retains not just *analogous* passion or the *comparable* seriousness of purpose of a holy calling but is holy work itself in every way as valid as Dunstan's. Indeed, he suggests that his poetic theology is more universal, since his art is not restricted to an institution but is as ubiquitous as the light of the sun, the sound of wind moving through palm fronds, or the lapping of waves against the stones of St Lucian beaches. The theme of the universality of light, of course, finds ample expansion in *Tiepolo's Hound* and becomes his method of using the kingdom of this world and the sun, not the Son, as his cosmic ground that seeks to annihilate the old divisions between Old and New Worlds, metropole and colony, painting and poetry, Jew and Christian, etc.[18] Indeed, the sacred, for Walcott, has always been the ordinary, the mundane, the passing of light – it is the very experience of time itself and the temporality of human existence – and the telluric impulse of art to render light is the acolyte's highest act of devotion. Poetry is his work of benediction; by implication, the secular, the temporal, and the earthly are indistinguishable from the sacred, the eternal, and the heavenly. These benedictions are the work of his metaphors, seeking to bridge the gap between these seeming impossibilities. Poetry is his method for not having to choose between secular scepticism and religious faith, hedonistic devotion to earth and pietistic devotion to heaven, poetry and painting, Europe and Africa, the metropole and the island, or, as we see in the opening scenes of *Omeros*, between the cosmologies of Native American, African, and Western societies.

It might not be unfair to characterize Walcott's blurring of these categories as a kind of indecisiveness. However, faith begins with the suspension of disbelief. In literary terms, this means that literature asks us, to invoke Giles Gunn again, to "assess the actual in light of its full potential for comprehension." In other words, we can understand Walcott's insistence on a suspension of disbelief as a serious and faithful articulation of trust that opens us to the boundlessness of the sacred. His indecisiveness, then, becomes his strength of inclusion and his willingness to bypass traditional binaries that would seek to circumscribe the sacred. It is perhaps useful to recall that religion has at least two root meanings: to read again and to bind together. If Walcott's poetry is religious, it is because it is a revisiting, a rereading of the familiar, and because, as he explains in his Nobel speech, it is an attempt to bind together the factions and fragments of Caribbean experience into an imagined and boundless whole: "Break a vase, and the love that reassembles the fragments is stronger than the love which took its symmetry for granted when it was whole".[19]

This love for the reassembled whole that poetry creates offers a different definition of the sacred than that presupposed by most traditional religions. If the sacred was once the original wholeness to which we seek to return, Walcott implies that it is the very gesture of reassembly, not the image of wholeness itself, that obtains as sacred. Holiness is not a thing or relic; it is desire, an act of perception; it is what love makes. Édouard Glissant once suggested that religious stories are traditionally considered sacred because they offer what he calls a "sacred root" that provides unassailable claims to place and to impermeable but ever-expandable borders.[20] Composite cultures like the Caribbean, on the other hand, must adopt myths from the fragments of atavistic cultures that have survived in the composite whole. Consequently, composite cultures make claims to place, to legitimacy, and to originality that are more tentative, ironic, and self-conflicted. Their stories are open-ended and express a "suspension of identity" as long as they refuse to accept facile closure or restoration of social wholeness. They are cultures, Glissant argues, whose writers "are situated on the frontier, on the border between two apparent or actual possibilities".[21]

Metaphors obtain their sacred function not because we believe that they summarize all possibility but because we can use them, again to recall Gunn's words, "to assess the actual in light of its full potential for comprehension." In this testing of metaphor, for Glissant, "the sacred 'results' not only from an ineffable experience of a creation story but also, from now on, *from the equally ineffable intuition of the relationship between cultures*" (*Faulkner, Mississippi*, p. 115 emphasis added). The origins of a culture, then, are not in the past but in a future possibility, in what is yet to be on the basis of the possibilities literature helps us to imagine. That is, as readers of literature of the New World, we are not in the business of finding but of *founding* culture.

The different and competing claims of stories in religion, whether it be the animism of African or Native American cultures, the mythology and rituals of the Hindus, or the monotheism of Methodism, initially present themselves as mutually exclusive choices to the poet and potentially divide communities against themselves. Ultimately it is the work of Walcott's poetry, however, to intuit what lies between them to which they are all subject. As he wrote in "Inside the Cathedral": "The only hope that artistic failure offers is, in fact, stronger than success; it is the nocturnal failure of the saint at prayer, the repetition of 'I am not worthy.' Repeated enough, a strange strength can grow as it does out of the mesmeric Litany. The subject's subjection" (p. 11). The only thing that makes secular literature different from religious literature, according to Walcott's logic, is that it confesses and exploits its failures.

For Walcott, the syncretism of the secular and sacred is not only a cultural and historical necessity for the Caribbean but it is also deeply personal. The dead haunt the edges of the physical work in his poetry, and some of those dead are distant ancestors and emblems of the Caribbean past. But as we saw in "The Bounty", the ultimacy of the dead and the question of their real or imagined presence is most directly and poignantly tested in the context of his immediate family. Their haunting presence is perhaps the most sacred core of his poetry because they put the entire question of poetry's relationship to the physical world in urgent relief. The suspension "between two actual or apparent possibilities" that Glissant describes is for Walcott a suspension of disbelief in the ultimate extinction of those he dearly loved. In this sense it remains appropriate to call his poetry a form of hopeful prayer since even if he remains sceptical of sectarianism, his poetry is fuelled by the persistent and nagging doubt that death is indeed the end.

Similar to his probing into the meaning of his mother's death in *The Bounty*, his deceased father, who died in 1931 when Walcott was a one-year-old, proves central to his poetics in *Omeros*. In the poem, he rejects atheism's radical certitude of nothingness even as he remains unable to declare the existence of a maker and God of love: "O Thou, my Zero, is an impossible prayer,/ utter extinction is still a doubtful conceit./ Though we pray to nothing, nothing cannot be there".[22] Or at least we infer he does, since these are words spoken by the ghost of his father, a double trick of metaphor, since his poetry projects the image and voice of the dead – a prayer to nothing – who speaks reassuringly that something is there, that metaphor is not mere imagination. Since the limits and bounds of life's materiality remain unknown and unknowable, the physical world blooms into perpetually immanent and sacred significance. As he articulates in *Another Life*, the artist must contemplate the intimation of "an oceanic nothing" even if the artist's assertion is always an "And yet, and yet" because:

> the same day will persist being good,
> either its nature has not learnt to forget,
> or fear was a faith it never understood;
> it hoisted, stubbornly, its yards and spinnakers,
> believed immortally in blue,
> and had, as usual, the old engine, love,
> nodded acknowledgement to the supreme maker's
> hand, yet could not tell you why, or how it moved,
> its bow of daylight driving to the dark,
> as if its love
> and the stunned blue afternoon were life enough.[23]

This is perhaps one of the most assertive passages in all of Walcott's poetry about the link between the beauty of light, the givenness and dumbness of a mute but regenerating world and the existence of a "supreme maker." Of course, Walcott is never pleased with the potential stasis of such declarations. Indeed, he escapes the clichéd conclusions of faith, without denying them, by reminding us of the fact that mute colour and light provide a self-sufficient bounty, one that points to, but does not need a maker for its significance.

Walcott's indecision is fruitful. Because it seems like indifference, nature's apparent self-sufficiency is almost an insult to the human experience of loss and death, and yet its self-sufficiency is precisely what constitutes its beauty and therefore the recompense it can offer. Loving the physical world, which perhaps begins as a symptom of metaphysical despair, becomes an expression of hope. As he declares in *The Bounty*, the unanswerable question of his mother's continued existence drives him to reach for her on the hem of the physical world through poetry, to learn again:

> my business and duty, the lesson you taught your sons,
> to write of the light's bounty on familiar things
> that stand on the verge of translating themselves into news:
> (*The Bounty*, p. 16)

A similar resolution appears at the end of *The Prodigal* where the hope and anticipation of seeing dolphins – and all of the profound sense of wonder at a surprisingly beautiful world – become intermingled and indistinguishable from the hope of seeing his twin brother again. He speaks of "those finished hopes/ that I would see you again, my twin, 'my dolphin.'/ And yet elation drove the dolphins' course/ as if both from and to you, their joy was ours".[24] The ambiguity of "finished" suggests both a realization that his brother is gone and that his hope is complete in seeing the dolphin. The ambiguity is further heightened by virtue of the dolphin's historical function as a kind of Hermes, an ambiguous sign of communication between the realm of the living and the realm of the dead, of resurrection in some Christian thought, and the human and natural realms of consciousness and experience. The tight rhymes and the pairings of the physical experience of the dolphins and the poet's metaphysical hope are equated, as if the hope and joy of both are simultaneously possible. Recognizing that he wouldn't have believed a prophecy that spoke of this future vision of dolphins, he acknowledges that the shape of faith, whether an expectation of beauty or of metaphysical transcendence, is the same. Thus, he notes: "they are here./ Angels *and* dolphins" (*The Prodigal*, p. 105 emphasis added). The physical vacillates between being a sign of the absence of the metaphysical and the immanent hope of the spiritual, and its undecidability means that hope remains alive and the poet alive to the world. We can hear this fruitful indecision in the concluding lines that describe the boat "getting no nearer or nearer [...] that line of light that shines from the other shore" (*The Prodigal*, p. 105).

Walcott was aware of this ambiguity from the beginning of his poetic journey. Describing himself on his knees on that hill at age fourteen to Edward Hirsch, he said: "I felt this sweetness of melancholy, of a sense of mortality, or rather of immortality, a sense of gratitude both for what you feel is a gift and for the beauty of the earth" (*Conversations with Derek Walcott* p. 99). Note that this sense of mortality – through the very paradox of the metaphysical hope mortality makes evident – suddenly becomes its opposite, a sense of immortality. This paradox of doubt's capacity to fuel belief was well expressed by Emily Dickinson: "we both believe and disbelieve a hundred times an hour, which keeps believing nimble".[25]

Tempered by the humility and humiliations of loss, art can become the substance of things hoped for. In the essay, "Inside the Cathedral," he remarks that it is the faith of art that "there is an earthly paradise, that there is no ambition that cannot be fulfilled, no faith that is not rewarded, in the exact manner that, desired hard enough, is prayed for. But only if it was good, and by good I realized I meant something that could bear pride but was not selfish, that could learn to love itself as it loved others" (p. 27). He ends the essay visiting Dunstan in the cathedral where he has begun his commissioned work, and despite their sectarian differences that have traditionally divided his island, Walcott states: "I could feel that he felt my pride and joy in his standing on the rail of the loft." He writes, "looking down with his grin of eternal friendship on the pews, the altar, and the years we had worked hard together, believing in the same thing: AMDG" (p. 29). Ultimately, the "subject's subjection," as he called it, or the acolyte's devotion to light that he describes in *Tiepolo's Hound* (2001), unites the idiosyncrasies of time, creed, and individuality, suggesting that we will never know for sure if his increasing reticence about God over the course of his career has been the result of growing doubt, or growing respect for what he feels subjected to.

Although his most recent book of poetry is full of lament, awareness of mortality, and even a declaration that "my gift abandoned me like a woman I was too old for", Walcott persists in the same task he began in adolescence (*White Egrets*, p. 69). He writes that even though the Caribbean remains relatively empty of the metropolitan standards of culture – opera houses, museums, and theatres –, "yet there are the days/ when every street corner rounds itself into/ a sunlit surprise, a painting or a phrase,/ canoes drawn up by the market, the harbour's blue/ the barracks. So much to do still, all of it praise" (*White Egrets*, p. 86). Perhaps, then, he still remains centrally concerned with the relationship between the mundane and the metaphysical as he was when he first began writing poetry. To borrow from the words of John Clare, Walcott's poetry declares that the world's "every trifle makes it dear".[26] Perhaps this heartbreaking praise of earth's bounty is really a yearning, a hopefulness, that life persists beyond the end. The actuality of his life and his physical experience are tested against this ultimacy, and while his poetry will not name that ultimacy, neither can it disavow it. In that it offers a possible portal to a metaphysics and yet ever and always a reminder of the finitude of death and biology, the earth remains perpetually the elusive and compelling terrain of the sacred.

The final poem of *White Egrets* declares poetry's brazen attempt to correspond to things, only to expose, yet again, the slippage of metaphor. In so doing, it opens up the space of metaphysical hope that lies at the root of his representations. The poem seems to express that it is enough, and yet too much, to hope that poetry can attain a kind of correspondence with the world of things, the world of light and beauty. Walcott announces that "this page is a cloud" on which emerge the colours, sounds and shapes of the island and its streets and villages. These images emerge, of course, simultaneously through his words on an otherwise blank page, suggesting the illusion of an exact echo or perfect correspondence between word and world as we read. As the poem describing his beloved St Lucia comes to an end, he writes: "a cloud slowly covers the page and it goes/ white again and the book comes to a close" (*White Egrets*, p. 89). If his poetry is a secular language of praise for this earth, here and now, it also always encounters the resistance and blankness of the indifferent world of nature. That is to say, its meaning relies on a chasm that opens between words and things, a chasm that admits the possibility of a cosmic "oceanic nothing" just as easily as it marks the space of metaphysical possibility. Standing over and against this space of potential nothingness, his language becomes sacred, in Glissant's sense of the word, because it imagines, almost promises, a new world of possibility. The implication here is that language is not sacred if it merely corresponds exactly to things, but only if we learn to hope that it does. It is as much a leap of faith, perhaps, to believe language could signify the realm of God and to speak the language of angels as it is to believe that it could capture the essence of physical life. Which is why it is as if at the end of his life, Walcott is always still beginning the work of praise of the earth. Language of the earth, *as such*, dislodges from the physical and occupies the ambiguous space of the metaphysical; poetry of the earth becomes the highest language of hope. If poetry merely ends at the edge of things and no chasm opens between, metaphor serves no purpose. Instead, as in this final poem, metaphor allows human hope to stand out in relief, against the blankness, as something we have chosen. Walcott's courageous refusal of triumphalism and yet persistent openness to possibility confuses the long-standing divide between poetry and revelation, between the word of man and the Word of God. We are forced to admit that the secular and telluric poet is perhaps also the oracle of sacred and celestial potentiality. And in our confusion, earth stands a chance, after all.

Endnotes

1. Rainer Maria Rilke, *The Essential Rilke*, Selected and translated by Galway Kinnel and Hannah Liebmann (New York: Ecco, 2000). p. 129.
2. Michel Serres, *The Natural Contract* (Ann Arbor: University of Michigan Press, 1995), p. 78.
3. John Haught, "Christianity and Ecology", *This Sacred Earth: Religion, Nature and the Environment,* Ed. Roger Gottlieb (New York: Routledge, 2003), p. 282.
4. *Blake's Poetry and Designs*, Eds. Mary Lynn Johnson and John E. Grant (New York: Norton. 1979), p. 209.
5. Derek Walcott, *White Egrets* (London: Faber and Faber, 2010), p. 34.
6. Wallace Stevens, "Sunday Morning", *Collected Poetry & Prose* (New York: The Library of America, 1997), pp. 53-56..
7. Giles Gunn, *The Interpretation of Otherness: Literature, Religion, and the American Experience* (Oxford: Oxford University Press, 1979), p. 89.
8. George Steiner, *Real Presences* (Chicago: University of Chicago Press, 1989), p. 216.
9. Mario Vargas Llosa, "In Praise of Reading and Fiction."<http://nobelprize.org/nobel_prizes/literature/laureates/2010/vargas_llosa-lecture_en.html>.
10. Derek Walcott, "The Muse of History", *What the Twilight Says: Essays* (New York: Farrar, Straus, and Giroux, 1998), p. 37.
11. Derek Walcott, *The Bounty* (New York: Farrar, Straus, and Giroux, 1997), p. 13.

12. I have written more extensively on this poem and its poetics of the environment in George B. Handley, *New World Poetics: Nature and the Adamic Imagination of Whitman, Neruda, and Walcott* (Athens: University of Georgia Press, 2007).
13. The poem, entitled "1944", was originally published in *The Voice of St. Lucia* on August 5, 1944. It was reprinted in *Crusader Nobel Laureates Supplement* on 22 Jan. 2000, p. 3.
14. See also the *Crusader Nobel Laureates Supplement* for the response by the priest, Friar C. Jesse F.M. I., entitled "Reflections on Reading the poem, '1944'".
15. It is at least reassuring to know that since that time, the Pope and a host of other religious leaders the world over, have begun to articulate a kind of worldly theology that would not be so threatened by the naturalism of the young Walcott. See, for example, *This Sacred Earth: Religion, Nature and Environment*, Ed. Roger Gottlieb (New York: Routledge, 2003) and *Holy Ground: A Gathering of Voices on Caring for Creation*, Ed. Lyndsay Mosely (United States: Sierra Club Books, 2008).
16. "The Art of Poetry XXXVII: Derek Walcott", Interview with Edward Hirsch, *Conversations with Derek Walcott,* Ed. William Baer (Oxford, MS: University Press of Mississippi, 1996), p. 99.
17. Derek Walcott, "Inside the Cathedral", unpublished essay, University of West Indies, St Augustine, Main Campus Library, (1987), pp. 1–26. Quote, pp. 12-13.
18. See my chapter "Impressionism in the New World", *New World Poetics*.
19. *The Antilles: Fragments of Epic Memory* (New York: Farrar, Straus, and Giroux, 1993), np.; and in *What the Twilight Says: Essays* (New York: Farrar, Straus, and Giroux, 1998), p. 69.
20. Édouard Glissant, *The Poetics of Relation,* Trans. Betsy Wing (Ann Arbor: University of Michigan Press, 1997).
21. Édouard Glissant, *Faulkner, Mississippi*, Trans. Barbara Lewis and Thomas C. Spear (New York: Farrar, Straus, and Giroux, 1998), p. 4.
22. Derek Walcott, *Omeros* (New York: Farrar, Straus, and Giroux, 1992), p. 75.
23. Derek Walcott, *Another Life* (New York: Farrar, Straus, and Giroux, 1973), p. 122; and *Collected Poems, 1948-1984* (New York: Farrar, Straus, and Giroux, 1986), p. 264.
24. Derek Walcott, *The Prodigal* (New York: Farrar, Straus, and Giroux, 2004), p. 104.
25. Emily Dickinson, *The Letters of Emily Dickinson*, Ed. Thomas H. Johnson and Theodora Ward (Cambridge: Belknap Press of Harvard University Press, 1958).
26. John Clare, "The Flitting", *John Clare: Major Works*, Ed. Eric Robinson and David Powell (Oxford: Oxford University Press, 2004), p. 250.

PATRICK A.B. ANTHONY

"WHEREVER IT IS LOVED FRIENDS GO": DEATH AND AFTER-DEATH IN THE POETRY OF DEREK WALCOTT

I first met Seamus Heaney through Derek Walcott. It was during Nobel Laureate week in Saint Lucia. For the past few years many great friends of Derek Walcott have visited the island during that week, among them the late Joseph Brodsky and Arthur Miller. Seamus Heaney and his wife Marie are regulars. In 2005 after the Derek Walcott lecture, Derek invited some of us to "let's go and have something to eat." The party included Seamus, Marie, Sigrid, Derek, Jean Antoine-Dunne, Thomas Dunn from Canada and myself. Since it was late, we headed to Domino's Pizza at Rodney Bay, Gros-Islet. When we arrived, Domino's Pizza had closed for the night, although the workers could be seen inside cleaning up. We sat on the benches in the small park in front of Domino's. This was no "*Ritorno a Milano*".[1] There was no "resting a cup of coffee in its saucer/*e'n la sua volontade è nostra pace*/ in His will is our pizza." (*The Prodigal*, p. 87). There was no pizza tonight and the laureates were hungry.

After some insistent knocking at the door of the pizzeria, someone opened to exclaim "We close!" "I know", I retorted, "but we have two Nobel laureates sitting there and they are hungry". Surprise mellowed into concern which spilt out into "but we shut down de machine aready." "You cannot start it back?" "No. You have to call de manager." Fortunately, Leslie Clarke, who owns the Domino franchise, is a good friend and knows Derek and Seamus. He was in my address book so I called him on his cell phone. "Leslie, Derek and Seamus are at Domino's, they are hungry and the place is closed. The workers say only you can authorise them to restart the machine". "I'll handle it," said Leslie. The rest is pleasant memory. We ate pizza to our hearts' content. To celebrate the memory we took a photograph standing right beneath the huge Domino Pizza sign. It's precious. I cherish that photo: Derek, Seamus, Marie, Jean, Thomas and me in blissful pizzerial satisfaction!

All of this is by way of introduction to Seamus Heaney's book *Finders Keepers*.[2] He autographed a copy for me with the Gaelic words "*Báil ó Dhia ar an obair*", which I later discovered meant "God bless the work!" I'd relished Heaney's *Selected Poems 1966-1987* [3] and as an islander could identify with "The land sustaining us seemed to hold firm/ Only when we embrace it *in extremis*./ All I believe that happened there was vision" ("The Disappearing Island", p. 261). It so happened that just about that time I was journeying through Philip Larkin's *Collected Poems*,[4] "falling and recovering" with him "In huge gesturing loops/ Through an empty sky" as he spoke of his life; "All that's left to happen/ Is some deaths (my own included),/ Their order, and their manner,/ Remain to be learnt." ("I have started to say", p. 185). The tense struggle in the poem "Trees" between despair, "The trees are coming into leaf.../ Their greenness is a kind of grief" and hope: "Last year is dead, they seem to say, / Begin afresh, afresh, afresh." ("Trees", p. 166) contrasts sharply with the nihilism and gloom of "High Windows": "And beyond it, the deep blue air, that shows/ Nothing, and is nowhere, and is endless". ("High Windows", p. 165). I was delighted then, in *Finders Keepers*, to stumble upon Heaney's essay "Joy or Night: Last Things in the Poetry of W.B. Yeats and Philip Larkin" (pp. 343-360). It deepened my appreciation of Larkin and helped me to understand "why Larkin's poetry at its best is read with such gratitude" (*Finders Keepers*, p. 350). For, as Heaney observes, "It too is sensitive to the dialectic between the cornucopia and the empty shell, obliged to try to resolve the imagination's stalemate between the death-mask of nihilism and the fixed smile of a pre-booked place in paradise" (*Finders Keepers*, p. 350).

Heaney's essay inspired the title of this paper, "Wherever it is loved friends go: Death and After-death in the Poetry of Derek Walcott". In the third section of the poem "The Acacia Trees"[5] Walcott writes:

> You see those breakers coming around Pigeon Island
> bowing like nuns in a procession? One thing I know,
> when you're gone like my other friends, not to Thailand
> or Russia, but wherever it is loved friends go
> with their different beliefs, who were like a flock
> of seagulls leaving the mirror of the sand, (*White Egrets*, p. 12)

Walcott's last two collections, *The Prodigal* (2004) and *White Egrets* (2010), are so preoccupied with aging and death that they seem to reflect what Heaney writes about Yeats's poem "The Man and the Echo" where "human consciousness is up against the cliff-face of mystery, confronted with the limitations of human existence itself" (*Finders Keepers*, p. 556). It is Walcott's effort to scale the "cliff-face of mystery" that this essay explores. In the poem "White Egrets" Walcott laments the death of the few friends he has left.[6] There is a tone of urgency as he confronts what Heaney calls "the demeaning realities of bodily decrepitude and the obliterating force of death" (Heaney, *Finders Keepers*, p. 346). The urgency is not only about the impending death of friends, but of his own demise.[7]

In her paper "'There is a sob in there somewhere', *The Prodigal* as Testimony of an Aging Walcott", Antonia MacDonald-Smythe claims that "Walcott intimately explores the aging process and the biological deterioration it engenders as bringing him closer to death; at the same time he becomes the synecdoche for the aging artist who capitulates to diminished social and cultural relevance".[8] MacDonald-Smythe is reacting to Walcott's response to Tony Mochama's query about *The Prodigal* being his "last book", and is exploring the meaning of Walcott's statement, "I said that just to get pity. There is a sob in there somewhere in that statement".[9] According to MacDonald-Smythe,

> it is around this sob that my interest constellates. Is this sobbing real or staged? Is it both? If real, does he sob in dread of the atrophying of the imagination that may come with having to remain at home? Is this sobbing the precursor to prolonged weeping, wailing and lamentation as he faces his mortality? Is he sobbing for himself or for the family and friends now dead? Veteran of threescore years and ten, perceiving himself as having therefore lived out his allotted time, mourning the recent death of his twin brother and his mother's less recent passing, Walcott, in *The Prodigal* seems concerned with his own mortality, mortality that he images as the enfeeblement of a body worn out by various excursions.[10]

Here MacDonald-Smythe's concern and mine converge. In *The Prodigal* and *White Egrets*, is Walcott weeping, wailing and lamenting for his mortality as MacDonald-Smythe suggests? Is he lamenting mortal losses as Sandra M. Gilbert claims poets have done for centuries: "Whether (with Dylan Thomas) counselling readers to 'Rage, rage against the dying of the light' or (with Walt Whitman) taking comfort in the serene arrival, 'sooner or later' of 'delicate death'"?[11] Herein lies our interest, as the poet stands before "the cliff-face of mystery". Can the " wilful and unabashed activity of poetry," as Heaney puts it, fortify the "spirit against assaults from outside and temptations from within – temptations such as the one contained in Larkin's attractively defeatist proposition that 'Death is no different whined at than withstood'"? (*Finders Keepers*, p. 360). How does Walcott confront the agonizing mystery of loss, pain, separation, death and dying? What is his perception of death and "after-death" in *The Prodigal* and *White Egrets*?

Homecomings

The Prodigal is about homecoming in many senses. It is about the prodigal son coming home to a recognition of the inevitability of loss and separation.[12] It is about recognition of loss of manhood in glimpses of beautiful women, Ilse, Roberta, Esperanza, Constanzia, and the Irish actress in Pescara.[13] It is a homecoming to the acceptance of old age and sickness: "Desire and disease commingling,/ commingling, the white hair and the white page/ with the fear of white sight, blindness, amputation,/ a recurring kidney stone, the plague of AIDS" (*The Prodigal*, p. 7)," and what he calls "these piercings of acute mortality" such as "the detached front tooth from a lower denture/ the thick fog I cannot pierce without my glasses/ the shot of pain from a kidney" (p. 53).

The wanderings and journeys of the author have come full circle in *The Prodigal*. He had vowed not to leave his people (p. 94) and wanted to protect and save them (p. 51) just as at the end of *Another Life* he had seen himself and Gregorias (Dunstan St Omer) as "blest with a virginal, unpainted world/ with Adam's task of giving things their names".[14] And so although he senses that his craft might ironically have been a kind of betrayal and questions the value of his life and work,[15] he has made the spiritual return home. He can now claim, "I have nothing more/ to write about than gratitude" (*The Prodigal*, p. 66).

The Prodigal is also about homecoming to oneself. It is about one man's quest for himself and the final discovery of that self. It begins with the author "wandering" through Greenwich Village ("the Village") in search of a subject other than himself only to end up in self-discovery (p. 6). Thus he asks, "Prodigal, what were your wanderings about?/ The smoke of homecoming, the smoke of departure" (p. 70), and finds the answer in his heart, though tired, a heart that sings of finally being at home. The only thing is that he is an old man by now who feels like he's in the evening of his years. Even this book (*The Prodigal*) he sees as "an old man's book" and possibly his last.[16]

Death and the colour "Ochre"

The Prodigal resonates with images of death and dying. The earth/ground/ death colour "ochre" is like a background tapestry for the wanderings of the prodigal, who hears "the dead sighing that they are still too cold in the ochre earth" (p. 54) Walcott's use of the colour ochre is a fascinating revelation of the poet/artist or poetry/painting dialogue which enriches so much of his work. As an artist he had found the colour ochre appropriate to so much of his own experience of the hues of earth and the ground. Not only were the roads or the earth ochre, but that colour became a vehicle for the communication of "the smell of the earth".

In an interview with Iyodele Hippolyte (broadcast on the National Television Network, NTN in St Lucia, during Nobel Laureate Week, 2007), Walcott spoke of how Harold Simmons had helped him to discover the St Lucian countryside. It is there that he first encountered the beauty of the ordinary St Lucian woman, the Martinas, Lucillas, and their odorousness, their "earth smell". He has immortalised it in section two of "Sainte Lucie", the central poem of the collection *Sea Grapes*:

> Martina, or Eunice
> or Lucilla,
> who comes down the steps

with the cool, side flow
as spring water eases
over shelves of rock
in some green ferny hole
by the road in the mountains,
her smile like the whole country
her smell, earth,
red-brown earth... [17]

It is that "red-brown earth" which is the colour ochre; and which is not just a colour, but for the artist/poet, is also a smell: the smell of the earth, the smell of the native woman. In the same poem, ochre is already associated with death: "the pomme arac dyes/ the earth purple,/ the ochre roads/ still waiting in the sun/ for my shadow". Why, because "In the empty schoolyard/ teacher dead today/ the fruit rotting/ yellow on the ground" (*Sea Grapes*, p. 37-38).

In her book *Color: A Natural History of the Palette*, Victoria Finlay writes, "Ochre – iron oxide – was the first color paint. It has been used on every inhabited continent since painting began, and it has been around ever since, on the palettes of almost every artist in history".[18] Of Aboriginal paintings which reflect their mythology of origins (what is called "Dreaming" or "Dreamtime") she states: "the material – ochre – with which these stories are passed on in rituals or on caves is not only from the land. It *is* the land."[19] She goes on to explain how red ochre has been used to paint bodies as "a funerary custom in Australia, Africa, America, and Europe for thousands of years".[20]

The colour ochre is mentioned at least fourteen times in *The Prodigal*. In *Tiepolo's Hound*,[21] his last work before *The Prodigal*, it is mentioned at least twelve times. There ochre is used to describe walls, dogs, reflection in water (shallows), a paint colour, and twice, the colour of land: "parched, ochre headlands" and "the ochre scars/ of garden clearings".[22] *Tiepolo's Hound* has been described as "one of the finest examples in poetry" of the coherence between painting and poetry,[23] but the use of the colour ochre is of interest here because it reflects a preoccupation with death and dying.

In *The Prodigal*, ochre is used to describe (a) walls (b) ridges (c) alleys and cul-de-sacs (d) canals and (e) meadows.[24] Despite these parallels with the use of ochre in *Tiepolo's Hound*, it is in *The Prodigal* that ochre becomes not simply a painter's colour, a "verbal brush stroke", as Baugh would say (*Derek Walcott*, p. 211), but a multiple metaphor. In *The Prodigal* it becomes a metaphor of death: "I hear the dead sighing/ that they are still too cold in the ochre earth/ in the sun's sadness" (p. 54); a metaphor of a season, like "*kawenm*": "In the country of the ochre afternoon/ it is always still and hot" (p. 64), "...in an ochre afternoon/ the enclosing harmony that we call home" (p. 82); as well as an extended metaphor as in "water lapping against eroding stone/ in the ochre country of the afternoon" (p. 64).

After Death

In the Prologue to his book *Between Cross & Resurrection: A Theology of Holy Saturday*, Alan E. Lewis captures the drama of Christian ritual. Alluding to how Christians celebrate Holy Week he states: "Through a few hours of worship and many of ordinary life, they relive annually the growing tensions of the climatic week; the grieving farewells, shameful betrayal, guilty denial, and agonizing fear of the night before the end; the long, dark, deadly day of pain and forsakenness itself; an ecstatic daybreak of miracle and color, song and newborn life..."[25]

Lewis's book is about Holy Saturday, the second day of the Easter Triduum. Of that day he writes, "The nonevent of the second day could after all be a *significant* zero, a *pregnant* emptiness, a silent nothing which says *everything*" (*Between the Cross*, p. 3). In his prologue Lewis captures all the agonizing mystery of loss, pain, separation, death and dying, and the hope of resurrection. These are the very themes played out in Walcott's later works such as *The Bounty*,[26] *The Prodigal*, and *White Egrets*, except for the "ecstatic daybreak of miracle and color, song and newborn life" (*Between the Cross*, p. 5) which represents the hope of resurrection. Of course Lewis is a theologian, Walcott, a poet. Theology can speak confidently about "after death" in terms of newness and resurrection. Reluctant to cast Walcott's craft in the mould of poetic theology, I resist such appellations as "after life", "new life" or "resurrection" which are ideologically charged. Let us then examine what happens after death in Walcott's oeuvre.

In *The Prodigal*, Part II Canto 9, Walcott writes:

I carry a small white city in my head,
one with its avenues of withered flowers, [...]
where my brother and our mother live now
at the one address, so many are their neighbours! (p. 51)

Already in *The Bounty*, Part Two Canto 1, Walcott had bewailed the number of friends he had lost.[27] In Canto 15 he names some.[28] In *The Prodigal* he gives a litany of dead friends whose names "the rain recited : "Alan, Joseph and Claude and Charles and Roddy.../ [...]/ For John and Inge, Devindra and Hamilton" (*The Prodigal*, p. 66). The litany continues, as noted above, in *White Egrets*: "Quick, quick, before they all die [...] some of the best already/ gone, Wilbert Holder, Claude Reid, Ermine Wright/" ("37", p. 71). It is how he speaks about his dead relatives and friends which will give us a key to his perception of what happens after death.

In Part Two Canto 13 of *The Bounty*, Walcott hints at the "after death" as he observes a tree. The heaving of the tree, which made him think the earth shook, evokes "if earth heaves like us/ then the dead, even in their silence, may still be breathing" (p. 38) In the next poem, Canto 14, Walcott again gently probes the imagination in its encounter with death and the "after death":

your soul travelled the one horizon like a quiet snail,
infinity behind it, infinity ahead of it,
and all that it knew was this craft, all that it wanted –
what did it know of death? Only what you had read of it,
that it was like a flame blown out in a lowered lantern,
a night, but without these stars, the prickle of planets, lights
like a vast harbour, or devouring oblivion;
(*The Bounty*, Canto 14, p. 39)

One of Walcott's boldest attempts to deal with "after death" can be found in the title poem of this collection. This poem is an elegy for Walcott's mother, Alix.[29] In Canto IV of "The Bounty" the poet asks, "But can she or can she not read this? Can you read this,/ Mamma, or hear it?" (p. 9). The question suggests that the poet is somehow uncertain whether the dead are capable of reading or hearing. However in "31/ Italian Eclogues", he puts the issue to rest: "Joseph, why am I writing this/ when you cannot read it" (*The Bounty*, p. 65). Although the dead may be incapable of reading or hearing, the poet is still wrestling with the notion of the "presence" of the dead. So he writes "No soul was ever invented/ yet every presence is transparent;/ [...] Faced with seraphic radiance/ (don't interrupt!), mortals rub their skeptical eyes" (*The Bounty*, canto v, p. 11). However, for he himself there is a certitude, a reality:

but there are inexplicable instincts that keep recurring
not from hope or fear only, that are real as stones,
the faces of the dead we wait for as ants are transferring

their cities, though we no longer believe in the shining ones.
I half-expect to see you no longer, then more than half,
almost never, or never then – there I have said it –

but felt something less than final at the edge of your grave,
some other something somewhere, equally dreaded,
since the fear of the infinite is the same as death, (*The Bounty*, pp. 11-12)

For Walcott, the grave is not final. Even if "There is no simile for our souls/ if they are winged but insubstantial" (*The Bounty*, p. 47), he cannot deny that he felt, "something less than final at the edge of your grave". There is "some other something somewhere". It is "infinite", "unendurable brightness" which causes the substantial to dread "dissolving to gases and vapours" (p. 12). One notion of "after death" in Walcott, then, is the substantial dissolving to gases and vapours. This concept is articulated again in poem "27" of *The Bounty* (p. 60).[30] As the poet contemplates the rain and the grey cloud that make "every headland a ghost" (*The Bounty*, p. 60), he is reminded that "all substance thins into mist" and that "the idea of eternity/is a razed horizon when the sky and the sea are mixed/ and the solid disappears like the dead into essences" (p. 60). So here we have two notions of "after death" in Walcott: (1) the substantial dissolving to gases and vapours and (2) the solid disappearing into essences.

As Handley observes, "What lies beyond the grave is feared, whether it is God or nothing, because it represents dissolution of the material substance we now are. He implies that existential atheism is as much an act of faith as dogmatic Christian faith; because both respond to what cannot be known with equal certainty, he offers instead agnosticism as his truest form of faith."[31] Yet, despite the dissolution into gases and vapours, or disappearing into essences, Walcott affirms that those "we still love exist but in another sense, that this shore cannot understand."[32]

Angels and Dolphins

Walcott's affirmation in *The Bounty* of an existence after death draws us to the closing line of *The Prodigal*, "that line of light that shines from the other shore" ("18", p. 105). Some see this line and the other closing lines of the poem as the homecoming of the weary voyaging "prodigal".[33] But these can also symbolize hope and faith. Walcott claims his heart clung to "those finished hopes/ that I would see you again, my twin, 'my dolphin.'" (*The Prodigal*, p. 104). "My twin, 'my dolphin'" is a play on the French "dauphin" which means "twin". Perhaps Walcott, for whom "Faith grows mutinous" (*The Bounty*, p. 9) was slowly coming back to some kind of belief, symbolized by "angels and dolphins". For him, both dolphins and white egrets evoke the elation of angels. The "dolphins seraphically soared/ to the harps of ringing wires and humming ropes" (*The Prodigal*, p. 104) while the white egrets "settle, but not too far off, like angels" (*The Prodigal*, pp. 72). When dolphins butt against the hull of the boat he's travelling on, Walcott exclaims, "What thuds against the hull, butting with such force?/ Angels are gliding underneath the keel." (*The Prodigal*, p. 102).

The Prodigal concludes with a spiritual communion between Walcott and his dead brother, Roderick, when what Walcott thought was a "belief in legend" that was "widening into mania" (p. 103) manifested in the apparition of dolphins. This seems a reclamation of some kind of belief in the "after death". For as Walcott clearly asserts:

> And had there been a prophecy that said: "Wait!
> On a day of great delight you will see dolphins."
> Or, in the ashes and embers of a wrecked sunset
> the same voice, falling as quietly as a flag, said,
> before the constellations arranged their chaos,
> "Those drifting cinders are angels, see how they soar,"
> I would not have believed in them... (*The Prodigal*, p. 105)

Why would he not have believed in them, we might ask? Walcott himself gives the answer: "being too old/ and skeptical from the fury of one life's/ determined benedictions" (*The Prodigal,* p. 105). But he goes on to state categorically that both angels and dolphins are here. Walcott, in old age, is really not as far "past faith" as he thinks. He might feel his "belief obliterated" (*The Prodigal*, p. 9) and that his "faith was strapped in" the night (p. 9), yet as Baugh observes, "The faith which, long ago, in 'Return to D'Ennery, Rain,' Walcott said he had lost was never really lost; it had barrelled too deep under the keel of his heart" (*Derek Walcott*, p. 229).

White Egrets

Walcott's last collection, *White Egrets* (2010), pulsates with probing questions and evocations about death, dying and "after death". White egrets frame the backdrop for his reflections like the huge bird, the "sepulchral egret or heron" (*White Egrets*, p. 10), that took his friend Joseph (Brodsky) away. When friends like that die, according to Walcott, "what you've also lost is belief in heaven" (*White Egrets*, p. 54). White egrets had always intrigued Walcott, and when he returns to the valley of Santa Cruz in Trinidad, he confesses "I have come back for the white egrets/ feeding in a flock on the lawn" (*The Prodigal*, p. 71). The egrets astonish "the page of the lawn" then "launch themselves with wings that, beating faster,/ are certain as a seraph's when they beat" (*White Egrets,* p. 8). Walcott believes the egrets will be there "after my shadow passes with all its sins/ into a green thicket of oblivion" into "...that peace/ beyond desires and beyond regrets,/ at which I may arrive eventually," (*White Egrets*, pp. 6-7). The egrets symbolize stability in a vulnerable and transient world: "Some friends, the few I have left,/ are dying, but the egrets stalk through the rain/ as if nothing mortal can affect them, or they lift/ like abrupt angels, sail, then settle again." (White *Egrets*, p. 9).

When Walcott wrote about the egrets in "33/A Santa Cruz Quartet, iii" [for Charles Applewhaite] in 1997, they were like "prayers without noise," rising into "the myth of a heaven that gradually pardons" (*The Bounty*, p. 73). By 2004, in *The Prodigal*, egrets were "feeding in a flock on the lawn/ [...] then suddenly but leisurely sailing/ to settle, but not too far off, like angels" (pp. 71-72). In *White Egrets,* we see the egrets "lift like abrupt angels, sail, then settle again" (*White Egrets*, p. 9). Their motion conjures up in the poet the memory of dying friends and fading hills: "Sometimes the hills themselves disappear/ like friends, slowly, but I am happier/ that they have come back now, like memory, like prayer." (p. 9).

Perhaps the enduring image which Walcott wanted us to recall of egrets is not that they were "like abrupt angels" (*White Egrets*, p. 9) with wings that "beating faster,/ are certain as a seraph's when they beat" (*White Egrets*, p. 8);

but rather, that they represented an affirmation of faith in the "after death". Egrets were "seraphic souls, as Joseph was", he writes, referring to his dear friend Joseph Brodsky. It is no mystery, then, why Walcott would close the title poem of *White Egrets* in stanza VIII with a description of their encounter, himself and Joseph, with the "sepulchral egret", "perhaps the same one that took him" (*White Egrets*, p. 10). The incident happened by the pool at a friend's house in St Croix. According to Walcott, what shook Joseph and caused him to point out "with a gasp" was that the "huge bird was suddenly there" and it "was such a spectral white" (p. 10). He closes the poem with those lines :

> Now when at noon or evening on the lawn
> the egrets soar together in noiseless flight
> or tack, like a regatta, the sea-green grass,
> they are seraphic souls, as Joseph was. (*White Egrets*, p. 10)[34]

Hic Jacet

In Part Two Canto I of *The Bounty*, Walcott, after bemoaning the "so many deaths" of his friends, "nothing short of a massacre" (*The Bounty*, p. 19) proceeds to write his own epitaph:

> So, for my *Hic Jacet*, my own epitaph, "Here lies
> D.W. This place is good to die in." It really was. (*The Bounty*, p. 19)

He who had written about the deaths of so many, so many elegies, could not resist the urge to write about his own death; for he knows that Basil, the death-figure is still "making his rounds" (*White Egrets*, p. 54) and that death is inevitable. It will not mutter "Maybe I'll skip this one" (*The Prodigal*, p. 86). As Walcott contemplates his own death, can we affirm that the faith which he said he had lost was never really lost?[35]

I have dealt elsewhere with Walcott's struggle with faith, his love/hate relationship with religion and Roman Catholicism, as well as his appropriation of Old and New Testament themes.[36] Is "the surge of happiness, inexplicable content" and the "fresh elation of dolphins" (*The Prodigal*, pp. 54-55) a sign of a deeper homecoming for Walcott? Do angels and dolphins represent and confirm some kind of faith? In the interview with Mochama on *The Prodigal* which MacDonald-Smythe quotes, Walcott acknowledges that *The Prodigal* "is about the final homecoming… It is a metaphor of opening arms and closing arms… it is also about death, blending with travelling and homecoming" (MacDonald-Smythe, p. 8). Is it a final homecoming to the inevitability of death and the possibility of an after-death?

From as early as the poem "Steersman, my Brother"[37] Walcott had struggled with the mystery of faith and death. An elegy written for his friend Julian John who had died suddenly while studying for the priesthood in France, "Steersman, my Brother" portrays the young poet praying "Restore, if even by your death, my faith (p. 41). Walcott, like Julian, was once a believer: "I had such faith as yours, but the tides/ Of bitterness broke over me, and the raft/ Of my saved cargoes perished" (p. 40). In "Return to D'Ennery; Rain" from the same collection Walcott acknowledges the loss of faith but refuses to apportion blame for his state.

Whatever Walcott's early struggles with faith[38] one can argue that the anguish of art and life has not left him untouched. The loss of so many friends and loved ones has confronted him with the inevitable question of his own mortality. We have witnessed his agony as he confronted the cliff-face of the mystery of death and after-death. When he wrote his epitaph in 1997 he was certainly not an old man

> "whose knees easily buckle,
> toothless at sunrise with white knotted hair,
> who sometimes feels his flesh cold as the stone
> that he will lie under" (*The Prodigal*, p. 87).

It is easy to write calmly "This place is good to die in" (*The Bounty*, p. 19) when one is not being constantly reminded of the "piercings of acute mortality".[39] Perhaps one can argue that since Walcott believed *The Prodigal* was his last book, then its closing line "that line of light that shines from the other shore" is more credible as an epitaph.

Pursuing this line of reasoning in the light of what was said above about angels and dolphins, one can affirm that Walcott has apparently arrived not only at "that peace/beyond desires and beyond regrets" where he eventually hoped to arrive (*White Egrets*, p. 6), but more than that, to some measure of serenity that comes with nascent faith. Thus, even if at one time he believed that his shadow might pass "with all its sins into a green thicket of oblivion" (*White Egrets*, pp. 6-7) we have seen how he has grown into acceptance of many things (a) angels and dolphins with all they symbolize (b) "some other something somewhere" (*The Bounty*, p. 12); and (c) that those "we still love exist/ but in another sense, that this shore cannot understand" (*The Bounty*, "27", p. 60).

In 1976 Derek Walcott celebrated the faith of his friend Dunstan St Omer (the Gregorias of *Another Life*) with the poem "For the Altar-piece of the Roseau Valley Church, Saint Lucia".[40] He hailed St Omer's faith "whatever one man believes he knows of God/ and the suffering of his kind" (*Sea Grapes*, p. 54), a faith which he has always admired in his friend, but which he does not possess. St. Omer's mural so moved Walcott that one senses evocations of homecoming to faith:

> after all that,
> your faith like a canoe at evening coming in,

like a relative who is tired of America,
like a woman coming back to your house [...] (*Sea Grapes*, p. 55)

Perhaps Walcott, the fortunate traveller, whose faith was once mutinous (*The Bounty*, p. 9) was growing tired of journeying and longing for home. If that be the case, then, *The Prodigal* and *White Egrets* may mark the final stages of the journey home; the canoe of faith gliding silently towards "that line of light that shines from the other shore" (*The Prodigal*, p. 105).

End Notes

1. Derek Walcott, *The Prodigal* (New York: Farrar, Straus and Giroux, 2004), p. 86.
2. Seamus Heaney, *Finders Keepers* (New York: Farrar, Straus and Giroux, 2002).
3. Seamus Heaney, *Selected Poems 1966-1987* (New York: Farrar, Straus and Giroux, 1990).
4. Philip Larkin, *Collected Poems* (New York: Farrar, Straus and Giroux, 1989).
5. "The Acacia Trees" is poem no. 5 in the collection *White Egrets* (New York: Farrar, Straus and Giroux, 2010), pp. 11-12.
6. "Some friends, the few I have left/ are dying," he writes in "White Egrets"; and again "Sometimes the hills themselves disappear/ like friends, slowly" but, "the egrets stalk through the rain/ as if nothing mortal can affect them", *White Egrets*, p. 9.
7. In poem "37" of *White Egrets*, for example, Walcott writes, "Quick, quick, before they all die [...] some of the best already/gone, Wilbert Holder, Claude Reid, Ermine Wright/...I must clear the house of my head, I must make room/for a shrine before they all die..."(p. 69). And about egrets Walcott writes "They shall/ be there after my shadow passes with all its sins,/ into a green thicket of oblivion" "White Egrets", *White Egrets*, pp. 6-7.
8. Antonia MacDonald-Smythe, "'There is a sob in there somewhere': *The Prodigal* as Testimony of an Aging Walcott", Bahamas: 26th Annual West Indian Literature Conference, 8-10 March, 2007. Unpublished, p. 6.
9. Tony Mochama, "A Day Out with Eccentric Nobel Laureate Derek Walcott", *Sunday Standard,* 28 May 2006.
10. "There is a sob in there somewhere", p. 6.
11. Taken from Sandra M. Gilbert's online description of her book, *Inventions of Farewell: A Book of Elegies* (New York: W.W. Norton & Co., 2001) <http://www.sandramgilbert.com/ inventions_ of_farewell_ a_ book_of _elegies_26295.htm.>

12. See: "…how the screaming gulls knew/ the names of all the women he had lost" and the "sweet meditation on a train/ even of certain griefs […]next to the stone sails of graves, his growing loss", *The Prodigal*, p. 4.
13. See: "the age in your armpits in the pleats of your crotch", *The Prodigal*, p. 8, or again "such an implacable lust that came with age –/ as a dirty old man leering at young things" (p. 32).
14. *Another Life* (London: Jonathan Cape, 1973) p. 152.
15. "Were your life and work/ simply a good translation?" *The Prodigal*, p. 61.
16. "In what will be your last book make each place/ as if it had just been made, already old, / but new again from naming it", *The Prodigal*, p. 99.
17. *Sea Grapes* (London: Jonathan Cape, 1976), pp. 46-47.
18. Victoria Finlay, *Color: A Natural History of the Palette* (New York: Random House, 2004) p. 26.
19. *Color: A Natural History*, p. 36.
20. *Color: A Natural History*, p. 38.
21. *Tiepolo's Hound* (London: Faber and Faber, 2000).
22. The following are the references to the word ochre in *Tiepolo's Hound*: "the ochre walls of the old cantonment in the still lagoon" (pp. 10-11); "the impasto indigo bay, the ochre walls of Provence"(p. 19); "as their ochre pot hounds forage"(p. 37) and "Ochre dogs sip it" (ibid.); "and whose/ range grew simple, olive, umber, ochre,/ his outlines smothered in a hundred hues"(p. 55); "all of that muted bliss contained in a red/ rusting roof, an ochre wall, patches of snow" (p. 62); "the ochre shallows/ reciting their lessons" (p. 67); "the beat of a brush reaching/ into its creamy palette, oranges, ochres" (p. 94); "On parched, ochre headlands"(p. 96); "the rough hills beyond with their receding/ indigos and often the ochre scars/ of garden clearings"(p. 111); "Each reproduction, even in monochrome,/ fresco or ceiling in a pale ochre wash" (p. 150).
23. According to Edward Baugh in his book *Derek Walcott* (Cambridge: Cambridge University Press, 2006), in *Tiepolo's Hound* Walcott has admirably illustrated the coherence between art and poetry: "At one and the same time the poet represents in words the life in paintings, or, more precisely, the life of paint, and life as painting, 'flesh becoming paint' (*TH,* p. 108), the identification of 'brushstroke and word'" (*TH*, p. 99).
24. In *The Prodigal*, ochre is also used to describe (a) walls: "curved facades gamboges and ochre" (p. 28); "the ochre walls of Parma" (p. 33); "Lemons of Montale against an ochre wall" (p. 88); (b) ridges: "after the white ridges,/ ochre scarps for a long while along

the grey lake" (p. 15); (c) alleys and cul-de-sacs: "over an ochre alley near the walls of Parma" (p. 94), "of brown and ochre cul-de-sacs, (p. 88); (d) canals: "the barge crawled along an ochre canal" (p. 3); (e) meadows: "the ochreing meadows" (p. 101).

25. Alan E. Lewis, *Between Cross & Resurrection: A Theology of Holy Saturday.* (Grand Rapids: Wm. B. Eerdmans Publishing Co., 2001), pp. 4-5.
26. *The Bounty* (New York: Farrar, Straus and Giroux, 1997).
27. "Now, so many deaths, nothing short of a massacre/ from the wild scythe blindly flailing friends, flowers, and grass,/ as the seaside city of graves expands its acre", *The Bounty*, p. 19.
28. "I look out of from Becune Point with deaths inside me [...]/ The clouds change governments,/ and Ben is gone, and John, Godfrey, and Quentin; the news/ is always of a fading..." The *Bounty*, p. 40.
29. According to Edward Baugh, this poem "completes, in effect, a trilogy for his mother, which spans thirty-five years or so, beginning with chapter 2 of *Another Life*, followed by chapter XXXII of *Omeros*", *Derek Walcott*, p. 203.
30. "'27' is the praise poem that all the poems work towards," writes Baugh, *Derek Walcott*, p. 208.
31. George B. Handley, "Derek Walcott's Poetics of the Environment in *The Bounty*", *Callaloo* 28.1 (2005), 209.
32. Of *The Bounty*, "27", p. 60, Baugh observes: "The statement 'those we still love exist' draws us to a simultaneous reordering of the words into 'those we love still exist', so that the full meaning is 'those we still love still exist'. There is a nice pun on 'sense', which also signifies that those we still love continue to exist in a being beyond accessibility to the mortal senses. This perception, of the ultimate insubstantiality of the sensuous substance of things, of nature, is all the more hard won in a poet who has so superbly represented that substance." *Derek Walcott*, p. 208.
33. Although some, like Baugh, interpret "that line of light that shines from the other shore" as "an extension of the sea-going, horizon-widening image" which Walcott always sought (*Derek Walcott*, p. 229), it is also open to other interpretations.
34. White egrets came to represent many things for Walcott. They inspired creativity: "Be happy now at Cap, for the simplest joys [...]/ for a line of white egrets prompting the last word," and productivity "be grateful that you wrote well in this place,/ let the torn poems sail from you like a flock/ of white egrets in a long last sigh of release." (*White Egrets*, p. 63). But they also evoked regrets, "the bleached regrets of an old man's memoirs":

    .... Watch those egrets
trudging the lawn in a disheveled troop, white banners

trailing forlornly; they are the bleached regrets
of an old man's memoirs, printed stanzas
showing their hinged wings like wide open secrets. (p. 46)

Another version of "the bleached regrets of an old man's memoirs", appears in the Faber & Faber edition of *White Egrets* and reads thus:

"...Watch these egrets
stalk the lawn in a dishevelled troop, white banners
forlornly trailing their flags; they are the bleached regrets
of an old man's memoirs, their unwritten stanzas.
Pages gusting like wings on the lawn, wide open secrets.

White Egrets (London: Faber and Faber, 2010), p. 47.

It is worth noting that the pagination for the Faber and Faber and Farrar, Straus, Giroux editions is sometimes the same, sometimes different by a couple of pages.

35. In the poem "Return to D'Ennery, Rain" he writes: "Why blame the faith you have lost? Heaven remains/ Where it is, in the hearts of these people", *In a Green Night: Poems 1948-1960* (London: Jonathan Cape, 1962), p. 34.
36. Patrick Anthony, "'Adam's Task': The Poetry of Derek Walcott and Caribbean Theology – A Study in the Relationship between Literature and Christian Theology". Unpublished MA Thesis. Catholic Theological Union at Chicago. 1987.
37. Derek Walcott, *In A Green Night*, pp. 39-42.
38. In the poem "The Schooner *Flight*", Walcott alludes to "the faith/ that had faded from a child in the Methodist chapel/ in Chisel Street, Castries", *The Star-Apple Kingdom* (New York: Farrar, Straus and Giroux, 1979), p. 18.
39. "And all the pieces that go to make me up –/ the detached front tooth from a lower denture/ the thick fog I cannot pierce without my glasses/ the shot of pain from a kidney/ these piercings of acute mortality", *The Prodigal*, p. 53.
40. Derek Walcott, *Sea Grapes* (London: Jonathan Cape, 1976), pp. 52-55.

WORKS CITED

Manuscripts

Correspondence with Derek Walcott. Ronald Bryden papers, Ms. Coll. 548, Box 1. The Thomas Fisher Rare Book Library, University of Toronto.

MacDermot, Galt. Letter to Derek Walcott. Derek Walcott papers, Ms. Coll. 136, Box 48. The Thomas Fisher Rare Book Library, University of Toronto. 10 Oct. 1992.

Toews, Jennifer. Foreword by Richard Landon, Preface by Ted Chamberlin. *How Beautiful My Brethren and Sistren: Derek Walcott, Life and Work*. Exhibition catalogue, October 2011- April 2012, The Thomas Fisher Rare Book Library, University of Toronto.

Walcott, Derek. "Carnival as Theatre". Ms. 1977? The University of the West Indies, Alma Jordan Library, St. Augustine.

———. *Marie Laveau. 1979.* Ms. Coll. 136, Boxes 24, 65. The Thomas Fisher Rare Book Library, University of Toronto.

———. *In a Fine Castle*. 1982. Ms. Coll. 136, Box 62. The Thomas Fisher Rare Book Library, University of Toronto. (Later reworked and renamed *The Last Carnival*).

———. *The Joker of Seville*. 1982. Ms. Coll. 136, Boxes 22, 62. The Thomas Fisher Rare Book Library, University of Toronto.

———. *The Last Carnival*. 1985, 1992. Ms. Coll. 136, Boxes 23, 34-37. The Thomas Fisher Rare Book Library, University of Toronto. (Later reworked, renamed version of *In a Fine Castle*).

———. *Beef no Chicken*. 1986. Ms. Coll. 136, Boxes 15, 34-37. The Thomas Fisher Rare Book Library, University of Toronto.

———. "Inside the Cathedral," Ms. 1987. The University of West Indies, Alma Jordan Lib., St. Augustine, pp. 1–26.

———. *Steel*. 1990-2005. Ms. Coll. 136, Boxes 28-33, 63, 66, 68. The Thomas Fisher Rare Book Library, University of Toronto.

———. *The Capeman*. 1995-96. Ms. Coll. 136, Boxes 15-16, 65, 70-71. The Thomas Fisher Rare Book Library, University of Toronto.

———. Draft notes, plot outlines, visuals and script insertions written for *American History X*, 1998. Director Tony Kaye (1952-) Ms. Coll. 348, Boxes 26, 27, OVS 22. The Thomas Fisher Rare Book Library, University of Toronto.

———. TS. *Tiepolo's Hound*. 2000. Several drafts. Ms. Coll. 348, Boxes 12, 14 and Item 15. The Thomas Fisher Rare Book Library, University of Toronto.

———. Guillermo Cabrera Infante review draft of "The Great Exile" for *The New York Review of Books,* March 28, 2002, Derek Walcott papers, Ms. Coll. 504, Box 1, The Thomas Fisher Rare Book Library, University of Toronto.

———. "Tribute to Elizabeth Hardwick", *New York Review of Books*, Jan. 17, 2008. Draft, Derek Walcott papers, 2009 accession. The Thomas Fisher Rare Book Library, University of Toronto.

———. "On the significance of Haiti", N.d. Draft notes for the Haitian Bicentenary, Derek Walcott papers, Ms. Coll. 504, Box 6. The Thomas Fisher Rare Book Library, University of Toronto.

———. Essay drafts "Heaney in Ireland", N.d. Derek Walcott papers, Ms. Coll. 136, Box 1. The Thomas Fisher Rare Book Library, University of Toronto.

———. Essay drafts for Arthur Miller Tribute. N.d. Derek Walcott papers, Ms. Coll. 504, Box 6, The Thomas Fisher Rare Book Library, University of Toronto.

———. "Good Old Heart of Darkness", N.d. Drafts of essay on Grenada. Derek Walcott papers, Ms. Coll. 136, Box 1. The Thomas Fisher Rare Book Library, University of Toronto.

———. *Omeros.* N.d. Ms. 0564:1:1, Box No. 20B. The University of the West Indies Alma Jordan Lib., St. Augustine.

———. *Omeros.* N.d. Ms. 0564:2:1, Box No. 20B. The University of the West Indies Alma Jordan Lib., St. Augustine. Trinidad.

———. *Omeros.* N.d. Ms. 0564:3:1, Box No. 20B. The University of the West Indies, Alma Jordan Lib., St. Augustine.

———. *Omeros.* N.d. Ms. 0564:4:1, Box No. 20B. The University of the West Indies, Alma Jordan Lib., St Augustine, Trinidad.

———. *Omeros.* N.d. Ms. 0565:5:1, Box No. 20B. The University of the West Indies, Alma Jordan Lib., St. Augustine. Trinidad.

Illustrations

O Babylon! Poster, Trinidad Theatre Workshop World Premiere, Little Carib Theatre

O Babylon!, 4th King

O Babylon!, Selassie

O Babylon! Stage sketches

O Babylon!, Sufferer

O Babylon!, Priscilla

O Babylon!, Aaron

Marie Laveau, Marie
Marie Laveau, Mourners
Marie Laveau, Dancer, Bamboula
Marie Laveau, Participants
Marie Laveau, Aborzor 'Zumba', Ex-Haitian Slave, Drummer
Steel, Zora
Steel, Kingdom of the Night, Arenkinian as Pluto
Steel, Steel Pan Drummers, Bandidos
Steel, Were You There
Steel, Growler
Steel, This is my Hill (Laventille)

Published Works

Walcott, Derek. "1944", originally published in *The Voice of St. Lucia*. 5 Aug. 1944. Reprinted in *Crusader Nobel Laureates Supplement* on January 22, 2000.

———. *25 Poems* (Port of Spain: Guardian Commercial Printery, 1948).

———. *Epitaph for the Young* (Barbados: Advocate, 1949).

———. *Poems* (Kingston: Jamaica City Printers, 1951).

———. *In A Green Night* (London: Jonathan Cape, 1962).

———. *The Castaway and Other Poems* (London: Jonathan Cape, 1965).

———. "The Figure of Crusoe: On the Theme of Isolation in West Indian Writing" [1965], *Critical Perspectives on Derek Walcott*, Ed. Robert D. Hamner (Boulder and London: Lynne Rienner Publishers, 1997).

———. *Malcauchon* or *The Six in the Rain* (University of the West Indies, Extra-Mural Dept., 1966).

———. *The Gulf and Other Poems* (London: Jonathan Cape, 1969).

———. *Dream on Monkey Mountain and Other Plays* (New York: Farrar, Straus and Giroux, 1970).

———. "Popular Poets are Now Being Severely Tested", *Sunday Guardian* 14 Feb. 1960, 7.

———. "Sparrow Shows Versatility in Range of Theme", *Sunday Guardian* 26 Feb. 1960, 16.

———. "Calypsonians! Danger Lurks in Tin Pan Alley", *Sunday Guardian* 25 Feb. 1962, 23.

———. "Poetry – Enormously Complicated Art", *The Trinidad Guardian* 18 June 1962, 3.

———. "A Fracas of Words and Music When Giants Meet", *Sunday Guardian* 27 Jan. 1963, 4.

———. "Alas! The Last Minute Road March is Gone", *Sunday Guardian* 3 Feb. 1963, 4.

———. "The West Indian Attitude to Cricket", *Sunday Guardian* 28 July 1963, 14.
———. "The King ain' Dead Yet", *Sunday Guardian* 2 Feb. 1964, 13.
———. "An Artist Interprets Cricket", *Trinidad Guardian* 1 Jan. 1964, 5.
———. "Spiritual Purpose Lacking", *Sunday Guardian* 5 Jan. 1964, 3
———. "Cheers for an Insincere Clown", *Sunday Guardian* 30 Jan. 1964, 5.
———. "Our Poetry in Song", *Sunday Guardian* 9 Feb. 1964, 13.
———. "Curious Mishmash of Style", *Trinidad Guardian* 12 Feb. 1964, 5.
———. "Efficient 'Birdie', Minus the Feather Ruffling", *Trinidad Guardian* 6 Jan. 1965, 5.
———. "The Mighty Terror – A Great Matador – With a Cape and a Hangover", *Sunday Guardian* 17 Jan. 1965, 3.
———. "Where Do They Get Their Style?" *Trinidad Guardian* 21 Apr. 1965, 5.
———. "Vintage Year for Calypso", *Sunday Guardian* 16 Feb. 1966, 6.
———. (Kaiso Man), "Laro 'Holes' Them at the OYB", *Trinidad Guardian* 10 Jan. 1967, 4.
———. "Every Politician should have a Cypher in his Back Pocket…The Clown Prince of Calypso Drops a Bomb", *Sunday Guardian* 15 Jan. 1967, 4.
———. "Dark Horses", *Sunday Guardian Magazine* 29 Jan. 1967, 4.
———. "It's Our Own Kind of Artist Figure in the Panmen, the Steelbandman, the Calypsonian", *Sunday Guardian* 5 Feb. 1967, 11.
———. "Where Exuberance Triumphs", *The Times* 8 Oct. 1968.
———. "Leaving School" [1965], *Critical Perspectives on Derek Walcott*, Ed. Robert D. Hamner (Boulder, Co: Lynne Reinner, 1997), pp. 24-32.
———. "Tribal Flutes", *Sunday Guardian*, 19 Mar. 1967, 2.
———. "Meanings", *Savacou* 2 (1970), 45–51.
———. *Another Life* (London: Jonathan Cape, 1973); (New York: Farrar, Straus and Giroux, 1973); fully annotated. Eds. Edward Baugh and Colbert Nepaulsingh (Boulder and London: Lynne Rienner, 2004).
———. "The Muse of History" [1974], *What the Twilight Says. Essays* (New York: Farrar, Straus and Giroux, 1998), pp. 36-64.
———. *Sea Grapes* (London: Jonathan Cape, 1976); (New York: Farrar, Straus and Giroux, 1976).
———. *The Joker of Seville and O Babylon!* (New York: Farrar, Straus and Giroux, 1978).
———. "Extracts from 'Marie Laveau'", *Trinidad and Tobago Review*, 3.6 (1979).

———. *The Star-Apple Kingdom* (New York: Farrar, Straus and Giroux, 1979); (London: Jonathan Cape, 1980).
———. *Remembrance & Pantomime* (New York: Farrar, Straus and Giroux, 1980).
———. *The Fortunate Traveller* (New York: Farrar, Straus and Giroux, 1981); (London: Faber and Faber, 1981).
———. *Midsummer* (New York: Farrar, Straus and Giroux, 1984); (London: Faber and Faber, 1984).
———. *Ti-Jean and His Brothers* (Port of Spain: Paria Publishing, 1984).
———. *Derek Walcott: Collected Poems: 1948-1984* (New York: Farrar, Straus and Giroux, 1986).
———. *The Last Carnival, Three Plays* (New York: Farrar, Straus and Giroux, 1986).
———. *The Arkansas Testament* (New York: Farrar, Straus and Giroux, 1987); (London: Faber and Faber, 1987).
———. "Caligula's Horse", *After Europe*, Eds. Stephen Slemon and Helen Tiffin (Mundelstrup: Dangaroo, 1989), pp. 138-142.
———. *Omeros* (London: Faber and Faber, 1990); (New York: Farrar, Straus and Giroux, 1990).
———. *The Odyssey: A Stage Version* (New York: Farrar, Straus and Giroux, 1993); (London: Faber and Faber, 1993).
———. *The Antilles: Fragments of Epic Memory. The Nobel Lecture* (London: Faber and Faber, 1993).
———. *The Bounty* (New York: Farrar, Straus and Giroux, 1997); (London: Faber and Faber, 1997).
———. "Reflections on Omeros", *South Atlantic Quarterly* 96.2 (1997), 229–46.
———. *What the Twilight Says Essays* (New York: Farrar, Straus and Giroux, 1998); (London: Faber and Faber, 1998).
———. *Tiepolo's Hound* (London: Faber and Faber; New York: Farrar, Straus and Giroux, 2000).
———. *The Haitian Trilogy* (New York: Farrar, Straus and Giroux, 2002).
———. *Walker and the Ghost Dance* (New York: Farrar, Straus and Giroux, 2002).
———. *The Prodigal* (New York: Farrar, Straus and Giroux, 2004); (London: Faber and Faber, 2004).
———. *Selected Poems by Derek Walcott*, Ed. Edward Baugh (New York: Farrar, Straus and Giroux, 2007).
———. "'Lament and Triumph, for Shirley Kelsick'. Walcott Laments Windies Decline", *Sunday Express* 1 July 2007, 51.
———. *White Egrets* (New York: Farrar, Straus and Giroux, 2010); (London: Faber and Faber, 2010).

Films, scripts, storyboards and scenarios

Derek Walcott. "Vangelo Nero", Film script. Ms. The Alma Jordan Library, The University of the West Indies, St. Augustine, 1972.

———. "To Die for Grenada", Film script. Ms. Coll. 136, Boxes 38-42; Storyboard in Box 67. The Thomas Fisher Library, The University of Toronto, 1983-1987.

———. *The Rig*, 1984.

———. *Omeros*, Screen Play. Ms. Dated April – May / 95. Composite, with several revisions and inserts throughout. Ms. Coll. 136, Box 14. The Thomas Fisher Library, The University of Toronto, 1995.

———. *A Maddening Space*, The New York Centre for Visual History, 1999.

Interviews and Conversations

Scott, Dennis. "Walcott on Walcott" [1968], *Conversations with Derek Walcott*. Ed. William Baer (Jackson: University Press of Mississippi, 1996), pp. 10-16.

"We are still being betrayed", Interview with Raoul Pantin, *Caribbean Contact* 1.7 (July, 1973), 14, 16.

Hirsch, Edward. "An interview with Derek Walcott" [1977], *Conversations with Derek Walcott*, Ed. William Baer (Jackson: University of Mississippi Press, 1996), pp. 50-63.

Ciccarelli, Sharon. "Reflections Before and After Carnival: An Interview with Derek Walcott" [1977], *Conversations with Derek Walcott*, Ed. William Baer (Jackson: University Press of Mississippi, 1996), pp. 34-49.

Thomas, Ned. "Interview" [1980], *Conversations With Derek Walcott*. Ed. William Baer (Jackson: University Press of Mississippi, 1996), pp. 64-69.

Sjøberg, Leif. "An interview with Derek Walcott" [1983], *Conversations with Derek Walcott*, Ed. William Baer (Jackson: University of Mississippi Press, 1999), pp. 79-85.

Hirsch, Edward. "The Art of Poetry XXVII" [1985], *Conversations With Derek Walcott*, Ed. William Baer (Jackson: University Press of Mississippi 1996), pp. 95-121.

Rowell, Charles H. "An Interview with Derek Walcott" [1987], *Conversations with Derek Walcott*. Ed. William Baer (Jackson: University Press of Mississippi, 1996), pp. 122-134.

White, J.P. "An Interview with Derek Walcott" [1990], *Conversations With Derek Walcott*, Ed. William Baer (Jackson: University Press of Mississippi, 1996), pp. 151-174.

Antoine-Dunne, Jean. "Derek Walcott in Conversation with Jean Antoine", *Poetry Ireland Review* 34 (Spring 1992), 72-85.

Presson, Rebekah. "The Man Who Keeps the English Language Alive: An Interview with Derek Walcott" [1992], *Conversations with Derek Walcott*, Ed. William Baer (Jackson: University Press of Mississippi, 1996), pp. 189-193.

Baer, William. "An Interview with Derek Walcott" [1994], *Conversations with Derek Walcott*, Ed. William Baer (Jackson MS: University Press of Mississippi, 1996).

Micheaux, Dante. "The Wolf Interview: Derek Walcott", *The Wolf Magazine*, 2009. <http://www.wolfmagazine.co.uk/21_walcott.php>

Secondary Sources

Aiyejina, Funso, and Paula Morgan. Eds. *Caribbean Literature in a Global Context* (St Augustine: UWI Faculty of Humanities and Education, and Lexicon Trinidad, 2006).

Allsopp, Richard, and Jeannette Allsopp. Eds. *Dictionary of Caribbean English Usage* (Oxford and New York: Oxford University Press, 1996).

Anthony, Patrick. "'Adam's Task': The Poetry of Derek Walcott and Caribbean Theology – A Study in the Relationship between Literature and Christian Theology", Unpublished MA Thesis, Catholic Theological Union at Chicago, 1987.

Aristotle. *Poetics* (Harmondsworth: Penguin, 1996).

Arnold, Matthew. *Culture and Anarchy*, Ed. J. Dover Wilson (Cambridge: Cambridge University Press, 1978).

Banks, Daniel. "From Homer to Hip Hop: Orature and Griots, Ancient and Present", *Classical World* 103.2 (2010), 238–45.

Baugh, Edward. *Derek Walcott* (Cambridge: Cambridge University Press, 2006).

Baugh, Edward. Ed. *Selected Poems by Derek Walcott* (New York: Farrar, Straus and Giroux, 2007).

Beckett, Samuel. *Collected Shorter Plays* [1984] (London: Faber and Faber, 2006).

———. "Breath", *Collected Shorter Plays* [1984] (London: Faber and Faber, 2006), pp. 209-11.

———. "Not I", *Collected Shorter Plays* [1984] (London: Faber and Faber, 2006), pp. 213-223.

———. *The Trilogy* [1959] (London: Picador Pan, 1979).

Benitez-Rojo, Antonio. *The Repeating Island: The Caribbean and the Postmodern Perspective*, trans. J, Maraniss (Durham and London: Duke UP, 1997).

Blake, William. *Blake's Poetry and Designs*, Ed. Mary Lynn Johnson and John E. Grant (New York: Norton, 1979).

Brathwaite, Edward Kamau. *The Arrivants: A New World Trilogy* (Oxford: Oxford University Press, 1973).

———. *Ancestors* (New York: New Directions, 2001).

Breiner, Laurence. *An Introduction to West Indian Poetry* (Cambridge: Cambridge University Press, 1998).

Breslin, Paul. *Nobody's Nation: Reading Derek Walcott* (Chicago: The University of Chicago Press, 2001).

Brodsky, Joseph. <http://www.poets.org/poet.php/prmPID/220>. Retrieved 16 Jan. 2012.

———. "On Derek Walcott", *New York Review of Books*, 30.17 (10 Nov. 1983), 39-41.

———. "Letters from the Ming Dynasty", *The New Yorker*, 28 Jan. 1980.

Burnett, Paula. *Derek Walcott: Politics and Poetics* (Gainesville: University Press of Florida, 2000).

Chamberlin Edward. *Come Back to Me My Language: Poetry and the West Indies* (Champaign: University of Illinois Press, 1993).

Clare, John, "The Flitting", *John Clare: Major Works*, Ed. Eric Robinson and David Power (Oxford: Oxford University Press, 2004).

Collymore, Frank. "An Introduction to the poetry of Derek Walcott", *Bim*, 3.10 (1949), 125–132.

Conrad, Joseph. *Heart of Darkness* (Harmondsworth: Penguin, 1973).

Dickinson, Emily. *The Letters of Emily Dickinson*, Ed. Thomas H. Johnson and Theodora Ward (Cambridge: Belknap Press of Harvard University Press, 1958).

Dougherty, Carol. "Homer After *Omeros*: Reading a H/Omeric Text", *South Atlantic Quarterly* 96.2 (1997) 335–357.

Eliot, T.S. *Selected Poems* [1954] (London: Faber and Faber, 1970).

———. "Tradition and the Individual Talent " [1932], *Selected Essays* (London: Faber and Faber Ltd., 1972).

———. "The Social Function of Poetry", *On Poetry and Poets* (London: Faber and Faber Ltd., 1956), pp. 15-25.

———. "The Music of Poetry" [1942], *On Poetry and Poets* (London: Faber and Faber Ltd., 1956), pp. 26-38.

———. *Notes towards a Definition of Culture* (London: Faber, 1948).

———. *Christianity and Culture: The Idea of a Christian Society and Notes Towards the Definition of Culture* (New York: Harcourt Brace Jovanovich, 1968).

Emery, Mary Lou. *Modernism, the Visual and Caribbean Literature* (Cambridge: Cambridge University Press, 2008).

Finlay, Victoria. *Color: A Natural History of the Palette* (New York: Random House, 2004).

Friedman, Rachel D. "Derek Walcott's Odysseys", *International Journal of the Classical Tradition* 14.3/4 (2007), 455–80.

Froude, James Anthony. *The English in the West Indies* (London: Longmans Green and Co., 1888).

Gilbert, Sandra. *Inventions of Farewell: A Book of Elegies* (New York: W.W. Norton & Co., 2001).
Glissant, Édouard. *Poetics of Relation* [1997], Trans. Betty Wing (Ann Arbor: The University of Michigan Press, 2010).
––––. *Faulkner, Mississippi*, Trans. Barbara Lewis and Thomas C. Spear (New York: Farrar, Straus, and Giroux, 1998).
Gottlieb, Roger. Ed. *This Sacred Earth: Religion, Nature and the Environment* (New York: Routledge, 2003).
Greenwood, Emily. "Re-Rooting the Classical Tradition: New Directions in Black Classicism", *Classical Receptions Journal* 1.1 (2009) 87–103.
Gunn, Giles. *The Interpretation of Otherness: Literature, Religion, and the American Experience* (Oxford: Oxford University Press, 1979).
Hall, Stuart. "Cultural Identity and Diaspora", *Colonial Discourse and Postcolonial Theory: A Reader*, Ed. P. Williams and L. Chrisman (New York: Columbia University Press, 1994).
Hamner, Robert D. Ed. *Critical Perspectives on Derek Walcott* (Boulder, Co: Lynne Reinner, 1997).
———. *Critical Perspectives on Derek Walcott* (Washington, DC: Three Continents Press, 1993).
Handley, George B. *New World Poetics: Nature and the Adamic Imagination of Whitman, Neruda, and Walcott* (Athens: University of Georgia Press, 2007).
———. "Derek Walcott's Poetics of the Environment in *The Bounty*", *Callaloo* 28.1 (2005) 201-215.
Hardwick, Lorna, and Classical Association, *Reception Studies* (Oxford and New York: Oxford University Press, 2003).
Hardy, Thomas. "In Time of 'The Breaking of Nations'", *Collected Poems of Thomas Hardy* (New York: The MacMillan Company, 1925).
Harris, Wilson. *Tradition, The Writer and Society* (London: New Beacon, 1967).
———. *The Unfinished Genesis of the Imagination* (New York: Routledge, 1992).
———. *The Mask of the Beggar* (London: Faber and Faber, 2003).
Hartigan, Patti. "The Passions of Derek Walcott", *The Boston Globe*, 25 Apr. 1993.
Haught, John. "Christianity and Ecology", *This Sacred Earth: Religion, Nature and the Environment*, Ed. Roger Gottlieb (New York: Routledge, 2003).
Heaney, Seamus. *Finders Keepers* (New York: Farrar, Straus and Giroux, 2002).
———. *Selected Poems 1966-1987* (New York: Farrar, Straus and Giroux, 1990).
Hunter, R. L. and Ian Rutherford, Eds. *Wandering Poets in Ancient Greek*

Culture: Travel, Locality and Pan-Hellenism (Cambridge and New York: Cambridge University Press, 2009).
Ismond, Patricia. *Abandoning Dead Metaphors: The Caribbean Phase of Derek Walcott's Poetry* (Kingston, Jamaica: University of the West Indies, 2001).
James, C. L. R. "The Mighty Sparrow", *The Future in the Present* (London: Allison & Busby, 1977), pp. 191-201. Originally published in *Party Politics in the West Indies* (Port of Spain: Vedic Enterprises, 1962).
———. *Beyond A Boundary* (London: Hutchinson, 1963).
Joyce, James. *Dubliners* [1914] (London: Penguin, 2000).
———. *Ulysses* [1922], Ed. Seamus Deane (London: Penguin, 1992).
King, Bruce. *Derek Walcott: A Caribbean Life* (Oxford: Oxford University Press, 2000).
King James Bible.
Kirk, G. S. *The Iliad, a Commentary* (Cambridge and New York: Cambridge University Press, 1985).
Kouklanakis, Andrea. "Thersites, Odysseus, and the Social Order", *Nine Essays on Homer*, Eds. Miriam Carlisle and Olga Levaniouk (Lanham: Rowman and Littlefield, 1999), pp. 35-53.
Larkin, Philip. *Collected Poems* (New York: Farrar, Straus and Giroux, 1989).
Lattimore, Richmond. Trans., *Homer The Iliad* (Chicago: University of Chicago Press, 1951).
Lévi-Strauss, Claude. *The Raw and the Cooked: Mythologiques,* Volume 1, (University of Chicago Press, 1983).
Lewis, Alan E. *Between Cross & Resurrection: A Theology of Holy Saturday* (Grand Rapids: Wm. B. Eerdmans Publishing Co., 2001).
Lewis, Gordon, *The Growth of the Modern West Indies* (New York: Modern Readers Paperbacks, 1968).
Lord Beginner, (Egbert Moore). "Victory Test Match", 1950.
Lovelace, Earl. "Watch, Your Freedom is in Jeopardy" [1968], *Growing in the Dark; Selected Essays,* Ed. Funso Aiyejina (San Juan: Lexicon Trinidad, 2003), pp. 65-67.
MacDonald-Smythe, Antonia. "'There is a sob in there somewhere': *The Prodigal* as Testimony of an Aging Walcott", Bahamas: 26th Annual West Indian Literature Conference, 8-10 Mar. 2007. Unpublished.
Marks, J. "The Ongoing Neikos: Thersites, Odysseus, and Achilleus", *American Journal of Philology* 126 (2005), 1–31.
McDermott, Harold N. "Ethnicity and the 'Mulatto of Style': Towards a theory of Theory of Caribbean Aesthetic in the Works of Derek Walcott 1948-1993", PhD Thesis, Unpublished. University of the West Indies, Mona, 2007.

Mochama, Tony. "A Day out with eccentric Nobel Laureate Derek Walcott", *Sunday Standard,* 28 May 2006.
Mootry, Maria K. "Three Caribbean Poets: Sea Imagery as an Index to their African Consciousness", *Pan Africanist* 1 no. 2 (1971), 22–27.
Morgan, Paula and Funso Aiyejina, Eds. *Caribbean Literature in a Global Context* (St Augustine: UWI Faculty of Humanities and Education, and Lexicon Trinidad, 2006).
Morton. Sarah E. Ed., *John Morton of Trinidad: Journals, Letters and Papers* (Toronto: Westminster Company, 1916).
Mosely, Lyndsay. Ed. *Holy Ground: A Gathering of Voices on Caring for Creation* (United States: Sierra Club Books, 2008).
Naipaul, V.S. *A Bend in the River* (London: Picador, 2002).
———. *A Flag on the Island* (New York: Penguin, 1969).
———. *The Middle Passage* (London: Picador, 2001).
———. *The Mimic Men* (London: Andre Deutsch, 1967).
O'Meally, Robert G. *Romare Bearden: A Black Odyssey* (New York: DC Moore Gallery, 2007).
Poets.org. "Derek Walcott", Accessed 16 Jan. 2012. http://www.poets.org/poet.php/prmPID/220.
Pollard, Charles W. *New World Modernisms: T.S. Eliot, Derek Walcott, and Kamau Brathwaite* (University of Virginia Press, Charlottesville, 2004).
Postlethwaite, N. "Thersites in the *Iliad*". *Greece and Rome* 35.2 (1988) 123–36.
Prinsep, James. *Banaras Illustrated* (Calcutta, Baptist Mission Press, 1831).
Questel, Victor, "Ash Wednesday", *Near Mourning Ground* (Port of Spain: The New Voices, 1979).
———. "Derek Walcott: Contradiction and Resolution – Paradox, Inconsistency, Ambivalence and their Resolution in Derek Walcott's Writings 1946-76", Diss. UWI, St Augustine, 1979.
Rilke, Rainer Maria. *The Essential Rilke*, Selected and Trans. Galway Kinnel and Hannah Liebmann (New York: Ecco, 2000).
Rohlehr, Gordon. "The Problem of the Problem of Form", *The Shape of That Hurt and Other Essays* (Port of Spain: Longman, 1991), pp. 1-65.
———. *Transgression. Transition, Transformation: Essays in Caribbean Culture* (San Juan, Trinidad and Tobago: Lexicon, 2007).
———. *A Scuffling of Islands: Essays on Calypso* (San Juan, Trinidad: Lexicon, 2004).
Rudder, D., "Another Day in Paradise", Lyrics Man, Port of Spain: Lypsoland CR023, 1995.
Scott, Dennis. "Walcott on Walcott", *Caribbean Quarterly* 14.1 and 2 (1968), 77–82.
Serres, Michel. *The Natural Contract* (Ann Arbor: University of Michigan Press, 1995).

Simmons, Harold. "A West Indian Poet Fulfils his Promise", *Critical Perspectives on Derek Walcott*, Ed. Robert D. Hammer (Boulder and London: Lynne Rienner Publishers, 1996,) p. 97.

Simone, Nina. "Why?" (The King of Love Is Dead) 'Nuff Said, Stereo LSP. 4965, New York: RCA, 1968.

Steiner, George. *Real Presences* (Chicago: University of Chicago Press, 1989).

Synge, John Millington, *Riders to the Sea, Four Plays and the Aran Islands* [1904], Ed. Robin Skelton (London: Oxford University Press, 1962), pp. 3-17.

Thalmann, William G. "Thersites: Comedy, Scapegoats, and Heroic Ideology in the *Iliad*", *Transactions of the American Philological Association* 118 (1988), 1–28.

"The Best Books of 2007", *Contemporary Poetry Review*. Accessed 2007. http://www.cprw.com/books07.htm

Tulsidas. *Sri Ramacaritamanasa: with Hindi Text and English Translation* (A Romanised Edition) (Gorakpur, India: Gita Press, No Date, but based on a 1968 edition, original text in Nagari with an English translation).

Vargas Llosa, Mario, "In Praise of Reading and Fiction", <http://nobelprize.org/nobel_prizes/literature/laureates/2010/vargas_llosa-lecture_en.html>.

Whitelaw, Billie. "A Wake for Sam", YouTube, accessed 9 Mar. 2013.

Williams, Denis. "The Concept of the Ancestor", *Image and Idea in the Arts of Guyana: The Edgar Mittelholzer Memorial Lectures*, 2nd Series, The National History and Arts Council, Ministry of Information, Georgetown Guyana, Jan. 1969.

Yeats, William Butler. "No Second Troy" [1916], *Collected Poems*, Ed. Richard J. Finneran (London: Macmillan, 1989).

NOTES ON CONTRIBUTORS

Patrick A. B. Anthony, a Roman Catholic priest from Saint Lucia, is the founding director of the Folk Research Centre (FRC) and director of the Pastoral Centre (AKFAPC) on that island. He holds a Masters degree in theology from Catholic Theological Union in Chicago and a doctorate in Literatures in English from the University of the West Indies, Trinidad. His doctoral thesis was on symbols, myths and rituals in Derek Walcott's plays. His area of interest is in the relationship between theology and culture, especially literature and theology.

Jean Antoine-Dunne is a Senior Lecturer in Literatures in English at the University of the West Indies, St Augustine and is also a painter and critic. She is co-editor of *The Montage Principle: Eisenstein in New Cultural and Critical Contexts* (2004) and Guest Editor of *Where is Here? Remapping the Caribbean*, Special Edition of the *Journal of West Indian Literature.* Vol 18. 2 (April 2010). She is one of the editors of the *Journal of West Indian Literature*.

Edward Baugh is Professor Emeritus of English, University of the West Indies, Mona, Jamaica. His recent publications include: *Derek Walcott* (Cambridge University Press, 2006), his edition of Walcott's *Selected Poems* (Farrar, Straus & Giroux, 2007), and *Frank Collymore: A Biography* (Ian Randle, 2009). His *Black Sand: New and Selected Poems* is due to be published in 2013 by Peepal Tree Press.

J. Edward Chamberlin is Professor Emeritus of English and Comparative Literature at Toronto University; but his interest in stories and songs has taken him around the world, to the Kalahari, Mongolia as well as to the Caribbean. He was Senior Research Associate with the Royal Commission on Aboriginal Peoples in Canada, and has worked extensively on native land claims in Canada, the United States, Africa and Australia. His books include *Come Back To Me My Language: Poetry and the West Indies* (1993), *If This Is Your Land, Where Are Your Stories? Finding Common Ground* (2003), *Horse: How the Horse Has Shaped Civilizations* (2006); *A Covenant in Wonder with the World: The Power of Stories and Songs* (2012); and *Island: How Islands Transform the World* (2013).

Rhonda Cobham-Sander teaches Caribbean and African Literature at Amherst College, in Massachusetts. She is co-editor of *Watchers and Seekers: Creative Writing by Black Women in Britain* and her critical essays have appeared in such journals as *Callaloo, Transition, Small Axe,* and *Research in African Literatures*

Rachel D. Friedman is an Associate Professor of Greek and Roman Studies at Vassar College in Poughkeepsie, New York where she teaches Greek language and literature and courses on classical literature in translation. A Hellenist by training, her most recent work is on contemporary receptions of Greek literature. She is currently writing a book on Derek Walcott and Homer with the working title *Reading Homer After Walcott: An Ecocritical Study*. The book, informed by recent work in ecocriticism, puts Walcott and Homer in conversation with each other as it explores the way that landscape shapes meaning in both poets' works.

George Handley is Professor of Interdisciplinary Humanities at Brigham Young University where he serves as Chair of the Department of Humanities, Classics, and Comparative Literature. He is the author, most recently, of *New World Poetics: Nature and the Adamic Imagination of Whitman, Neruda, and Walcott* (University of Georgia Press, 2007) and an environmental memoir, *Home Waters: A Year of Recompenses on the Provo River* (University of Utah Press, 2010). His articles have appeared in *Callaloo*, *Mississippi Quarterly*, *Interdisciplinary Study of Literature and the Environment*, *Modern Fiction Studies*, and other journals.

Barbara Lalla is Professor Emeritus, Language and Literature, UWI, St Augustine. Major Publications include novels: *Cascade: A Novel,* and *Arch of Fire* (translated *Flammendes Land*). Other books include *Postcolonialisms: Caribbean Re-reading of Medieval English Discourse*; *Defining Jamaican Fiction: Marronage and the Discourse of Survival*; Companion volumes with Jean D'Costa, *Language in Exile: Three Hundred Years of Jamaican Creole* and *Voices in Exile*; *English for Academic Purposes; Writing about Literature* in collaboration with Paula Morgan, as well as several edited works such as Created *in the West Indies. Caribbean Perspectives on V. S. Naipau*l, and *Beyond Boundaries: Cross-Culturalism and the Caribbean Canon,* both co-edited with Jennifer Rahim; and *Studies in Caribbean Language* with Pauline Christie and others.

Harold McDermott currently serves as director of the Language Technology and Research Centre at the University of Technology, Jamaica. He has authored several texts in Communication Studies and Literatures in English at the Caribbean Advanced Proficiency Examination level and has published a number of articles on Caribbean literature in international journals.

Antonia MacDonald is a professor in the School of Arts and Sciences, and Associate Dean in the Graduate Studies Program at St. George's University, Grenada. She writes on contemporary Caribbean women writers (including Maryse Condé, Jamaica Kincaid and Michelle Cliff) and, more recently, Derek Walcott and on St. Lucian Literary Studies. She has published articles in the Journal of West Indian Literature (JWIL), Callaloo, Anthurium and MaComere and is the author of *Making Homes in the West/Indies*.

Paula Morgan is a Senior Lecturer in the Faculty of Humanities and Education, The University of the West Indies, St Augustine, and is a former Head of Department of Liberal Arts and Coordinator of the Cultural Studies Graduate programme. Her primary area of research, teaching and publication is gender and ethnic relations in the Caribbean and the African Diaspora. Dr. Morgan has produced and /or co-authored five books.

Kenneth Ramchand is a former President of the University of Trinidad and Tobago and is Professor Emeritus in West Indian Literature, The University of the West Indies, St Augustine and Professor of English Emeritus, Colgate University, New York. He has published extensively (books and essays) on West Indian writing and is currently preparing a volume of Selected Essays for Peepal Tree Press.

Louis Regis is a Lecturer in Literatures in English at the University of the West Indies, St Augustine, and Head of the Department of Literary, Cultural and Communication Studies. His publications include *Black Stalin Kaisonian* (Mona: Arawak, 2006) and *The political calypso: True opposition in Trinidad and Tobago* 1962-1987 (Mona: University of the West Indies Press); and (Gainesville Fl: The University of Florida Press, 1999).

Gordon Rohlehr is Professor Emeritus, West Indian Literature, The University of the West Indies, St Augustine. His books include *Ancestories: Readings of Kamau Brathwaite's Ancestors (*2010), *Transgression, Transition and Transformation* (2007). *A Scuffling of Islands: Essays on Calypso* (2004), *The Shape of that Hurt and Other Essays* (1992), *My Strangled City and Other Essays* (1992), *Calypso and Society in pre-independence Trinidad* (1990) and *Pathfinders: Black Awakening in the Arrivants of Edward Kamau Brathwaite* (1981).

Jennifer Toews is the librarian in charge of the Derek Walcott papers at the Thomas Fisher Rare Book Library, University of Toronto, Canada, and also a huge fan of his work.

GENERAL INDEX

THEMATIC INDEX

DISCUSSION OF WALCOTT'S WORK BY TITLE

Poetry

Plays

Criticism and Prose

Film scripts

Interviews with: